Women and the Creation of Urban Life

NUMBER SEVENTY-TWO:
*The Centennial Series of the Association
of Former Students, Texas A&M University*

Women and the Creation of Urban Life

DALLAS, TEXAS, 1843–1920

Elizabeth York Enstam

TEXAS A&M UNIVERSITY PRESS
COLLEGE STATION

The paper used in this book meets the minimum requirements
of the American National Standard for Permanence
of Paper for Printed Library Materials, Z39.48-1984.
Binding materials have been chosen for durability.

Library of Congress Cataloging-in-Publication Data

Enstam, Elizabeth York.
    Women and the creation of urban life : Dallas, Texas, 1843–
1920 / Elizabeth York Enstam.
        p.   cm. — (Centennial series of the Association of Former
Students, Texas A&M University ; no. 72)
    Includes bibliographical references and index.
    ISBN 0-89096-799-7
    1. Women—Texas—Dallas—History. 2. Women—
Employment—Texas—Dallas. 3. Women—Texas—Dallas—
Economic conditions. 4. Work and family—Texas—Dallas—History.
5. City and town life—Texas—Dallas—History. 6. Dallas (Tex.)—
History. 7. Dallas (Tex.)—Social conditions. 8. Dallas (Tex.)—
Politics and government. I. Title. II. Series.
HQ1439.D36E57   1998
305.4´09764´2812—dc21   97-40990
                                                                  CIP

Contents

Illustrations

Tables

Acknowledgments

A project that lasts for twenty years acquires its own history and turns its author into something of a permanent fixture in the local libraries and reading rooms. The archivists and librarians who helped me begin the research for this book have retired, left to accept other positions, or entered their second careers. One married and moved away to live in Ireland. Recently, I have remembered them all as I waited for their replacements to find the materials for me to check various details one last time.

Friends who read the early drafts of this study will most likely not recognize the final product. Nonetheless, they participated in the form it has taken. The comments of David Weber, Willard Hamrick, Susan Pacey, Bonnie McKee, Charlotte Phillips, Neila Patrick, Raynall Barber, and the late Myrtle Buckley led me to search for more precise bearings within the rich, but overwhelming resources that I found in those first years.

As the field of women's history developed, the growing numbers of publications and their increasingly sophisticated scholarship raised additional questions for my research and required repeated reorganization of my materials. I am especially indebted to Judith McArthur, Nancy Baker Jones, and Elizabeth Hayes Turner, not only for specific suggestions for my manuscript, but also for allowing me to read early drafts of their work. The quality of their scholarship explicitly established the standards to which I have aspired.

The perceptive responses of several scholars did much to shape the manuscript during its final stage, which lasted almost four years. Judy Mohraz warned me not to bury my interpretations within the narrative; Peter Stearns alerted me to the need for a sharpened focus on my overall purpose. I am indebted to Robert Fairbanks, not only for his astute advice, but also for his faith in the project during some dark times. And I am grateful to Zane Miller for his long, thoughtful letters with sound advice and helpful comments, particularly about the book's organization and structure.

Jackie McElhaney has my special gratitude for reading multiple drafts of several chapters and for years of generosity in sharing her research files. In addition, on countless occasions she has alerted me to valuable sources discovered during her own research. Michael Hazel read and commented on the manuscript, then helped immensely in finding and reproducing several of the photographs. Special appreciation goes to Mary Ellen Holt, first for her help in locating materials in the Dallas Historical Society's collection, and second, for her wonderful practice of calling me whenever she finds items of possible use in my research. With kind consideration for my deadlines, Gaylon Palotti provided copies of photographs from the Historical Society's files, while Gretchen Boettcher and Carol Roark helped me locate numerous others in the Dallas Public Library's collection. My thanks, also, to Jim Foster for permission to use some existing prints. For years, the Inter-library Loan staff members—and especially Don Mahon—have immeasurably increased the resources available to me.

During the decades of this research and writing, my daughter Gwendolyn grew up and went off to graduate school to become a medievalist. For many years she and my husband Raymond shared their home with ever-growing stacks of paper that had a perverse way, at one time or another, of cluttering every flat surface in our house. Under such annoying circumstances, I have always appreciated their encouragement—and their forbearance.

Finally, my gratitude to the Texas A&M University Press staff; and to the anonymous readers for both their general remarks and specific suggestions.

To all these members of my "village" I must say, your help has been invaluable. I only hope that I have used it wisely, and in the ways you intended. The final results are my responsibility.

Introduction

When Margaret Beeman married John Neely Bryan in February 1843, she became the first white woman to live where the city of Dallas would be.[1] Seventy-six years later, on July 4, 1919, Nona Boren Mahoney presided when the Dallas Equal Suffrage Association met to celebrate ratification of the Nineteenth Amendment to the United States Constitution. Between the dates of these two events, the place called Dallas grew from a single log cabin into a city of more than 150,000, and life assumed many of its modern forms. Whether the effects of those eight decades were greater for women or for men is debatable, but for everyone, life changed in basic and lasting ways that affected employment, work in the home, and participation in the community. Women achieved many of those changes and, in the process, shaped essential elements of city living.

This book investigates women's lives and work during the years when Dallas developed from a frontier settlement into a modern city. Founded in 1841 and incorporated in 1856, Dallas offered advantages for such a study. Especially convenient was the city's youth, for great-grandchildren of the original settlers were available to recall family stories and census and city directory listings were relatively small, providing population surveys and samplings of manageable sizes. Moreover, with its founding during the decades when Americans began aggressively settling the trans-Mississippi frontier, the city's origins held few mysteries. In the 1840s, real estate speculators like Neely Bryan planted settlements as if they were crops, and subsequent local leaders solicitously tended their growth. Advertisements in the pioneer newspaper and articles in the earliest city directories proudly announced each acquisition, as residents built the institutions and established the practices characteristic first of antebellum, and then of modern, urban places.

In admittedly broad strokes over a period spanning nearly three generations, this book seeks to evaluate what women have done, not in comparison to or contrast with the achievements of men, but simply within one city's development. Although the study of local history threatens a myopic preoccupation with details, it also focuses direct investigation onto the inner workings of the American past, on how, in the nation's various sections, particular people—female and male—faced crises, built their lives, and adapted to change. Whatever the vast impersonal "forces" that "swept" the land, specific people in specific places exercised choices about living, and dealt with the consequences. Concentration on a single community breathes a special vitality into the shards of information that survive from past lives.

The research for this study began with a simple question and an unrealistic expectation of uncomplicated answers: When, and at what level of development, did women's work become important and noticeable in Dallas? Men built the city, this initial question assumed, while women helped and contributed now and then, once in awhile, and maybe on occasion did something of value. Despite the question's inadequacy, the search took a fortunate direction, not only for information about women's achievements but also for the context within which they worked and for the ways in which change in that context affected what they did.

Economics seemed the most obvious factor upon which to begin organizing the initial research, for, almost always and everywhere, people went to a new place hoping for a better life. Memoirs, personal reminiscences, business advertisements in the newspaper, comments in the letters of travelers, the county tax rolls, the federal censuses, and, for later years, listings in the city directories —these provided evidence of the ways women labored in the building of this new place.

The sources that revealed women's economic roles also defined the stages of Dallas's growth. The agricultural village of the 1840s developed into a country market town by 1850.[2] In the early 1870s, the coming of the railroads produced first a frontier "boom town" and then, with the rapid growth of population and the expansion of markets and trade, a regional distribution center for North Central and West Texas, the Indian Territory, and much of Arkansas. By 1880, Dallas was a commercial city, characterized less by size than by increasingly sophisticated business transactions, a widening array of economic services, and the earliest evidence of a diverse, if stratified, social structure. After 1900, banking and finance, insurance, and real estate joined the wholesale and retail trades to confirm the city's identity as predominantly "white collar" and devoted to "clean" industry.

For women, the stages of Dallas's economic development had their most visible effects in employment outside the home. Rapid growth during the 1870s and 1880s stimulated market demand for traditional female skills, while after 1900 changes in business methods and organization brought new opportunities for wage earners. Because American towns and cities offered the kinds of occupations defined as "woman's work" and suited to then-current notions of propriety, the increasing numbers of employed women became a prime characteristic of modern urban life. From 1880, when somewhat dependable census figures first became available, women formed an ever-growing component of the Dallas labor force.

Consideration only of the marketplace, however, obscures much of women's economic participation by neglecting its domestic aspects. This study's earliest findings revealed the importance of women's work in providing the original settlers with what they needed to live. In ways so basic as to be primal, women's daily labor constituted the foundation of the entire range of local economic activities. After 1890, industrialization altered domestic work as much as paid employment and changed the methods, the processes, and even the nature of household tasks. At least as important as the actual work done in the home was its position within the urban economy at every stage of the city's development. Along with employment, this study considers the relationship of domestic labor to the marketplace. Despite the difficulty of estimating its worth in numbers or measuring it in dollars and cents, work performed in the home held fundamental value for the overall economy.

A city is more than its economic system, but historically, business and industrial development has been the basis for, and indeed often caused the social changes identified as urban. As early as the second decade of settlement, the 1850s, Dallas residents had built a rich cultural life. Long before the town had paved streets, much less indoor plumbing even for the wealthy, the pioneers organized their relationships into a complex level of community. By 1880, with an economy based upon the transactions of trade and commerce instead of the direct produce of the land, Dallas functioned as a city, despite a population of only 10,358. Alongside the robust businesses were growing ethnic diversity, the appearance of differing lifestyles, regular church services and socials, thriving commercial entertainment, and privately sponsored cultural events, all offering a greater variety of associations and aesthetic experience than the country or the smaller towns. "[I]t is art, culture, and political purpose . . . that define a city," wrote Lewis Mumford in *The City in History.* From the earliest cities in the Neolithic period, people moved into urban areas in search not only of economic opportunity but also of a richer, fuller life.[3]

During the seventy-seven years encompassed in this study, women did much to establish the social and cultural infrastructures in Dallas, as well as the public institutions and agencies that characterized life in a modern urban place. Camouflaged within families, hidden behind prescriptions of propriety, and ignored by the definitions of history, women nevertheless were full participants in the creation of urban living. This study's first four chapters examine women's lives in the urban frontier—their integration in the preindustrial economy, participation in the country market town, work in the railroad "boom town," and innovations in the young commercial city. From the very beginning and at every level of development, women's work was "noticeable"—indeed, vital—in its value to Dallas. The early research, in other words, yielded the answer to the book's original question of when and how women's work affected what Dallas became.

For the late 1890s and the two decades before 1920, that question proved to be inadequate. After 1900, women in Dallas altered social policies in ways that enabled them to share, to an unexpected degree, political power and community authority. During the years when women were becoming a significant and indispensable proportion of the city's paid labor force, housewives founded numerous organizations and institutions that proved to be permanent assets for urban life. Indeed, privileged white women initiated many of the services and resources that became part of the definition of "urban." Chapters five through nine give accounts of these accomplishments and assess their roles in establishing Dallas as a modern city.

For all aspects of women's work, the focus on a single place conveys a strong awareness of agency in human affairs. With regard to employment, business ownership, and the professions, women succeeded or failed as individuals. For civic programs, they usually worked through groups, yet the personal inclinations of officers and founders inevitably influenced both the selection and definition of every organization's purposes. Study of both venues of women's work, the marketplace and the community, required recognition of the specific human agents who set local events in motion and sustained their momentum. The resulting short biographical profiles emphasize, with the unique, even the anecdotal, this study's roots in the humanities. Such glimpses of personalities allow presentation of the city's female population not only in statistical aggregates, but also by accumulating, through the successive chapters, images of the diversity that characterized even apparently homogeneous lives. Still, each individual, whatever her eccentricities and personal uniqueness, had counterparts in cities throughout the United States, and each proved to be a woman of her times.

Among the most extraordinary of the Dallas women leaders were the African Americans. Although they were dominant among the city's minorities, the dearth of information about their lives did as much to determine the study's focus on Anglo-European Americans as the fact that Anglo-European American traditions then defined the city. African Americans shared much of mainstream culture, despite strict segregation and pervasive racism. As they created a vibrant, cohesive society of their own, black people in Dallas participated in two cultures, constantly challenging the established social structure while developing separate, vital forms of community.

For the city's Hispanic residents, sources of information proved even more elusive than for African Americans. Before 1900 Hispanic surnames appeared in the city directories, and by 1910 three *barrios* existed in or near Dallas. A fourth, named "Little Mexico," emerged around 1914. Located about a mile north of downtown, this neighborhood grew after 1916 to include perhaps ten thousand people as refugees from the Mexican Revolution fled into Texas.[4] Day-to-day work resembled that done by the majority of Dallas residents, but for Hispanic women, much of the fabric and texture of life has been woven of cultural threads distinct from those of the Anglo-European American groups. Understanding their experience required more than analysis of city directories and manuscript censuses or perusal of news stories and the records of voluntary associations. In addition to the separate treatment which such considerations demanded was the fact that only after 1917 did immigrants from Mexico begin forming a visible community in Dallas. Effective Hispanic participation in the city's public life and politics came after 1960.

From this study's initial search for women's "noticeable" work, a single theme emerged through the evaluation of their achievements: during the city's development from agricultural village to modern urban community, women achieved genuinely public and community roles. Of all their accomplishments, the most unexpected lay in their growing participation in the public culture, in Thomas Bender's terms, as the "subtle power to assign significance and meaning to various cultural phenomena."[5] By 1920, when women at last exercised the right to vote, their influence already extended from the curriculum in the Dallas public schools to local and state political issues and even to questions of public behavior.

Five aspects of women's work revealed how their roles were changing during times when female lives were supposed to be only private. The first aspect was their participation in the urban economy, through both employment in the marketplace and traditional work in the home. Defined most explicitly on the unindustrialized frontier by the production of necessary goods from raw materials, domestic labor evolved by the early twentieth century into its present form as services, yet remained as vital to the daily functioning of the city's labor force as to the pioneer farming families. At the same time, the changing marketplace demanded ever more, and more diverse, workers, with the result that by 1920 Dallas women were present, if only as "tokens," in every category of occupations. Through paid employment and work in the home, virtually the entire adult female population of every class, race, and ethnic group—and hundreds of girls between the ages of ten and eighteen—participated in the development of the city's economy.

Second, women did much to establish fundamental elements of the social structure. Beginning in frontier times with the basic institutions of home, school, and church, women helped to create new, if stratified, forms of community during the 1870s and 1880s, when Dallas experienced both the abundance of industrialization and the strain of the "boom-bust" national economy. With such occasions as the church socials that strengthened congregations and the benefit recitals sponsored by the music study club, women drew relatives, friends, and newcomers into the patterns of association most often found in urban areas.[6] In yet another facet of social formation, married women in Dallas, like their counterparts elsewhere, defined essential characteristics of the modern middle class through their growing authority in family life. Long recognized as an integral component of urban places, the city's middle class exhibited, most visibly through its young matrons, the values and tastes that came to influence both wage earners and the elite.

The third aspect of women's community involvement occurred with the initially circumspect, even timid, assumption of leadership roles in institutions and organizations that characterize modern urban life. Most likely because of changes in the structuring of men's work after the arrival of the railroads, middle- and upper-class women quietly accepted public functions always before performed by men. Most surprising, this profound change never became an issue for public discussion. Presumably, Dallas residents accepted the "high culture" of education and the fine arts as somehow related to nurturance and traditional domestic qualities, and thus as appropriate for women. However delicately effected, this alteration in public gender roles violated custom and propriety by giving women unprecedented prominence in community affairs. Its immediate results were permanent, and highly visible. With the Dallas Public Library (1901) and the one-room gallery that became the Dallas Museum of Art (1909), privileged white matrons founded the first of numerous civic and municipal institutions that would alter women's social roles as much as they changed the city.

The library and the museum are relevant to the fourth expression of women's community involvement, that of drawing the city into national trends. Both these institutions enhanced connections with the wider American and Anglo-European cultures. Similarly, numerous programs launched by the women's clubs were typical of nationwide social programs, then defined as "Progressive" and now seen as related to the origins of social welfare legislation in the 1930s.[7] At first funded in Dallas solely by private efforts, the resulting agencies in time acquired public money and, together with more traditional charitable and philanthropic organizations, established the basis for the city's first system of regular, inclusive public assistance. As much as the merchants, bankers, and business owners with their growing markets and new sources of capital, women linked Dallas with widespread social movements, adapting solutions introduced in other cities to problems in Dallas and tailoring out-of-state methods to local resources, political realities, and human needs.[8]

When their purposes collided with entrenched policies, women learned the strategies and tactics of political action. The resulting campaigns defined the fifth, increasingly overt and public, aspect of women's work in the community: their entrance into politics in the name of numerous social causes. After 1900, women drew into the political arena issues usually considered to be domestic and private. Unavoidably entering the formal, recognized channels of power and authority, they took strong positions with regard to the making of decisions and the setting of policies, especially those affecting families and homes.[9] However carefully presented in proper "ladylike" terms, these actions had profound implications. They not only violated perceived divisions between public and private, but also they challenged society's most basic organization of work and relationships.

That is, they challenged *gender*. For the matters of direct concern to home and family, the private female "domain," women employed the social prescriptions of gender to expedite what they wanted or needed from public sources. In essence, they evaded gender restrictions by applying gender definitions to suit their purposes.[10] A fundamental concept of the social fiction of the "separate spheres," gender could have defeated their efforts and blocked their intentions. Instead, women made it their strongest tool for influencing public decision making, and for justifying their access to power within the community. As a result, the organizations women formed, the associations through which they worked, the institutions and agencies they founded and ran—all affected the lives of thousands of people outside their own families and made possible cultural and personal experiences rarely, if ever, before available in Dallas.[11]

Although man was not this study's measure of woman's accomplishments, nineteenth-century attitudes and definitions of gender inevitably affected the process of analyzing women's work within the context of Dallas history. People's expectations affected their behavior as much as the actual situations they faced, and their beliefs about the "natural" ordering of human life determined their reactions even (perhaps especially) to new conditions. Usually complementary and cooperative, occasionally contradictory and in conflict, social prescriptions designated as female or male affected every aspect of the building of Dallas and the creation of urban life.[12]

Throughout the years included in this study, women worked both alongside and apart from the men now remembered as the founders and builders of Dallas. By assigning women vaguely to "social" and "cultural" life, historians traditionally have shortchanged their accomplishments.[13] In truth, women helped to build the definitive forms of urban life by establishing organizations and agencies that altered the responsibilities and functions of Dallas government, amended the public conception of political issues, and changed the city's physical structure. Women assumed community leadership in perpetuating the traditions, learning, fine arts, and customs of the larger culture. In the process of initiating, developing, and sustaining much of what we now recognize as distinctly urban living, women stretched, redefined, and at times erased the essentially artificial boundaries projected between female and male, between the "private" and the "public" as aspects of human endeavor.[14]

As a case study with characteristics of a synthesis focused on one city, this book seeks to do more than merely reveal what Dallas women have done. During the past two decades, scholars have examined women's lives and work in dozens of monographs and hundreds of articles. With their findings, these authors have formulated guiding interpretations for women's history in the United States. Application of these major theories to a single community offers an opportunity to illuminate the integral significance of women's work, in all its diversity, magnitude, and variety, for one place during a period of eighty years. Thus considered, women's achievements may assume their rightful stature, not relative to or in contrast to those of men, but simply as work which was necessary for any society and which, left undone by women, very likely would not have been done at all. At every turn, women's accomplishments in Dallas reverberate throughout the nation and serve to illuminate more completely one aspect of human experience, the creation of urban life.

Part I
The Urban Frontier

Chapter One
Agricultural Village and County

"Our spring went dry this year by the middle of May," Mercy Ann Mathis wrote to her family in Tennessee, "and that would make me sick of Texas if nothing else to lug watter [*sic*] a half mile . . . I am no better satisfied," she continued, "nor do I like Texas any better . . . nor I never shall."[1] The streams in Dallas County were not always as dry as in 1858, of course, nor all pioneer women so disappointed in their new homes. But long after the years of settlement and in many households later than 1900, lugging water was among the tasks typical of women's work in rural areas and Dallas alike.

On the frontier, especially, the home was the basic social institution, and it served public as well as private functions. The first schools and worship services were held in the settlers' log cabins, where mothers taught classes for the local children and invited itinerant ministers to preach. The home was the center of recreation and social events, too, as well as the hospital and the mortuary. Most fundamental, however, the pioneer home was the unit of production, where families grew and manufactured for themselves the majority of things they needed to live. A woman's skill at using the raw materials she produced and her knowledge of the offerings of the natural world were crucial to the survival of her family and, later, to its prosperity and success. For family and community life, women's work was integral both to the settlement of Dallas County and the establishment of Dallas the town.

The first woman to live in Dallas was Margaret Beeman Bryan, but only a few scraps of information about her life have survived. In the photograph taken perhaps ten years after her marriage to the city's founder, John Neely Bryan, she looks very young, pale, and fine-boned, with dark hair and eyes. Her delicate appearance is deceptive, however, for in the 1850s she supported four children alone during six years when Neely drifted through California, the Rocky Mountains, and the Indian Nation. Years later, when a family friend recalled the beauty of her hands, her son responded with a somewhat tart *non sequitur,* that those hands "should have been beautiful," because they carried one end of the chain used to measure the first lots in Dallas.[2] He neglected to mention the more frequent uses to which his mother put her hands, the work typically done by women on the frontier to sustain their families.

Married at eighteen to a man almost twice her age, Margaret Bryan "set up housekeeping" in 1843 with household articles that her mother had brought from Illinois.[3] Bryan came to Texas with a group that included her parents and siblings, plus two uncles and their families. As one of the earliest immigrants to Dallas County, she knew what "pioneering" meant, yet in 1914, when she was eighty-nine, she recalled her early married life fondly. "[M]y husband and I crossed the [Trinity] River many times in our little canoe, dug out of a cottonwood tree, and your magnificent buildings have taken the place of our little rude log cabin, with clapboard roof and puncheon floor. . . . My husband and I lived happily in that lonely log hut."[4]

For several years their "log hut" and one or two others *were* Dallas. Neely Bryan had claimed the land beside the best ford on the Trinity River, and by mid-decade two major immigration routes led travelers through his "town."

Margaret Beeman Bryan and her husband, John Neely Bryan, about 1853.
Courtesy Historic Photograph Collection, Dallas Public Library

Opened in 1840 to run between Austin and the Red River village of Preston, the north-south Preston Road crossed the river at Bryan's claim. Three years later, in 1844, the Republic of Texas built the northeast-southwest National Central Highway, which joined the Preston Road about a mile north of Bryan's ford and funneled traffic to his ferry instead of the rival crossings nearby.[5] Appointed postmaster, Bryan handled the few pieces of mail coming by mule twice a month from Bonham and made his home the Dallas post office, as well as its tavern and inn.

The pioneers who trickled in were mostly farmers, but by 1848 Dallas had seven physicians and three general stores.[6] The owner of one store, Charles Durgin, succeeded Bryan as postmaster but turned the office's duties over to his wife. Elizabeth Thomas Durgin very likely was the first woman in Dallas to work with her husband in a family-owned business. In addition to her share of minding the store, she organized the post office by sewing pockets onto a length of canvas, embroidering the alphabet on some; labeling others "bills," "notes," or "receipts"; and hanging the canvas on the wall. However simple, this letter file was an improvement over the bags into which her husband and his partner had dumped the mail.[7]

Becoming the temporary county seat in 1846, Dallas was more an agricultural village than a town. Trade in the general stores often took the form of barter, as people paid for merchandise in kind—a side of bacon, maybe, or a bag of wheat. When Addie Dye McDermett came with her family in December 1847, she found "a doll village . . . of small log cabins, the largest not exceeding 12 x 14 feet," built on the sandy soil of the riverbank. Neely Bryan had hired a surveyor to draw a plat, but Dallas had no streets. "A network of picturesquely winding paths . . . connected the houses," McDermett remembered, and all were "more or less weed and grass grown."[8] Thanks to the traffic of the two major roads, the "doll village" held promise for business owners, as travelers to the west and south increased the demand for goods and services.

More important were the farmers moving into the surrounding area. From the time of earliest settlement, Dallas and Dallas County grew together. Other inland American cities originated as places of defense or as civilization's "spearheads" in the wilderness, and their leaders worked for years to develop a "hinterland."[9] In contrast, Dallas and its surrounding countryside were interdependent, linked in a close, almost symbiotic process of development. Merchants, craftspeople, and professionals in the village depended for their livelihood upon the agricultural trade; in turn, farmers needed the services, manufactured goods, and markets available in the village shops and stores.

For its first three decades, Dallas and the county were dominated not by single men intending to make their fortunes quickly and move on, but by families, married couples who meant to build homes and rear children. In a pattern common to other times and other frontiers, those first to arrive often drew relatives after them. One such family was that of Nancy Jane Hughes Cochran, who came with her husband and three children from Missouri in 1843. Pleased with the abundant yields of their first year's crops, the Cochrans wrote letters with such glowing accounts of their success that Nancy Jane's brother and six sisters moved with their families from Tennessee. One sister's family settled in East Texas, near Tyler, but the brother and five other sisters claimed homesteads that stretched over much of what became the northern residential area of Dallas.[10] Enmeshed in family relationships despite their move west, such women pioneers were unlikely to experience the loss of status and respect sometimes suffered by frontier wives who were isolated by distance from the support of kin and community traditions.[11]

In 1850, the federal census takers failed to distinguish the residents of Dallas from those in the county, where men outnumbered women by 25 percent among adults over the age of nineteen. Many nineteenth-century frontier areas, in fact, had about one-fourth more men than women. Like all the women in Dallas County, the single men attached themselves to families, living either with the employers who hired them as farm hands or with relatives, sometimes their fathers and brothers in all-male households. The sex ratio changed little during the following decade, as the county's white population almost tripled. Among the 207 slaves present in 1850, females predominated at 54 percent. By 1860, the sex ratio was more even, with women accounting for 52 percent of the 1,074 African Americans.[12]

For almost a decade, the only social institution on this frontier was the home, and every family's life centered there, beginning with its support and sustenance. Indeed, the entire Dallas County economy of the 1840s was based in the individual home, with its few links to the marketplace in Dallas. As the site for manufacturing and processing goods, the home was a workplace, a unit of production and not merely a site of consumption. Women's work was integral to that home-centered economy, with every family's prosperity dependent upon their production, along with that of the men.[13]

The specific tasks of women's work differed little from county to village, and those who lived in the growing settlement of Dallas had the same chores as their neighbors on the farms. Although the men hunted frequently, the women provided most of the food supply. Food production was, in fact, every woman's primary responsibility. Margaret Bryan fenced her garden with brush and grew vegetables to accompany the "buffalo, deer, and turkey for meat with wild honey for sweets" on her dining table.[14]

Of all the foodstuffs, vegetables were the most labor-intensive. In a growing season lasting from late February until mid-November, a garden meant almost daily work for eight to nine months of the year, with watering, cultivating, weeding, and then gathering as the produce ripened.[15] Early and late plants flourished in the frequent rains and mild temperatures of spring and autumn, but the Texas climate required adaptations in gardening methods developed in the eastern states. Learning by trial and error, the pioneers lost a few summer crops before they began to sow the vegetable seeds among the corn plants, which provided shade and held moisture around the roots. Herbs grew in separate, more protected plots for use in foods and "home remedies."[16]

A variety of techniques, also learned in the Southeast and Midwest, preserved foodstuffs for winter. Women laid cabbages, beets, turnips, and potatoes on mounds of earth, covered them with cornstalks, and then buried the entire pile beneath a thick layer of dirt. They dried grapes and peaches on racks in the sun before storing them in cloth bags; they made wild grapes, plums, and berries, as well as domestic peaches and cherries, into jellies, jams, and preserves. In addition to saving eggs in brine, some women knew how to pack butter in layers of salt for the winter, and many years later one pioneer's daughter fondly remembered its "nutty taste."[17]

Women processed all the meats, both wild game and animals raised for slaughter. "Hog killing time" came for housewives in Dallas as for those in the county, with grinding sausage, boiling lard, packing organ meats, curing bacon and hams. The mild climate that grew vegetables so abundantly led to problems with meat. Because cold weather usually lasted only a few days at a time even in the winter months, on many occasions the hog products spoiled when the temperature rose before preservation was completed.[18] Serving chicken for Sunday dinner was not dependent on the weather, but the process took several hours, from killing, defeathering ("picking"), and disemboweling the bird to cutting up and soaking the pieces in salt water before cooking. For many years, women in Dallas performed farming chores by milking cows, slopping pigs, churning butter, gathering eggs, and feeding chickens.[19]

After the growing, gathering, preserving, and processing of foodstuffs, actual meal preparation was almost a full-time job in county and "town" alike. Fresh-baked breads, vegetables from the garden, meats taken from the home supply—cooking such foods over an open fireplace took hours, and most families ate three full meals a day. Because the majority of Dallas settlers were native southerners, both their foods and cooking methods were typical of the South, where pork products, chickens, whole-grain breads, and honey and molasses were the dietary staples. Baked goods made with white flour and desserts prepared with sugar were rare luxuries. Even between-meal snacks consisted of "real" food, perhaps an egg or a potato roasted in the hot ashes of the fireplace.[20]

Cooking involved auxiliary tasks. Water had to be drawn from the well, carried from a nearby spring, or dipped from a barrel that the men hauled by wagon from the nearest creek. The fire had to be fed, too, and women chopped kindling as they needed it from firewood sawed and stacked by the men. If the fire died, someone went to a neighbor's home for live coals or started a new fire with a flint, kindling, and "punk," a highly flammable fungus that grew on decayed wood. If punk was not available, gunpowder could substitute—risky, but effective.[21]

Feeding the family was the women's most urgent work; clothing them was next in importance. Women as well as men dressed deer hides and bearskins for jackets, pants, and moccasins. Wealthier families had fabrics brought by wagon train from Jefferson or Shreveport and hired seamstresses to "live in" for several weeks each season to repair old garments and make new ones. As soon as they could produce cotton and wool for their own use, most women sewed their families' clothes from homespun.[22] Serviceable, tough, and often ill-fitting, the value of frontier clothing lay not in its cut, style, or fit, but in how long it would last.[23]

After completing all the tasks necessary to process raw cotton and wool—washing, carding, combing, dyeing, spinning, and weaving—women sewed homespun into dresses and men's shirts. They blended cotton and wool fibers into cloth called "jeans" for men's work clothes and suits; spun sewing thread and rubbed it with beeswax to prevent fraying; cut buttons from gourds and covered them to match the garment; and made dyes from bark, berries, the hulls of green nuts, and wood chips from particular trees.[24] Only after 1872–73 and the arrival of the railroads did Dallas stores offer plentiful supplies of commercially manufactured fabrics and notions, leaving just the cutting and sewing to be done by hand.

Families with several daughters or even one woman slave could achieve a higher standard of living than those with only one or two adult women. If the household possessed such luxury goods as counterpanes, linens for dining table and beds, blankets, comforters, and pillows, the women had to make them. Nancy Jane Cochran made featherbeds for her home and for her children's wedding gifts with feathers from the chickens and geese she had brought from Missouri.[25] Lights, also, improved daily life, and providing them was the women's work. In the 1840s, beef tallow and wild honeybee wax were used for candles and for tapers, with the latter wound around a bottle, then unwound as they burned. A family with fewer hands for work had to rely on a wick laid in a saucer of fat.[26]

Frequent pregnancies accompanied most women's prime working years. Like preventive medicine in general, prenatal care was unknown, and Dallas County women left no evidence regarding their knowledge of contraception. According to the Census of 1850, the average frontier home in the county had four children under the age of fifteen. Individual households, to be sure, had the eight to twelve children so often assumed to be characteristic of nineteenth-century farm families, but others had one, two, or none. Few women lived in a

statistically "average" home, and, because the census takers did not count mis-
carriages, infant deaths, or stillbirths, only family stories preserved memories of
an individual's unsuccessful pregnancies.[27]

Combined, as it had to be, with the hard work of providing for a family,
frequent childbearing contributed to health problems, premature aging, and,
for some women, a shortened life span.[28] The first white woman to arrive in
Dallas County was Charity Morris Gilbert, who in 1842 lived for a few months
on the Trinity River's banks, west and south of where Dallas would be. The
mother of eight children, Gilbert was forty-one, but members of the Beeman
family remembered her as an old woman. Her husband and sons disliked working the sticky black soil of Dallas County, so the family moved to Bonham in
Fannin County. There Charity Gilbert bore four more children, for a total of
eleven. She died in 1854, at the age of fifty-three.[29]

Other pioneer women seemed virtually indestructible, frequent childbearing and hard work notwithstanding. During the 1850s and 1860s, Mary Amery
Jackson spent the majority of her working years on a farm in Dallas County.
Born in England in 1828, she immigrated to Texas with her husband and eight
children, and long afterwards her son remembered how his parents toiled to
rear a family on the frontier. When Mary Jackson died in 1915 at the age of
eighty-seven, she had outlived her husband by twenty-eight years.[30]

Producing food and clothing left women little time for anything else, including the children. A mother constantly busy providing her family's livelihood
could barely think about the children's physical safety, much less supervise their
moral and social training. Youngsters learned appropriate behavior through close
association with adults during the working day. Full-time devotion to special
childhood needs was a maternal ideal that came into vogue decades later, primarily among the urban middle and upper classes. Children in farm families
were about as likely to be tended and even disciplined by older siblings as by
their mothers.

Household chores were delegated to daughters as they grew up, but when
there was too much for the girls to do—or if the family had only sons—pioneer
mothers pressed the boys into service to spin and weave, churn, carry in water
and firewood, and make candles. Many years later, one man thought he must
have spun enough thread during his childhood to reach from Dallas to El Paso.
Another complained that just as he mastered the craft of making candles, people
stopped using them. One household task could be a paying occupation, for
mothers allowed sons who churned extra butter to sell it to housewives in Dallas. By the 1850s and very likely earlier, the village was a market where farm
women could sell butter, eggs, and garden vegetables and so add small amounts
of cash to their family economies.[31]

The work necessary to feed and clothe the family made house cleaning, like child rearing, a lower priority, but when women found time to clean, they made their own implements. Scalded corn husks mopped rough puncheon floors; clumps of wild straw tied to sticks became brooms; rushes from stream banks scrubbed cedar water buckets and churns.[32] Washday required soap, bleach, and starch, all made by recipes that varied only slightly from household to household.[33] As with the cooking and laundering, cleaning the house meant chopping kindling and firewood to heat the water carried from the stream or drawn from the well.

Health care was yet another of the women's responsibilities, one that chose its own time to demand their energies. Entire families came down with chills and fever almost upon their arrival in Dallas County, where the most common illnesses were malaria, pneumonia, typhoid fever, and vague, undiagnosed "fevers." Even the "childhood" diseases often were deadly, with measles, whooping cough, and diphtheria claiming numerous victims. Methods of treatment were basic and almost always "homemade." With quinine very expensive and often unavailable, a native plant called "snake root" could relieve the symptoms of malaria. A salve for burns came from jimsonweed and "candy for colds" from the horehound plant. "Scurvy root" relieved soreness of the mouth and gums. Additional medicinal herbs grew in the women's gardens, and family lore included the ways to prepare and use them.[34]

When someone died, preparations for burial were the women's work. Most frequent were the losses of children. Nationwide, one child in five died before its fifth birthday, and, with their large numbers of young children's graves, nineteenth-century cemeteries in Dallas County fit the national statistics.[35] Female neighbors came to help wash and dress the body and to provide emotional support, just as they came to help with the ordinary housework when serious illness struck or a new baby was due.[36]

Even under normal conditions, the time needed for homemaking, whether on the frontier or in long-settled areas, now appears as daunting as the work itself. Washing, bleaching, and starching the laundry, for example, filled an entire working day. Ironing took another. The laundering was done once a week or perhaps twice each month; other household tasks, too, were periodic instead of daily. Thorough cleaning of a cabin was far less urgent than meals and clothing, but it was a major job, requiring a full day with several women working together. A year's supply of soap took a full week of constant attention, longer if the family was large. In some families, the women made soap and candles twice a year.[37] In order just to keep up with the main chores, women had to do several things at once—mend or weave while the bread baked, spin as the soap cooled, roast sweet potatoes or corn in the fire beneath the pot boiling the dirty clothes.[38]

Margaret Bryan did this work for the members of her household, which by

1850 included fourteen persons. The Bryans' double cabin—two separate cabins with a roofed "dog-trot" or breezeway between them—sheltered Margaret, Neely, and their three children, the oldest of whom was five; the four children, aged three to ten, of Margaret's uncle; and five boarders, who included three men, a teenage boy, and a five-year-old girl. With eight young children and five adults eating three meals a day, Bryan undoubtedly needed frequent help, which came, most likely, from her mother and sisters. Just as they took in orphaned children, both relatives and those of neighbors, pioneer women spent days and sometimes weeks with other families in times of crisis or when the workload was heavier than usual.[39]

Everyone, in fact, could expect some degree of community support. Such help amounted to an exchange of services, that, for all its casual nature, operated as a system among women and men alike in the nineteenth-century rural economy. When a birth was imminent, for example, the neighbor women attended the expectant mother, and often one among them was an experienced midwife. Neighbors came in times of sickness and death, too, to do household chores, tend the ill, or bury the dead. Barn and house raisings, corn huskings, and quilting bees also were occasions when the pioneers shared major work. They cooperated in the same way to slaughter and butcher the hogs, then salt and cure the meats. A family owning one of Dallas County's few ox-powered cotton gins routinely interrupted its own work to accommodate any neighbor who brought a wagon load of cotton. One farmer set her field hands to splitting rails for a neighboring widow, only then sending the men to cut timber for use on her own farm as ox yokes, plow stocks, garden palings, and boards.[40]

However much it resembles the bartering of goods without cash, the exchange of services was less precise with regard to value, although the monetary worth of "exchanged" chores could be estimated in terms of the time actually spent doing the work. Instead of a swapping of personal favors, however, the practice seems to have been more a matter of "pitch in and help whenever you can," a customary expression of community, rather than a formal arrangement. A century later, the work of that "moral economy" is virtually impossible to evaluate by a monetary standard, such spontaneous cooperation now being almost incomprehensible. Ultimately, the system's value lay not only in the amount of labor expended, but also in the sense of security gained through the resulting personal ties.

Forced into self-sufficiency by their distance from established towns and cities, the settlers expressed a market orientation at least as early as the 1850s. Particularly, they hoped that the railroads would soon reach the Three Forks area. Dallas County had numerous creeks and springs but lacked a navigable stream: the Trinity was a temperamental river, either flooding or drying up, almost always choked with silt and clogged with tree roots. Wheat and corn were the cash crops, for flour and meal went overland to market much more easily than bales of cotton. Farmers traveled into Dallas and often farther east to Jefferson, Texas, or even to Shreveport, Louisiana, to exchange their produce for manufactured goods.[41]

Close as they came to self-sufficiency, the rural pioneers never were completely independent. Their need for services and goods they could not produce at home sustained the merchants, craftspeople, and professionals immigrating to Dallas.[42] The production of food, clothing, and shelter for immediate use was more important than a cash crop, especially just after their arrival, but from the time of first settlement, people throughout the county needed salt, sugar, flour, coffee, and other groceries; farm tools and shoes; and repairs on implements and household items. The trading of farm produce for commercially manufactured wares linked the production of the agricultural home with the marketplace. Indeed, the domestic, or use, economy did not merely support, but actually generated, the local market.

However well their wares sold, the general stores did little to alter the distinctly rural nature of life in Dallas. Goods manufactured in New England and the Northeast had a long, expensive journey to Texas, and store owners had to transport merchandise overland from Jefferson, Shreveport, or Galveston in ox-drawn wagons. Because animals could not be watered during the dry months, the freight shipments stopped altogether in July and August, making fabrics, groceries, farm tools, and iron implements scarce until the autumn rains.[43] Regardless of the supplies, the available goods hardly affected women's work, for nothing resembling a commercial food industry existed. No breads could be purchased already baked, no vegetables were available canned or frozen, no meats could be had already butchered, much less packaged.

In the earliest years, travelers passing through the Three Forks remarked upon the crude living conditions of its settlers, and much later the son of one pioneer family reasoned that only poverty could have driven anyone to "such a wilderness."[44] This assumption was not entirely accurate, for, as on many frontiers, settlers in Dallas County tended to be people "on the way up," who already had spent a number of years searching for a place where they could "make it." The primitive conditions of "starting over" coexisted with evidence of former prosperity.

One-room log cabins with chimneys of native stone were small and cramped, hardly luxurious even with puncheon floors instead of dirt. Many settlers began their new lives with such crude furnishings as bunks built into the walls and corn shucks for mattresses, while others managed to transport a few pieces of good furniture from their former homes.[45] One family brought a large cherry chest, a small table for the Bible, and bedsteads with hay ticks to go beneath their featherbeds.[46] Among the incongruities travelers in Texas reported were log cabins with libraries and fine furniture, and women who wore silk dresses and real jewels to frontier parties.[47]

Whatever their supplies, goods, flocks, and herds, the early Dallas County pioneers certainly brought their skills, experience, intelligence, and customs. For the times, they had a fair amount of education, too. In 1850, 89 percent of the county's 2,536 white adults could read and write—a proportion much higher than that usually assumed for frontier populations. Women were more than twice as likely as men to be illiterate: of 285 white persons over the age of nineteen with no schooling, approximately 67 percent were female.[48]

On every frontier, the wilderness was cultural as well as physical. Throughout the 1840s and well into the next decade, education in Dallas and Dallas County was a matter of "catch as catch can," depending on whether parents could teach their children or find someone to do so. Few settlers had much formal schooling, but almost anyone who could read and write seems to have been able to attract pupils. Fourteen-year-old Rebecca Baker taught thirty students in her parents' cabin. In what later became the Dallas area called Oak Cliff, Mary Hord began teaching her children, then soon found herself with an entire class of little girls. Because their homes were twelve to forty miles away, they slept in her loft and paid twelve and a half cents a day for meals and tuition.[49] In Farmers' Branch, then about fifteen miles to the northwest, Mary West held classes in her cabin until a man teacher opened a school nearby, then resumed giving lessons when he left after only four months.[50]

While women were more likely to teach in early Dallas County homes, fathers also took responsibility for their children's education. In the late 1840s, William Brown Miller hired a young widow, Sarah Gray, and paid her way from Kentucky to Dallas County to tutor his daughters. Every frontier included people who were suspicious of culture and learning, if not of basic education, and Miller shocked such conservative neighbors by instructing Sarah Gray to teach his daughters dancing along with reading, writing, and sums.[51]

Like schooling, churches had their origins in private homes. In religious gatherings during the 1840s, women were always present and usually constituted the majority. In Farmers Branch, a Methodist layman called his neighbors together each week for worship. Because the men were "Sunday hunters," most of those attending were women and children. Very likely, Nancy Jane Cochran arranged the first formal worship held in Dallas County in her cabin in 1844. Despite acceptance of piety as a desirable female trait, records of women's early religious work are rare, with Cochran's being one of the few documented instances. A decade later, in 1856, she donated the land for a church about ten miles northwest of Dallas, paced off the lots for building and cemetery, drew up the deed herself, and named the church Cochran Chapel in her husband's memory.[52]

Hard work, personal sacrifice, and community participation did not earn equality, although the pioneer women of Texas enjoyed a legal status notably better than that of their sisters in the older states.[53] Texas women who were single, widowed, or divorced had, except for the vote, the same rights as men, including, oddly enough, the right to run for and hold most state offices. In contrast to English common law, which erased a wife's legal existence, the Texas Constitution of 1845 incorporated certain principles of Spanish-Mexican law and gave a married woman the right to hold separate property in her own name. She also owned an equal share of the community property that she and her husband acquired.

Except to prevent the sale of her separate property, however, she had few rights of control over anything except her personal effects. Without her consent, her husband could rent or mortgage her property and take all income and profits from it, although he could use such gains only for the family's support. As manager of the community property, he also controlled her wages, earnings, and bank accounts, including money she deposited before marriage. Concerned more for the welfare of families than individuals, the framers of the Texas constitution wrote into law a wife's right to reclaim control of her separate property if her husband mismanaged it or the income it produced.

Moreover, her interest, if not her right, in the homestead was recognized by the legal requirement that she give separate and independent consent to its sale. Otherwise, the family home and lands belonged to her husband, regardless of the labor she invested in their establishment and maintenance. Although Texas never adopted the common-law tradition of the legal fiction of husband-wife unity, later decisions by the state's courts suggest an assumption that marriage was not a partnership but an adversarial situation in which the husband's interests and decisions worked for the relationship, while the wife's worked against it. In Texas, as elsewhere in the United States, a woman was incapacitated legally less by her sex than by her marriage.

Whether—and how many—husbands actually exercised their legal right to their wives' butter and egg money we can never know, nor can we know how many married women found their inferior status galling, inconvenient, or incapacitating. More marriages were broken by desertion, or certainly by death, than by divorce. One clue to women's opinions of marriage as a legal situation, though, may lie in a widespread enigma: frontier widows tended, far more often than widowers, to remain unmarried. Even relatively young women with considerable property, a powerful aphrodisiac in any century, remained widows. While some undoubtedly felt that the deceased husband was irreplaceable, others probably wished to protect their children's interests. Yet others may have come to relish the responsibility and independence they discovered as widows or that they had known earlier as single women. According to the conventional wisdom, men sought new mates as soon as possible; otherwise, many felt they had to break up their families and distribute their children among relatives or neighbors.[54]

Whether or not frontier marriages were what we would call happy, the most important aspects of people's lives centered in their homes.[55] The pioneers knew the satisfaction of producing with their own hands the things they needed, and their wealth grew directly from their personal skills and energy. The labors of wife and husband were not separated from their commitment to each other and to their children, who saw their parents labor at concrete tasks that produced immediate results and thus knew, to a large extent, what would be expected of them as adults. By joining the family workforce at an early age, children learned through experience to meet those expectations.

Social life grew out of the family-based processes of making a living. Originating in the work of furnishing homes, quilting bees often were parties for everyone and not just occasions for the women to sew. The men and boys went as eagerly as their wives and sisters, but spent the time playing ball, wrestling, or talking, while the women worked. After the quilting frame was raised again to its storage place near the cabin ceiling came the time for dinner and then dancing, often into the wee hours of the next day. As late as the 1870s, barn and house raisings, too, brought people together for work within the system of labor exchange, while simultaneously enabling rural settlers to form the social relationships that made them a community.[56]

Their descendants chuckled over stories of "wild" forms of frontier entertainment and treasured family memories of gentler diversions. In 1846, the county's first grand jury handed down fifty-five indictments for "gaming." Nearly thirty years later, the editors of the city directory noted that the accused had included "some of the most reputable and responsible men who ever lived in the community."[57] By contrast, the Christmas and New Year's celebration of 1849 was more decorous. On that occasion, ten couples danced the minuet and the Virginia reel to fiddle music on the puncheon floor of the log "Dallas Tavern" owned by Margaret Bryan's brother. There was no Christmas tree, but Santa Claus visited the children.[58]

Like celebrations, family structure was traditional. Early Dallas County families tended overwhelmingly to be nuclear, consisting of a wife, her husband, and their children. Only after fifteen or more years did some of these households become extended to include three generations living under the same roof. Unmarried men were not unusual on any frontier; more surprising were the widows who sought a better future for themselves and their children. As single persons, such women claimed headrights of 320 acres and established their homes and farms. Youngsters of these and other pioneer families grew up to marry neighbors and form stable webs of kinship, many of which endured throughout the twentieth century.[59]

The presence of the father in the home insured patriarchal authority, although the men often were away, taking care of farm matters or following an additional occupation. The freighting business, for example, involved driving wagons to Jefferson, Shreveport, Galveston, or Austin. For weeks at a time, a freighter's wife cared for home and children alone, except for occasional help from a female relative or perhaps, a servant. Similarly, attorneys practiced law all over their judicial districts, following the court from one county seat to the next and leaving wives to add the management of farms or, if they lived in Dallas, small businesses to their usual family responsibilities.[60] Despite frequent or extended absences, however, a father's "place" was in the home.

Economically if not legally, the married couple was a partnership, with, as a general rule, the husband's work contributing to the family's long-term interests while the wife produced goods for immediate consumption. The home-centered, unindustrialized economy was by nature a use economy, with much of its production (and especially that of the women) intended for consumption by the producers. While 50 percent is a safe estimate for the wife's contribution to the family's livelihood, both modern scholars and people at the time have asserted that, in terms of actual labor performed, the women did more, and more different kinds of, work than their husbands to sustain the frontier homes.[61] As Nancy Jane Cochran's son wrote, "[T]he pioneer women contributed more to the development of the country, and to the advancement of civilization than did the men. They contributed, in their sphere, as much as the men to the physical development of the country."[62]

Women often labored in the men's "sphere," too. When husbands were away, wives tended the larger farm animals and worked to produce the cash crop, in addition to their regular chores of milking twice a day and tending the smaller livestock and fowl. During the busiest seasons of planting and harvesting, the women joined the men in the fields as a matter of course.[63] At times, women helped with the "men's work" even when the men were present. Immediately after the three Beeman families arrived in 1840 at White Rock Creek, some eight miles from Neely Bryan's claim, they built a log blockhouse for defense. A man they knew had died at the hands of Indians a few months earlier. With her infant son in one arm and her rifle in the other, Margaret Bryan's mother, Emily Beeman, regularly took her turns at sentry duty.[64]

For untold generations, women did the work of producing food, clothing, and household furnishings. Before industrialization in both Europe and America, the home was the economic center of society: almost all goods were produced in someone's home, and, for most of human history, women performed many of the tasks required to support their families. Judging from pioneer reminiscences of other areas, Dallas and Dallas County differed little from frontiers elsewhere, whether midwestern or southern, northern or Texan, rural or "urban." With adaptations to fit the climate and the available materials, women's work in the home was similar everywhere.[65]

The skills and knowledge that women used so adeptly in early Dallas and Dallas County homes were oriented—like Texas law—not to individual opportunity but toward maintenance of a family.[66] In the frontier home, success, to say nothing of survival, depended upon the work of wife and husband as a team or partnership. The initial drudgery, isolation, and hardship in time gave way to prosperity, a higher standard of living, and, very likely, enhanced status in the new community. The frontier, in fact, seems to have benefited women most as members of families. Indeed, the argument could be made that, given the nature of the work required to earn a livelihood, men also fared better within families. In private ways that rarely were acknowledged or even noticed, women always participated in the development of community, most especially in the economy. For village and countryside alike and in the basic social institutions of home, school, and church, women's work was integral and essential to the founding of the new community.

Chapter Two
The Country Market Town

"[T]his morning I went up in town," Frances Killen Smith wrote in her diary, "but was too proud to look at the know nothing flag as I went by."[1] Basing his campaign on the principles of the Know-Nothing, or American Party, Sam Houston was running for governor in June 1857, against the states' rights ticket of the Democrats. His speech in Dallas aroused great excitement, but had Fanny Smith been enfranchised, she would have voted against "old Houston." However fervently she may have participated in family discussions or expressed her opinions to friends, she lacked the right to vote. Turning her eyes from the Know-Nothing banner had to be the extent of her political action.

Given women's visibility in Dallas during the 1850s and 1860s, Fanny Smith's interest in politics was not surprising. Except for voting and holding office, women were active participants in the community, and female names frequently appeared in the newspaper and in public records. Women executed wills and administered the estates of male relatives, were parties to lawsuits, taught in schools, worked in family businesses, ran their own shops, entered contests and exhibitions at the county fair, spoke and performed at public events, organized holiday celebrations, attended political rallies, and marched in parades.[2] Although the town's few voluntary associations had only male members, women performed in a musical society and helped to plan its programs. They also formed two "ladies' aid" groups during the Civil War. In a social and cultural, if not exactly a physical, wilderness, virtually everything women did helped to build the community.

As the county seat and the area's marketing center, Dallas in 1857 was a logical campaign stop for a gubernatorial candidate. Although the population had reached perhaps 400—in 1858, the special state Census of Incorporated Places would list 430—hundreds of visitors regularly came into town. Farmers sold their crops or traded them for supplies in the general stores, attended the county and district court sessions, had tools and implements repaired, and caught up on the local news. Travelers crossing the Trinity River to reach the territories farther west and south needed temporary lodging, as well as goods and services. Excepting only the fact that its population nearly tripled between the federal censuses of 1860 and 1870, Dallas seemed typical of country market towns throughout the South.

Among the earliest institutions were a newspaper and a school, both forging links between the growing settlement and the larger society from which its residents came. When Lucy Jordan Latimer and her husband arrived in July 1849, their ox-drawn wagon carried her rosewood piano and his printing press and boxes of type. Wake Latimer published the *Cedar Snag,* soon renamed the *Dallas Herald,* while Lucy taught school and music lessons and played piano solos for such events as the dedication of the new courthouse in 1851. Between 1852 and 1854, Wake served as chief justice of Dallas County, and Lucy worked with his partner to write and edit the paper.[3]

The farming families in Dallas County socialized and formed neighborly ties through occasional barn raisings and quilting bees, but town life, by its very nature, required a kind of sustained cooperation rarely experienced—or needed— in rural areas. One example was the way Dallas leaders worked to win the 1850 election to become the county seat, and another was their successful lobbying of the legislature for incorporation in 1856. Both achievements carried notable advantages. For economic as well as political reasons, becoming the center for local government did more to insure a settlement's permanence than any other factor. When people came to conduct legal business during the county court's regular sessions, they also traded in the stores. Incorporation was in some ways still more important, for it made Dallas a legal entity and gave residents the right to act as a body through elected leaders to incur debts, enter contracts, bring lawsuits, adopt and enforce ordinances, and control future development.[4]

In addition to Dallas's status as the local political and administrative center, the occupations of its residents clearly attested to the place's urban character. A number of residents still listed their occupations as farming, but most were engaged in trade and commerce. Of the "middling sort" who were neither extremely wealthy nor very poor, a majority owned businesses, such as the general stores, the *Dallas Herald,* and at least one "exchange office" that provided monetary services, though not actual banking.[5] By 1858, the proprietors of a few small industries could be counted among them—the carriage manufacturer, brick makers, and saddlers—along with craftspeople, including the tinsmith, the saw-grist miller, the blacksmiths, milliners, and dressmakers. The professions offered less security than trade and business. Attorneys sold insurance and real estate, and more than one physician ran a drug or dry goods store.

Also significant was the fact that relationships among the residents were more complex than those in a village or rural community. In 1849, the town's first voluntary association, the Tannehill Lodge of Freemasonry, was organized. After completion of their meeting hall in 1853, the Masons reserved its upper story for their own uses but opened the first floor for rental. The Masonic Hall became the town center, available for church services, gatherings where men discussed public business, programs and performances for everyone's entertainment, and meetings of the literary society and the lyceum.

The variety of available goods and services indicated a considerable degree of specialization in occupations by the late 1850s, with women active in the growing market economy.[6] In 1852, Frances and Thomas Crutchfield opened a two-story hotel in a frame building, with room and board available for $12.50 to $15.00 a month and a full meal for twenty-five cents. An obvious business for a town growing where two major roads converged near a ferry crossing, the Crutchfield House also served as the post office and the stagecoach depot. Like Charles Durgin before him, Postmaster Crutchfield left the mail to his wife, but like her, had numerous duties. In addition to managing the guest accommodations, Frances supervised the hotel's kitchen and dining room. Thomas ran the stage office, posting schedules and selling tickets for the coaches that left several times each week for Austin, Houston, and Shreveport.[7]

The growing economy also attracted Sarah and Alexander Cockrell in 1852, when Alex bought Neely Bryan's ferry license and the remainder of his headright. Sarah had lived as a frontier farmwife in Dallas County for six years, but now she began a business career that would affect the town's development for the next four decades. With several black servants to relieve her of the heaviest household chores, she worked with her husband during the 1850s in a series of ventures: a construction business that included the making and delivery of bricks, a wooden toll bridge to replace Bryan's ferry, a saw-grist mill half a mile south of town, the construction of a two-story brick building for rental to small businesses, and the planning of a three-story hotel. Judging from letters to her daughter in later years, Sarah Cockrell's formal schooling had ended at the elementary level. Because Alex was illiterate, she kept the business records, managed the money, and handled the correspondence—all tasks which she could perform in the "appropriate" place, their home.[8]

In April 1858, Alex was shot during a quarrel with a personal rival who happened to be the town marshal. Left the richest person in Dallas, Sarah had to assume full responsibility for their four children, the oldest of whom was eight, and for the business ventures they had run together. The remaining thirty-four years of her life exemplify the ways southern women successfully balanced the obligations incurred through widowhood against the demands of propriety: Cockrell tailored the public aspects of managing several businesses to suit her private needs.[9] After winning a lawsuit to collect money that the marshal owed

Alex, she began reorganizing her business affairs around her family duties. First she fulfilled the construction company's existing contracts, then closed it and the saw-grist mill. Both would have required her to travel.

The two businesses she chose to run not only allowed her to be with the children, but also provided services vital to Dallas. After Alex's toll bridge collapsed in August 1858, Sarah renewed the license to put the ferry back into service and thus maintained access to the major roads south, west, and north. Also important for the town's development was the hotel, completed late in the summer of 1859 and named the Saint Nicholas. Lauded by the *Herald* as if it were a public service instead of a private business, the Saint Nicholas (later, the Dallas Hotel) had suites for families and parlors for special occasions, as well as rooms for individual guests. With tall mirrors and polished floors, chandeliers and ornate furniture, the hotel immediately became the local social center and the site of formal balls, dinners, and cotillion parties. Equally important in the community's point of view, the hotel provided accommodations for travelers and visitors, including potential investors and business owners.[10]

In that same year, 1859, Sarah Cockrell applied to the legislature for a charter to build a permanent bridge across the Trinity River. Business owners and farmers needed a dependable link between countryside and markets, for, while the ferry was adequate most of the time, seasonal rains frequently sent the

The Dallas Hotel, originally named the Saint Nicholas, in 1859. The building burned in the fire of 1860. Sarah Cockrell opened a two-story building across the street as the Dallas Hotel, which was renamed the St. Charles about 1870. Courtesy Dallas Historical Society

river over its banks to a width of half a mile and more.[11] As owner of the ferry license as well as of the land providing access to the bridge, Cockrell was the logical person to undertake such a major project.

The community's response must have surprised and disappointed her. Fifty-five business owners and professional men signed a petition against the bridge, arguing that toll charges would anger farmers and discourage investors. Years later, descendants of the pioneer families recalled the tolls as expensive. Yet, in a time when privately owned toll bridges were common, the actions of the petitioners suggest a degree of sex prejudice along with their commercial concerns.

Subsequent events revealed Sarah Cockrell's tenacity and, perhaps, her political skills. For many years, family legend has claimed that she traveled to Austin to speak on behalf of her project, thus becoming the first woman ever to address the Texas Legislature. The House and Senate journals record no such appeal, but she well may have addressed the committees on roads, bridges, and ferries. Moreover, Cockrell family friend Nicholas Darnell was speaker of the house, with the influence to sway the votes of fellow lawmakers and the power to control the progress of bills. Whatever her role in the proceedings, in February 1860 the Cockrell bridge charter easily passed the legislature, 26-0 in the senate and 59-2 in the house.[12] Sarah Cockrell received no unusual favors: the other bridge charters issued by the Eighth Legislature also went to private investors, who would charge tolls to recoup their investments and justify their risks.

Merchants especially needed a dependable means across the Trinity River. In 1856, the owners of the Gold and Donaldson Dry Goods Company advertised a wide range of merchandise, much of it for use in the home. Tableware, wooden tubs, and churns shared shelf space with a variety of fabrics that included cashmere and visette silks alongside the muslin, gingham, and flannel expected in a frontier emporium. The proprietors stocked items as small as dress trimmings, ribbons, buttons, and combs, as well as implements like tinware and such major appliances as stoves for kitchen and parlor.[13] One European visitor included the Gold and Donaldson general store in his travelogue and observed, "Here you may get salt pork, whiskey, wine, arak, sugar, salt, coffee, tea, and other articles necessary for life, all scattered chaotically about. Outside are farming implements, ox hides, and hides of buffalo and bear; all kinds of iron utensils and implements, carts, chests, boxes, kegs, etc."[14] An odd assortment of luxury goods mingled with basic groceries and tools.

Despite the availability of commercially made wares, people continued to rely on the use economy of the home, where women produced and processed foods and fabrics, sewed clothing, and maintained living conditions. Manufactured goods and purchased groceries eased women's work somewhat, but as yet did little to change it. For those who could afford to buy such items, commercially produced cloth, sewing thread, buttons, trimmings, soap, and candles saved many hours of labor.

In Dallas as in the county, meal preparation remained the primary task of every day, beginning with foodstuffs that required all the steps of basic processing before they reached the table. Living in a town offered a few advantages, such as purchasing butter from a farmwoman's sons to save a few hours each week. Even without a butcher's shop, fresh meat was available, if only on occasion. An impromptu market opened in the town square between 4 and 6 A.M. whenever a local farmer hauled a slaughtered animal into Dallas, hacked off hunks of beef with a meat ax, and estimated their prices without the use of scales. During the nine months between March and November, all such meat had to be cooked immediately after purchase to prevent spoilage in the warm climate.[15] The alternatives to cold beef were game from the men's hunting, chickens raised in the backyard, or ham and pork from the previous season.

All purchased items had to be hauled into Dallas in ox-drawn freight wagons. Supplies were especially scarce during the dry months of July and August, and housewives frequently did without groceries for a week or more. When the wagons arrived at last, one pioneer's son recalled many years later, "there was something of a public rejoicing . . . [and] a hogshead of sugar lasted no longer than it took the merchant to weigh it out to his customers."[16] Transportation costs raised prices, and people frequently complained. With corn selling for thirty cents and wheat for a dollar a bushel in 1853, seven dollars was a lot to pay for a bag of salt. An acre of land brought only one to five dollars.[17]

However much or little a particular family purchased, commercial household items, fabrics, and groceries linked women's work to the marketplace in readily evident ways. Indeed, the main purpose of trade and commerce ultimately lay in supplying the home and improving life within it. Less obvious than domestic ties to trade was the basic economic importance of traditional female tasks, and these differed little throughout the nation. In urban as in rural areas, work in the home preceded all other activities: the production of meals and clothing, and the maintenance of comfortable shelter remained fundamental to the local economy.

Traditional female skills were part of the public economy, too, and sewing was the first of the home crafts to earn money in the marketplace. Dallas County's wealthier families regularly hired local seamstresses, sometimes to live in during the week and go home on weekends, but more often to stay for several weeks in the spring and fall to make new clothing and mend old garments. Women throughout the county also took in sewing. Addie Dye McDermett's sister Martha had a small business as a "tailoress" before her marriage to Margaret Bryan's brother, William H. Beeman.[18]

In 1859, the exhibitions at the first county fair included the arts and crafts of homemaking. Sponsored by the Dallas County Agricultural and Mechanical Association, the fair drew two thousand visitors to view items produced in people's homes—the women's vegetables, butter, candles, and soap alongside the men's flax, livestock, sorghum molasses, wheat flour, and corn. Wool carpeting and homemade fabrics, such as jeans and white linsey, shared the display tables with crocheted articles, quilts and blankets, ladies' riding hats, woolen net shawls, and silk net gloves. A competitive spirit flourished, with one young woman entering several contests in the hope that surely she would win a prize in one, if not in all.[19] As a major outlet for creative expression, as well as a vital home-making skill, needlework dominated the women's exhibits.

The needle arts also provided respectable trades for women in dressmaking and millinery. In September 1856, Maria Bingham, a fifty-one-year-old widow from Virginia, advertised the opening of her millinery shop to sell bonnets in silk, velvet, leghorn, and straw, as well as dresses in the latest styles. Later notices in the *Herald* added her offers to cut and make dresses, and to accept orders for both plain and fancy sewing. Her business must have been limited, however, for almost every woman in Dallas could sew with some degree of skill.

By 1859, Bingham also faced professional competition, as two newcomers advertised their services for dressmaking and millinery, one calling herself a "fashionable mantua maker and milliner" able to make dresses, trim bonnets, and do "Fancy Work."[20] The next year, 1860, Maria Bingham was running a boardinghouse "for gentlemen," in addition to her dressmaking and millinery. Whatever the insecurities of her craft, an accumulation of property over the years gave evidence of at least modest success: in 1871, Bingham advertised four full-sized town lots for lease, plus an entire block of eight others.[21]

While almost every woman could sew, relatively few could teach, another extension of women's traditional work in the home. During Dallas County's earliest years, the 1840s, teaching was gaining acceptance throughout the United States as an occupation appropriate for women, while at the same time female education was changing. Significant improvements began in 1821, when Emma Willard opened her seminary in Troy, New York, and won public support for a challenging course of study for girls. Appealing to patriotism and national pride, Willard argued that America needed educated women—Republican mothers—to run well-ordered homes and rear morally upright children, especially sons.[22]

During the 1830s and 1840s, Willard's graduates, and those of Mary Lyon at Mount Holyoke in Massachusetts, found teaching positions throughout the South, where higher education for women indicated gentility and upper-class status. Southern female seminaries and academies reformed their curricula to equal those of the best male schools, and in 1838 the world's first college for women, the Georgia Female College, opened in Atlanta. As a population, antebellum southern women showed higher illiteracy rates than men, but those who could afford a formal education had a choice of good institutions.[23]

The teachers who immigrated to Dallas during the 1850s clearly had benefited from the trend. Their advertisements in the *Herald* included their credentials, along with impressive lists of the courses they offered. Despite a frequent turnover of teachers, each year the Masonic Hall housed a Young Ladies' School that accepted small boys; often a separate "male school," taught by a man, also offered lessons there.[24] Before 1860, at least half the town's teachers were women, some of whom taught with their husbands. Married couples ran coeducational institutions with males and females in separate classes; almost always, the husband was principal and his wife assistant principal or "head of the female department." Willing to accommodate special needs, one school in 1859 offered night classes for students unable to attend during the day.[25]

Girls in Dallas appear to have enjoyed equal opportunities for education. Descriptions of courses varied little from school to school, with quality dependent solely upon the teacher's academic background. Money was the main factor in any child's access to schooling, although by 1859 the state allotted tuition funds to each county for pupils unable to pay.[26] The children of wealthier families had instruction in the fine arts, as well as basic education. Late in the 1850s, Lucy Latimer was one of several women who offered piano lessons, and a "Professor" Howard ran a dancing school, which closed its spring term with a fancy-dress party for the pupils.[27]

Religion, like education, was a primary form of cultural expression. Women were present and slightly in the majority when the earliest congregations were organized in Dallas, the Methodists in 1850 and the Disciples of Christ in 1852.[28] For a number of years, these groups, and other Protestants as well, were unable to support full-time pastors or to erect church buildings. Nonetheless, by 1856 the town's residents could attend worship services every week, if not always of their chosen denominations. Ordained ministers of several Protestant faiths lived in or near Dallas. They supported their families with other occupations and took turns preaching in the Masonic Hall each Sunday.

As much as religious expression and schooling, forms of recreation also revealed development in the community's cultural life. In the spring and summer of 1856, the "musical amateurs of Dallas and vicinity," both women and men, gave concerts of vocal and instrumental music in the Masonic Hall. Organized by July into the Musical Association of Dallas, the group presented several subsequent programs, at least one consisting of a series of *tableaux vivants*, that is, appropriately costumed individuals posing in "representations of classical, historical, and other scenes."[29] No record has survived of the group's founders or officers, but its existence shows the participatory nature of people's diversions, as well as the fact that women were active in community life. Women and men played instruments and sang in these formal "concerts" and entertained friends and relatives during gatherings in private homes.[30]

Performances often included classical music along with popular. In the early 1860s, Sally Reinhardt presented her piano students in recitals and won praise from the *Herald* only slightly less lavish than that awarded to her solo concerts. A native of Saxony, married to a watchmaker and jeweler, and the mother of two young sons, Sally Reinhardt could tune, repair, and restring pianos as well as give lessons. She also was a singer of some vocal range and accomplishment, for at her own concerts she performed selections by Beethoven and Donazetti, along with such lighter music as the "Last Rose of Summer," the "Star-Spangled Banner" (not yet the national anthem), and the "Bird-Song, after the manner of [Jenny] Lind." Reinhardt sang for public occasions, too, such as the ceremony in April 1860 to present the Texas Rangers with a silk flag sewn by a group of women.[31]

Residents also observed traditional celebrations. At the May Day festivities held in 1858 in a wooded area outside town, twenty-one-year-old Juliette Peak, later to become Dallas's first philanthropist, was crowned Queen of May. During the county fair of 1859, a "tournament" expressed the southern fascination with medieval times. On this occasion, the "Knights" of Dallas, Tarrant, the Prairie, and the Old Dominion competed not in jousting but in horsemanship. "Sir Prairie" won the competition and had the honor of crowning the Queen of Love and Beauty at a formal ball in the Dallas Hotel that night, when dancing lasted till "a late hour." In contrast, on Sunday evenings, dog fights attracted spectators to the street corners around the public square.[32]

Amateur performances and holiday festivals were not the only diversions available. In 1857, residents could view "the paintings of the Hudson schollars," perhaps reprints of works by the Hudson River School and possibly the property of a local resident, on exhibition at the courthouse.[33] Professional performers toured Texas, including an actress who in 1859 presented a well-received program of readings from Shakespeare and *Hiawatha,* and the family-run circuses which visited each year. However small and perhaps shabby those troupes may have been, each managed its own kind of panache. In 1859, an all-female silver coronet band led a circus parade into Dallas.[34]

Although women participated in entertainment and public programs, formal organizations like clubs and societies were reserved for males. The appearance of voluntary associations, in fact, was additional evidence of the community's increasingly urban nature. Excepting the *Herald*'s notices for the Musical Association, no evidence exists for women's organizations before 1861. Fraternal groups were the earliest voluntary associations in Dallas, and as early as 1856, a lyceum met regularly for lectures on science. The Dallas Historical Society convened each third Thursday evening "at early candle light," probably to discuss national, ancient, or medieval rather than local history. All the officers and, more than likely, the members of both these latter groups were men, although announcements in the *Herald* often invited "the ladies" to attend the programs.[35]

Dallas residents had contact with the wider culture, too. The *Herald*'s editors stocked a public reading table in their offices with the current issues of such magazines as *Harper's, Godey's Lady's Book, DeBow's Review, New York Musical World,* and the *National Democratic Review.* Newspapers from other places also were available—the *Rising Sun* of Newberry, South Carolina; the *Messenger* from Woodville in Tyler County, Texas; and the *Southern Intelligencer* from Austin.[36]

Of these publications, *Godey's Lady's Book* was the most significant historically, not only as the first American mass-circulation magazine, but also for its major influence on women's roles in the United States during the mid-nineteenth century. As popular among southern as among northern women, *Godey's* was edited by Sarah Josepha Hale, a New England widow who took up a career to support five children. Making the magazine famous for its fashion plates and columns on etiquette and manners, Hale advocated higher education for women and urged them to enter the professions, especially medicine. At the same time, she considered the duties of the private "sphere" far more valuable to society than business, politics, or any aspect of public life. Her editorial policy did much to help develop the concept of domesticity into a widely accepted ideology that defined women's roles in home life.[37]

With its explicit designation of the home as the female's "natural sphere," the concept of domesticity pervaded American culture by the 1850s. Elaborated into a doctrine of social organization, its tenets idealized motherhood and attributed to womankind a "moral nature" superior to men's. These ideas spread throughout the nation through popular fiction, the women's magazines, and even school textbooks. Frontier conditions did not hamper the acceptance of domesticity, although they may have interfered with its actual practice. Even if Dallas women managed to read *Godey's* regularly, the requirements of pioneer life could frustrate role expectations in small towns as in the county.[38]

As elsewhere in the South, family life in Dallas remained solidly patriarchal, with fathers retaining traditional authority within their households. Merchant families resided, as they had for centuries in both Europe and America, in the buildings where their businesses were housed, usually living in rooms behind or upstairs over their stores.[39] Such arrangements enabled mothers to share in tending the store and fathers to perform their duties in disciplining the children. During the 1840s and the 1850s, the growth of cities and the spread of industry in the Northwest and Midwest increasingly drew fathers away from their homes to work, and the ideal of domesticity combined with these conditions to give mothers a new kind of authority.[40] These social changes would not reach Texas until the late 1870s, when, in a predominantly agrarian state, they mostly benefited middle- and upper-class urban women.

During the 1850s, Dallas seemed in many ways less a frontier than an ordinary country town, and women's lives reflected the community's development. Nineteen years old in 1857, Fanny Smith clearly preferred to be with friends in Dallas than on her parents' farm.[41] Her father was an ordained Methodist minister who took his turns preaching in the Masonic Hall. As the owner of twenty slaves, he was a small planter and one of the county's wealthiest men, a position that allowed his daughter considerable leisure. Fanny enjoyed a pleasant life of visiting friends, reading novels, shopping in Dallas, and attending religious services and other public gatherings. She learned to play the violin and was good enough at the piano to perform in the Musical Association's programs.

Fanny's skill at horseback riding and driving the buggy enabled her to go into town alone or with women friends.[42] Such trips by unescorted women were evidence that, as one long-time resident recalled, Dallas in the 1850s was "as quiet, law-abiding a community as could be desired."[43] Lawbreaking involved personal rivalries and feuds and relatively minor incidents of vandalism, such as young men shooting up the dinner bell in front of the Crutchfield House or, on one memorable Christmas Eve, tearing down and burning the abandoned log courthouse built years earlier by Neely Bryan.[44] Such antics did little to threaten white people's safety or property, and women apparently had few fears about traveling in and around Dallas. Children, too, enjoyed a degree of personal freedom almost unthinkable a century later; as adults, they remembered happy days of playing in thickets and ponds near the town. Young girls, one woman recalled, grew up "as fond of sport" as their brothers and as "skillful in use of the rifle" and in horseback riding.[45]

One of Fanny Smith's good friends was her former piano teacher, Lucy Jordan Latimer. Reared and educated in Tennessee, Latimer lived in one of the town's nicest residences.[46] With a black woman to do the hardest household chores, she had time each week to receive her numerous women friends and to visit their homes for tea. She enjoyed the annual commencement exercises of the local schools, and regularly attended Sunday school, prayer meetings, Bible classes, and church services. When Lucy went by stagecoach to visit out-of-town friends, Fanny came to "take care of things." Married and mother of three children, Lucy Latimer hardly was "house-bound."

Owning slaves did not free middle- and upper-class southern women from housework, however, whether they lived in town or the country. While Fanny Smith had no farm chores, she washed windows, mopped floors, ironed, and cooked. She sewed daily, and almost every entry in her diary mentions a sewing project—quilting, embroidering, knitting, and making lawn and calico dresses and crinoline petticoats. Apparently Fanny made all her own clothes and turned to "old Mrs. Bingham" for help only with the cutting of elaborate garments. She even worked on wheat cloth sacks for the storage of farm produce.[47]

The early years in Dallas County undoubtedly were hard and sometimes lonely for many of the first women settlers. But within a decade, their daughters' lives, and their own as well, were integrated into the community, with numerous relationships and acquaintances among the town dwellers and those of nearby county areas. While men's social lives were structured by membership in the Masonic and Odd Fellows lodges, Fanny Smith's diary records a more casual network among the women, based on spontaneous visiting and afternoon tea rather than the formal rituals of "calling" that developed decades later, or the planned meetings of clubs and societies. For women, the resulting community included relatives and friends, residents of county and town, both married and single, who sought each other's company often and shared work and troubles, as well as local news and enjoyable occasions.

Just as the fraternal organizations signified an inclination toward exclusivism among the men, women in Dallas appeared to separate into specific groups, perhaps even into "cliques," if not yet into identifiable classes.[48] Associating mostly because of kinship or perhaps, similarities in background and education, certain women were often mentioned in Fanny Smith's diary as her mother's friends, others as her own. Still others who were equally prominent (especially from a historical point of view) she never mentioned.

Essentially, Dallas was a community in the classic sense, of people tied together by place, with interests and concerns shared because of that place. One pioneer remembered those early days as a time "when we were all free and equal, and seemed to be on the same footing."[49] The lack of great differences in wealth did much to create that sense of equality. Those who owned less could realistically aspire to possessing, someday, as much as their richer neighbors. The few Catholic families could not leaven evangelical Protestant dominance, and most residents were of southern origin, including some who recently had lived in midwestern or border states.

In contrast to the large slave populations elsewhere in the South, black people were scattered among the white families in Dallas and Dallas County. On farms and in town, owners and slaves worked alongside each other in the fields and the houses; for African Americans, social and community life appeared to operate around the edges of white culture.[50] In August 1863, for example, three young people, two "colored Sisters" and a "colored Brother," were baptized in a nearby creek and received into membership in the Pleasant View Baptist Church, located about seven miles northeast of Dallas.[51] During the Civil War years, black people in the town held suppers and "entertainments" to raise money for the poor, often in the same places where similar events were given by whites at different times.[52]

African Americans could do little to weaken the town's cultural homogeneity or to affect its social values, which weighed most heavily upon themselves. In 1852, a young black woman named Jane Elkins was tried, convicted, and hanged for murdering her employer with an ax as he slept. Jane's mistress had hired her out to keep the man's house and care for his young children after his wife's death. But female slaves had other "duties," too, and after living for years in the household of a widow, Jane Elkins may have found these especially onerous. Because the county's criminal records burned long ago, only one brief account of her trial survives, that in John Cochran's history of Dallas County.[53] Cochran remembered the identities of prosecutor and judge, but Jane Elkins had no defense attorney before an all-male, white, southern jury during a time of rising sectional tensions over slavery.

A decade later, only about 5 percent of the county's 1,329 households owned slaves. Nonetheless, on February 23, 1861, local voters endorsed, 741 to 237, Texas' secession from the United States.[54] Women enthusiastically attended public meetings and parties to celebrate the news of secession and later, to see the men off to war. In May 1861, fifteen young women, each carrying a white banner bearing the name of a southern state, marched behind a brass band in a parade through town.[55] A month later, a group of women held a program to present the silk flag they had made for a local volunteer company, the First Texas Light Artillery. Lucy Latimer's thirteen-year-old daughter, Josephine, wore a white dress to deliver a speech in which she hoped that the flag's "beautiful stars and brilliant bars . . . [would] never be trampled upon by a victorious and insolent enemy . . . nor trail the dust of a dishonorable retreat."[56]

The war years brought few changes to Dallas, although residents noticed almost immediate effects. By December, the sudden scarcity of goods sent prices soaring to levels almost triple those of June. Women accustomed to paying ten cents a yard for calico found that it suddenly cost twenty-five cents, with the best quality forty-five cents; spools of thread that formerly sold at three for twenty-five cents were a quarter each. The price of needles and pins doubled. At the same time, demand for farm produce dropped, with wheat bringing less than fifty cents a bushel.[57]

Whatever the wartime hardships, Dallas was untouched by fighting and never threatened with invasion. Designated one of the state's eleven military supply depots and recruiting stations, the town prospered during the war years but in size, gained only the few Confederate officers stationed in the town, their families, and the enlisted men under their command. As the marketplace for wheat, corn, fodder, and meat from several surrounding counties, Dallas was an obvious site for a quartermaster's post. Mexican merchants in San Antonio also sent their agents to buy flour, which they later sold to the army on the Texas coast and the western frontier.[58]

Volunteer soldiers often—perhaps usually—depended upon volunteer labor back home for clothing and supplies. In September 1861, the governor of Texas asked the women of every county to organize societies to supply the state's troops with clothing, and the *Herald* published letters from enlisted men describing their needs.[59] In response, about twenty-five women in Dallas met at the courthouse to form the Ladies' Association, the town's first women's organization. The group elected officers and divided into committees to decide what kinds of clothing the soldiers needed, to purchase fabric and distribute it for cutting and sewing, and then to collect and store the completed garments for shipment to the men.[60]

Throughout the war years, in fact, the men's needs took precedence over other concerns, and the usual household tasks virtually ceased whenever wives, mothers, and sisters had to provide clothes for relatives at war. As one woman remembered many years later, "When the soldier boys wrote . . . [and asked] for more clothes, it was a hurry up job. We would work almost night and day to make the cloth, then neighbor women would come and help cut and make garments."[61]

The war created a limited number of paying jobs for women. A weaver could earn $10 a yard, the employer providing the thread. Planning to sell clothing to the men in military camps, one merchant provided fabric and thread and paid twenty-five cents for each pair of pants sewed. A good seamstress could make six pairs (or $1.50) a day.[62]

For women in the countryside, war brought much more work with the crops. For everyone, whether in town or country, the conflict meant return to the household-based economy, with a degree of self-sufficiency much like the conditions of frontier days. In addition to resuming hand manufacture, women had to find or invent substitutes for goods and groceries made scarce by the Union blockade. They cut the ribs of old umbrellas for darning needles and sharpened them with a grindstone; hoarded sewing needles and pins "as if they were diamonds"; roasted and ground rye, barley, okra seeds, or corn meal to replace coffee; and scooped up the dirt from meat house floors to recover the salt. For soda, they sifted and then boiled wood ashes into lye and boiled the lye back into powder. The final product was very strong, but adequate for baking once experience taught the women how to use it.[63] People felt isolated, one old-timer recalled many years later, "cut off from the rest of the world and compelled to live at home."[64]

Community ties served women well. The families of soldiers could expect material aid, as well as moral support, from friends and neighbors. In 1863, Dallas women formed a society to help those left behind and held benefit programs and social events to earn money and gather goods for both the soldiers in the field and their relatives at home. The county commissioners, too, provided a little money for the families and widows of the soldiers.[65]

Emancipation threatened the southern social hierarchy as nothing else could, and once black Texans officially were free, race relations ceased to be cordial even on the surface. Former Confederates seized any excuse to vent their bitterness upon people forced to seek work as servants. Men who were kind and generous to white friends and neighbors became violent toward African-American women employees with little or no provocation. Beatings, whippings, even murder could result from the failure to bake a pan of bread just right or a mother's attempts to protect her young daughter from rape by a white landowner's favored black overseer.[66] Whites who wished to help the new citizens found very limited options and great danger.

Without even minimal cooperation from the white community, the Freedmen's Bureau agent could claim only one achievement: he managed to stop Josephine Latimer Scott's piano renditions of "Dixie," which he called an insult to common decency and the American flag.[67] The local courts never tried anyone indicted for violent crimes against the freedmen or the white Unionists, and the company of troopers from the Seventh Cavalry could insure order and enforce fair labor rules only with their presence. Efforts to establish a school for African-American children also failed, although not entirely because of white resistance. Many of the parents were mothers supporting their families alone, and for them the most pressing matters were basic needs.[68]

Despite social tensions, Dallas was growing, if more modestly than its boosters would have preferred. In 1860, the town had 775 persons, of whom 97 were slaves. Of the 678 white people, 131 were foreign-born, most in northern and western Europe but a few in Poland and Hungary. About 100 more were former members of La Réunion, a Fourierist community which existed for a few years (1856–60) about three miles west of Dallas. After La Réunion disbanded, around 100 of the "French colonists" added their skills in millinery, brick making, dressmaking, carpentry, masonry, and midwifery to the services available in the town. More easily than other foreign-born immigrants, they assimilated into the community through business relationships, intermarriage, and political leadership, beginning within a decade to accept public offices as marshal, county clerk, city treasurer, mayor, and alderman.[69]

Along with the growth of Dallas was a rate of mobility matching that in many areas of mid-nineteenth-century America. While Dallas County's total population had more than doubled within the decade, only half of the 435 families named in the federal Census of 1850 were listed again in 1860.[70] Assuming that, as the *Herald* reported, Dallas did not grow during the war years, the town's population mushroomed after 1865 to the 1,299 persons counted in the special

Census of 1868. Of these, 39 percent were African Americans, the highest proportion of the town's population that this group would reach before 1920.[71]

Whatever the personal tragedy of war and the turmoil of Reconstruction, the nature of women's work in the home and their participation in community life changed little during the 1860s. Judging from advertisements in the *Herald,* postwar growth resulted in an immediate, if small and indeterminate, growth in female employment. The children of white immigrants increased the demand for schools, and dressmakers and milliners, also, found larger numbers of customers among the newcomers.

Whatever the strength of domesticity as an ideal, throughout the 1850s and 1860s, women in Dallas did whatever was necessary, including the performance of familial legal duties. Despite the importance of their traditional work, especially during the war years, only men served in the visible, recognized, and titled positions, as judge, county commissioner, sheriff, marshal, mayor, prosecutor, alderman. Women's participation in public programs was acknowledged with appreciation, but their labor in the home and in family enterprises tended to be taken for granted, if not actually ignored. So integrated within tradition and custom as to be indistinguishable from the functions of family and community, women's day-to-day domestic achievements merged with habit and routine. The very basic nature of these tasks made them invisible, unlikely to be recognized or commemorated. Perhaps, given the sheer necessity of domestic work, it was unthinkable and indeed unimaginable, that its products and services should not be available. Thus, people probably were incapable of perceiving the centrality of women's fundamental participation in the town's development.

Chapter Three
Frontier "Boom Town," Inland Distribution Center

"All Dallas has gone wild," Catharine Coit wrote to relatives in South Carolina after a shopping trip in September 1873. "There is such a rush to get rich that everybody is trying to do something to get money to invest in *lots* before it's too *late*. Ladies [are] turning teachers, dressmakers, boarding house keepers, etc."[1] Two railroads had come, the north-south Houston and Texas Central in July 1872 and the east-west Texas and Pacific six months later, in February 1873. Almost overnight they turned Dallas into a "wide open boom town," but at an irreversible social cost. Loss of traditional community, a growing degree of persistent poverty, higher rates of crime, division into neighborhoods segregated by race, occupations, and wealth—these conditions first appeared during the 1870s and grew more pronounced in the following decades.

The "boom" began during the late 1860s and resulted from several factors. Renewed immigration at the war's end, growth of the cattle industry, expansion of flour milling and cotton processing, plus merely the rumors of the railroads combined to attract travelers, immigrants, job seekers, and merchants. When the trains arrived, they joined the freight-wagon companies to make Dallas an inland distribution center with markets in the smaller towns nearby, and customers hundreds of miles to the west on the Texas plains.

For women, the 1870s brought the seeds of change in public roles and community relationships. First and most obvious, the railroads stimulated employment, both with jobs that were unrelated to domestic tasks and with the growing market demands for the skills of housework. Unexpectedly but perhaps more clearly than during any other decade, the town's needs revealed the basic importance of traditional work in the home, not merely for families, but also for Dallas. Of equal, if less noticeable, significance were the earliest lasting female voluntary associations, the ladies' aid and industrial societies in the churches and the Ladies' Hebrew Benevolent Association in the synagogue.

Dallas in 1872. Courtesy Historic Photograph Collection, Dallas Public Library

However conservative their initial activities, these groups were the first local indication that American women would be active participants in the rapid development of an urban, industrialized society. In Dallas, the religious societies almost immediately began creating new forms of community. Within two decades, the social impulse they expressed would, here as elsewhere, initiate unprecedented roles in public life for women.

By 1870, Dallas had a total of 2,103 persons, an increase of nearly 40 percent over the 1,299 counted in the town's special Census of 1868. This growth helped to fuel a rate of construction that produced 725 new buildings in 1873 alone.[2] The vibrant business activity encouraged Sarah Cockrell to revive her ten-year-old plans for a major bridge across the Trinity River. In July 1870, the legislature granted a charter for the Dallas Wire Suspension Bridge Company to the four men who joined Cockrell in the new corporation, with the authority to choose "such other persons as they may associate with them." During the following months, around one hundred individuals invested a total of fifty-five thousand dollars to form the stock company.[3] Sarah Cockrell held the controlling number of shares—yet never served on the company's board of directors. Choosing her oldest son and her son-in-law to represent her interests, she bowed, as her son later wrote, "to the conventions of her day regarding a woman in a public corporation."[4] Despite such obeisance to propriety, many years later a contemporary remembered her as "the life and mainspring in the final building of the bridge."[5]

Praised by the 1873 city directory as "the most magnificent . . . in the frontier states," the bridge pleased investors, too, with annual dividends of over 100 percent. Its stocks were, as one man recalled, "in great demand," but its very importance caused resentment. Accustomed to an economy based as often upon exchange or barter as upon cash, farmers considered the tolls expensive. Nearly a decade of public agitation would lead the county to purchase the bridge in 1881 and open it for traffic free of charge.[6]

The bridge played a crucial role in lifting Dallas to a new status as the regional inland distribution center. While the trains gave storekeepers direct connections with their suppliers, the bridge expedited freight traffic between Dallas merchants and those in smaller towns and rural villages.[7] For the first time, wholesalers opened warehouses and prospered alongside the retail dealers.[8] Wagon yards and livery stables multiplied as new transport companies shipped hardware, dry goods, groceries, and tools. The teamsters who brought buffalo hides and bones to market in Dallas delivered freight on their return trips, hauling manufactured goods to places several hundred miles away on the West Texas plains.[9] Together, the railroads and the new iron bridge enabled the town's merchants to supply customers in a vast hinterland.

With the bridge nearing completion early in 1872, Sarah Cockrell expanded her business interests. Expecting the railroads to increase the importance of local milling and wheat marketing, she purchased a one-third interest in an existing mill; three years later, she bought the remaining stock. In partnership with her son and son-in-law, she formed S. H. Cockrell and Company, giving her own name to this private corporation, in contrast to her reticence regarding the public bridge company. Although Dallas rapidly was becoming a major cotton depot and compressing center, wheat remained important as a cash crop. By 1877, the county's flour mills were earning almost three million dollars annually. Within the following three years, they were selling several grades of wheat flour in a marketing area that extended from Shreveport in the east to San Antonio in the south, and included numerous small towns along the Houston and Texas Pacific Railroad's line.[10] Equipped with the most modern steam-powered machinery, Cockrell's new venture was "on the cutting edge" of the local economy.

The town's prosperity grew from sources other than legitimate business, too, as vice flourished in the form of gambling, drinking, and prostitution. By 1874, a total of 167 saloons gave Dallas a reputation as a "fancy town" among the cowboys and farmers' sons, and attracted some notorious characters as well. Professional gamblers such as Wyatt Earp added Dallas to their regular circuits through the Southwest. Doc Holliday's dental practice ended in 1875, when the town marshal reportedly invited him to leave after a saloon shooting.[11] Along with the saloons and the gamblers came increased demand for prostitution, but before 1880 no census data existed on the numbers or identities of the women.

In addition, perhaps a score of actresses and "variety girls," considered by "polite society" to be barely a step above the prostitutes, appeared in the city directories for one or two years, then were replaced by others.[12]

Almost overnight, it seemed, the country market town disappeared before a crush of newcomers, about 6,500 in 1873 and 1874. Many were transients who had lost their jobs in other states, for the "boom town" years in Dallas coincided with a nationwide "bust," a six-year depression which, except for that of the 1930s, was the worst economic downturn in United States history.[13] A "Help Wanted" ad in the *Herald* could attract as many as twenty applicants, and those unable to find work sank into the category of "tramps." Living in tents and huts in the Trinity River bottoms, some men survived by burglarizing homes and businesses, while others begged from door to door, usually in the mid-morning hours after husbands left for work: women were notably more compassionate about handing out food.[14] Equally precarious were the situations of families, usually with at least one employed member, who weathered the housing shortage in whatever shanties and shacks they could find, or in tents pitched around the edges of town.[15]

While men often had trouble finding employment, women enjoyed multiplying opportunities, almost always related to work in the home. Many continued to take in sewing as they had for years; others opened small businesses in their homes; and a few ran dressmaking and millinery shops in rented rooms downtown. The larger shops employed up to a dozen seamstresses and sometimes included daughters working as apprentices to their mothers.[16] Despite their apparent success, the vast majority of the millinery and dressmaking shops lasted for about five years; only one continued to be listed in the city directories for as long as fifteen.

Among the town's new residents, the demand for education increased. Most of the schools listed in the city directories or advertised in the *Herald* were small and private, enrolling between twelve and thirty pupils in the teacher's home. These schools revealed much about living conditions in Dallas during the "boom town" years. After Marie L. Lamoreaux came from Michigan in 1878 for reasons of health, she decided to open a school for the children who sometimes worked as paper boys or bootblacks or at odd jobs, but who mostly seemed to roam the streets. Hanging blackboards and maps around the unplastered walls of the "two-room box" where she lived with her husband, Lamoreaux soon realized that their families needed the children's earnings. The youngsters came to her classes only on Sundays and then more for the food she served than for the lessons. A meal of soup, bread, butter, and cakes, she learned, was the most effective educational motivation she could offer.[17]

Teachers' families, too, needed money. In 1870, John and Catharine Coit left the farm they had homesteaded in 1856 near Plano and moved into a frame "box house" in Dallas. John joined a law office but complained in a letter to his brother that Dallas was "now one of the most expensive [towns] in Texas." For additional income, Catharine opened a school for girls and little boys. A graduate of Harmony College in South Carolina, she undoubtedly was one of the best-educated residents of Dallas, and her surviving letters reveal a lively, complex mind, well qualified to teach. Her first class of sixteen pupils paid a total of forty-six dollars a month, a sum with which, she wrote to a relative, "we can get along I hope very well."[18]

For the next two years, the front room of the Coit home served the family of seven as a living room and doubled as a bedroom for parents and daughters. The attached "shed room" did triple duty, as dining room and kitchen, as the sons' bedroom at night, and as a schoolroom on weekdays. Cooking, cleaning, teaching—Coit did them all on crutches, for three years earlier a knee injury had required the amputation of one of her legs. The return of a former servant to help with household chores was welcome indeed, but just as their situation improved, John died of pneumonia in 1872.[19] Now the sole support of her family, Catharine Coit closed the school and took her children back to the farm.

Lucinda Coughanour very likely was the best-known Dallas teacher during the 1870s, and her career exhibited the strength of traditional values. A native of Tennessee who grew up in Kentucky, Coughanour taught in several local schools after 1862, then opened her Select School for Young Ladies in 1873. She offered the standard classical curriculum, but her students learned, as one of them remembered, "a great deal besides what was in their text books from this gracious, intellectual woman."[20]

While twentieth-century women have tended to reenter the labor market after their children reach school age, Coughanour stopped teaching for the birth of her son in 1872, then opened the Select School a year later. She, in fact, taught throughout her childbearing years, finally retiring when her youngest child was almost ten. The reason for these working years must have involved the family's economic security. In the 1870s, Dallas had more attorneys than the small community needed, and for a number of years Robert Coughanour sold both real estate and insurance from his law office.[21] With his practice well established by 1881, Lucinda closed her school for the last time.

The schools in Dallas reflected the town's increasing diversity and gave parents choices regarding the type of education their children would receive. In 1872, the earliest tax-supported public schools opened, one for "colored" and two for white pupils. They operated for only five months each year.[22] Students able to pay tuition could choose among a variety of private institutions, including the Ursuline Academy, the German and English Private School, and the School of Congregation Emanu-El. A black minister ran the private Union Bethel Academy for African Americans. Of all these, only the public schools hired women teachers.

By contrast, the Dallas Female College employed a majority of women on its teaching staff. Run by a Methodist minister and by 1870 officially affiliated with his denomination, the institution offered the standard classical curriculum. Like many women's colleges at the time, a special elementary department accepted children, especially welcoming the younger sisters and brothers of the students in its degree program.[23] Women also found faculty positions in the co-educational Dallas Male and Female College and the Lawrence Commercial College.[24] Not yet dominating the profession in Dallas, women held barely more than half of all the teaching positions in the colleges, public schools, and small private schools.

Among the "ladies rushing to get rich" was a growing number of married women. Before 1870, wives "helped out" in small family firms, but virtually all employed women were single or widowed. After 1873, the listings of "two-career" families increased in the city directories, with wife and husband sometimes in the same kind of work—as merchants, for example, or cooks. One couple ran a saloon, and both spouses were named as proprietors. In another case, the wife was a merchant of fruit and confectionery, her husband a dealer in wholesale fruit. Usually, wife and husband were in unrelated ventures, with the woman's work a variation on homemaking—a laundry, dressmaking or millinery shop, hotel, restaurant, school, or boardinghouse. One woman was a florist, her husband clerk of the district court. The sheriff's wife was a dressmaker; the mayor's wife ran a day boardinghouse with meals for single professional men who lived in their offices.[25]

Such women faced an awkward situation with regard to Texas law. When a matron opened a business under her own name, legally she could use only her separate property for its establishment and operation. Nonetheless, her profits, like those of her husband's enterprises, were community property; thus both were under his control and were vulnerable to his creditors. Although she owned, equally with her husband, the community property amassed during their marriage, she could not draw upon it for business purposes. As manager of the community property, however, her husband could use it at will, as well as any profits it produced. A wife's status as *feme couvert* shielded her from legal responsibility for her contracts. This provision might be seen as an advantage but it could discourage other merchants from dealing with her.[26]

Few married women seemed daunted by these conditions, perhaps because husbands viewed their wives' businesses as temporary family ventures and willingly accepted responsibility for any risks the women incurred. On the other hand, few people knew much about the law, and most probably assumed that, aside from criminal behavior, individuals could do whatever they chose. As a general rule, especially in small towns, where face-to-face transactions predominated, any merchant's relationships with customers and creditors depended more upon shared values and personal trust than upon law and the courts. When opportunity beckoned, thousands of matrons in nineteenth-century Texas operated stores in their own names.

Aside from owning small businesses, single women and widows were more likely than matrons to accept jobs unrelated to traditional roles, such as telegraph operator, owner of a cigar and tobacco shop, wholesale cotton buyer, or coeditor of a local periodical. As a general rule, even job opportunities new to Dallas took familiar forms. After 1873, numerous out-of-state companies advertised in the *Herald* for "lady agents" to sell products like hair goods, patent medicines, and cosmetics. The saleswomen could set their own hours, work out of their homes, and sell exclusively to other women. Similarly, in the late 1870s, Sanger Brothers Dry Goods Company began hiring women to sell such "women's goods" as dresses, hats, notions, fabrics, and sewing machines, and to fill orders for clothing to be custom made by the store's seamstresses, dressmakers, and milliners.[27]

Despite the fact that most women were in the job market for only a short time, changes in the town's economy drew increasing numbers, as well as a growing proportion, of the female population into paid work. By the end of the decade, 29 percent of women aged sixteen and over worked outside the home for pay or ran their own businesses. Comprising about 20.5 percent of the town's labor force, the great majority were in occupations directly related to homemaking. Nearly 70 percent were in some form of domestic service; 76 percent of domestic workers were black. In fact, by 1880, African Americans were nearly 70 percent of the female labor force in Dallas.[28]

Approximately two hundred adult African-American women aged eighteen and over lived in precinct 1 (Dallas and its immediate environs) in 1870. Of these, 25 percent lived with the white families for whom they worked as servants. The rest resided in independent black households, more than half (53 percent) of which sheltered nuclear families composed of the wife, her husband, and their children. Another 14 percent of black households were extended families with three generations living together; 23 percent more were "augmented" with additional adults who may have been either relatives or friends. Children in such complex households grew up with several caretakers—parents' siblings, grandparents, or other kin—and mothers had help with familial responsibilities. The African American population was young, with 24 percent of its members under thirteen years of age and 58 percent under twenty-one. Single parents headed 29 percent of all the black families in and around Dallas, and almost always the parent was the mother, usually living with her minor children in her white employer's home.[29]

Although they were most vulnerable to the strain of rapid urbanization, black people were creating a vital, if separate, community. During the 1870s, perhaps the most stressful decade in the city's history, they organized four churches, established their families in traditional structures, and began educating their children. Many purchased homes, too, often from whites who hoped to insure themselves of domestic help by selling land so that potential servants would live nearby. In a newspaper interview given many years later, in 1923, a former slave named Nettie Johnson revealed the distrust felt by African Americans: "I thought the white folks was just tryin' to get hold of money and give me nothin' for it." In 1870, the land seemed expensive at $1.50 an acre.[30]

However disadvantaged in transactions with whites, women like Johnson were not a passive labor force. In July 1870, a number of laundresses met to plan a strike for better pay, demanding $1.50 for each dozen socks, with "bachelors' socks five cents extra."[31] The *Herald* failed to report the outcome of their action, but with an unknown number like Nettie Johnson in debt to white employers for their homes, probably they were unsuccessful.

Recognized as the least accurate of all the federal censuses, the 1870 returns were particularly suspect with regard to women's occupations. Of 267 African-American females between thirteen and seventy years of age in precinct 1, this census claimed that 17 percent were domestic servants, 35 percent keeping house, and 33 percent unemployed. More likely, sizable numbers of those listed as being without employment or as "keeps house" actually were earning money as farm laborers or independent laundresses for neighboring white families. For white women also, the 1870 census seriously distorted the truth by recording only four—a "performer," a domestic servant, a music teacher, and a schoolteacher—as employed outside their homes. Along with others who advertised small businesses in the *Herald,* this census listed Sarah Cockrell, Lucinda Coughanour, and Maria Bingham as "keeps house," a designation that satisfied nineteenth-century gender expectations and rules of propriety but served only to distort the reality of women's lives.

More than any other occupational category, the skills of homemaking were in demand throughout the "boom town" years, not only because of the numbers of immigrants, but also because so many of them were male. While most previous settlers had come with their families, those who arrived in the early 1870s were predominantly young single men. Outnumbering women in 1873 by more than two to one, their most immediate needs were for meals and lodging.[32] The solution was to board.

Teaching required an education and millinery and dressmaking, years of training and practice, but almost anyone could rent out extra rooms and serve two meals a day. In 1870, Dallas had two hotels and two boardinghouses; in 1873, the city directory listed two hotels and thirty-three boardinghouses. Some boardinghouses actually were small, more or less exclusive hotels with complete staffs of maids, porters, and cooks. Others supplied only the most basic furniture, requiring the boarders themselves to bring such additional comforts as featherbeds, blankets, pillows, linens, even chairs.[33] Women who took in "day boarders" provided one or two meals daily but no lodging; wives of small business owners were very likely to board their husbands' employees.

A nineteenth-century woman lost only a little social prestige if she taught school, somewhat more by going into millinery or dressmaking. She had to be careful with a boardinghouse, which would attract a consistent clientele. Lawyers, physicians, and ministers seemed drawn to certain boardinghouses, while skilled workmen such as carpenters, stonemasons, and blacksmiths chose others. Those accepting actresses and "variety girls" raised questions about their owners' morality, and some were thinly disguised brothels. Despite the delicate matter of reputation, the boardinghouse offered a direct way to turn homemaking skills into profitable employment.

Moreover, the boardinghouses performed several functions for the town. When a boardinghouse keeper gained a reputation for "setting a fine table," families chose her home for Sunday dinner or to celebrate a special occasion. After the meal, guests gathered on the porch or verandah to socialize. More basic than their function as restaurants, the boardinghouses eased the critical housing shortage. Young married couples boarded until they could find or afford a house, and unmarried men who lived in their offices or businesses went to a boardinghouse for meals.[34] Because single males comprised the vast majority of their customers, the boardinghouses enabled a minority of women to keep house for a majority of men and, sometimes, to provide the men with surrogate families.

Simply by the nature of their services, boardinghouses underscored the importance of work traditionally done in the home. Shifting such work from the domestic use economy into the marketplace, the boardinghouses lifted the labor usually done in private out of its invisibility within individual homes and into public view in the realm of trade and commerce. Taking housework into open participation in the marketplace, the boardinghouses met the basic needs of the town's growing labor force. More than any other female occupation, keeping a boardinghouse indicated the fundamental economic importance of women's traditional work in the home.

The majority of Dallas women continued, unpaid, to perform domestic work within the privacy of their homes, and this work had changed little since the early years of settlement. A few in rural Dallas County still spun and wove after 1873, but, like housewives in town, most now purchased fabric and notions to sew clothing. In country and town alike, women provided much of their families' food by gardening and keeping cows, chickens, pigs, and sometimes hives of bees.[35] Unlike the commercial manufacture of textiles and goods for the home, food preparation remained a part of domestic production, with many town housewives using their backyards to perform essentially the same work as women in the county.

With food production as with the boardinghouses, women's work joined the market economy. As Dallas grew, so did the demand for garden vegetables, dairy products, poultry, and cured meats. A housewife could get a dollar for a water bucket full of tomatoes or a bushel of turnips. Bakers and hotel keepers advertised regularly in the *Herald* for eggs, butter, chickens, and lard, sometimes offering to pay in gold for these and other foodstuffs. Grocers, also, needed milk, buttermilk, and fresh vegetables, and boardinghouse owners drove through the countryside in search of fresh produce and dairy products.[36]

While food production and preparation were much the same everywhere, the frontier town made child care in some ways more worrisome. Located at the best place to cross the Trinity River, Dallas attracted cattle drives headed for markets farther east and north. Two or three thousand longhorns running down Main Street and stampeding across fences, gardens, and yards were dangerous enough, but the drovers were at least as bad. Leaving the animals to graze outside town, they returned to race their horses through the streets "yelling like Comanches," one man remembered, "and firing their guns." No one thought that the cowboys "meant any harm," but women "gathered up their children from playing in the sand piles of the streets and crouched with them in their houses until the frolic was over." Another man recalled that the "cracking of pistols was the signal for me to run home."[37]

Primitive physical conditions, more than boisterous behavior, led a young Dallas lawyer, John M. McCoy, to write to his fiancée in 1872, "Ladies usually do not like Dallas, at least at first." In letters to his parents two years earlier, McCoy described business and public buildings alike as crude, with bare interior walls that were "very frequently unsealed and [o]pen to the naked rafters [which are] often staring you in the face." Even the houses of the wealthy, he continued, "are the most ordinary kind—they are generally simply weatherboard without plastering." He had not seen "a carpeted floor, be it parlor or kitchen," since traveling south of Kansas City. Living in Dallas, he commented, was simply "pioneer life."[38]

Among the pioneers were six Ursuline nuns, Dallas's first order of women religious.[39] Their lifestyle was communal in nature, yet their work differed little from that of other women in the town. The Ursulines arrived in February 1874 with $146, a few furnishings donated by their Galveston convent, and whatever odds and ends they could carry on the train. Opening a school for girls of all faiths, the sisters lived, taught classes, and accepted boarding students in a four-room house, one of the "flimsy frame boxes" hurriedly constructed by contractors to profit from the rapid immigration. Each pupil paid an entrance fee of $5, plus $17 a month for board, tuition, stationery, and instruction in the basic academic subjects, as well as all kinds of fancy sewing. Laundry was $3 per term.[40] These charges were typical for schools at the time, and the Ursuline Academy's first class of seven quickly grew to fifty.

Accustomed to life in an established convent, the sisters missed the more comfortable living conditions in Galveston. During the unusually long and cold winter in 1874–75, water froze indoors overnight and broke the pitchers on their washstands. Rain and melting snow dripped through the roof, splashing and steaming off the stove to wet furniture, clothing, and bedding. When summer came, the low ceilings and thin walls provided little more than shade. In opening a day and boarding school, each nun had housekeeping chores, whether washing clothes, cleaning, cooking, milking, sewing, or nursing students who fell ill. Like other women pioneers, the nuns had to learn how to garden in the blistering summers.

The bishop had purchased the house for them, and their priest helped in every way he could, yet their existence remained Spartan to the point of privation. With families feeling the depression's pinch, tuition payments often were late, and some never came at all. Nonetheless, the Ursulines refused to delay their plans. In October 1874, barely nine months after their arrival, construction began on their permanent convent and school. Only five months later, in February 1875, the sisters and their students moved into the new building, described by the city directory as "second to none in this city for beauty of finish and convenience of design."[41] By 1879, the academy had more than two hundred day students and as many boarding pupils as it could accommodate.

For other homemakers as for the Ursulines, domestic life in Dallas remained much like that in the country. Without organized public services and utilities, families had to make all their own household arrangements. Indoor plumbing did not exist; kerosene lamps and purchased candles lighted homes. Most people dug their own wells and drew water with a rope and bucket; for some, the force pump was an appreciated modern convenience. Others bought water, either from vendors who sold barrels of spring water door-to-door, or from the city-owned pumping station and pressure tower. Water from the Trinity River was fit for little except putting out fires. Often muddy and always polluted, it ruined laundry and made people sick. Until a commercial steam laundry opened around 1881, wealthier women sent their families' clothing to Shreveport for cleaning.[42]

Along with food production and sewing, care of the sick remained the wife's responsibility. People with serious, even life-threatening illnesses were nursed at home, for only the destitute used the one-room public hospital, opened in 1873 and later "improved" with construction of an adjoining kitchen and privy.[43] Henrietta McCoy Taggart's experience with family illness was common. Taggart moved with her family to Dallas from Kansas in 1876, and soon afterwards her five-year-old daughter became very sick. With carefully administered doses of quinine and calomel (a form of mercury!), Taggart spent weeks nursing the child through the chills and fever of an undiagnosed illness. Lacking confidence in the local physicians, she wrote to her parents in Indiana after the little girl recovered, "I was my own doctor this time and succeeded pretty well, too, I think."[44]

Five months later, the child and her little sister came down with whooping cough. The older girl recovered quickly, but the younger developed bronchitis and possibly pneumonia. For two weeks, Henrietta Taggart hardly left her daughter's bedside day or night. By this time the family had found a doctor whom they trusted. Although he came to their home almost every day, he later credited the mother's care and attention, more than medication, with the child's survival. Such labor took its toll: Taggart found herself unable to sleep when her patient at last began to recover. Nursing duties did not end with the immediate family, and, between the illnesses of her children, Taggart nursed her aunt through a severe case of typhoid fever.[45]

A good example of how a family could retain its traditional functions even in a frontier town, the McCoys and the Taggarts provided these benefits to each other. The first of the McCoys arrived in Dallas in 1845, and additional relatives followed during the next twenty-seven years. Although they established four separate households by 1882, the McCoys and the Taggarts remained an extended family, as close-knit and involved in each other's lives as the Dallas County families whose children intermarried and lived near their parents' homesteads. During the mid-1880s, the McCoy women had the emotional support, household help, and companionship they had known in the agricultural community they left.[46]

The McCoys transported their customary relationships into Dallas along with their household goods, but newcomers without family ties had to depend upon other kinds of association. Caroline Landauer Dysterbach lacked the family support enjoyed by the McCoy women, but in other ways she lived much as she would have in her native Germany.[47] Born in 1850 in a village near Heidelburg, Caroline Landauer met Polish Abraham Dysterbach after she immigrated with relatives to New Orleans. Soon after their marriage in 1872, they came to Dallas, where he opened a business to sell livery goods, feed, hardware, groceries, and whiskey to hunters and settlers traveling west.

Caroline made their home in the rooms upstairs. Without female relatives but with the help and companionship of other Jewish women, she bore five children there. Like the wives of many craftsmen and small business owners, Caroline worked in the store, then managed it alone after her husband's retirement around 1889. The greatest changes in her life may have been those resulting from the family's growing prosperity, which during the 1880s, made possible the purchase of a house and the separation of residence from source of livelihood.

The Dysterbachs began their lives in Dallas during years when the town was acquiring a new degree of diversity. In 1872 the Catholics established their first parish, and in 1876 the Jews formed their first synagogue. At the same time, growing differences in occupation, income, and race sharpened segregation in the residential neighborhoods. These years produced the earliest signs of patterns of living that signaled the presence of identifiable classes. A sampling of 193 listings in the city directory for 1875 found the home addresses of bankers, jewelers, attorneys, physicians, and real estate and insurance agents likely to be separate from their places of business, a development associated with the appearance of the modern middle class. Small shop owners and craftspeople, on the other hand, still tended to live upstairs or in rooms behind their stores and shops.[48] While they might well reach middle-class status in income, they continued to follow the traditional urban ways, with wives active in day-to-day commerce and parents sharing a genuine partnership with regard to family duties.

Even more clearly indicative of class segregation was Dallas's first exclusive residential area, called "The Cedars" and located a few blocks south of downtown. Including homes that ranged from moderately expensive to mansions, this neighborhood not only attested to degrees of wealth new to Dallas, but also to the lifestyle defined as "middle-class."[49] By mid-decade, another such neighborhood appeared along Ross Avenue and its adjacent streets, all to the northeast of downtown. Increasingly sequestered by the separation of residence and workplace, the wives living in these areas narrowed their associations to those with people much like themselves, except when they hired servants or went to shop in the stores.[50]

More surely than income, race determined where wage earners could live. About two miles northeast of the town square and beyond the exclusive homes on Ross Avenue was "Freedmantown," the settlement where former slaves clustered around a pre–Civil War cemetery. African-American homes also spread to the south along the Houston and Texas Central Railroad tracks in a second community called "Stringtown," which connected Freedmantown with a third black area, later to become known as "Deep Ellum."[51]

In addition, a small number of African-American residents lived among the white wage earners in "Frogtown," located along the Trinity River a few blocks north of the courthouse. Originally a respectable "addition," after 1873 Frogtown rapidly lost its prosperous families to the new, more prestigious neighborhoods, and evolved into Dallas's first "red-light" district. Another area of "ill repute" grew during the 1870s—"Boggy Bayou," with its expensive "upscale" brothels south of the courthouse along the river. Deep Ellum, too, harbored prostitution, along with a reputation for crime and violence.[52]

The 1870s were a time of "pioneering" for Dallas, as for its people. Throughout the decade, the business district looked like that of a frontier town, despite the presence of several large buildings and imposing hotels. Grainy photographs show square, one- and two-story buildings lining dusty unpaved streets. The front doors of stores and shops opened onto wooden boardwalks, some roofed and made into porches, and others uncovered, bare to the weather. Rails for horse-drawn streetcars ran down the middle of Main Street, which was lighted at night by gas lamps posted at a few corners.[53]

Gradually, rustic conditions were giving way before the beginnings of urban services and conveniences, some provided by private companies, others by volunteer groups, and yet others by the city government. In the early 1870s, the city council passed ordinances requiring the penning of livestock, the banning of garbage and wastes on the streets, and the appointment of a public health officer.[54] Gas mains, telephones, volunteer and then salaried firemen, regular letter carriers, policemen in navy blue uniforms with brass buttons—all first appeared in Dallas during the 1870s. So did three streetcar lines, whose mule-drawn cars stopped wherever people flagged them and let passengers off at their own front doors.[55] Despite these advances, inconveniences remained. The streets turned into muddy bogs in wet weather, and men cut the mud off their boots with hunting knives. During the dry season, water wagons ran throughout each day to sprinkle the streets and keep down the dust. Board walkways existed only in front of those stores whose owners chose to construct them.[56]

As during the 1850s, cultural and social life attained a degree of sophistication beyond that consonant with the primitive physical conditions. In 1871, a group of men pledged six dollars a year to become stockholders of a public library. Every day except Sunday, the reading room made a collection of one thousand volumes available from 7 A.M. until 6 P.M.[57] Commercial entertainment flourished, with performances of popular plays at the two opera houses; at least one restaurant was considered "suitable for ladies" after an evening at the theater.[58] Traditional festivities were well attended, and Dallas residents celebrated Mardi Gras with parties, balls, parades, and special sales by the merchants. In 1878, they attended a "Merry Maifest," a German festival sponsored by the Turnverein Society.[59]

National political movements reached the frontier "boom town," too, through speakers who visited to lecture on the major social issues of the day and on other topics of general interest. Among the lecturers was Elizabeth Cady Stanton, who in 1848 had helped launch the original crusade for American women's rights. In 1875, Stanton was sixty-eight years old and, in the words of the Herald, "somewhat advanced in years . . . with hair almost white." She was still vigorous and enthusiastic about her cause, though, and her large, "fashionable" audience in Field's Theater warmly applauded her remarks. Entitled "Our Girls," this particular address was considered the most successful in her touring lecture repertoire. The *Herald* found Stanton's speech "comprehensive, tasteful, and, at times, quite eloquent," as she combined "profound, brilliant, and exalted thoughts with the best of all human qualities—good, sound common sense."[60]

Victoria Woodhull, the first woman to run for president of the United States, also visited Dallas in 1875 and again in 1876. Although Woodhull shocked most Americans with her private life and her advocacy of "free love," the Dallas newspaper described her as "genteel and attractive . . . self-possessed, ladylike, and dignified."[61]

Customary lifestyles remained strong despite—or perhaps because of—the upheaval and confusion of the "boom town" years. Nuns in a semicloistered order did not escape the chores of homemaking and housekeeping, and even with her business ventures operating at the heart of the Dallas economy, Sarah Cockrell seemed preoccupied with domestic matters. She employed a cook, a laundress, and a maid to do most of the housework, but she still centered her life at home. In the fall of 1870, she purchased a new iron stove for her kitchen and bragged in a letter to her daughter, "I can cook everything I want too [*sic*] at the same time. I had rather cook for 20 on it than for 2 on the fireplace." She pieced a quilt, oversaw the harvesting of cabbages and potatoes, made ketchup and preserves, and won a silver cup and napkin ring in the wine competition at the county fair. When Margaret Bryan and three of her grown children, all of them sick, arrived one day at her door, Cockrell took them in for a week, then rented a house for them.[62]

Despite her lifelong interest in business and the success of her numerous ventures, Cockrell's values remained traditional, especially with regard to her children. She sent her sons to school in other states, and one graduated from Washington and Lee. Her only daughter, Aurelia, was reared to be a southern lady, with piano lessons and enrollment in classes taught by Lucinda Coughanour. Aurelia's short life (she died in 1872, at the age of twenty-two) was comfortable and privileged, and her letters contained no hint that she might follow her mother into business.[63] Instead, like other daughters of Dallas pioneers, Aurelia Cockrell expected a life devoted to home and family. Only the exigencies of widowhood or the extraordinary demands of a raw frontier could yet turn most women from their traditional roles. Despite the social approval—indeed, adulation—it received, the economic significance of work in the home went unnoticed. When the *Herald*'s editor reported in 1876 that fifteen hundred women and girls were "units in the producing class of Dallas," he meant those who held paying jobs.[64]

However strong their commitment to domesticity and family life, more than paid employment drew women out of the home during the 1870s. Like the Catholics and the Jews, the major Protestant denominations built houses of worship in Dallas during these years, and to do so they needed women members. Sarah Cockrell gave land and money to the Methodists, and the present First Methodist Church in downtown Dallas commemorates these gifts with a large stained glass window in the main sanctuary. Similarly, a Mrs. Bullington donated the lot for the Presbyterians' first building. The Baptist congregation owed its very survival to Lucinda Beckley Williams.[65] In 1872, upon the advice of the departing pastor, Williams persuaded eighteen women to form a ladies' aid society. Raising five hundred dollars to lay the foundations of a church building, the women more or less shamed the men into action. The latter chose a "search committee" for a permanent minister and solicited donations from the area's established Baptist congregations.[66]

Within two years, female members of other denominations also organized aid societies. When the Methodists chose a new pastor in December 1874, a male church leader asked the women to prepare for his arrival. Twelve cleaned the parsonage, while others went in pairs through the business and residential areas to solicit donations for furniture, bedding, kitchenware, and linens. In this quiet, almost surreptitious way, a task that was domestic in nature drew a small group toward participation in the public realm and hinted at the direction of future changes in women's relationship to Dallas.

Modestly active religious roles for women actually were not new among southern evangelicals. After the nationwide revivals that began in 1802, Protestants in the South organized missionary societies. These, along with church work in general, became by the 1830s the center of social life for white women in many communities.[67] Sometimes with fewer than a dozen members, the "ladies' aid" or "ladies' industrial" societies in Dallas were organized with formal constitutions and by-laws. By 1874, both the Methodists and the Presbyterians in Dallas had such women's groups to raise money for their churches, as well as to visit the sick and get relief to the poor, regardless of sect or denomination. The Presbyterians sewed calico dresses, shirts, and aprons to sell; like the Methodists, they held oyster suppers, ice cream and strawberry "socials," and teas. Most popular with both denominations were "evening entertainments," programs of music and recitations presented by young women members of the church in the parlors of the town's best hotels, with refreshments served after the performances. Within two years, the Presbyterians raised almost five hundred dollars for church improvements, in addition to the money they spent on clothing and food for the poor.[68]

The women's aid and industrial societies were important for reasons other than raising money for charity and the churches. Visits to the sick and the bereaved strengthened ties within the congregations, while the "socials" created the kind of community based on members' choices, not merely on the random associations typical of traditional communities. Meetings to sew and to plan their money-raising events provided the women with companionship; the programs they presented served the same purpose for everyone who attended. For young single Protestant women and men, the strawberry festivals, oyster suppers, and evening entertainments were among the few acceptable occasions to meet and get acquainted.

In a period with few kinds of public entertainment, church programs reached beyond specific denominations and sometimes beyond faiths. In January 1876, the *Herald* urged readers to attend the Ladies' Hebrew Benevolent Association's ball and help raise money to build the synagogue. Jewish residents were quick to answer community needs, the paper's editor noted, and they deserved the town's gratitude.[69] Such occasions often became communitywide social events, increasing acquaintances and creating more numerous opportunities for contacts and friendships among Dallas residents. In these modest, almost unnoticed ways, the women's first voluntary associations began the process of altering female roles in the town's life, at least among families with comfortable incomes.

Both positive and negative elements of modern urbanization appeared in Dallas before the population reached ten thousand. The "boom" years advanced the town's status as the regional inland distribution center but stripped away the traditional community once so comfortable for white residents. The hardships and dislocation of rapid immigration and the suffering of persistent poverty accompanied the first public library, a growing number of public and private schools, and the aquisition of basic services and conveniences. Along with diversity in religion and and ethnicity came the earliest evidence of class distinctions and the first signs of new community roles for women through participation in voluntary asociations. As some women went outside their homes for the sake of the church and the poor, others joined the growing female labor force. However unsettling, unprecedented change was also producing stable, if unfamiliar, patterns of living and new, more varied opportunities for cultural experiences and personal relationships.

Older residents, especially, understood the significance of what they were witnessing. In July 1875, 122 original settlers met in the courthouse to form the Dallas County Pioneers' Association, electing two women as vice-presidents and four others to the executive committee. Nearly half (55) of the charter members were women. The organization's purpose—indeed, its very existence—sprang from an awareness of how much the pioneers had accomplished. Perhaps it resulted, too, from a sense of nostalgia, if not regret, at the passing of traditional community, in which members once had felt "free and equal," with all "on the same footing."[70]

Chapter Four
The Young Commercial City

"We will pay our expenses, or close our doors." With this terse promise in May 1886, the Ladies' Charity Association opened the Woman's Home and Day Nursery, a shelter for indigent women and their children. The combination of defiance and defensiveness made the motto peculiar for a charitable organization, except perhaps as a reply to husbands who had issued dire warnings about financial risks and threatened not to bail the association out of debt. The Home's Board, however, managed to pay its bills for almost twenty years, and, besides the help it provided for several thousand women and children, the Woman's Home held another significance. Founded and run by women specifically to meet the needs of women, the home heralded genuinely public female roles.

"Doing good works" was an activity long accepted for privileged women. Providing food, clothing, shelter, and medical care to the poor and unfortunate obviously resembled homemaking and thus constituted a "natural" female task. From all appearances, the Ladies' Charity Association merely followed custom, when in reality, almost any effort to alleviate suffering involved matters of community concern. The Woman's Home was the first in a series of institutions, all founded by women, to apply domestic and therefore "private" solutions to community problems. Members of a generation that expected clear differences between the public and the private "spheres," the Ladies' Charity Association began smearing those boundaries by assuming public responsibilities in Dallas.

The most obvious change for Dallas during the 1880s was a population almost quadrupled in size, from just over ten thousand in 1880 to more than thirty-eight thousand by 1890. Amid the trends and pressures of the resulting social upheaval, the dozen members of the Ladies' Charity Association were almost invisible. Hundreds of other women entering the "public realm" through the paid labor force were more difficult to overlook, as unprecedented prosperity in business and commerce created a robust demand for varied skills in the marketplace. Because Dallas lacked virtually every kind of urban service and convenience, the town seemed to offer unlimited possibilities for the energetic and ambitious. Local newspapers, and very likely general opinion as well, focused on the opportunities for business owners and job seekers.

Other kinds of activity revealed the strain of living in times when old social forms were crumbling but their successors had not yet emerged. Rapid growth brought prosperity, along with rising poverty, increasing crime, and the loss of traditional community. Districts of the city evolved toward separate functions— business, industry, or residence—while the emergence of identifiable classes not only destroyed the earlier frontier sense of egalitarianism, but also segregated the residential neighborhoods by race, ethnicity, income level, and men's occupations. In specifically urban kinds of pioneering, women helped, through both the community and the marketplace, to shape life in Dallas during these turbulent years.

Along with differentiated classes and segregated neighborhoods, voluntary associations characterized modern urban life in the United States. Forming nuclei around which new kinds of community developed, the earliest and largest for women in Dallas were the ladies' aid, industrial, and benevolent societies in the churches and the synagogue.[1] In 1880, the Baptist missionary society and three ladies' aid societies (Baptist, Jewish, and Methodist) enrolled fewer than 150 women; within a decade more than a score of religious groups together claimed nearly 800 members. The missionary organizations sometimes managed to involve entire congregations in their programs, while the aid and industrial societies hosted fundraising events which, as social occasions, cemented relationships within congregations.[2] Convinced that they obeyed an authority superior to that of mortal man—whether pastor, deacon, or husband—evangelical women sometimes had men's support and at other times defied male ridicule and criticism to follow their own sense of purpose. Women's religious groups became tiny enclaves of community within the city's burgeoning population of strangers.

Among the missionary societies nationwide, those devoted to foreign missions attracted even more members than the Woman's Christian Temperance Union. Each week the local chapters met to study and discuss standardized lessons mailed out by the national denominational organizations, as well as the interdenominational Woman's Union Missionary Society. They raised so much money to support the missionaries that male religious leaders, usually without success, coveted the women's treasuries for home missions. In Dallas, the Presbyterians, Baptists, and Methodists met together when foreign missionaries visited the city. Usually unmarried women who traveled widely to speak about their experiences in Asia and Africa, the missionaries reported on the success of their programs and exhibited mementos and works of art from the "heathen" lands.[3] For residents of a small parochial city, the missionary societies not only allowed public expression of personal faith, but also provided contact with the world beyond Dallas. Curiosity about exotic, unfamiliar ways of life, plus a normal human desire for adventure may have been as important as religious devotion in producing the largest of the nineteenth-century American women's movements.

Organized nationally in 1874 in Cleveland and in 1882 in Texas, the Woman's Christian Temperance Union (WCTU) also claimed an exalted purpose, but involved its members more in political and social than religious issues. The WCTU's first Dallas union was formed in 1884 by a national representative from Ohio. City directories reported total memberships ranging from 72 members in 1891 to 26 in 1898; by 1914, the local organization had three unions of 170 women. However unexpectedly small (given the WCTU's reputation and influence), this membership produced an impressive list of achievements, including an annual "rest cottage and nursery" for women attending the State Fair, a shelter for homeless newsboys, a boardinghouse for employed women, and several petitions to the city council to hire a police matron. In addition to their own programs, the WCTU in Dallas supported various campaigns led by other local women's groups. The organization backed the efforts of the Dallas Woman's Forum to win passage of a city ordinance to regulate foods and drugs, and joined the Texas and the Dallas Federations of Women's Clubs in working for a state law to control child labor.[4] With its central tenet that alcoholic beverages threatened families and its national motto "Do Everything," the WCTU pulled women out of the home in defense of the home. In the process, the organization became a major force in defining new female roles within a changing American society.

Contemporaneous with the missionary societies and the WCTU were the women's study clubs, inspired by the desire for self-improvement and continuing education. Like members of the religious groups, women in the clubs were active in churches or synagogues, if only to attend worship services regularly. But individuals gave their best energies to either religious or secular associations. Drawing mostly from the middle and lower-middle classes, the missionary and ladies' aid societies included wives and daughters of prosperous wage earners like construction contractors and typesetters but less often attracted those who belonged to the culture clubs. Women in literary and music organizations tended to come from more privileged families. While the church groups retained their religious focus, the literary and music study clubs became vehicles for widening community interests among women, particularly with regard to improving the living conditions in Dallas.[5]

American women's literary groups dated from the year 1800, when the first was organized in Chelsea, Connecticut. Societies were meeting regularly in southern cities by the 1880s, although in Texas the first culture club for women may have been the Electro Auto-Biological Society, founded for the study of science in Galveston in 1856.[6] The earliest in Dallas was the Pearl Street Reading Club, organized on March 6, 1880, when twelve neighbors met in a private home. Everyone had some light sewing or darning "to employ our fingers," and one young mother brought her seventeen-month-old son. For the next sixteen years, at a two-hour meeting each Saturday afternoon in a member's parlor, the women took turns reading aloud from works of history, the fine arts, and literature.[7]

The Ladies' Literary Society was more typical of future women's clubs. Organized at about the same time as the Pearl Street Reading Club, the Literary Society's programs consisted of musical performances, "pronouncing exercises," short selections from chosen works, and business sessions. Perhaps wealthier than the Pearl Street women and better able to afford child care and household help, members devoted a few hours each week to entirely nondomestic activity.

While the Pearl Street readers kept to their original purposes, the Literary Society launched a community project upon receiving a charter in 1882 to open a public library and free reading room. With support from sixty stockholders, who included twenty-five life members, for the first time in Dallas women organized a public institution. All previous attempts to found a library in the city had been made by men. By 1889, the library owned nearly two thousand books and subscribed to numerous periodicals. Its president was a man, but the other officers were women, presumably members of the Literary Society.[8]

Like serious literature, classical music had female devotees, and in 1884 they organized the city's first music study club, the Ladies' Musicale. In antebellum times, guests often sang and played instruments at dinner parties and other gatherings in private homes, and the Musicale's programs reflected this custom.[9] The club's main condition of acceptance was possession of "more than mere mechanical ability," an evaluation made by those who already belonged. At each monthly meeting, always held in a private home, members performed instrumental and vocal solos and sometimes invited their families and friends. In a time when popular and commercial shows dominated public entertainment in Dallas, these were the earliest regular performances of classical music.

The president and founder of the Ladies' Musicale, Belle Fonda Schneider, in many ways was more visible in community life than her husband, despite his numerous business ventures. In later years, local historians and raconteurs remembered her more often for a feud with actress Sarah Bernhardt than for her leadership in cultural and charitable organizations. Schneider was a native of Kentucky and claimed descent from one of the oldest Dutch families of New York. When she moved to Dallas soon after her marriage in 1879, she was recognized as a "society" leader immediately upon her arrival.[10] Formal dinners, fancy-dress balls, and her fluent French aside, wealth and unquestioned social status enabled her to lead a life that was considerably more public than propriety allowed. Through work with the Ladies' Charity Association, the Ladies' Musicale, and later the Derthick Musical and Literary Club, Schneider was a leader in two important aspects of urban life in Dallas, founding both institutions to foster the fine arts and organizations to relieve poverty and need.

Participants in a nationwide movement, the charter members of the Ladies' Musicale and the other culture clubs were influenced by the activities of women elsewhere. In the fall of 1885, a young Dallas matron visited her mother-in-law in St. Louis and, while there, attended a literary society meeting. Discussions with friends after she returned home resulted in the Dallas Shakespeare Club in the winter of 1886. A month later, a group in another exclusive neighborhood organized the Standard Club to study, as their name implied, the "standard" American and English authors. The Shakespeare Club barred men, but the Standard Club met in the evenings and sometimes included presentations by the members' husbands.[11]

By August 1888, a third organization, the Dallas Chautauqua Literary and Scientific Club, was meeting regularly to study the assignments in history, literature, Bible, astronomy, and physiology in the curriculum designed by the summer faculty at Lake Chautauqua, New York. After six years, the local Chautauqua created its own program, renamed itself the Pierian Club, and collected a four-hundred-volume library to supplement the holdings of the library founded by the Ladies' Literary Society. Housed in a member's home, the Pierian library was open to nonmembers one day each week, and by 1900, the club sent a regular traveling library into the rural areas of Dallas County. Building its own library also was one of the earliest projects of the Quaero Club, founded in 1892 by women in Oak Cliff to study English literary masterpieces.[12]

With their avowed purposes of self-improvement, the study clubs included women with varying degrees of formal education. Some had attended female academies and seminaries for only a year or two, while a few were college graduates. One held a degree from Vassar. Within their own social stratum, these women were pleasantly inclusive, and their clubs welcomed Jewish and Catholic members as well as Protestants, Episcopalians as well as evangelicals, daughters of Dallas founders as well as newcomers.

Among the Jewish women were members of the Sanger family. German immigrants from a long line of peddlers and traders, two Sanger brothers served in the American Civil War and then joined the "terminal merchants" moving northward ahead of the Houston and Texas Central Railroad. In 1872, the pair opened a dry goods store in Dallas, and by the mid-1880s both were wealthy enough to build fine homes in the Cedars. Their wives and children enjoyed such opulence as to be viewed, according to the matriarch of another Jewish merchant family, as "the very epitome of royalty." Admiration for the Sangers pervaded blue-collar homes in Dallas, too. A Protestant woman whose father was a construction contractor in the early 1900s remembered naming her paper dolls after the Sanger daughters.[13]

With the luxuries went a sense of social responsibility born, perhaps, of memories of years of hard work and insecurity. Fanny Fechenbach was a native of Wurtemburg, Germany, who in 1866 moved with her parents to Cincinnati and then, ten years later, to Dallas. She married Alex Sanger in 1879 and, as their wealth accumulated, became a knowledgeable collector of European paintings and antique furniture. A founder and board member of early charity efforts, including the nonsectarian Woman's Home and Day Nursery and the Dallas Orphans' Home (later the Baptist Buckner Orphanage), she earned recognition as more than a "society" leader.

After she died in New York City in November 1898, an estimated five hundred mourners met the train returning her remains to Dallas. Attending her funeral the next day were several thousand "of every class . . . from the street laborer who had at some time received her far-reaching charity, to the merchant prince and the banker."[14] Other privileged Jewish matrons followed Sanger's example of social concern. After 1900, their names appeared among the founders, officers, and committee chairs for such institutions as Dallas's first settlement house, the free kindergartens, and the free medical clinics for children.

The organization of the women's clubs was, as much as any other development during the 1880s, evidence that the old sense of frontier egalitarianism had dissipated. At least as significant as the sheer numbers and diversity of newcomers were the more pronounced differences among them in terms of wealth, education, culture, and background—all factors as potent in new cities as in old. "Leveling" pretenses ceased, as residents acknowledged distinctions among themselves and as exclusivist tendencies found expression in social events such as those sponsored by the Idlewild Club. Formed by a group of wealthy young men in 1884, the club held its first Grand Ball that winter, and the debutantes arrived in carriages driven by white-gloved servants.[15]

Self-proclaimed status notwithstanding, the emerging elite often was difficult to distinguish from the middle class. Earning social standing through success in their chosen fields of endeavor, Dallas's privileged classes rarely could depend upon inheritance or family. The newly prominent would serve their adopted city well, providing a stable core of permanent families as the coming decades alternated between expansion and prosperity, and upheaval, depression, and loss. From their ranks would come both the city's social activists and its leaders in social and cultural, as well as economic and political affairs.[16]

The number and vitality of the women's organizations were a prime indication that, during the 1880s, Dallas was acquiring a modern middle class. Previously defined in terms of wealth, by 1850 the term "middle class" connoted a good deal more than the earlier, simpler definition based upon occupations. In many respects, the middle class in the United States emerged as much from urban living conditions as from the prosperity resulting from industrialization. Well before 1880, the term came to connote a way of life characterized by privacy, a predominantly nuclear family structure, and sufficient wealth to employ at least one servant.

Members of the middle class chose their associates and friends more frequently in clubs and societies, less often through daily contacts at work or casual neighborhood acquaintances. Interactions with members of other classes and ethnic groups were frequent but brief, if only because Dallas had grown larger. For women, daily life became private almost to the point of seclusion, with few spontaneous encounters and chance meetings. Their excursions into public areas were restricted, too, with certain neighborhoods and downtown streets forbidden to those who wished to maintain a reputation as a "lady."[17]

The fact that husbands left home for most of each day changed familial relationships, altering the balance of power within the middle-class family. Of necessity, mothers assumed much of the authority once wielded only by fathers, to manage homes, domestic affairs, and the education and training of children. Presiding over houses too elaborate in construction and decor for one woman to maintain alone, middle-class matrons spent much of their time supervising servants, whether full staffs or merely a cook and a laundress who came once a week.

Women, in fact, created many aspects of the middle-class lifestyle, defining its values, directing its daily routines, and upholding its standards of personal behavior. A wife confirmed the family's status through her management of its resources for purchases of clothing and home furnishings and accessories, and through her use of social occasions to display the material proof of her husband's financial success. As the arbiters of a complex system of etiquette and manners, women regulated such rituals as mourning and the rounds of formal calls, as well as the rules of dress appropriate for certain times of the day.[18] Emulating the fashions and behavior of the upper class, middle-class women in turn influenced the values, ideals, and standards acceptable among the elite.

During the 1880s, this generation of young upper- and middle-class matrons, most of them recent immigrants to Dallas, initiated forty years of social change and reform in the city. Simply being newcomers freed them from a number of customary restraints. The vast majority were native southerners who grew up on plantations or in small towns. Mostly in their late twenties and thirties, they moved to Dallas soon after marrying and, unlike daughters of the original settlers, were separated from the influences of their birth families and extended kin networks.

In a city less than fifty years old, other social restrictions were weaker, too, if not eliminated. With traditional community structures overwhelmed by the huge population growth, the privileged women turned to the literary and music societies as a major source of friends and acquaintances who shared their values and interests. For secularly oriented women, the voluntary associations provided outlets for energies and concerns that were entirely apart from the conservative authority of religion and churchmen. Indeed, in many urban congregations, members of the missionary and ladies' aid societies, also, ran their organizations in quiet autonomy. In addition to assuming almost sole responsibility for homes, children, and servants, city matrons found themselves with an amount of independence that perhaps was unprecedented among women.[19] Married to the business owners who "pioneered" in the city during the 1880s, the privileged wives themselves became pioneers as, however unintentionally, they built the foundations for new community roles for women in Dallas.

While some urban dwellers clung to their rural ways and remained apart from the new forms of community developing around them, the first clubwomen were urbane in outlook. Oriented toward cooperation and interdependence, they adapted easily to urban life. In so doing, they differed from the immigrants who clung to their former rural lifestyles, in which each family had lived in near self-sufficiency and socialized mostly on such work occasions as barn raisings and quilting bees.

During the next several decades, the middle- and upper-class women, including about twenty leaders of the city's club movement, were well equipped to take advantage of the loosening of traditional restrictions. Wealth gave them not only household help and extensive leisure, but also access to books and periodicals, and opportunities to travel to the great cities of the United States and Europe. Educated to appreciate libraries and art museums, the theater, and classical music, the clubwomen set to work building the organizations and institutions that would express and perpetuate their interests and, they believed, be assets for the city. At the same time, they acknowledged the plight of the less fortunate and, circumspectly at first and then with increasing confidence, established permanent sources of relief and aid.[20]

For the next thirty years and more, the clubwomen of this Dallas generation would cooperate in numerous cultural and civic projects. Such personal associations bred relationships comparable in quality and duration to those with family members. Working together through the years would not prevent personal conflicts and subtle competition, or preclude disagreements about methods and procedures for achieving goals. Whether these privileged matrons of the 1880s actually formed a "women's culture" or merely established pockets of "sisterhood" within the clubs, their years of association resulted in a network of companionship that very likely was strong enough to connote, at least for specific purposes and functions, a separate community of women.[21]

However we describe their personal relationships, the clubwomen's programs and projects produced associations that were as important for the creation of urban living as their husbands' businesses were for economic development. Without long-term programs and articulated strategies for achieving goals, the women as yet had little need to challenge male authority or to develop a political culture. Sharing fundamental values, particularly regarding their concept of womanhood and the duties and authorities that devolved upon females, the privileged matrons began extending familial responsibilities into the community. One result was the foundation of a social infrastructure that would define and serve Dallas for decades.[22]

The associations of middle- and upper-class women manifested one type of community within an increasingly diverse population; among other people in the city, more varied social structures and types of relationships existed. Instead of a classic community bound together by frequent association and the shared interests of place, Dallas residents were forming numerous small communities, easily discernable by 1880 and still multiplying decades later. The most obvious of these "chosen" or "associative" communities were built around ethnicity.[23] By 1892, the city directories listed more than a dozen African-American churches, all representing evangelical faiths. A Scandinavian Club existed as early as 1875 and a Swedish Lutheran Church by 1884, while Swiss men enjoyed a social club, and Irish and Italian men had formed benevolent associations.

Of the ethnic groups, the Germans had the most, and the most varied, manifestations of a separate community. During the 1880s, Dallas German immigrants established three churches (Methodist, Lutheran, and Presbyterian), two schools, several men's social and singing societies, and a German-language newspaper. Their only women's organization was the Ladies' Aid Society founded at the request of the German Methodist bishop in 1886. Within a few decades, they and other immigrants of European origin would assimilate into the American-born community. At the same time, African Americans in Dallas formed institutions that were similar to those of the white majority but adapted to their own uses in a rich, vital separate community.

Religion, personal interests, neighborhoods, occupations, and professions were, like race and ethnicity, the bases for new kinds of community. Formed around the voluntary associations, churches and synagogues, neighborhoods, and places of employment, some of these new communities had overlapping memberships, while others remained discrete.[24] Individuals who belonged to more than one found enduring relationships in some, while in others they encountered acquaintances with whom they had less contact. Like most cities, Dallas also had residents who seemed to "float" outside all the communities and never achieve, or claim, places.

Alongside these adaptive and creative developments were the negative aspects of urban life. Newspaper writers seemed almost as alarmed by the divorce suits—by 1881 at least one each week and often three or more—as by the frequency of suicide. Although dependable figures do not exist, the suicide rate appears to have been higher for women than for men. The reported incidents were divided almost evenly between females and males, but in Dallas men outnumbered women.[25] Crime increased, too, by 25 percent during the period from January 1886 to January 1888, for example, as rapid population growth strained the city's ability to absorb newcomers, much less provide them with adequate jobs and living conditions.[26]

Perhaps most troubling were the delinquent boys between the ages of seven and sixteen, some of them orphans and others the sons of parents who exercised little or no control. Between April 1889 and April 1890, the city recorded 104 arrests of children under ten and 729 of youngsters between ten and twenty, mostly for theft and burglary or, in the case of young girls, for shoplifting.[27] Legal procedures specifically for juveniles did not exist, and after their convictions, children were jailed with adult offenders. Hoping to get several boys released, members of the WCTU visited the sheriff in 1892, only to learn that, without homes, the children would have to serve out their sentences. The women organized the Newsboys' Relief Association to seek foster parents in several small towns within a fifty-mile radius of Dallas, but failed to locate families willing to accept such responsibilities.[28]

Late in 1892, the association opened a shelter, only to find themselves at odds with their beneficiaries. Left alone for a few hours one evening, the boys literally took the house apart, dismantling even the electric lights in attempts to learn how they worked. Another incident illustrated more baldly the social chasm between the children's expectations and those of their self-appointed benefactors. At a Sunday afternoon tea, one seven-year-old interrupted the hostess's "nice talk" by demanding, "Give us less talk and more cake!" With nicknames like Fish Fin, Daigo, Corndodger, and George the Indian, the newsboys had their own culture and values, their own ways of surviving street life. Such children had little use for the "home teachings" and "better influences" that middle-class women thought important. Once the boys realized that the association members would not buy newspapers, they stopped going to the shelter. Only bootblacks continued to draw on the women's charity.[29]

Women and young children may not have suffered more from the dislocation of rapid change, but they got more sympathy than the starving male "tramps" who lived in the river bottoms. Images of distress seemed to be everywhere. Leaving five children, a penniless woman died of pneumonia in the St. Charles Hotel, where "charitable ladies" had cared for her and paid her expenses. An elderly woman entered the cotton mill's office to get warm but was too ill to leave. The marshal sent her to the public hospital at city expense. A young widow, mother to three children and unable to find work, died of malnutrition and illness. The newborns left on doorsteps were fortunate; many others were abandoned along alleyways or country roadsides.[30]

Apart from the ladies' aid and benevolent societies, few institutions existed to alleviate any kind of distress. Buckner's Orphanage took in children, the county poor farm accepted people officially designated as permanent paupers, the public hospital had a few beds for indigent patients, and several ethnic groups ran charity organizations for their own members.[31] The city offered limited amounts of relief, but only after those needing aid visited the mayor, who then sent a police officer to investigate. If the petitioner was designated "worthy," her or his name went on the list of "regular pensioners on the city's bounty."[32]

While privileged young matrons benefited from the ethos of unrestrained private enterprise, they also tried to alleviate some of its consequences. In 1886, Belle Schneider chaired the first Crystal Charity Ball, which earned one thousand dollars for Dallas's poorest residents.[33] More lasting was her leadership, as president of the Ladies' Charity Association, in founding, also in 1886, the Woman's Home and Day Nursery, a shelter for "respectable [needy] women." Along with lodging, the nonsectarian home provided day care for the children of employed mothers, especially those supporting their families alone; on occasion it also took in elderly widows and even entire families when husbands were ill and unable to work. These early cross-class efforts were not matched by racial compassion. The home's founders and board members ignored the city's African-American poor, who remained entirely dependent upon aid from friends, neighbors, and acquaintances—usually, though not always, of their own race.

The Ladies' Charity Association supported the Woman's Home mostly with donations from individuals. With Dallas designated the permanent site for the Texas State Fair, the association earned additional money by running a lunch stand each October during the fair. The group found physicians who were willing to donate medical services and for a short time received ten dollars a month from the city government. In March 1886, members of the Ladies' Musicale, some of them also officers of the Woman's Home, raised funds with a production of *The Mikado*.[34] Often the study club's regular performances, too, were recitals benefiting the home, as were plays presented by the Dramatic Club.

With growing demand for its services, the Woman's Home took in more than 1,100 "suffering and destitute women" by 1895; by 1901, it helped more than 1,960. Accepting infants abandoned anywhere in Dallas County and mothers and children brought by police officers, the home sheltered 15 to 20 residents each month. When the Woman's Home and Day Nursery closed in 1905, other institutions, also founded and run by women, were providing similar services.[35]

However deeply rooted in compassion, the Woman's Home was a prime example of the way urban rationality replaced frontier spontaneity. Providing carefully planned, systematic aid, this kind of organization would replace the customary neighborliness of the rural network of service exchange and the incidental handouts of traditional charity. With their efforts to help indigent and employed women, the members of the Charity Association exhibited an awareness of conditions beyond their own comfortable lives and established the pattern of social concern for Dallas women for decades into the future. Between 1890 and 1930, women's organizations provided, and indeed often were the *only* sources of the kinds of social services becoming common in American cities.

The clubwomen's benevolence took less direct forms, too. In February 1891, two hundred women agreed to support plans to provide employed women, particularly those new to the city, with nutritious meals and "suitable" living conditions at prices they could afford. For many people, wages failed to meet even basic needs, and women's earnings usually could not cover the cost of safe lodging, much less the added expenses of nutritious food, adequate clothing, and fuel. Supported by donations from businesses and individuals, the Girls' Co-Operative Home and Training School was chartered and opened on June 1 in a house originally built as a private residence.[36]

Described as beautiful and spacious, set upon "a wide spreading lawn," the home was "centrally located in a first-class neighborhood, and within a three-minute walk from the center of the city." Rooms rented for three to five dollars per month, meals were two dollars a week, and lunch each day cost ten cents. With a five-hundred-volume library and free courses in telegraphy, typewriting, stenography, and dressmaking, residents found opportunities to improve their work skills and train for better jobs. In 1908, the Girls' Co-Operative Home became the Dallas chapter of the Young Women's Christian Association.

Middle-class women, too, benefited from the sense of social responsibility felt by the club leaders. The Woman's Exchange, a quasi-private sales outlet for women's handicrafts, was based on the philosophy of "helping others help themselves." Organized in April 1887 under the charter of the Literary Club's public library, the purpose of the Exchange was to give women a way to supplement their family incomes despite the social prejudice against female employment. Such housewives could sell their handicrafts through the Exchange with confidence that their identities, and thus their "difficult situations," would remain secret. Staffed as well as organized by women, the Exchange accepted handsewn articles, baked goods, sweets, and condiments for sale on a consignment basis. In order to help pay its expenses, the Exchange also operated a "lunch room," where "ladies out shopping" could eat or "drop in and get the ever refreshing cup of tea." The small restaurant served breakfast, lunch, and dinner "in Old-Fashioned Southern Style."[37]

With fifty members by 1889, the Woman's Exchange in Dallas never enjoyed a profit and struggled to remain open. Throughout the United States, very few of the Woman's Exchanges were self-supporting, much less profitable. As one critic wrote, they were essentially charities, and while they maintained high standards for the goods they handled, their boards ignored basic rules of business management.[38] Perhaps more serious was the fact that their wares would by nature appeal only to a limited middle- and upper-class market, one soon saturated with handmade luxury items. The Exchange in Dallas closed within five years, yet it serves as evidence of women's active responses to the hardships of urban conditions.

In the midst of fundamental change, traditional impulses also continued to move people, and religious faith inspired the city's first philanthropist, Juliette Peak Fowler.[39] The daughter of a wealthy family who pioneered in Dallas in the 1850s, Fowler had a happy and privileged early life. Tragedy struck within two years of her marriage, when she lost two infant children and her husband, all to different causes. Clinging to the belief that so many deaths must have some larger meaning, she returned to Dallas around 1862 to care for her aging parents. During the following years, she judiciously managed the property and invested the money left by her husband and later by her parents, then she sought ways for her wealth to help others.

When she died suddenly in 1889, her will included provisions for several individuals, plus a bequest of land and a trust fund to establish a home for aged women. Unanticipated problems delayed fulfillment of her wishes, beginning with an unsuccessful legal challenge to her will by disgruntled siblings. In 1903, Fowler's sister and executrix, Sarah Peak Harwood, donated the money, property, and state charter to the Texas Convention of Christian Churches, which used Fowler's bequest to operate an orphanage for several years. At last, in 1911, the first building of the Juliette Fowler Home opened as a residence for the denomination's elderly women. The first Dallas resident to plan long-term benefits for numerous people, Fowler must be counted among the innovative women of her generation.

The Fowler Home, the Woman's Home and Day Nursery, the Girls' Co-Operative Home, and the Woman's Exchange did more than meet women's needs. In efforts to ease problems that were peculiar to women, the founders of these institutions expressed empathy and caring for those of other classes, religions, and, often, ethnic groups. By applying the quality of nurturance to community problems, they extended into public life a trait associated with the most private images of "true womanhood," domesticity.[40] Going outside their homes to perform a customary role, such groups contradicted and, in time, sabotaged nineteenth-century social expectations.

Impressive even in their earliest accomplishments, the women who were beginning to define permanent roles for themselves in civic life were few in number. With approximately two hundred members altogether by 1890, the Shakespeare, Standard, Quaero, and Pierian Clubs and the Ladies' Musicale reached beyond members' personal interests and relationships into the community, creating social occasions for relatives and friends and transforming feelings of concern into practical ways of easing at least some of the misery they saw in Dallas.[41]

Through two conduits, both originating in the culture clubs, women of the dominant American-born majority were redefining their duties in community life. Charity and philanthropy long had been accepted female responsibilities, but after 1885, women in Dallas extended them beyond the traditional forms into a wider expression of social concern. Moreover, such women now planned and presented an increasing number of the city's cultural events and performances. In the past, men had, almost always, initiated and sponsored such occasions. These actions indicated a quiet shift in public gender roles and the beginnings of pervasive, almost surreptitious change in the city's most basic social organization, the division of labor in the building a community.

As they altered female public roles, the women's clubs also drew Dallas beyond local and even regional confines. By their very nature, the art exhibitions and musical performances connected sponsors, viewers, participants, and listeners with the larger culture. Few institutions could express more clearly than libraries, however limited their holdings and clientele, the impulse to relate local life to a wider experience. Similarly, visiting missionaries and the weekly lessons distributed by the national foreign mission organizations gave churchwomen glimpses of life in far-flung areas of the globe. In an apparent contrast, the Dallas women's efforts to meet people's needs seemed to respond only to local concerns and limited purposes. But the founders of the Woman's Home and Day Nursery, the Girls' Co-Operative Home, and the Woman's Exchange were following examples set in other places in the United States. As a result, charitable work, as much as cultural projects, participated in national trends.

More visible in Dallas than the work of the clubs and charitable institutions during the 1880s was the rapid increase in female employment. Unlike those who worked for wages, the privileged women of the middle and upper classes usually stayed in their "place," confining their activities to their exclusive neighborhoods and to the commercial innovation designed with them in mind, the department store. They acquired former residences to house their charitable institutions, and when they shopped downtown, kept to the "respectable" side of the street. Of necessity, employed women seemed to be everywhere as they went to and from their jobs in the mills, offices, hotels, and manufacturing plants. The clubwomen barely caused a ripple in the community's consciousness. The presence of wage-earning women in the public realm was undeniable, and it was growing.

With 27 percent of all females aged sixteen and over employed by 1880, women constituted 20.5 percent of the labor force. The city directories listed more every year, and the opportunities were a direct result of the developing economy. Still dependent upon supplying the needs of consumers, Dallas by 1880 exhibited the earliest signs of functioning as a city rather than as a town. Its economy increasingly depended upon the transactions of buying and selling, with cash as the medium of exchange; the reliance by farmers and merchants upon the simple trade or barter of farm produce became ever less frequent. In 1880, the county tax rolls showed four businesses—a dry goods company, a wholesale grocery house, and two banks—with taxable assets greater than those of the largest local landowners.[42]

Probably nothing indicated the nature of the Dallas economy as much as the character of institutions that dealt with money—the savings and loan companies, investment agencies, and banks. Their function of making savings available for capital investment depended upon the prosperity already achieved by local businesses and farms. As much as growth in the retail and wholesale trades, the seasonal extension of credit to farmers laid the foundation for the city's future position as a regional center for banking and finance.[43]

Like trade, commerce, and banking, industry depended upon consumer demand, which grew simply from the concentration of people with their business and personal needs. Construction, printing and publishing, and the repair and manufacture of farming equipment dominated the industrial base in Dallas. None of these by itself could define the local economy by attracting large numbers of specific kinds of wage earners. Rather, the needs of consumers determined the nature of the city's manufacturing, just as the wholesale and retail trades shaped its commercial activities.[44]

Firmly established as an inland distribution center, Dallas also was a communications and transportation hub for mail, railroad lines, and telephone and telegraph connections, all of which allowed business owners direct access to new markets and sources of investment. As the city's merchants forged trading relationships in St. Louis, Chicago, and Kansas City, they strengthened existing ties in New Orleans, Galveston, and Houston. Businesses based on older technologies prospered, too, with the freight wagon and stagecoach companies carrying manufactured products from Dallas to the small towns and rural communities of North and West Texas.[45]

As in the earlier stages of economic development, women were present, operating their own businesses, accepting paid jobs, and continuing their traditional work in home production for immediate use and, often, for sale. And as in other southern urban areas, the majority of women wage earners were black, comprising only 23 percent of the female population but 67.8 percent of the female labor force. Of white women living in Dallas in 1880, only 13.8 percent listed occupations; 76 percent of African-American women aged sixteen and over were employed.[46] The city was in step with national trends, for although social disapproval of female employment remained widespread, white women throughout the United States were entering the labor force in unprecedented numbers. The profile of Dallas women's occupations would show significant change during the next forty years. But roughly between 1880 and 1892, the majority of the city's female labor force, both employees and business owners, remained in work that in its products, if not in methods and technology, resembled traditional tasks in the home.

Mere expansion of the population increased demand for workers in occupations that were domestic in nature. Between 1880 and 1890, the city directories recorded nearly a fivefold increase in dressmakers and milliners, while the number of boardinghouse keepers multiplied almost nine times. Domestic service translated into such commercial jobs as hotel chambermaid, as well as offering positions in private homes. Among the dozen white laundresses were two who owned laundries, while numerous African Americans took in washing at home or worked for male-owned commercial laundries as finishers, starchers, "bluers," assorters, and ironers.[47] Whites benefited most from specialization in jobs related to housework. Large hotels hired them as "waiters," "linen room keepers," and "matrons" (caretakers) for the ladies' waiting room at the railroad depot.

Of 510 black women employed in 1880, 84 percent divided almost evenly into laundresses who worked out of their homes and domestic servants for private employers. While only about 20 percent of the domestic servants lived with their husbands, 40 percent of the laundresses were married and, whenever possible, working at home.[48] Two African-American women turned their domestic skills into small businesses, one a restaurant and the other a laundry. Both had two or three black female employees, but neither appeared in the city directories for as long as five years.

Despite medicine's relationship to age-old female roles, only two women physicians practiced in Dallas during the 1880s. One was in partnership with her husband, also a doctor.[49] The growing nationwide acceptance of female teachers made education easier to enter, and in Dallas two developments during the 1880s were especially significant. Women came to dominate teaching in both public and private schools, and for the first time black women found positions as teachers.[50] For a few years in mid-decade, all the white public schools had female principals. By 1889, the fourteen public schools employed only one woman principal, even though female teachers outnumbered males by four to one. The sex ratio differed for African Americans. Twelve black women and eleven black men taught in the public schools by 1889, but no African-American women were principals.[51]

Proportionally fewer women were in private education, although white matrons owned eleven of the nineteen private schools for young children. Female teachers in these small institutions outnumbered males almost two to one.[52] Women taught college-level courses at St. Mary's Institute, where the only two men on the faculty were piano instructor Hans Kreissig and the school's founder and philosophy professor, Bishop Alexander C. Garrett, the rector of St. Matthew's Cathedral.[53] Several small private schools for African-American children operated for one or two years and well may have had black women teachers. In 1880, the largest private school in Dallas was an academy for black students, taught entirely by African-American men.[54]

As significant for Dallas as the growing numbers of women in the labor force was the increasing variety of female occupations, an early indication of the way women would spread throughout the Dallas economy during the next thirty years. In addition to the jobs related to traditional roles, a limited number of "white-collar" positions were opening. The dozen female office clerks, telegraph operators, and cashiers of 1880 combined with stenographers, "typewriters," and bookkeepers to total seventy by 1889–90. Private businesses as well as the telephone company were hiring operators, and, as the decade passed, more women found sales jobs in dressmaking and millinery shops. The larger dry goods companies employed three times more saleswomen than a decade earlier. Perhaps because it resembled writing, editing was an acceptably "ladylike" occupation, and by the mid-1880s the city directories listed seven Dallas women as editors, one for the "society" page of the *Morning News* and the rest for small publications such as the newsletter of the Buckner Orphanage.[55]

Women found limited opportunities in industry, with the 1890 census counting 394 in manufacturing jobs. Before 1880, the town's two dominant industries, flour milling and cotton processing, hired only men. After 1885, women took jobs in several new manufacturing plants, including the Dallas Cotton Mill, three men's shirt manufacturers, a lithograph firm, and a paper and box company. With the growth of printing and publishing, women worked as bookbinders, press feeders, and compositors for the daily newspapers, while two opened their own shops as job printers. Still, according to the city directory for 1889–90, the categories of office, sales, manufacturing, and trade all together accounted for only 9 percent of employed women.[56]

Of white married women, only 3.9 percent were employed in 1880. By contrast, 58 percent of black matrons worked for pay. By mid-decade, the city directories listed a few whites who earned money in a variety of ways, usually in work related to their husbands' occupations, if not to traditional female roles. A physician's wife sold drugs, along with toilet articles, books, and stationery. In one case the wife owned a restaurant, her husband a meat market. A woman managed the theater belonging to her husband; another ran the hotel over her spouse's saloon. A number were partners with their husbands in such small businesses as a meat market, a lunch stand, a floral shop and greenhouse. Visible only in the city directories, such women disappeared in the crudity of census categories and the assumptions of census takers. Especially if their businesses were located in their homes or if they worked part-time, the census listed them under the term "keeps house."

A few women found employment in which they became harbingers of the future. The female cashier of a land mortgage firm was a company officer, not a clerical worker; like her, numerous others would serve during coming decades as officers and managers of small businesses that were usually family-owned.[57] Retail dealers sold boots and shoes, clothing and notions, hair goods, second-hand garments, and, in one case, masquerade costumes. Artists worked in their homes, while photographers ran their own shops and hired female photo printers. With choices influenced by propriety, custom, and legal constraints, women who operated businesses unrelated to traditional roles were, almost always, widowed or single. The female president of the East Dallas Bank; the owners of a furniture store, a drug company, and a stone quarry; and the proprietor of a firm manufacturing pumps, gas, water, and steam fittings—all were widows who had taken over family businesses, as was the owner-president of a tent, awning, and mattress firm.[58]

Like the previous decades, the 1880s in Dallas were pioneering years, though not for clearing forests, breaking prairie sod, or building log cabins. Instead, individuals and the city government were developing the physical infrastructure of urban life. Despite a nationwide depression, the appearance of Dallas changed dramatically, as individual property owners, investors, entrepreneurs, private organizations, and the city and county governments erected new buildings. In 1890 alone, a total of 769 went up. The best structures incorporated elements of styles ranging from Second French Empire to Romanesque, Italianate, Queen Anne, and Byzantine. Many were imitations of the design and construction experiments introduced in Chicago after the Great Fire.[59]

Additional basic services accompanied the splendid new buildings. Dallas acquired telephone lines, paved downtown streets and sidewalks, and, in 1888, a steam-powered railway to replace the mule-drawn streetcars. By 1883, a privately owned electric plant enabled the city to install street lights downtown. The conveniences, however, as yet extended less to the general public than to businesses and the homes of the wealthy.[60]

Even as the commercial sector grew and developed, numerous aspects of the preindustrial economy lingered. Although the home was no longer the unit of production or the source of livelihood, housewives continued to provide vital goods and services to the family economy through household production. Their work in the home remained necessary to the daily functioning of the labor force and the ranks of management. An unknown number of women—many, in view of the frequent reports of farm animals roaming the streets—continued to pro-

By the late 1880s, Commerce Street looked like a city. The building draped in flags, banners, and bunting was erected by Jay Gould to house the offices of the Texas and Pacific Railroad. Courtesy Historic Photograph Collection, Dallas Public Library

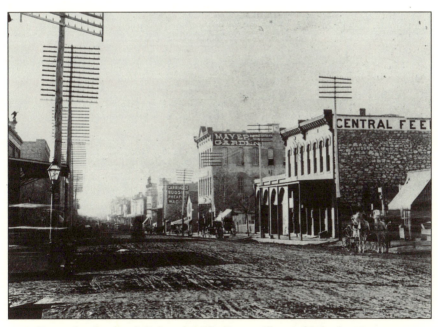

Except for the electric light poles, Elm Street still resembled a frontier town. Courtesy Historic Photograph Collection, Dallas Public Library

duce much of the food for their families' tables. At the same time, ever larger numbers of urban housewives were buying foodstuffs from neighborhood grocers, from farmers who sold produce door to door, and from neighbors who sold surplus vegetables and dairy products produced in their backyards. In 1884, the city chemist complained, "Anyone that owns a cow [is] . . . selling milk to somebody."[61] This fact made his job of citywide milk inspection virtually impossible but serves as evidence that numerous women raised livestock inside the city limits.

The Ursuline nuns, for example, continued to rely upon traditional ways. Their convent and school depended upon garden produce as well as cash payments for tuition and fees. In the early 1880s, the sisters purchased a farm just beyond the city limits. Two nuns rose before dawn each day, rode the streetcar to the end of the line, milked the cows, and then returned with fresh milk for breakfast. Later becoming the students' favorite place for field trips and special school events, the farm enabled the nuns to raise vegetables and keep livestock to feed themselves and their boarding students.[62]

Long after the coming of the railroads, housework changed little in town or country. One local woman's records of her production have survived. Ettie Fulkerson Cockrell was married to Sarah Cockrell's youngest son and lived a few miles southwest of Dallas on his family's original homestead. In 1885, Ettie earned $125 and in 1886, $175 by selling her turkeys, eggs, and butter in the city. She spent the money for household items, including a carpet for her parlor, curtains, a hanging lamp, and a highchair for her seventeen-month-old son. Her butter sales alone carpeted the dining room and paid the cook.[63] Urban homemakers, too, participated in the market economy by selling their surplus dairy and meat products, eggs, and vegetables to their neighbors or to hotels, bakeries, restaurants, and grocery stores.[64]

Unfortunately, Ettie Cockrell and her counterparts in Dallas kept no records of the foodstuffs they produced for immediate use by their own families, making it impossible to estimate the value of their contributions to their households, much less to the Dallas economy. As trade and commerce grew, the visibility of home and use production faded before the need for cash to acquire manufactured goods. Within the family economy, purchased items and services replaced the products of personal knowledge and skill as the basis of livelihood, in people's perception if not always in reality. Even for those who continued to produce foodstuffs and sew clothing, participation in economic life and status within the community related increasingly to money income. Ettie Cockrell's account book and the random memories of urban women's descendants remain the only sources acknowledging even the existence of the use economy within the home.

Ettie Cockrell's mother-in-law, the city's most successful businesswoman, focused her attention on real estate. Listed in the 1880 census as a "capitalist,"

Sarah Cockrell sold, rented, and leased both city lots and county acreage to the railroads, the City of Dallas, churches, individuals, and business firms. In 1884, she opened the Sarah Cockrell Addition, an exclusive residential subdivision adjacent to the Cedars, just south of downtown. Because the real estate addition, like the flouring mill, was a private corporation, giving it her name did not violate her traditional values. Along with one son, she also participated in the local construction boom, commissioning a prominent North Texas architect to design a five-story office building, which opened in 1885.[65]

Cockrell's lifestyle and behavior did little to signal the social changes affecting many other women's lives. In tailoring her business interests to the values of home and family, she managed the public aspects of her life from the "proper," private setting and thus preserved traditional appearances. Whatever people thought about her business success and frequent involvement in lawsuits, she was vastly respected. When she died on April 16, 1892, all the departments of city government closed during the funeral services, and the members of

Sarah Horton Cockrell, about 1885. Courtesy Dallas Historical Society

the city council attended in a body. Declaring her "a very mother in Israel" and "one of the founders of our city," her obituary lauded her "nobility of soul, unostentatious charity, and hearty hospitality."[66]

Sarah Horton Cockrell's business career spanned the development of Dallas from a country market town to a commercial city. For more than forty years she had participated in the growth of an economy built upon commerce and finance and based primarily on cash. By the end of that time, the rapid increase of the female labor force was an additional sign of a modernizing economy, as was the appearance of a middle class as identifiable by lifestyle and values as by income. As areas of the city turned into homogeneous districts composed exclusively of businesses, manufacturing plants, or private homes, the residential neighborhoods in turn became segregated by class, ethnicity, and race. Obvious differences in wealth and standards of living erased any surviving remnants of the fabled frontier egalitarianism.

But if certain urban characteristics provoked division and separation, others fostered new kinds of cooperation and community. Alongside the voluntary associations organized for professional, business, and labor interests were those devoted to religious purposes and to cultural and educational progress. Still others grew out of concern for the increasing rates of poverty, crime, suicide, and vice, and from genuine desires to improve people's lives. The developing urban social structures, forms, and practices were oriented toward the increasing opportunities for diverse and varied friendships, acquaintances, and experiences. At the same time, they provided means to alleviate the suffering of dislocation and the general upheaval that accompanied rapid growth and change. By 1892, Dallas had reached the end of its frontier period. In an almost mythic way, Sarah Cockrell's death signified the city's passage from pioneer conditions into established urban ways of life.[67]

Part II
Creating Urban Life

Chapter Five
Women and the Urban Economy

"All I ever asked was to be treated as man's equal," Clara Badder told a *Morning News* reporter in 1895, when she worked as an abstractor in the county clerk's office. Before moving to Dallas with her family, Badder was the deputy registrar of deeds in Huron County, Michigan. Once she had wanted to be a lawyer, but because her mother disapproved, she "settled for" work as an abstractor instead. Still, Badder believed, by taking jobs formerly reserved for men, women like herself were advancing female equality more even than the suffragists. Like a man, she insisted, a woman "should be left to follow her own talents and inclinations . . . guided solely by adaptability and reason." She was rearing her own daughter to be self-supporting.[1] In this short interview, Clara Badder expressed the rising expectations of women in her generation, for occupations based upon ability and interests instead of sex, for fair and equal treatment on the job, even for personal independence and respect.

The increase in employment after 1880 was the most visible aspect of women's entry into public life. Widely perceived as threatening to accepted social customs and patterns of living, the growing female labor force also was a major characteristic of the modern urban economy. Increasing from 26.1 percent in 1900, by 1920 36.2 percent of Dallas women spread into virtually every type of occupation, but as a population clustered in certain kinds of work. Employment more than tripled among matrons, from 5.6 percent in 1900 to 19.5 percent in 1920, and grew among single females from 40.5 percent to 58.3 percent. Equally significant were the women's identities: for married and unmarried alike, the most growth occurred among those who were white and native-born with native-born parents. The largest increases came, that is, among the majority of the population and not among immigrants or minorities.[2]

Women were a fresh source of labor, and many who entered the job market for the first time found new kinds of work. While a growing economy demands a *larger* work force, a changing economy needs people with *varied* abilities and skills. Thus, women's employment in Dallas indicated, more clearly than men's, the economic trends under way in the city. Throughout the nation, much of the innovation and growth occurring in business and industry were possible because thousands of women could meet the job market's new demands.

Developments in the home economy abetted the trends. As machines and factories took over manufacturing, the labor of supplying a family's basic needs required fewer hands. At the same time, domestic tasks were evolving from production into service work, providing higher levels of health and comfort to the families they sustained. Retaining its position at the base of the Dallas economic structure, the home became more closely linked to the marketplace. Yet, because the site of domestic labor was within the "private realm," work in the home became less visible and its significance to the community less obvious, especially in comparison with the quickening pace of female employment.

Cities consistently had higher employment rates for women than either rural areas or the nation as a whole. In every census year, female employment figures for Texas cities were larger than those for the state or the nation.[3] As in Europe and elsewhere in the United States, the availability of suitable work was the single most powerful determinant of the employment of women, and urban places were more likely than rural areas to offer jobs that women could do. Despite the presence in Dallas, well before 1920, of such heavy industries as petroleum processing and the production of cotton oil, cement, and iron and steel, the city's predominant economic activities retained their orientation toward supplying consumer needs, thus offering work attractive to women. In 1900, females aged sixteen and over who earned wages made up 24.4 percent of the city's labor force; by 1920, they accounted for 28.1 percent.[4] Integral to the city's development, the growth in women's jobs was, as much as any other factor, evidence that Dallas had achieved a modern economy.

While the number and kinds of jobs increased overall, industrialization took a measurable toll on traditionally female occupations. Seamstresses still found plentiful jobs with shops and department stores, mattress and awning firms, and clothing manufacturers, but the nationwide shift to ready-made clothing caused the numbers of white dressmakers to drop. By 1920, their proportions declined to 1 for every 115.4 white women, down from 1 for every 37 white women aged sixteen and over in 1880. Among African Americans, by contrast, discriminatory policies in department stores produced the opposite effect. "We always had dressmakers," recalled the daughter of a physician, "because I couldn't . . . stand the idea of . . . having a saleslady tell me that I couldn't look at the dresses, that I'd have to go back to the dressing room and have her bring me what she wanted me to have."[5] From 1 for each 105 black women over sixteen in 1900, the numbers of African-American dressmakers in Dallas increased by 1920 to 1 for every 70.[6]

Other occupations that were domestic in character also grew, if only slightly. While clothing factories and textile mills were replacing dressmakers, women who ran hotels, boardinghouses, and lodging houses became somewhat more numerous. In 1920, Dallas had a boardinghouse for every 301.3 white persons, as compared with one boardinghouse for every 374.7 in 1880. Until the advent of apartment buildings after World War II, private lodging houses (including both boardinghouses and places offering furnished rooms without meals) increased proportionally a little faster than the city's population. Similarly, women continued to turn food production and preparation into small neighborhood businesses, such as grocery stores and, less often, bake shops, confectioneries, meat markets, and fish and oyster stores.[7]

Teaching opportunities multiplied between 1900 and 1920, as the Dallas population nearly quadrupled, from 42,638 to 158,976. Outnumbering men almost five to one, women educators advanced into administrative positions as primary school supervisors, registrars, and principals' assistants. In 1910, six of nineteen principals were women. By 1920, however, only men held positions as principals. White teachers found an increased demand for private education. The Dallas public schools required female teachers to resign when they married, and running their own schools enabled married women to continue in their professions. Private kindergartens and elementary schools multiplied, as did schools of elocution and physical culture, along with studios for art, music, and dance. Julia Jackson Shamburger rode horseback to take half of the federal census for Harrison County in 1900 and used the money she earned to go to business school. In 1915, married and living in Dallas, she began teaching business classes in her home, then built a separate building next door for the Shamburger Business School.[8]

Of the six "colored" public schools, one had a woman principal in 1900. That number grew to three by 1920, when African-American women teachers outnumbered their male colleagues by four to one. For members of both sexes, becoming a teacher indicated personal and family success, as well as progress by the race; early in the twentieth century, the faculty in the Dallas public schools included former slaves and their children.[9] Education was one of the very few occupations offering African Americans professional dignity, status, a secure future, and opportunity for advancement.

More than in teaching, women continued to accept jobs in basic housework. In 1900, almost 90 percent of domestics—housekeepers, chambermaids, laundresses, cooks, servants—were black. The African-American teachers, practical nurses, dressmakers, and those "hired by business" made up only 8.4 percent of the black female labor force. By 1920, 91.1 percent remained in some kind of domestic service, despite significant decline in these occupations. The multiplication of commercial laundries, for example, replaced many self-employed laundresses, but expansion in other kinds of work, especially during and after World War I, also attracted women away from all areas of domestic service.[10] Although African Americans were a declining proportion of the Dallas population, down from 21.1 percent in 1900 to 15.1 percent by 1920, they made the city's female occupational profile resemble those of other southern cities. Throughout the South, black women drove employment rates upward as sharply as did immigrant women in the more industrialized North.[11]

Perhaps better than any other commercial institution, the department store illustrates how the modern economy multiplied occupations for women. Offering services in addition to merchandise, the stores hired staffs that ranged from on-site hairdressers and "shampoo girls" to candy makers, nurses for employee health problems, and teachers to instruct new employees and train demonstrators for special promotions. Women held clerical positions as billers, copyists, auditors, authorizers, advertising managers, "stock girls," "cash girls," and "office girls," but as sales personnel, they clustered in the departments offering "women's goods." African Americans usually were "markers," wrappers, porters, folders, assorters, and elevator operators, who worked more or less out of the public's sight.[12] The department stores pulled women into the labor force while maintaining a facade that suggested adherence to social tradition.

Older than occupations in the department stores were those in printing, work that was distinctly not domestic. First hiring females in the 1820s, printing firms nationwide included an ever larger proportion of women among their employees, from 9.1 percent in 1870 to a high of 20.3 percent in 1905. Thereafter, in one of the most clearly documented instances of widespread sex discrimination within a skilled trade, the numbers of female printers declined rapidly.[13] Few women in Dallas found work in composing, printing, or proofreading, despite the city's position as a regional publishing center.

As late as 1920, the city directory listed only sixteen women even in the socially approved positions of writer, reporter, and editor. Except as stenographers and clerks, women were much less likely to work for a daily newspaper than to edit specialized periodicals with limited circulations. As owner-editors, women usually had either previous experience in journalism or family connections in printing and publishing. A leading clubwoman and suffragist, Nettie Baily Ford was editor and publisher of *Texas Motherhood Magazine*, the official organ of the Texas Congress of Mothers. She was married to a print shop owner. Before launching the "society journal" *Beau Monde*, Alice Parsons Fitzgerald wrote for several newspapers in Missouri. After moving to Texas, she worked as society editor for the *Dallas Times Herald*.[14]

One journalist used the authority of her profession to advance the women's efforts for social change and reform. A native of Michigan with nine years of experience in writing and editing, Isadore Miner (later Callaway) wrote book reviews and edited the *Morning News* "women's page" for twenty-three years, from her arrival in Dallas in 1893 until her death in 1916.[15] She had divorced a husband who refused to support her but called herself a widow, no doubt because of the prejudice her generation harbored against divorcees. Personally active in numerous women's organizations, Callaway wrote a weekly column as "Pauline Periwinkle," through which she advocated the clubs' programs, from woman suffrage to patronage of art students. Above all, she used her pen to educate the public about injustice and human need, to ridicule the positions she considered to be unreasonable and prejudiced, to condemn callousness and lack of caring, and in general to explain and publicize the significance of the women's purposes for Dallas and for Texas.

Isadore Callaway (Pauline Periwinkle), about 1909, when she was president of the Dallas Federation of Women's Clubs. Courtesy Historic Photograph Collection, Dallas Public Library

Unexpectedly having had to learn to support herself, "Pauline Periwinkle" was well aware of the enterprising women who launched numerous kinds of businesses in Dallas. By 1920, the city had nearly one thousand female proprietors, although their proportion of all employed women was less than 1 percent, and little changed since 1880.[16] For these as for many men, business ventures tended to be connected with personal relationships. First run by sisters Lena and Amelia, the neighborhood grocery store of L. Engers & Company operated for nearly two decades between 1895 and 1915. At one time or another, Lena Engers employed her entire family, including father, mother, brother, and all her sisters.[17]

In other cases, sisters ran dressmaking or millinery shops together or sold insurance; in fewer instances, brothers and sisters co-owned such businesses as photo finishing shops or hotels. Wives and husbands often operated "mom-and-pop" stores, such as small neighborhood groceries and in one case, a wholesale house for fancy goods, notions, and "gentlemen's furnishings." Those listing themselves in the city directories as china decorator, hemstitcher, "poultry fancier," costumer, and teacher of crocheting and embroidery may have been mothers of very young children or women who, lacking other training, turned their domestic skills into paying occupations. Some found a permanent niche in the marketplace. The "fancy cake baker" of 1896 was running her own bake shop in 1900; the woman who sold potato chips out of her kitchen in 1902 was operating a potato chip factory in 1912.[18]

Domestic characteristics lingered in much of female employment, but in each successive year between 1900 and 1920, compilers of the city directories found women in jobs that females had not held before. The earliest seem to have appeared suddenly, between 1900 and 1905, in such listings as laboratory assistants in drugstores, engravers for jewelry stores, and draftsmen for architects. Although women in these jobs were more "tokens" than pioneers opening new occupational areas, after 1910 their numbers grew.

A few African Americans were leaving domestic service to run lodging houses, boardinghouses, neighborhood grocery stores, and beauty parlors. In 1919 and 1920, the black-owned *Dallas Express* announced the opening of additional businesses with women proprietors, including an insurance office, the Little Ford Express Company, and "the largest and most commodious [hotel] . . . for colored in Texas." The city directory for 1920 listed one black woman as proprietor of a theater, another as owning a restaurant, and yet another as running a small company to manufacture clothing. A fourth was a photographer.[19] Numerically, the black population was growing in Dallas, but entrepreneurs of both sexes found their markets and opportunities confined to the African-American community. At the same time, they were protected from white competition.

While the majority of female entrepreneurs operated businesses related to homemaking, widows owned every type of business imaginable, from dry goods stores, publishing companies, and newsstands, to foundries and manufacturing plants for iron work. Some were merely figureheads for firms run by sons or other male relatives, but most ran the businesses they owned. The city directory listings contain a few clues to a woman's actual role. When the company name was not followed by that of a male officer or manager, obviously the female proprietor ran her firm. The presence of male officers, however, was not necessarily significant. Even after 1900, widowed business owners sometimes remained as circumspect as Sarah Cockrell, privately retaining control while delegating the public aspects of their affairs to male relatives. Only family records or the memories of descendants can attest to whether a woman who modestly remained "behind the scenes" actually kept the books, managed the finances, and made the decisions for day-to-day operations.

In many cases, a woman's own employment history was the best evidence of her role. If she worked in the family business before widowhood, she was likely to remain actively involved. Even when they were not related to the owners, such employees as bookkeepers, cashiers, and stenographers often became partners and/or company officers. Of the women listed in the 1920 city directory as business partners, officers, or owners, 70 percent were, according to the best available information, active in the firms. Only family memories or records could reveal how "silent" the other 30 percent were.

Among the most successful was Carrie Marcus Neiman, who, with her husband and brother, founded the firm of Neiman-Marcus in 1907. Remembered many years later by her nephew as his mentor, Neiman never finished high school, yet, before the age of twenty-one, she was a top saleswoman and the head blouse buyer for a leading department store in Dallas. Commercial manufacturers of fine women's clothing faced stiff competition from designer-dressmakers in Europe and New York, as well as in local areas. Throughout her career, Carrie Neiman served as a link between her wealthy customers, many of whom would not make purchases without her advice, and the clothing manufacturers, who relied on her judgment regarding style, colors, cut, and fit. In these ways, Neiman influenced development of the modern fashion industry.[20]

Like widows, women in business with their husbands faced no special restrictions, but matrons running their own firms were caught legally between past and present. In response to women's increasing participation in the marketplace, the Texas Legislature passed a law in 1911 intended to benefit married women who ran shops and stores in their own names.[21] The statute enabled a matron to reclaim the status of *feme sole* for the purpose of engaging in trade, by applying, with her husband and in writing, to the district court in the county where she would establish her business. The resulting license gave her the rights

Carrie Marcus Neiman, age twenty, 1903. One of the three partners who founded Neiman-Marcus in 1907 and a fashion adviser throughout her lifetime, not only to Neiman-Marcus customers but also to clothing manufacturers in New York. Courtesy Stanley Marcus

to make contracts freely and to sue and be sued in the courts. The law also made her separate property liable for her debts and obligations, a condition important for gaining the confidence of creditors.

But the matron's business license did not release her from the state's community property laws. Allowed to invest only her own money in her business, she could never draw upon any of the joint holdings built up during her marriage, although her husband, as manager of the community property, could use them at will. Worse, her profits, like his, were community property and thus were under his management. For this reason, she could not legally invest her profits in her firm, and, because her profits were community property, they could be attached for her husband's debts.

A second statute passed in 1913 gave married women sole control of their separate property (except for its sale) and the rents, profits, and dividends it produced. Along with exclusive control of her earnings and bank accounts in her name, a matron gained the right to use her profits to benefit her business. Falling well short of full equality, the laws of 1911 and 1913 carried definite advantages, although few married women in Texas seem ever to have been daunted by legal considerations when deciding to open businesses.

After 1910, the most significant change in female employment in Dallas was the rapid increase in clerical occupations, primarily among single women. Alongside printing, publishing, and retail and wholesale marketing, insurance companies were multiplying. By 1920, they totaled one hundred for fire and fifty for life insurance. All needed competent office workers, and they swelled the so-called "white-collar" segment of the city's labor force. As early as the 1890s, women had taken various kinds of office positions, as copyists for insurance offices, abstractors for land-title research companies, and attendants and assistants to physicians and dentists. Before 1900, the stenographers, typists, cashiers, clerks, and bookkeepers altogether numbered fewer than one hundred; between 1910 and 1920, the stenographers alone almost tripled, from 1,106 to 3,247. At the same time, this occupation's personnel went from 73 percent to 90 percent female in only ten years. By 1920, office work was the city's most rapidly growing form of female employment.[22]

Dominating an area of employment did not insure equal pay. In 1920, an experienced female stenographer in Dallas could earn between $75 and $135 a month, those specializing in legal work $150. Experienced male stenographers earned $100 to $175. In nonclerical, "blue-collar" work, too, women's wages lagged behind those earned by men. A woman marker and "assorter" for a commercial laundry made $100 per month, compared with $150 for a male marker and "bundler." By contrast, black male "hands" at the cotton oil mill earned between $3.75 and $4.05 a day, while a white waitress at the Sanger Brothers lunch counter earned $3.75 plus tips for three hours' work.[23]

Increased demand for clerical employees came not only from business firms, but also from public agencies created as local, state, and federal government took on new roles.[24] As a regional retail and wholesale center and a major agricultural market, the city had strong banks. This financial vitality was a major determinant in the 1914 selection of Dallas as headquarters of the eleventh district of the Federal Reserve Bank.[25] By 1920, Dallas women were sorting currency for the Federal Reserve, as well as working as deputy collectors for the IRS, clerks for the U.S. Post Office, and secretaries in the women's division of the Municipal Free Employment Bureau. In city and county governments, too, women held various administrative positions, becoming deputy probation officers, deputy county clerks, deputy county health officer, manager of the city Social Service Department, director of public welfare, and manager of the Dallas Mexican Labor Exchange.

Expansion of private charity and social service organizations opened additional clerical and administrative jobs. By 1920, the Young Women's Christian Association had hired women for such positions as general secretary, publicity secretary, recreation secretary, county secretary, secretary for its cafeteria and rest room, director of its school of commerce, and house secretary of its home for young employed women. The Woman's Christian Temperance Union, the Anti-Saloon League, the larger churches, and cultural and educational groups hired multigraph operators, typists, clerks, and stenographers.

By 1920, the population profile of stenographers and typists in Dallas matched almost exactly that of the rest of the United States. Slightly more than half were twenty-four or younger, and only 15 percent were married. The vast majority, 88.5 percent, were white women, native-born of native-born parents. Needed less for the production of goods at home, unmarried daughters of middle-class (and, increasingly, of the more prosperous wage-earning) families had the highest level of education yet achieved by any segment of the population.[26] Not only were they the largest group in American society with the degree of literacy needed for office work, but they also possessed the good manners that enhanced a firm's image. For numerous reasons, the new positions fit well with current notions about what women could—or should—do.

The increase in female white-collar employees was evidence of two significant developments in the Dallas economy: expansion of the service sector, and business firms' adoption of modern corporate organization and business methods. Both innovations generated an enormous need for record keeping, intra- as well as interoffice correspondence, and such publications as annual reports and financial statements.[27] In ways that changes in men's jobs did not, the rapid growth in this aspect of women's employment reflected the city's economic development and its growing similarity to larger cities in the Northeast and Midwest. Between 1900 and 1920, the profile of the female labor force changed significantly more than either that of the male force or that of the city as a whole. In two areas the changes were dramatic—specifically, the decrease of 26.1 percent in domestic service and the increase of 21.4 percent in office positions. Except for the men leaving domestic service, the male occupational profile changed little during these decades.[28]

Nationwide, office employees in large companies tended to have their wages and opportunities depressed as large numbers sought work, but in small local firms, clerical jobs could lead to better positions. As early as 1910, Dallas women with clerical or stenographic experience seemed able to reach the managerial levels of almost any kind of company. By 1920, from businesses dealing in credit and loans to those in printing and publishing, from hardware firms to boiler and steam-heating equipment installers, from engineers and roofers to soft-drink companies, women with backgrounds in office work managed an astonishing variety of companies in Dallas. With regard to upper management positions, women fared best in family firms after widowhood, or in partnership with relatives and friends.[29]

Later seen as a "dead-end" occupation, stenography could open opportunities.[30] Between 1910 and 1920, nearly a dozen women ran their own businesses offering the services of stenography, multigraphing, and notarizing. One specialized in legal work, another owned an agency for temporary office help, and yet another operated a "stenographic exchange" as an adjunct to her business school. Attorney Helen Viglini used her experience in office work to challenge tradition. Possibly the first female lawyer to practice in Dallas, Viglini worked as a stenographer, then as an executive secretary to support five children while she read law in a friend's library. In 1919, she passed the bar examination with the second highest score in Texas. When Viglini became a prosecutor during the early 1920s, she very likely was the first woman district attorney in the state. After her return to private practice, she became the first to argue a case before the Texas Supreme Court.[31]

In the professions other than teaching, women's progress was slower than in business, although not so glacial as in law. In 1920 only three female attorneys practiced in Dallas.[32] By 1900, virtually all of the city's nurses were women, some of whom found positions as superintendents of small private sanitariums, hospitals, and infirmaries owned by local physicians. Nurses also worked with the city health department and as "health superintendents" for manufacturing companies and department stores, as well as for clinics in settlement houses and other volunteer-supported organizations.

Women doctors (never more than six at any given time) usually limited their practices to women and children and sometimes volunteered as staff physicians for orphanages and rescue homes. If not specializing in gynecology, obstetrics, or pediatrics, women tended to enter areas of medical practice outside the mainstream—as osteopaths, for example, or as chiropractors. By 1920, however, individuals worked in all the orthodox fields of medical training and practice, including internal medicine, dentistry, and optometry. Women found positions also as anesthetists, medical technicians, pharmacists, bacteriologists, and pathologists.

The ministry presented especially stern resistance to female participation, and, except for volunteer workers, most Protestant women in religious service were missionaries. Between 1900 and 1920, a half-dozen female Christian Scientists made their livings as practitioners, a function central to their church's teachings and beliefs. Congregations with female pastors were small and outside the Protestant mainstream. The Reverend Mrs. Alice Baker, for example, led the Truth Seekers Spiritual Church, which she had founded.

By contrast, Carrie Bryant Chasteen had an unusual career. Ordained in 1909 by the Oak Cliff Christian (Disciples of Christ) Church, Chasteen had served before her marriage as pastor of a church in Little Rock. After marrying a minister, she traveled widely with him and earned a reputation as a gifted speaker before settling into the role of "preacher's wife." In 1929, she was appointed Dallas' first "municipal minister," a ceremonial office in keeping with the contemporary vogue for public acknowledgment of female abilities, but one offering little genuine progress toward equality of opportunity or real integration into the profession.[33]

World War I encouraged trends already in motion and in some ways served as a watershed in the history of American women's employment. Most obvious to people at the time was the spectacle of women filling vacancies left by men who were away in military service. For the first time in Dallas, women became messengers for Western Union and operatives in the cotton gin manufacturing plant. Inspired by "patriotic duty," one applied for work in a railroad freight office. She pronounced herself "well and strong, . . . able to do a man's work" and said she preferred leaving the "work of offices and stores . . . to more delicate women."[34] The federal government opened a special school to train women ticket agents for the railroads, and in December 1918, one of its first graduates accepted work at the Union Terminal Station in Dallas. Patriotism had influenced her to leave an art career, she told the *Morning News*, but so had "a desire to prove that women could do men's work."[35] With managerial positions in offices, heavy labor in factories and railroad yards, and even the far lighter (but traditionally male nonetheless) work of conducting streetcars, women took jobs that were new to females.

The war effort also created employment in traditional areas, with 118 Dallas nurses enlisting in response to the military's appeal. Funded through the Bureau of Labor, the United States Government Employment Bureau opened at City Hall to help employers find replacements for male bookkeepers, stenographers, and cashiers, as well as operatives to staff garment and box factories. Both the navy and the army recruited women as stenographers, typists, and telephone operators, the latter for duty in Europe. In August 1918, forty-five hundred women were working in the city's factories and industrial plants; by late September, their numbers had reached six thousand. Within those few weeks, some companies doubled the numbers of women on their payrolls. The Government Employment Bureau was, according to a *Morning News* headline, "Deluged With Applicants to Take Places of Men." Its female director, however, assured the public that women were accepting jobs only out of patriotism or to "keep their minds occupied" while their men were in danger.[36]

When white women advanced into supervisory positions in offices and factories, they left vacancies for black women who wished to leave domestic service. Nationwide, such shifting within the female labor force was more common than actual growth in the numbers of employed women. The national female labor force did not increase significantly in size between April 1917 and early 1920, but women found better paid and more desirable work. Local figures approximated those for the nation. From 25.4 percent in 1910, the female portion of the Dallas labor force increased only to 28.1 percent within the decade. Depending on location, the 1920 Census found one-fourth to one-third of the nation's female population in paying jobs.[37] With so small an increase, World War I was perhaps most important for sharpening American perceptions of change.

For the most part, employers were pleased, if often surprised, that women performed "men's jobs" as well as men, "and sometimes better." In January 1920, a number of Dallas business owners petitioned the city council to amend the ordinance that forbade the hiring of women to operate elevators. When the ordinance had been suspended during the war, employers had found women to be "as prudent and careful as men in such positions."[38] Perhaps also as a result of wartime dislocations in the job market, women took such occupations as press repairer for a publishing company, bell captain for the Adolphus Hotel, meat cutter for caterer Simon David, and architect for a manufacturer of agricultural structural steel.

More than the war, economic growth after 1919 drew increasing numbers of women into the labor market, and revealed changing public attitudes about females in the paid work force. Prosperity eased competition for jobs. According to the Federal Employment Bureau in Dallas, a few women returned "cheerfully to domestic pursuits with the peace," but for those who chose "to retain their positions, in most cases, it is said, the natural expansion of business will care for them, as well as all soldier employees."[39] With the post-war increase in women's employment came awareness of the fact that wage-earning women had problems and needs not shared by unemployed females or by men. In 1920, the *Morning News* carried a regular weekly column entitled "For and By Business Girls," which dealt with such topics as when to leave one job to search for another. In similar recognition of the most rapidly growing segment of the labor force, the privileged women on the YWCA board voted to sponsor a series of courses to upgrade the skills of office workers and thereby enable them to improve their earnings.[40]

During these years, too, women's professional organizations flourished. While the Graduate Nurses' Association was organized in 1907, women in other occupations seemed to realize the value of new contacts during the war years. In 1917, the Dallas Women's Advertising League formed "to prepare members to fill the vacancies created in the advertising field by the men who had gone to war" and, undoubtedly, to share news and information about job opportunities. The charter members of the Dallas Business Women's Club, founded in October 1918, had years of employment experience, as did those who in July 1919 revived a pre-war organization as the Professional Women's Club of the YWCA. Soon afterwards, the two groups joined forces and affiliated with the Texas Federation of Business and Professional Women's Clubs.[41]

Despite the increasingly "white-collar" nature of the city's economy and the war's effects, the profile of women's occupations in Dallas changed little. In 1920, the largest single category of female jobs remained domestic and personal service, with 34.7 percent of employed women working as servants, waitresses, housekeepers, laundresses, and laundry operatives. Clerical occupations employed another 27.1 percent, but, when combined with the telephone and telegraph operators (5.8 percent) and the clerks and saleswomen in stores (11.8 percent), raised white-collar occupations to 44.7 percent of employed women.[42] The 7.3 percent employed as seamstresses and dressmakers in factories and mills could be classified in either "traditional" or "new" occupations: although engaged in the manufacture of products once made at home, they left home to earn wages by tending machinery in very nontraditional ways. They brought the total of "new" occupations to 52 percent from 44.7 percent. Added instead to the ranks of the 'traditional' jobs for a total of 44.0 percent, they make this classification only 0.7 percent lower than the "new." Whatever the shape of the female employment profile in 1920, the trends were clear, with the most growth occurring in occupations unrelated to domestic tasks and the most shrinkage in areas that were similar to housework.

As in the rest of the United States, the vast majority of employed women in Dallas in 1920 were single (divorced, widowed, or never married), but in all four marital conditions, the proportion of those employed had risen everywhere. Among the city's wage-earning matrons, 44.8 percent were black and 48.7 percent were native white women with native-born parents. For the first time, the female labor force was almost equally divided between native whites and native African Americans. Black women mostly did work related to homemaking, while white women dominated sales, office, and factory positions.[43] African-American women drove all female employment figures sharply upward. Even so, contrary to popular assumptions, employed African-American men outnumbered wage-earning black females in every age group, though not by margins as large as those by which men in the white labor force outnumbered women.[44]

By 1920, only 8.9 percent of employed black women had found work other than domestic occupations. A few held sales and office jobs in businesses owned by black men, and a total of forty worked as bookkeepers, cashiers, office clerks, stenographers, and typists in small firms. Black dentists and physicians hired office attendants and assistants, while men's clubs such as the Knights of Pythias and the National Woodmen employed clerks and office managers. It is likely that these women, like their white counterparts, were younger and better educated than those in more traditional domestic occupations.

Except for changing more slowly, black women's employment history on the whole resembled that of whites. Both groups earned money first through skills they practiced in the home, but by 1920 were moving into other areas as the economy produced new demands.[45] African-American seamstresses working for stores or clothing manufacturers may have been middle-aged while the office workers were younger and better educated. The porters, laborers, elevator operators, "janitresses," packers, assorters, and wrappers hired in white-owned department stores, bakeries, and wholesale houses also may have been older. Only six black women were trained nurses, but seventy-seven others worked as practical nurses. The city directories sometimes listed black women merely as "employee" or "helper"; fifty-eight were semiskilled operatives for textile and clothing manufacturers.[46]

Ministers, politicians, and moralists of both sexes portrayed the employment of women outside the home, especially after marriage, as a new and socially undesirable change. By abandoning their private, domestic "place" to join the wage market, critics claimed, women violated the "natural" order. Employed matrons endangered the very survival of home and family, while single women raised serious issues of social control with regard to gender. Not only were unmarried females exercising personal independence by earning wages, they were also creating new lifestyles.[47]

Social criticism met the entry of women into "men's jobs," yet in a milieu that strictly separated female and male "spheres," the simultaneous entry of men into women's traditional areas of work occurred almost unnoticed. One of the earliest results of industrialization, for example, was the male takeover of clothing manufacture. Although men had worked as weavers and tailors for centuries, the making of clothing continued to be a major responsibility of women. As late as 1910, female designer-dressmakers dominated professional aspects of the industry, while women monopolized others as home crafts. After 1886, scores of women accepted employment as spinners, weavers, and seamstresses in the Dallas Cotton Mill, which was owned, managed, and supervised by men. Similarly, of four large millinery manufacturers in Dallas, three were owned and run by men. The founder's widow operated the fourth. Each employed as many as forty women milliners and trimmers, while the millinery firms owned by women were smaller and short-lived.

Men also had taken over areas of work based entirely on general domestic tasks. To be sure, the process did not begin in Dallas. For centuries, men had worked as bakers, brewers, and tavern owners, and the trend accelerated with the passage of time, even though provision of food and beverages was an age-old female responsibility. By 1910, all but 7 of Dallas's 30 hotels were owned by men, as were 95 of the city's 97 restaurants. Women ran 87 of the 107 boarding-houses and lodging houses and undoubtedly did the day-to-day work of running the rest. Grocery stores, laundries, and clothing shops, all related to work done for centuries by women, more often were owned by men, who also took most jobs as cooks in hotels, restaurants, and cafes.

The significance of these observations lies not so much in one sex's encroachment upon the other's work as in the way such information supplements understanding of the processes by which industrialization affected employment and the demand for labor. Widely perceived as a one-way process, in which women flocked into and usurped men's jobs, the changes more often involved a swapping about of work between women and men, usually somehow skewed by the application of gender expectations to the marketplace.[48] Instead of a rational integration of the labor force on the basis of skills, education, experience, and expertise, employers and managers practiced and employees accepted, an arbitrary application of sex roles within the workplace. At the same time, they accepted an extension of the paradigm of separate spheres to situations in which it was particularly irrelevant.

Few could deny the female presence in the marketplace, but social commentators and theorists tended either to express frustration about assessing the economic importance of labor in the home, or to overlook it altogether.[49] The inability to apply accepted economic terms and measurements to the value of domestic work led not to new definitions and methodologies for assessing that value, but to the habit of ignoring work in the home as an integral factor in production. But if an economy is the sum total of the work by which people acquire the goods and services they need, then evaluations of that economy must include all the labor necessary to produce those goods and services, regardless of where the labor is performed, by what methods and technology, under what system of remuneration, and by whom. Although done out of the public view and without pay, work in the home was—and is—as much a part of society's system of providing for the population as any other work.[50] Analysis of the Dallas economy before 1920 must include the work done in homes alongside that of the marketplace.

By 1900 and on some streets earlier, physical conveniences such as paved streets and gas and electric lines were combining with commercially manufactured products to change the nature of domestic labor. Although retaining some production like that in the agricultural family economy of the frontier, by 1890 work in the home had begun its evolution into services in the urban family economy. Increasingly, domestic labor involved less manufacturing and more cleaning—that is, fewer handicrafts and more maintenance chores. Contrary to later beliefs, certain things did not change. Before 1945, middle-class housewives gained leisure because they could afford to hire servants, not because mechanical appliances eased or shortened their work day. Even as services rather than production, work in the home remained time-consuming and arduous and continued to be of basic importance for the day-to-day lives of the Dallas labor force.

Still the foundation of the city's economic functioning, work in the home made it possible for husbands, sons, and, in a growing number of families, daughters to be at their jobs each day. Between 1900 and 1920, federal censuses and city directories reported the occupations of entire families. Each almost always included one adult woman without a listed occupation, who nonetheless worked full time preparing meals "from scratch" and performing the maintenance tasks of sweeping, dusting, mopping, laundering, ironing, and mending. Factories and mills relieved housewives of the responsibility for producing goods but left to them the final chores of completing manufacture before use, as well as the ongoing care and upkeep of purchased items.[51]

Life in many Dallas households was surprisingly rural. Well into the twentieth century, thousands of families of both races lived on unpaved streets without water and sewer lines. Electric power and gas service were expensive, if available at all. Downtown streets and the exclusive white neighborhoods acquired basic physical amenities by the 1890s, and the African-American area of "Freedmantown" had them by 1913. Other city folk lived more like farmers. They had backyard wells and privies and disposed of their own household wastes and garbage.[52] Before 1900, wealthy families stabled horses for their carriages on their urban properties, while, as late as the 1930s, the less wealthy, both white and black, used their backyards to keep small gardens, milch cows, flocks of chickens, and perhaps a hog or two.[53]

Whites and African Americans alike produced and processed foods, gathering eggs and milking cows daily, churning butter, and killing chickens for Sunday dinner and sometimes for breakfast. Once a year at "hog-killing time," they, like farm women, spent days processing bacon, hams, pork, sausage, and lard. During the summer, they dried black-eyed peas, apples, and peaches for winter and boiled fruit into preserves, jams, and jellies. Urban dwellers ate like rural families, too, and every day wives prepared three full meals from foodstuffs that—whether they came from the backyard garden or smokehouse, the neighborhood grocer, or the farmers and other vendors who sold produce door to door—were whole and unprocessed.[54] Among those who gardened and raised livestock, barter survived well past 1920. In childhood, one woman heard a classmate taunted as "so poor your mama has to pay her dressmaker in eggs."[55]

Like their frontier predecessors, women in Dallas kept no records of the amounts, much less the market value, of their produce. In 1901, the United States Bureau of Labor conducted a study of the food purchases of 11,156 families in thirty-two states and the District of Columbia, and the South Central District included Texas. The study's findings make possible at least a general estimate of the monetary value of household production by Dallas housewives, and its percentage of the family diet.[56]

The purchases of individual families varied, but, regardless of class, their predominantly southern origins and Dallas's inland site undoubtedly affected their diets. A reasonable assumption is that the city's residents ate more bacon, chicken, pork, and ham than fish, beef, and rice.[57] Women could produce and process the latter four items, as well as several varieties of home-baked breads. According to the chart of food costs, an urban housewife's production could be nearly 80 percent of her family's total food supply, an amount close to that produced by the rural pioneers. By raising livestock and cultivating gardens, city families, like those on the frontier, might need to buy only sugar, salt, flour, cornmeal, coffee, and tea. Into the 1930s and perhaps later, many Dallas women continued to produce foodstuffs, as "country ways" lingered in an environment otherwise urbanized.

Work with foods had changed little in sixty-odd years, but few if any women continued to spin and weave. After the 1870s, commercially manufactured fabrics, as well as paper dress patterns and sewing machines, made household sewing easier, although the amount done in any particular home depended upon the wife's time and skill. Some mothers sewed only their daughters' undergarments, but, because ready-made clothing often was ill-fitting and unfashionable, many continued to make their own and their children's clothes. For all major stores, "piece goods" remained the department most important to sales and profits.[58]

Turn-of-the-century urban housewives probably spent less time sewing than cleaning. "Whenever anybody needed the broom," Hazel McCarley Winterbauer remembered, "we always knew where to find it. Mama had it."[59] Married to a construction contractor and the mother of seven children, Ida Young McCarley spent much of her working years fighting dirt, and her daughter's memories contrasted the home's earlier relationship to the overall economy with that in the new century. Except for food preparation, household tasks were evolving from production and manufacturing into services, tending toward more cleaning and maintenance and less making of goods.

The difficulty of McCarley's household labor was due to the fact that her neighborhood was one of those lacking basic physical conveniences. Large windows for cross-ventilation during the long dry summers made sweeping and dusting necessary every day. The rains of winter and early spring turned the street to mud, which women like McCarley had to scrub off their linoleum rugs on hands and knees with soap and rags. In homes lacking electric power, the cleaning appliances then on the market were useless, even had they been affordable.[60]

As on the frontier, household work often required the completion of auxiliary tasks first. The bedroom and sitting room stoves burned coal, but firing the kitchen range required chopping firewood and kindling. Drawing water from the backyard well, whether by a force pump or with a rope and bucket, and carrying it inside was a major household chore. The weekly laundry took around fifty gallons; scrubbing the linoleum rug in one room could use as many as four. Baths for the family probably used fifty more.

Women like McCarley taught their children to help at an early age. Children went home from school to draw pails of water, chop kindling and firewood, carry buckets of coal, clean ashes out of the stoves, empty chamber pots, wash dishes, and scrub cooking utensils with sand from "washed-out" places in the yard. Even in rural areas, women no longer made candles, but everywhere children as young as six could clean and polish the oil lamps. Ida McCarley's daughters inherited the chore of ironing as soon as they were old enough to lift the heavy flatirons heated on the kitchen range. Like washing, this task took an entire day, partly because McCarley wanted even the bed linens and dishtowels pressed.

Precisely the same tasks made up daily life in May Cole Deatherage's home, with the difference that Deatherage could afford to hire household help. After marrying a physician in 1893, her life revolved around family duties, especially rearing two children and caring for her invalid mother-in-law. She did not garden or raise livestock. Deatherage's leisure resulted from her employment of a cook to prepare three meals a day and a laundress to wash and iron the clothes weekly.[61]

Still, May Deatherage was hardly a "lady of leisure." Much of her time went into daily supervisory and managerial tasks, such as planning meals, placing orders with the neighborhood grocer and butcher, purchasing foodstuffs and household goods from door-to-door vendors. Having had a good deal of experience before marriage in sewing for herself and her younger siblings, Deatherage made many of her own clothes and almost all those of her daughter. She also did the dusting, sweeping, mopping, and general "straightening up," although the fact that her home was located on a paved street made her cleaning chores lighter than Ida McCarley's. Water and sewer lines enabled the family to replace the backyard well and privy with indoor plumbing, and her husband's earnings allowed his family to have electric power and gas service. May Deatherage could own mechanical household implements, making cleaning more thorough, if not always lighter or less time-consuming.

By 1900, two widely owned "modern conveniences," the kitchen range and the ice box, enabled a woman to give her family a higher standard of living but did little to increase her leisure. Allowing women to shop for foods less often and to serve more varied meals, neither appliance shortened preparation and cooking time.[62] Commercially processed foods were limited in variety and often poor in quality; breads, cakes, and pies from the bakery were expensive for wage-earning families. Whatever their source, foodstuffs arrived in every kitchen needing all the steps of basic processing. For that reason, as yet only hired servants could significantly shorten a housewife's day.

Daughters could be spared to seek employment, but the woman who stayed at home worked full-time, too. When dairy owner Ben King once bragged that his wife did not "have to work," she set him straight: "Women who go out to jobs get to come home at night. I just work all the time."[63] A leader in the middle-class African-American community in Dallas, Mary King's daily work differed little, if any, from Ida McCarley's, whether in cleaning, gardening, processing foodstuffs, or cooking. For both housewives, paving of the street where they lived, the extension of water and sewerage services, and the installation of electric power and gas lines—improvements in Dallas, in other words—did more than household implements to ease their lives. Yet, until the development of the commercial food industry after 1945, even citywide conveniences and new household implements had a relatively minor effect on the amount of time required for domestic labor.

As life in the city became more rationalized and planned, it also grew more complicated by urban attitudes: home production waned, but standards of cleanliness rose. The puncheon floors and fireplaces of frontier cabins needed little cleaning, even if anyone had the time. Maintaining possessions, such as linoleum rugs and kitchen ranges, claimed many of the hours freed from home manufacture. When women sewed more numerous garments and adorned them with embroidery, smocking, pleating, lace, or crocheted trimmings, they had to give such clothing special attention in laundry and ironing.[64] Oil lamps and gas lights, wool rugs and lace curtains similarly required special and frequent care.

Alongside the rising standards of household cleanliness, a married woman found her duties further enlarged by "scientific motherhood." In addition to requiring more attention to children and their particular needs, this nationwide movement demanded that mothers become knowledgeable about the most recent information on children's health, care, and nurture. The result was another kind of work, one that required many hours to read books and articles on child care, nutrition, sanitation, and health.[65] Needless to say, the new ideals for mothering were more accessible to those who could afford household help than to less affluent women.

Childrearing methods became as indicative of the middle-class lifestyle as hiring servants, accumulating possessions, and obeying elaborate rules for manners, etiquette, dress, and taste. For achieving these qualities—this lifestyle—a family's real standard of living, as well as people's perception of its standing in the community, came not merely from the husband's earning capacity, but also from the wife's "refinement," "accomplishments," and maternal expertise.

After 1870, access to goods and, to a large extent, social status, depended increasingly upon monetary income. In an urban economy, services, like goods, usually required cash. Money became the sole source of livelihood when wives, for whatever reason, did not garden and keep livestock. Rented living quarters frequently lacked the space for producing foodstuffs, and many women reared in cities and towns never learned the skills needed to produce and process home-grown produce. Under such circumstances, direct material contribution to the family economy required paid employment. In 1900, over 94.4 percent of the married women in Dallas worked only in the home. By 1920, this percentage had declined to 81.5, with married women constituting about a third of the female labor force.[66]

The shifting of housework toward services and away from production did not remove the home from its basic position within the local economy. Women continued to labor at the fundamental level of livelihood, albeit less in the acquisition of goods than in their care and upkeep. Machine manufacturing enabled many more people to acquire things once available only to the wealthy. Urban living, with all its pleasures and comforts, tended to make domestic tasks different but not fewer or easier. In the early twentieth century, the housewife in Dallas worked at the heart of the use economy and linked it with the marketplace in two major ways. First, she kept goods usable, whether she purchased them or produced them herself. Second, by providing family members with regular meals, wearable clothing, and healthy, comfortable living quarters, the housewife enabled them to go out to work each day. She, in other words, supported the city's labor force.

By 1920, women riddled the Dallas economy. Not only were they entering all kinds of employment, but also their labor was essential, indeed integral, to the economy. The profound changes occurring throughout the city's marketplace demanded ever larger numbers of workers and ever more varied skills. From the limited production of goods and the provision of basic services in the home, to the most abstract and rationalized occupations of the marketplace, women were working in virtually all sectors of the economy to provide people in Dallas with what they needed to live.

Chapter Six
City of Women

"Our Texas clubs are just beginning to aspire to that higher plane of club life where the desire for self-culture and the enjoyment of the individual are not the only aims, but where associated with these is a desire to promote the welfare of humanity, to better the communities in which we live, and to advance in every way possible the noblest ideals of womanhood." In the spring of 1898, May Dickson Exall welcomed the trustees of the Texas Federation of Women's Clubs to their first annual board meeting in Dallas. As president of the city's Federation of Women's Clubs, Exall endorsed the state organization's promise to "encourage woman's work for woman's good" and then, in her expression of purpose, projected its commitment into public affairs.[1]

During the next three decades, the Dallas Federation both led and supported a series of campaigns for civic reform, all originating in the women's clubs, but all bearing implications that reached far beyond the personal benefits of club membership for urban housewives isolated in middle-class homes. Intended to improve living conditions for city residents, these programs were evidence of a shift in gender roles with regard to public responsibilities. The clubwomen first took up community tasks that male leaders could no longer accept, then turned their energies to problems usually left for private solutions. In the process, they not only dealt with local issues, but also connected Dallas with the wider culture in ways similar to those by which businesses were linking their markets with the national economy. The origins of this genteel activism lay in the 1890s, when the women's clubs affiliated into a movement and promoted the causes of Progressivism in Texas.

At the turn of the century, Dallas clubwomen seemed to be everywhere at once. Beginning with such modest "village improvements" as planting shrubs around the courthouse and placing spittoons in public buildings, they came to exercise community-wide influence by founding permanent public institutions.

When they established agencies for social aid, sought reforms in the state's prisons and asylums, and worked for laws that altered the roles of government, the clubwomen embraced the philosophy of the political and social movement known as Progressivism. They saw that much more needed to be done, too, about women's legal rights, female access to higher education and employment opportunities, even the general lack of respect accorded to work in the home. As they sought solutions for these and numerous other social problems, the women used traditional approaches and adapted to the local situation strategies developed by clubs elsewhere in the United States.

Not only in Dallas, but throughout the nation, a half-century of pervasive change in women's lives was finding expression in the popular culture. Two terms used widely during the 1890s, "The New Woman" and "The Woman's Century," referred, respectively, to the increase in women's activities and public visibility, and to a growing, if sometimes grudging, admiration for their achievements. Writing in 1896, the *Morning News*'s "Pauline Periwinkle" encouraged married women to take advantage of the opportunities available to their generation. "One of the most alluring of the many phases of the new woman movement," she wrote, "is the promise it holds for the middle-aged woman of the future."[2] College-educated and devoted to her career, the "New Woman" usually was portrayed as unmarried, but large numbers of urban matrons shared the trend through membership in voluntary associations.

Few female club members in Dallas had experience in any aspect of public life. Their organizations were young: the oldest of the study clubs appeared in 1880, and all seven together enrolled about two hundred members by 1890. Two institutions already founded by clubs—the Woman's Home and Day Nursery and the Girls' Co-Operative Home—were located in residential neighborhoods.[3] The Woman's Exchange operated in a rented room downtown, but dealt entirely in the products of domestic crafts. Holding their meetings in private homes and hosting only quasi-private events, the women's voluntary associations as yet performed few, if any, functions recognized as essential by the community.

Yet, before they organized the federations that would take them into civic life, Texas women entered the most public of arenas, politics. On May 10, 1893, forty women and nine men met in the parlor of the Windsor Hotel in Dallas to elect officers and adopt a constitution and by-laws for the Texas Equal Rights Association (TERA). Fourteen of the charter members, including Vice-president Sarah L. Trumbull and Treasurer Lucy Knowles, lived in Dallas. The other thirty-five came from such small towns as Tyler, Circleville, and Granger, as well as the state's large cities.[4] Perhaps most significant, the majority of the leaders were former or current officers of the Woman's Christian Temperance Union (WCTU) and thus were experienced in dealing with both local public officials and state lawmakers.

The Texas suffragists based their justification for the ballot upon such traditional American principles as "No taxation without representation" and "Governments derive their just powers from the consent of the governed." Mothers should help to make the laws under which their children would live, the suffragists insisted, but voting alone was not enough. Women were needed as full participants in American political life, serving on juries, on city councils, and in legislatures, where their superior moral qualities could end corruption in government and clean up politics.[5]

The suffragists were joining a nationwide movement that dated from 1848, and the issue was familiar in Texas as well. At the state constitutional conventions of both 1868 and 1875, delegates had, if unsuccessfully, raised the question of enfranchising women. Only occasional speeches by WCTU leaders kept woman suffrage from fading entirely in Texas, but the next decade opened with more promise.[6] In 1890, Wyoming entered the Union with a provision for equal suffrage already in its constitution, and three years later Colorado became the first state where male voters approved a referendum to give women the vote.[7]

On March 13, 1894, Dallas suffragists organized their own Equal Rights Association (DERA). Mostly middle-class and married to business and professional men, the local suffragists were active in the city's culture clubs as well as in the state suffrage movement. The DERA's treasurer, Lucy Knowles, was an officer of the Woman's Home and Day Nursery, as well as treasurer for the Texas suffrage organization. President Sarah L. Trumbull was the TERA vice-president and, as a state organizer, led the founding of societies in Belton, Denison, Fort Worth, Granger, San Antonio, and Tyler. As avid a suffragist as her generation produced anywhere, Trumbull urged Dallas women to assert themselves "for home and country." She hoped during her lifetime to see women endowed with their proper rights, voting in elections and holding seats in the legislatures to fight directly for "equality, right and justice."[8]

In January 1895, the suffrage society in Dallas opened its own clubrooms in a building on Main Street. By claiming public space in the city's business district, the suffragists' bimonthly meetings symbolically announced their intentions to participate fully in public life. Moreover, the issue inspired discussion throughout the community. The *Morning News* published a special column, then expanded it into a full weekly page of news about women's club work and the suffrage campaign in Dallas and elsewhere. Equal rights for women provided topics for debates at the Dallas High School and the Young Men's Christian Association.[9] With 130 members by April 1895, the Dallas suffragists had the largest local society in Texas.[10]

At the state level, interest in the vote was curtailed by women's lack of experience in public life and civic affairs. In 1895, a suffrage bill was introduced in the House of Representatives in Austin, but it died in the committee on constitutional amendments.[11] The TERA could not press its cause effectively, largely because the movement had no base among women upon which to build. Too many Texas women could see little value for themselves in the franchise.[12] Without public opinion organized behind it, woman suffrage was not a serious issue for state lawmakers. Rather, it was merely a topic that arose now and then. The support of Spiritualists and Freethinkers made interesting news stories but could not give suffragists the acceptance and status that the Democratic, Republican, and Populist parties withheld.[13]

The suffrage societies foundered and disappeared by 1897, but the suffragists were leaders in other associations with statewide memberships. These would establish the basis for new public roles for women. Only days after the first suffragist meeting in the spring of 1893, several Dallas women helped to organize the Texas Woman's Press Association (TWPA). Belle Smith, former editor of a short-lived Dallas literary journal called the *Round Table*, became the TWPA's first president. Aware of the power of the press in "moulding [*sic*] public opinion," the twenty charter members sought to relate their professional interests to their "special nature" as women.[14]

Concerned also about serious social problems, the Dallas members of the TWPA hosted the launching of the Texas Woman's Congress. With this organization, they joined another nationwide movement, this one begun in 1873, when the Association for the Advancement of Women (AAW) held the first of its conventions in midwestern and northeastern cities. Known as the "Woman's Congress," each annual meeting featured papers, reports, and discussions of widespread problems and injustices in American life. By combining literary and cultural interests with social concern, the congress inspired clubwomen in various states to organize their own annual congresses.[15] Southern women launched their region's club movement during the 1880s. Beginning with intellectual and spiritual purposes, they later added town improvements and social and charitable projects to their studies of Browning, Shakespeare, and the Bible.[16]

During the State Fair in October, 1893, Dallas members of the TWPA hosted the first annual meeting of the Texas Woman's Congress. Taking advantage of special train fares available to fairgoers, delegates from fourteen cities and towns represented study and culture clubs, temperance groups, and missionary and ladies' aid societies. In 1894, at its second meeting the Woman's Congress changed its name to "The State Council of Women of Texas." The word "congress" was "too political," they decided, and they defined ambitious, if somewhat vague, purposes: first, "To make better known to the general public the magnitude and variety of woman's work for humanity"; and second, "To bring together women for all lines of work, [including] . . . religious, domestic, educational, philanthropic, professional, patriotic, . . . [as well as both] personal culture and altruistic effort through literary and study clubs, musical societies, art leagues, etc."[17]

Only seven women attended the suffragist program at the State Fair that year, but several hundred, including the TERA officers and members, went to the Council of Women's sessions. At the meetings in 1894, 1895, and 1896, delegates discussed plans to "create and foster" public interest in numerous social projects, including kindergartens in the public schools; public libraries for all communities; a state school for "the feeble minded," with manual training courses; and a state home for the "physically afflicted." Although the council explicitly refused to work for woman suffrage, its aims included essentially feminist demands, such as an equal "standard of purity" for both sexes, recognition of the real importance to society of women's traditional work in the home, and equal admissions policies and opportunities for girls in professional and industrial training programs in schools and colleges supported by public funds.[18] Even for these goals, leaders expected the Council of Women to serve only as a forum of communication.

Already, for many clubwomen, talk was not enough. With each passing year, attendance at the council's programs declined, and in 1897 the Texas Federation of Women's Clubs assumed leadership of the young club movement in Texas. Founded in Waco by leaders of the Women's Council, the Texas Federation intended for its members to enter public affairs "indirectly"—always behind the scenes, that is—and through personal contacts. Four Dallas clubs sent delegates: the Current Events, Standard, Shakespeare, and Pierian. Like those from other places, the city's representatives came from study and culture groups only; the missionary and temperance societies were forming separate organizations to coordinate their projects in regional and state arenas.[19]

The events in Waco again reflected nationwide developments. Founded as a national organization in 1890, the General Federation of Women's Clubs recognized its purpose to be not merely the discussion of problems, but also the initiation of solutions. By coordinating the interests of the various types of women's clubs, the national leaders intended to bring the values and principles of "woman's sphere" into every aspect of American life. Viewing the community as an extension of the home and thus as an appropriate arena for woman's influence, they planned to present the findings of their investigations to lawmaking bodies and to urge reform.[20] As early as 1892, five years before the founding of the state federation, at least three Texas clubs sent delegates to the General Federation's meeting in Chicago.[21]

After 1897, women's organizations throughout Texas federated within their local communities. In 1898, three literary clubs—the Pierian, Standard, and Shakespeare—joined the Ladies' Musicale and Oak Cliff's Quaero Club in the

The Dallas Shakespeare Club, about 1895. On the front row, right,
May Dickson Exall, the club's president, and Sally Griffis Meyer,
future president of the Dallas Art Association. Courtesy Dallas Historical Society

Dallas Federation of Women's Clubs. Affiliated with both the Texas Federation and the national General Federation, the local clubs had access to the experience and ideas of women elsewhere in the United States and to the support of their counterparts throughout the state. By 1902, the Dallas Federation enrolled ten member organizations with a total of 246 women. After 1905, such diverse groups as the Woman's Auxiliary of the Typographical Union, the Graduate Nurses' Association, and the Council of Jewish Women provided a broader base among women's organizations.[22]

The Dallas Federation leaders began their community service by founding the public library, a relatively uncontroversial project that carried no political connotations but promised permanent benefits to the city. During the previous forty years, Dallas residents had attempted at least five times to establish a library. The 1894 effort emerged directly from the women's difficulties in finding books and reference materials for their club reports. In 1888, the library run by the Ladies' Literary Society had closed, and its books were packed away in the City Hall basement. At the same time, women's literary societies seemed to spread like prairie wildflowers in spring. In addition to the Shakespeare, Standard, and Quaero clubs and the Chautauqua, by 1894 the new organizations included the Clionian Club, dedicated to discussing the works of Oliver Wendell Holmes; the Fin de Siècle Club, reading the novels of Charles Dickens; and the Athenian Chautauqua Circle, studying Byron, Livy's histories, Norse legends, and songs and legends of the Middle Ages. Relatively few people shared these interests, and the meetings called to discuss a city library were sparsely attended.[23]

Led by May Exall, the clubwomen in Dallas accepted the recommendation of the Texas Federation of Women's Clubs to concentrate their energy and resources on founding a permanent library. The first president of the Dallas Federation, Exall was a native of Texas and a Vassar graduate, as well as president of the Shakespeare Club. Remembered by her grandchildren as petite and very dignified, she would become the *grande dame* of Dallas women's clubs and, over the next fifty years, a leader in women's organizations. Enlisting the aid of several businessmen, Exall appointed a committee to target a list of "prominent citizens [about half of whom were women] and moneyed men" for donations. Within a few weeks, the committee raised twelve thousand dollars, then turned to Andrew Carnegie's library program for help. After the city government promised to donate a site and pledged four thousand dollars for annual operation and maintenance, Carnegie sent fifty thousand dollars to the Library Association.[24] The Dallas Public Library was the first institution founded by women to be built on public property and supported by tax money.

On October 22, 1901, the library opened with a special ceremony. With 11,436 books by its first anniversary, the library reached a total circulation of 83,006 among the 5,400 white persons "qualified" to have readers' cards. Almost at once, the librarians began attempts to reach across class barriers into a wider "public" by expanding services beyond middle- and upper-class patrons. On the advice of public schoolteachers, they gathered a separate collection for children who had to end their formal education in the seventh and eighth grades to help support their families. In addition, by 1904 the library regularly sent books into white working-class neighborhoods for readers' shelves in the settlement houses.[25]

Efforts on behalf of black readers were less energetic. In 1907, the Public Library Board in effect refused to help the Ladies' Coterie Club establish a library for African Americans. When Coterie Club officers Genevieve Cooper and Mrs. R. T. Hamilton met with the library trustees and requested support, May Exall responded with apparent warmth, promising to do everything "in [the board's] . . . power" to help. She then assigned the matter to an all-male committee, which several months later reported that it could not find "such general support from your people [*sic*] as would justify them in endorsing [a library for black citizens]." The committee added, preposterously, that such support "might

Dallas Carnegie Library in 1901. Courtesy Historic
Photograph Collection, Dallas Public Library

be construed as taking sides in the question and do more harm than good [within
the black community]."[26]

May Exall and the members of the Public Library Board, among them the
most activist white clubwomen in Dallas, endorsed a committee report that they
would never have accepted for their own programs. A graduate of Fisk University's college preparatory course, Genevieve Cooper was a former public schoolteacher who held a certificate from a normal school. Married to the first black
dentist to practice in Dallas, she was a natural leader of African-American women
—May Exall's exact counterpart in the black community. Hamilton, too, was a
civic leader, wife of a physician, and possibly a former teacher. No records survive of either woman's reaction to the library board's response. While they must
have resented the board's patronizing decision to donate to the Colored Reading Room all duplicate copies in the city library's collection, most likely they
accepted the books graciously. The Coterie Club continued its efforts until 1912,
but only in 1935 did the Dunbar branch library open for African Americans in
Dallas.[27]

As with the founding of the library, the names associated with art in Dallas
were, except for two professional male artists, those of women. Belle Gay Smith,
a native of Mississippi who moved to Dallas in 1878, presented the city's first
exhibitions. A charter member and several times president of the Standard Club,
Smith edited the *Round Table* in 1889–91, organized the Art Students' League

in 1893, and served on the boards of the Public Library and the Art Association. Soon after her husband became secretary of the Texas State Fair and Dallas Exposition in 1886, she accepted appointment as superintendent of the Fair's Ladies' Department. That year, for the first fair, she organized a small exhibit of paintings by San Antonio artist J. R. Onderdonck. Throughout the 1890s, artist Frank Reagh traveled to cities in the Northeast to select works by recognized artists, enabling Smith and her committee to present a larger and increasingly sophisticated art show each year at the fair in Dallas.[28]

Aside from these exhibitions, people interested in viewing paintings and sculpture had to rely on the generosity of local collectors. The most prominent was Katherine Lamar Crawford. Born in Oxford, Mississippi, educated in Europe, and married very young to L. Q. C. Lamar, Jr., Katherine for several years served as official hostess for her father-in-law, the United States Secretary of the Interior during the 1880s. Widowed in the early 1890s, she moved to Sherman, where she headed the Art Department and taught French at the North Texas Female (later Kidd-Key) College until she remarried in 1896. In the art gallery of her new home in Dallas, Crawford opened her collection to the public several times each year, displaying works by such artists as Van Dyke, Kung-Meyer, and Bougereau, along with her own paintings. On other occasions, she hosted lectures, special exhibitions, musical performances, and receptions for visiting artists.[29]

The "public" who attended Crawford's showings and programs belonged to her social stratum, but the Dallas Public School Art League worked to cultivate an appreciation of fine art in a more general audience, and particularly among schoolchildren. First organized in 1895, the league's members also were the Mothers' Club of the McKinney Avenue School, and their first project was to purchase reproductions of major paintings to hang in the classrooms and halls. With less diversity than they would achieve later, the public schools included pupils from differing ethnic backgrounds and classes. Alongside the privileged children of the Art League's members in the McKinney Avenue School were those of Russian and Polish immigrants who lived on adjacent streets. In 1899 and again in 1901, the league brought the Texas Federation of Women's Clubs' Traveling Gallery to Dallas for viewing by the general public, as well as by the schoolchildren, whose classes visited the showings. Each of the exhibitions, consisting of about one hundred reproductions, was followed by a series of free lectures.[30]

Whatever the influence and generosity of local collectors and interested mothers, only the stability and leadership of a permanent museum could make art a regular part of urban life. The origins of the Dallas Art Museum lay with those of the Dallas Public Library, where May Exall and the Dallas Federation reserved a room and installed special lighting for a gallery. During the library's formal opening in October 1901, the Dallas Federation's Art Committee held an exhibition of works by foreign and Texas artists. With the admission fees, the group began a fund to purchase works of art for a permanent collection.[31]

Chaired by May Exall, the Art Committee of the Dallas Public Library joined the Public School Art League in January 1903, to form the Dallas Art Association. Of the twenty-one trustees, eighteen were women who represented the clubs and the annual State Fair of Texas exhibitions, while the remaining four were prominent business and professional men. Six years later, in April 1909, the association gave its collection to the city, then moved the works of art from the public library to the Fine Arts Building in Fair Park. The city paid for operating expenses, maintenance, and staff, while the association remained trustee of the collection, with sole authority for purchases. After 1910, the museum's board worked to enlarge its base among the city's population with receptions and teas, as well as exhibitions of drawings by public schoolchildren and paintings by local artists. Again an organization founded and run by women had become a permanent municipal institution, located on public property and supported by tax money.[32]

Like interest in art and literary studies, classical music was mostly a pursuit of the middle and upper classes. During the 1890s, the meetings of the Ladies' Musicale and its successor, the Derthick Musical and Literary Club, were the only regular performances in Dallas. In contrast, popular music was thriving, with six or more professional bands and orchestras and at least three amateur groups available to play for parties, dances, and holiday celebrations. Male singing societies, such as the Frohsinn, the Schweizer Maennerchor, and the Quartette Club, sometimes featured classical selections along with their performances of popular songs and folk music.[33]

Between 1895 and 1910, the most dependable sources of classical music were the women's societies. The Saint Cecelia Club, the Schubert Choral Club, the Wednesday Morning Choral Club, the Apollo Club—all met once a week to study choral music for women's voices. They sponsored public appearances by major artists and instrumental ensembles, but their own periodic recitals were private and sometimes were given as benefit performances for various charities.[34]

The most adequate extant documentation is that of the Saint Cecelia Club, organized in 1895 by Alice Bryan Roberts. A graduate of the Cincinnati College of Music and for many years a voice teacher, Roberts, as president of the State Association of Musicians and Musical Societies, was active in fostering the study of classical music throughout Texas.[35] Beginning with twenty-five charter members, the Saint Cecelia Club soon expanded into a mixed chorus for its three or four annual recitals. Sponsoring two to four concerts each year by nationally recognized musicians, Saint Cecelia members, by the end of their seventh season in 1902, had presented a total of sixteen concerts by major artists and had sung in twenty-two choral recitals.[36]

Unfortunately, Dallas lacked enough lovers of classical music to provide adequate support for even a few annual performances. Too often, Saint Cecelia Club members had to make up for poor box office receipts; in 1907, the club went into debt to pay its expenses, then disbanded. For many years afterward, Alice Roberts continued to bring classical musicians to Dallas, herself arranging appearances by major artists and frequently supplementing inadequate ticket sales with a personal check.[37]

Poor attendance at classical performances did little to encourage the organization of a symphony orchestra. Eight years after a first attempt in 1890, Belle Schneider reorganized the Ladies' Musicale as the Derthick Musical and Literary Club, with the express purpose of raising money for the Symphony Club. The climate for classical music had not improved, however, and Music Director Hans Kreissig struggled for six years before again disbanding the orchestra in 1904. Before 1920, citizens' groups and local musicians made three more attempts to form a symphony for Dallas. All failed.[38] An orchestra required more time, energy, and money than volunteers could manage, and the women's usual methods of raising funds were inadequate. For many years, people who cared for classical music had to rely on a succession of societies and clubs to sponsor performances by major artists, orchestras, and opera companies.

Unlike other American cities, where wealthy patrons endowed the museums, libraries, and orchestras, Dallas had only its devoted volunteers, mostly in the women's study clubs. As a dependable core of visitors to exhibitions and audiences for concerts, recitals, and lectures, the women's most basic service in the creation of the city's formal aesthetic life was that of patrons: they read and discussed the books, listened to the musical performances, viewed and sometimes purchased the paintings. With programs in the public schools, women hoped to create a wider future audience for the arts; through scholarships, they supported the training of young performers and artists. By sponsoring lectures and courses, they hoped to increase appreciation for the fine arts in Dallas. They may have had some small degree of success. After a series of art lectures in 1902, owners of several furniture stores believed that they could see improvement in the quality and taste of purchases for private homes.[39]

Like women, men supported learning and the fine arts. During the 1850s and 1870s, men organized the earliest library associations and debating and literary societies, while male singing groups and choruses presented public programs. But after the coming of railroads in the early 1870s, male energies focused on jobs, careers, professions, and businesses; men spent most of each day in offices, factories, and shops. Their lives were very different from those of the pioneers of the 1850s and 1860s, who casually went to the Dallas Historical

Society meetings "at early candle light" and laid aside whatever they were doing when the Masonic bell rang.

Except for the professional artists and musicians, men virtually ceased by the mid-1880s to organize events and occasions in the city's formal cultural life. Individuals among the male business owners and community leaders responded willingly when the clubwomen asked for donations or invited them to serve on boards or committees. But by 1906, as one clubwoman wrote to the *Morning News*, women were taking up community work that men "have not the time to do."[40] Until well into the twentieth century, women founded the institutions and organized the events of formal aesthetic life in Dallas, adding variety to the resources and experiences available to urban residents and visitors.

An older female endeavor than nurturance of the arts was charity, and in the work of easing poverty and suffering, women were highly visible. The mid-1890s were a time of nationwide economic depression. In Dallas during those years, an outbreak of smallpox accompanied the closing of businesses, the collapse of the city treasury, and the rise in poverty caused by widespread unemployment. When an unusually cold winter aggravated the problems in 1894, a Methodist leader named Virginia Johnson asked a prominent businessman to go with her to the mayor to discuss a citywide relief effort. The public response was gratifying. More important, a year later several men founded the United Charities, the first attempt in Dallas to organize the collection and distribution of charitable donations.[41]

Certain kinds of need, however, outstripped regular contributions, and, throughout the 1890s, women outside the clubs also worked to alleviate suffering. Their efforts extended beyond periodic donations to the actual founding of major institutions, some providing aid and relief for only a few decades and others continuing to serve the community a century later. While such women were members of the "New Woman" generation, often their work stemmed from venerable traditions.

Accepting an invitation from the bishop and several Catholic physicians, the Sisters of Charity of Saint Vincent de Paul sent two nuns to Dallas in 1896. The city needed them: one public hospital, the two-year-old Parkland Memorial, existed for a population of more than forty thousand persons. Except for a few private infirmaries and clinics run by individual doctors, most families cared for their sick at home.[42] Belonging to the order whose American chapter was founded by Elizabeth Ann Seton, the first American-born saint, Sisters Stella Dempsey and Mary Bernard Riordan began their work by accepting patients into a four-room cottage the bishop had purchased for their living quarters.[43]

In addition to her nursing duties, Sister Mary Bernard directed construction of the new hospital. Opened in July 1898, the one-hundred-bed Saint Paul Sanitarium had brick walls fifteen inches thick and ceilings twelve feet high,

St. Paul Sanitarium, about 1900. Courtesy Historic
Photograph Collection, Dallas Public Library

features that helped to cool the building during the summer. In winter, steam
heat and a fireplace warmed each room. The large garden on the grounds provided vegetables for the diet kitchen and helped to control expenses. In 1900,
the nuns opened Texas' second nursing school, which received its state charter
of incorporation six years later.[44] For the next sixty-one years, the Saint Paul
Sanitarium Training School accepted both female and male students into its
programs. A century later, Saint Paul Hospital continued to be a major source
of health care in Dallas.

Religious commitment inspired Protestants, too, to support institutions of
caring. For several years during the mid-1890s, the Charity Chapter at the Episcopal Saint Matthew's Cathedral paid the rents of several elderly women, some
of them ill and all destitute. Around 1898, the churchwomen decided to con-
solidate their efforts in a house donated by one of their members. Named Saint
Matthew's Home for Aged Women, the institution operated until 1920 with
support from the Episcopal Diocese of Dallas.[45] Several years earlier, another
group of women began a day nursery, which in 1897 became Saint Matthew's
Home for Children. Under the auspices of the diocese, the orphanage operated
for fifty years.[46]

The occasion for founding the Virginia K. Johnson Home and Training
School was more dramatic, if no less urgent. In 1893, a well-known prostitute
wrote to Virginia Johnson pleading for help in leaving the "sporting life." After
agonizing over the letter, Johnson presented it to the missionary society of which

she was president. The group accepted the project, and at the age of fifty, she began her life's work. The result of Johnson's labors was a "rescue home" called Sheltering Arms, where young women could find living quarters, education, and job training. Thereby, the Methodists hoped, the women might avoid a life of prostitution.

A native of Missouri and educated by private tutors, Virginia Johnson during the Civil War was suspected of being a Confederate spy and was imprisoned by Union officers. After that, she certainly possessed the confidence to challenge propriety. The earliest organized attempts to "rescue" prostitutes began in New York City in 1836, but the Social Purity Movement continued to be questionable for female reformers. Rescue work involved association with known prostitutes, visits into the least reputable areas of town, and sympathy for unmarried pregnant women—all of which stretched well beyond the limits of behavior acceptable for middle-class women. Still, the courage required to challenge the pressures of propriety earned admiration. A Methodist bishop dubbed Johnson "Saint Virginia" for her efforts to save "fallen" women.[47]

Under the auspices of the Methodist Church and with Virginia Johnson as administrator, Sheltering Arms became the Ann Browder Cunningham Home in 1897 and later, in 1911, the Virginia K. Johnson Home and Training School. In a large three-story brick building on an eighteen-acre campus in Oak Cliff, the home operated until 1941, seven years after Johnson's death. By this time it had evolved into a haven for unwed mothers, rather than a shelter for reforming prostitutes. During its three incarnations after 1894, the home helped around three thousand women and over fifteen hundred children.

However impressive, women's community work during the 1890s was marred by its lack of compassion toward African Americans. Public spirit and aesthetic interest failed, almost entirely, to extend to that one-fifth of the city's population who were black. With help from only a handful of white individuals, African-American residents in Dallas built their community life parallel to, but separate from, that of the dominant white majority. With the emergence of a strong class of professionals and owners of small businesses came the values and lifestyle recognized among whites as middle-class. By 1900, 39 percent of married black women were employed outside their homes, down from 58.2 percent in 1880.[48]

Growing prosperity accompanied acceptance of the values reflected in a sermon preached in March 1893 by the pastor of New Hope Baptist Church. Urging his congregation to "rise above prejudice, passion, and sensation and vote for the best interest and welfare" of their community, the minister recommended the examples of "the Chinaman in acts of frugality and economy . . . [and the] white man . . . [in] making preparation for the . . . future."[49] Home ownership and improvement, thrift, education, and hard work were the values that middle-class whites assumed to be their own. African-American citizens considered these values to be the foundation of citizenship and therefore, a means to dignity and equality. Centering their cultural life in the churches, black people also developed an increasingly active network of voluntary associations, another sign of an emerging middle-class, indeed of an elite, among them.

During the 1880s, men had organized the Mystic and Stag clubs and by 1893, they had a literary society as well. The first culture club for African-American women was the Ladies' Reading Circle, which began meeting in its own clubhouse in 1891. Four years later, black women formed a new chapter of the Methodist missionary society, the King's Daughters, with a membership that included teachers and the wives of physicians. By 1902, the Women's Auxiliary of the Negro YMCA was giving "entertainments" to raise money for that institution's reading room. Among delegates attending the Colored WCTU's annual meeting in Terrell were several Dallas women, one of them an officer in the organization.

Like Mary King, the African-American clubwomen were community leaders, many of them middle-class homemakers married to professionals or owners of small businesses. Others, such as Julia Caldwell Frazier, were music teachers or public schoolteachers. An admired Latin scholar for whom a Dallas public school is named, Frazier was born in Alabama and became the only woman in her graduating class at Howard University in 1888. With her stern dignity, awe-inspiring decorum, and skirts kept long even after styles changed in the 1920s, Frazier was remembered by one former student as "a lady of the old school." Club notices in the earliest extant issues of the *Dallas Express,* for 1919 and 1920, frequently included her name among the members of women's literary societies.[50]

With the club movement, African-American women, like their white counterparts, were joining a long tradition. A generation before the Civil War, in 1831, free black women in the Northeast began organizing literary societies for self-improvement, as one means of overcoming racial prejudice. When Dallas clubwomen joined the newly organized Texas Federation of Colored Women's Clubs in 1906, they pledged to work for "better homes, schools, and churches" and for "the betterment of the race."[51] Unimpeded by attitudes that frequently hampered southern white women, African Americans could have put their energy and faith in the promise of America to work to benefit the entire city.

While the women's clubs in Dallas were products of a particular social milieu, they did much to shape the city's future. For both races, widespread social changes were improving middle-class women's lives and making it possible for them to become more active in their communities. Averaging less than four children by 1890, native-born white women found themselves devoting many fewer years to familial duties than their mothers and grandmothers.[52]

Thanks as much to improvements in sanitation and standard of living as to medical advances, by 1900 a white woman reasonably could plan to celebrate her seventieth birthday, an African American to reach her sixty-fifth year.[53] Between 1870 and 1900, the phenomenal growth in industry and commerce boosted more families than ever before into the middle class, often enabling even young married couples to hire household help. By the turn of the century, middle-class white women and a relatively small but growing number of African Americans enjoyed a significant amount of leisure.[54]

Equally important, the increase in wealth made daughters less necessary for labor at home and thus they were more likely than in previous generations to graduate from high school and go to college. By 1900, 53 percent of girls aged five through fourteen attended classes during the nine-month school year in Dallas, compared with 52.8 percent of all boys. In both races, young women were more likely to stay in school after age fourteen than their brothers. Among whites, 32.6 percent of females and 28.1 percent of males between fifteen and twenty were still in school, compared with 25 percent of black females and 24.2 percent of black males. These figures would change little until 1916, when the state's compulsory education law took effect. In 1900, only eight white men and twenty women graduated from the public Dallas High School; one man and one woman received diplomas from the city's "colored" high school.[55]

The quality of instruction in the past is difficult to assess, but young women from privileged white Dallas families had local access to an education similar to that offered in well-known eastern schools. Saint Mary's Institute opened in 1889 and by 1892 was granting bachelor's degrees.[56] Except for two men—the school's founder, Episcopal Bishop Alexander C. Garrett, who lectured in psychology and logic, and Hans Kreissig, professor of music—the Saint Mary's faculty members were female. Almost all were unmarried, with degrees from such respected institutions as Chicago, Columbia, Cornell, Smith, Wellesley, and Toronto, as well as the state universities of Texas, Michigan, and Illinois. Like the most prestigious women's colleges, Saint Mary's did not require its faculty to have degrees beyond the bachelor's level. Although they taught all the courses offered at men's schools, women faculty members everywhere served primarily as examples of "womanliness," grace, and refinement. Scholarship, while appreciated, was of secondary importance.[57]

Saint Mary's curriculum balanced a rigorous program of academic studies with sports and physical activity, requirements first instituted at Vassar in the late 1860s.[58] With a daily schedule beginning at 6 A.M. for classes, exercise, and study, the college was unlikely to produce graduates who would become home-bound wives or develop the vague ailments, mysterious illnesses, and general ennui which seemed to plague many middle-class women a generation earlier.

Perhaps the most obvious results of female education were the voluntary associations, some organized to recreate members' happy memories of their school years and others growing from a desire for continued learning. The clubs and societies, though, had unexpected effects on their members. Begun for development of personal interests and self-improvement, the local clubs and, later, their state associations provided women with the skills necessary for participation in public life.[59] Sallie Griffis Meyer was one of the few club officers in Dallas who grew up in the city. During the 1890s, Meyer was so shy that she burst into tears the first time she read a paper before the Pierian Club. In 1909, however, she accepted the presidency of the Art Association, an office she held for the next seventeen years. Developing into a community leader, she also served on the board of the Dallas Public Library and in 1901 helped to write the state's first child labor law.[60]

Such self-confidence, acquired in part through learning to speak before a group, was as important as the mastery of parliamentary procedure. As women practiced the skills of defining goals and formulating strategies, they came to trust the good intentions and to respect the expertise of other women, as well as to take pride in their own capabilities. Being assured of the support of one's peers was at least as necessary as the ability to manage a budget or lead a committee.

The ladies' aid, industrial, and missionary societies also provided such experience. In 1894, Lucinda Williams, who in 1872 had saved the First Baptist Church from extinction, became president of the Baptist Woman's Missionary Union. At the first meetings she chaired, Williams found the formal rules of order unnecessary. Instead, she "very much needed to encourage free speech," for many women were "timid and backward about talking [before the group]." Once they decided to speak, they tended to ramble. "Sometimes there were little talks entirely off the question," requiring Williams to nudge the discussion back to the problem at hand, while trying to insure each speaker "a fair hearing." Years later, after decades of leadership in Baptist organizations, she remembered chairing these early sessions as "the most taxing" work she ever had done. Yet, within a short time, the Baptist women learned not only to run local meetings, but also to plan and manage their annual conventions without male assistance.[61]

Whether secular or religious in orientation, the women's organizations served important social purposes by directing community energy and thereby shaping life within the city. The matrons who were doing so much through their clubs to create the urban lifestyle also gave each other a genuine sense of belonging. Their clubs and societies reached beyond the traditional bonds of family and fostered special relationships among themselves.[62] Members joined for personal reasons, whether from a sincere impulse toward self-improvement and a genuine interest in history, literature, and music, or merely from a wish to know "the right people." Unlike kinship ties and neighborhood acquaintances, these associations were based upon conscious choices. Alleviating the isolation of the home, the clubs provided the companionship that former generations had taken for granted in the country market town. Perhaps more for women than for men, friendships now developed not within the rhythms of daily life and work structured around the family, but during more formal, arranged occasions and especially through selective association.

As much as trade, commerce, and finance, the women's organizations drew city residents beyond a local, provincial focus into heightened awareness of the world beyond Dallas. Through the Council of Women and its successor, the Federation of Women's Clubs, the culture clubs affiliated with state and national organizations. The missionary societies, too, belonged to regional, state, and national groups within their denominations. As local activities taught them the skills for public participation, affiliation with state and national associations gave women contacts with the trends and developments of the larger world. Influenced by examples from older northeastern and midwestern cities, Dallas women found themselves called to new roles in community life after 1900.

Perhaps the decade's most significant evidence of a new outlook among Dallas women appeared in 1895, in a seemingly trivial incident that attracted little or no public attention. Weary of having their children's clothing ruined by mud and dirt, three or four mothers asked the Board of Education to spread gravel on the playground of the McKinney Avenue School. The board denied their request, so the women gathered in their leader's parlor and, now numbering an even dozen, decided to chip in five dollars apiece and buy the gravel. After a sympathetic member of the school board donated the gravel from a creek-bed on his property, the mothers used their money to pave the school's walkways and plant shrubs on the grounds. With the remaining funds, they purchased reproductions of paintings to hang in the classrooms and halls. Calling themselves the Public School Art League, they sponsored exhibitions of the Texas Federation of Women's Clubs' Traveling Gallery in 1898 and 1899. In 1903 they merged with the Public Library's Art Committee to form the Dallas Art Association.[63]

In 1895, the Public School Art League continued its dual life. As the McKinney Avenue Mothers' Club, members soon returned to the Board of Education. The men needed little urging to replace the school's rickety furnace, but in 1898 they balked at the request for installation of indoor toilets. When the women appealed to the mayor, he refused even to meet with them. Undaunted, the mothers chose a committee to visit his office every day until he agreed to hear their concerns. In a very short while, the McKinney Avenue School had modern plumbing—on the inside. Outside, raw wastes from the toilets drained into one end of the school yard instead of flowing into the storm sewers. As a result, one mother recalled many years later, "a pond of green slimy water stood in a grove of plum trees."[64] Once again, repeated visits to the mayor's office got results, and the city extended a closed sewer line to the school.

In a time when people expected women to limit their interests to the "private realm" of the home, the McKinney Avenue mothers were, in the name of home and family, questioning the judgment of elected officials and demanding that public money be spent in certain ways, as well as assuming that they had the right to make such demands. In these simple, mundane matters affecting day-to-day life—gravel for a playground, a new furnace, indoor toilets, a sewer line—the women inadvertently took the elementary steps of political action.[65] Very likely, these little-known events were Dallas women's first direct encounters with government. They certainly foretold both women's immediate political future and their unexpected effectiveness in altering life in Dallas and shaping the city's physical, as well as its social, structures.

Historically, perhaps the most significant fact about these first "political" women was their identity. Their president was Olivia Allen Dealey, in whose parlor they met to discuss the playground gravel. A native of Lexington, Missouri, and descended from five generations of newspapermen and journalists, "Ollie" Allen continued the family tradition when she married the business

Olivia Allen Dealey (front row, center) *and her family, about 1900.*
Courtesy A. H. Belo Corporation Archives

manager of the *Morning News,* George Bannerman Dealey. In addition to rearing five children, Olivia Dealey directed the Public School Art League until it joined the Dallas Art Association in 1903. For decades she chaired committees and held offices in this and numerous other civic and cultural organizations, and worked to establish the College of Industrial Arts (later, Texas Woman's University) in Denton.[66] Overshadowed by her husband throughout her life, Dealey was as much a community leader as her better-known spouse.

Relatively wealthy, socially prominent, and married to successful professionals and businessmen, the twelve McKinney Avenue mothers were typical of the women who, in 1898, federated their several culture clubs into a movement and proceeded to found permanent institutions in Dallas. Educated and privileged housewives, most without experience in the work force or in public life, the clubwomen soon would realize that they could not achieve their goals except by dealing with elected officials and learning the machinations of public policy making. In their quest to improve education and make the city a cleaner, healthier place to live and rear their children, they, like the McKinney Avenue mothers, learned that they possessed useful qualities, particularly an unsuspected capacity for leadership and the courage to defy convention, however circumspectly. Most significant, along with perhaps a dozen men, they were Dallas's earliest social reformers. Through the institutions they founded and the principles they held, the clubwomen's activism did much to shape the city's future.[67]

Chapter Seven
City of Mothers

"Some of these patients are not of our church," a lay worker at the Saint Paul Free Clinic warned Sister Brendan. The young nun seemed personally offended, for observers saw her stiffen before she replied firmly, "But they are humanity."[1] Her words expressed the attitude of many women in Dallas during the early twentieth century. Whether Catholic, Protestant, or Jewish, religiously inclined or secularly oriented, privileged white women crossed religious, class, ethnic, and, once in awhile, even racial boundaries as they worked to alleviate the effects of poverty, prevent illness, and help newcomers adapt to the city. In the process, they came to view relief and assistance as community responsibilities instead of occasional, individual acts of mercy. As "Pauline Periwinkle" wrote in 1912, the women believed their programs to be "entitled to public support" and deserving of a permanent place in community life.[2]

Between 1890 and 1920, women in Dallas founded hospitals, orphanages, homes for the aged, and rescue homes for "redeemed" prostitutes. All except the last were considered proper causes for women's nurturing talents, and even the rescue homes earned their founders a kind of scandalized respect. Day nurseries and kindergartens, settlement houses, medical clinics for children, and milk stations for infants were compatible with traditional female concerns, too, but they were more than adaptations of customary impulses to changing times. In cooperation with public agencies, these organizations became the foundations of a comprehensive citywide system of aid that, at first by implication and then explicitly, redefined relief as an ongoing function appropriate to the community. Originating with privately funded agencies, the values invoked by the clubwomen's programs spread in time into the public culture and produced physical improvements in the conditions of life in Dallas.[3]

In applying the values of the private realm beyond the home, women stretched more than the traditional ideas about charity. In effect, they advocated an expanded definition of public responsibility, one that could include the well-being of citizens. Extending their help into matters always before considered private, the women practiced an inclusiveness that recognized (if it did not always appreciate) the increasing diversity of the urban population. With modest amounts of money raised from private donations and such activities as craft bazaars and food sales, women pioneered in establishing modern forms of relief in Dallas.

Few sources reveal conditions in the city's turn-of-the-century immigrant and working-class neighborhoods as clearly as the minutes of the trustees who ran the settlement houses and infant welfare stations. Combined with clubwomen's responses, the descriptions of the problems found in these districts explain clearly why permanent social welfare agencies offering numerous kinds of services came to characterize modern urban life.

Dallas women had few local precedents for what they set out to do. During the 1870s and 1880s, public awareness had focused, without much sympathy, on able-bodied "tramps," most of them young unmarried men in search of work. Cigar, paper and box, and cracker factories, the cotton mill, shirt makers, print shops, leather goods manufacturers, and newspapers—during the 1890s, all drew job-seekers who both enlarged the population and stimulated the demand for consumer goods. But regular seasonal closings, market fluctuations, and periodic layoffs combined with the depression of 1893–97 to produce a degree of suffering that Dallas residents had not experienced before. City conditions concentrated people's misery, making it more noticeable to the privileged, and more troublesome than if it had been only, scattered through the countryside.

For the two decades after 1900, the city's poor clustered in four areas. The cotton mill district in South Dallas was home mostly to native-born American wage earners, as was the area just south and west of downtown, formerly known as Boggy Bayou and now called the "Reservation" for its lingering association with prostitution. "Frogtown," also an older neighborhood and a "red-light district," included thousands of new immigrants who outnumbered its "demimonde." Frogtown's public school, Cumberland Hill, enrolled pupils from at least sixteen nations, with later reports claiming twenty-eight. Farther to the east and about two miles from downtown was the fourth location of concentrated poverty, a settlement of Russian and Polish Jews located just beyond the comfortable homes on McKinney Avenue and its adjacent streets.[4]

In the early 1900s, the main sources of relief were still ladies' aid societies in the churches, benevolent associations in synagogues, fraternal lodges, and ethnically oriented charities like the German Ladies' Aid Society. Reserving their ministrations for persons known to them in some way, these groups, like the city government, sometimes sent a committee to investigate requests for aid.[5]

Such charitable groups usually were successful in gathering Christmas and Thanksgiving donations, as well as occasional communitywide collections for the victims of natural disasters and "acts of God." As a general rule, specific causes got better responses than constant requests for food, clothing, or money. Private charity, in short, mostly involved "taking care of our own" and responding to crises and natural disasters.

The sources of public assistance were fewer, and the funds available were more limited. The state gave pensions to veterans and the widows of veterans, while the city and the county provided most of the meager aid available at the local level. In 1876, Dallas County opened a poor farm, where law-abiding paupers found shelter and prostitutes worked off their fines for "vagrancy." The county commissioners, like the city government, gave food, fuel, and small monthly payments to individual applicants who passed inspection as the "worthy poor."[6] First opened in 1873 and named Parkland Memorial in 1894, the city-supported hospital for years served only the destitute. Ignorance and public apathy allowed the mentally ill to be treated more like criminals than patients. The state asylum in Austin accepted a limited number of persons adjudged "lunatics" at hearings in the county courts, but until a second asylum opened in 1919 in the town of Rusk, others were simply locked into local jails.[7]

In the mid-1890s, whites could find long-term help from only three private sources, each limited to a specific clientele: Sheltering Arms (later the Virginia K. Johnson Home) took in girls and young women who were "in trouble"; the Buckner Home accepted orphans; until 1905, the Woman's Home and Day Nursery housed unemployed and indigent women and their children. African Americans had to depend on neighbors, relatives, and friends.[8] By definition barred from these institutions, the numbers of poor people increased rapidly during the depression of 1893–97. Overwhelming the city's tiny relief fund and straining the resources of benevolence groups, their suffering provoked the earliest step toward a system of inclusive public assistance in Dallas, the organization of the United Charities by several businessmen in 1896.[9]

The charitable organizations and institutions founded in Dallas between 1901 and 1920, including the United Charities, were pioneering efforts for a community where little or nothing like them had ever existed before. Instead of the entrenched methods and established philosophies encountered by reformers in other cities, the Dallas clubwomen found a kind of frontier, with only a few antebellum forms of charity that were inadequate for the growing need. Provision of regular, systematic public aid throughout the city—at first for whites and later for minorities as well—would, to a large extent, emerge from the women's pioneering efforts.

Influenced by the ideals of Progressivism, Dallas clubwomen believed that government responsibilities should expand beyond a vague promotion of "the general welfare." Between 1895 and 1920, their social projects would introduce the Progressive agenda into the city, especially in urging higher standards of public health and safety and concern for the well-being of women and children. Like other southerners who called themselves "progressive," the women usually favored prohibition and studiously ignored or avoided racial issues. Many were slow to support woman suffrage. But they agreed with their northern counterparts that immigrants, the disadvantaged, and especially children must be saved from poverty and disease and from lives of crime and dissipation.[10]

Concern for children's welfare appeared in Dallas with efforts to provide early childhood education. During the 1880s and early 1890s, clubwomen concentrated on the special needs of women. While they did not forget women after 1895, their primary attention turned to children, beginning with the need for safe and affordable day care. The first day nursery for children of employed mothers opened in the Woman's Home in 1886, and at least one other existed by 1897. By 1901, two years after organization of the National Federation of Day Nurseries, women in Dallas were running four free day nurseries for children of employed mothers. Although they provided a high quality of all-day care and, for each child, a daily bath and lunch, the nurseries did little to prepare children for school.[11]

Kindergartens, which originated in Germany in 1840 and spread throughout the United States after 1860, served this need.[12] With their own children enrolled in private kindergartens during the 1890s, middle-class Dallas women were convinced that the children of poor families, too, needed to be taught the basic principles of nutrition and personal hygiene, along with games and songs that prepared them for elementary school. During their preschool years, the children of foreign-born parents, the women believed, should learn the rules of social and ethical behavior and become acquainted with American culture. With a depressed economy curtailing city expenditures, appeals to the Board of Education failed to get kindergartens opened in the public schools.

The women decided to do the job themselves. By 1899, three different groups were running free kindergartens, all supported by money raised at such events as ice cream festivals, music programs, teas, and church suppers. In 1900, the women pooled their resources in the Dallas Free Kindergarten and Industrial Association and opened a kindergarten in an old blacksmith shop. Soon afterward, in 1901, the cotton mill's owner donated a room, a piano, and a matron's salary for a second kindergarten and day nursery for children of millworkers. The clubwomen saw this gesture as an attempt to forestall their current work for a state child labor law, but they agreed to provide teachers, lunches, and daily baths for the children. Around this time, too, the association opened the Dallas Kindergarten Training School for teachers.[13]

Attendance at the free kindergartens was often irregular, but not always because the pupils lacked clothes. Mothers who earned money by taking in laundry needed help, and sometimes they kept children as young as four at home to work. When the cotton mill closed each summer, entire families worked in the fields near the city. In the wage-earners' neighborhoods of South Dallas, the clubwomen found the kind of mutual aid that they called "genuine charity. . . . Among these people, each is willing to help his neighbor and does so."[14]

The needs of the children could not be separated from those of their families. To deal with these myriad problems, the clubwomen turned to the means that had proven so successful elsewhere, the settlement house. This movement began with the opening of Hull House in Chicago in 1889, and by 1900, settlement houses came to number nearly one hundred nationwide. The Kindergarten Association in Dallas opened Neighborhood House, located about a mile north of downtown, where the staff could work with both residents of Frogtown and the poor immigrants living near McKinney Avenue. Children from Polish and Russian Jewish families, as well as those of German, French, and English immigrants, attended the kindergarten in Neighborhood House. Their varied backgrounds required, among other things, that Christmas celebrations be "wholly non-sectarian."[15] By 1905, the association's three free kindergartens altogether enrolled more than 370 youngsters.

Settlement houses laid the foundations for the new profession of social work.[16] By 1908, Neighborhood House was home for eight social workers, who made between forty and sixty calls each month at the homes of foreign- and American-born immigrants. In monthly cooking classes for women and girls, the social workers stressed cleanliness and basic nutrition. Like the special courses for mothers in child care and development, the cooking classes were part of an effort to help wage-earning families and the poor improve their health. Other courses offered instruction in basic sewing skills, while a weekly rummage sale made secondhand clothing available at very low prices. In addition, the social workers trained young women (all of them white) for jobs as domestic servants, still the largest occupational category for females in Dallas. The classes, clubs, meetings, and home visits put the social workers in contact with the families of more than three thousand children each year.[17]

To support the expanding work, the Free Kindergarten and Industrial Association raised money with handicraft bazaars, rummage sales, lunches in the Titche-Goettinger Department Store, food sales at the State Fair each year, and donations from business firms and individuals. Lawrence Neff assigned the copyright to his book, *The Legal Status of Women in Texas,* to Isadore Callaway, a member of the Kindergarten Association, and all profits from its sales went into the association's treasury. On numerous occasions, Presbyterian, Methodist, Baptist, and Catholic churches and organizations like the Council of Jewish Women allowed the kindergartens to use their buildings. Such help amounted

*Neighborhood House, about 1915, after moving from its original location
to the corner of Cedar Springs and Collins.* Courtesy Historic
Photograph Collection, Dallas Public Library

to "in kind" donations of janitorial services, rooms, heat, and electricity. After
1908, Kindergarten Association members joined the other clubwomen in holding cups on busy street corners to gather money from passersby on "Tag Day,"
the main annual fundraising event of the city Federation of Women's Clubs.[18]

Unlike traditional charity, which supplied basic needs and met emergen-
cies or natural disasters, the assistance provided at Neighborhood House was
intended to enhance the immediate quality of life and equip the "working poor"
with the skills needed to improve their standard of living. By 1910, Neighborhood House was essentially a community center for those who could not afford
health care or recreation. With a full-time nurse, free facilities for bathing, a
recreation program in its gymnasium, and musical and dramatic performances
in its auditorium, as well as mothers' clubs, parents' meetings, boys' clubs, and,
by 1916, a chapter of the Campfire Girls, the settlement house had contact with
virtually everyone in its service area.[19] Now located nearer its Frogtown clientele in a $25,000 building owned by the Kindergarten Association, Neighbor-
hood House's social workers also did case work for United Charities.

As community support grew for preschool classes, kindergartens opened
in the Dallas public schools and the Kindergarten Association shifted its resources to education for older children. By 1916, the top floor and mezzanine of
Neighborhood House had living quarters for seventy-five boarding students, as

well as for the social workers who were their teachers. A year later, in 1917, state legislation made kindergartens mandatory in all Texas public schools. The law should have eliminated the need for those run by volunteers, but in 1919, the Free Kindergarten Association continued to instruct one hundred children between the ages of three and seven in South Dallas. In conjunction, the association operated a day nursery for seventy-three children whose mothers worked in the cotton mill.[20]

To their traditional charity and benevolence, the major Protestant denominations added the new methods of helping those in need. Methodist deaconesses, trained in social work as well as in the tenets of their faith, ran two settlement houses that were also religious missions, Wesley Chapel and Wesley House.[21] Wesley Chapel opened in 1903 in the "Reservation" area, where at least thirty saloons and forty brothels flourished in a neighborhood of approximately three thousand immigrants from numerous European nations. With the avowed purpose of helping these newcomers achieve stable families despite their surroundings, the deaconesses organized a mothers' club, maintained a playground, taught a kindergarten for about forty children, and offered free bathing facilities. They also gave religious instruction through street worship, home Bible study groups, and "cottage prayer meetings." In 1904, the Dallas Public Library began stocking the chapel's bookshelf, a service that helped to widen the library's "public."

Opening near the cotton mill in South Dallas in July 1909, Wesley House offered a free medical clinic. In addition to leading a mothers' club, weekly story hours for children, and Sunday school classes, the deaconesses at this settlement house regularly went into the city's slums to care for the sick, many of whom were too poor to own night clothing or bed linens. Support for both settlement houses came from the Methodist women's City Mission Board, and volunteers from several congregations and physicians donated their services.

Throughout the United States during the early years of the twentieth century, "scientific" or "educated" motherhood joined domesticity and "true womanhood" as popular guidelines for women's lives. Meshing with development of the Progressive philosophy of "child saving," maternalist concern for children's needs grew into a movement that produced several national associations with specific fields of interest.[22] By 1912, public awareness of children's issues persuaded a reluctant Congress to establish the United States Children's Bureau. Poorly funded and underappreciated, the agency nonetheless was effective, as its women officers made it the major source of information about children's health and provided individuals in every state with encouragement in their struggles to improve children's lives.[23]

In Dallas, widespread interest in children's well-being inspired efforts to improve the public schools. In 1905, mothers' clubs in six neighborhood schools allied to form the Mothers' Club Congress, which then joined several additional groups in 1909 and renamed itself the Council of Mothers. Patterned after the National Congress of Mothers founded in Chicago in 1897, the local organization would participate in numerous reform efforts during the next two decades. With concern for schools growing throughout the state, one hundred delegates from other communities met at the First Methodist Church in Dallas during the State Fair in 1909 to form the Texas Congress of Mothers, electing officers, adopting a constitution and by-laws, and defining a dues structure.[24] A year later, in 1910, the organization adopted *Texas Motherhood Magazine,* edited in Dallas by clubwoman Nettie B. Ford, as its official publication. This magazine became Texas mothers' major source of the latest information about nutrition, sanitation in the home, and child care and health.

Alongside the settlement houses were traditional social service institutions, for Catholic nuns had a long history of concern for children. Two orders of women religious opened schools in Dallas after 1896; two others sought to meet more basic needs. In 1905, Bishop Joseph Dunne founded Saint Joseph's Orphanage and asked the Sisters of Charity of Saint Vincent de Paul to run it temporarily.[25] Two years later, when the Sisters of the Incarnate Word took over, they found themselves responsible for thirty-three children living in a frame building that badly needed repairs. On their first day, the Incarnate Word nuns found no food in the house and no credit with the neighborhood shop owners. Their first order of groceries cost three cents more than they had; one of the children donated those last three pennies. With a parish fund of only one hundred dollars a month, the sisters solicited food, money, and clothing from their Oak Cliff neighbors.

Saint Joseph's was well off by comparison with the Good Shepherd Home. Opened in 1909 by the Sisters of Our Lady of Charity, the Good Shepherd was a shelter for young girls, some in serious trouble with the law and others seeking refuge from dangerous or unstable home situations.[26] For over a decade, the home was a rectangular frame building of whitewashed planks with a flat tar paper roof. Because each convent of their order was autonomous, the sisters had no general fund and no mother house to which to appeal. Donations of vegetables and fruit from Protestant neighbors augmented the foods from the nuns' garden and livestock. Earning money by running a commercial laundry, the nuns also did plain and fancy sewing and baked fruitcakes and altar breads for sale. By 1920, when construction began on their permanent building, the Sisters of Charity were feeding, clothing, and educating ninety young girls, some of whom came into their care through such public agencies as the police and the courts. A year later, they moved with the children into their new home, which they named Mount Saint Michael.

Whatever their religious orientations, women involved in social services soon found that one kind of problem led to others. After working for several years with the Dallas Free Kindergarten Association, Blanche Kahn Greenburg in 1910 asked her friends to donate milk each day for the children in the nursery at the cotton mill and the free kindergarten in East Dallas. Despite provisions of the city's pure food and drug ordinance of 1907, the milk sold in small neighborhood groceries was rarely, if ever, inspected. Often unsanitary if not diluted, it contributed to the health risks facing children of the poor. In April 1913, Greenburg decided to expand the milk donations into a program. Calling together a dozen women and men, she led in organizing the Dallas Infants' Welfare and Milk Association.[27] The group's main purpose was to supply clean, whole milk to indigent families with young children, but they also planned a free medical clinic for infants.

A native of New Orleans and married to the rabbi of Temple Emanu-El, Greenburg was a future vice-president of the Dallas Equal Suffrage Association.[28] In 1913, she invited male city leaders to serve as directors and committee members for the Welfare and Milk Association. Community support came immediately. Merchants contributed furniture and supplies and agreed to place boxes for contributions in their offices and stores. The physicians who volunteered for the free clinic wrote a series of articles on infant care, prenatal health, and dental hygiene. These guidelines were published by the *Morning News*, first in regular daily issues and later as pamphlets for free distribution. The city Federation of Women's Clubs donated money from its Tag Day collections. In stores and the lobbies of banks and hotels, women sold buttons inscribed with a child's picture and the plea, "Help Feed This Baby."

In June 1913, the first milk station opened in a small building that mill owner J. T. Howard erected in the Trinity Play Park for the children of employees in his cotton mill. Certified by the city chemist and later by the Tennessee Dairy chemist, milk went free to those unable to pay and sold at cost to others. In a rare example of cross-race compassion, albeit proffered in a demeaning manner, the association agreed that black mothers could buy milk at reduced prices—but only so long as they came to the side door and not "in such numbers" that they were "objectionable to white people."[29] Later in 1913, a second clinic and milk station opened in Neighborhood House for the Frogtown and Cumberland Hill areas. In 1922, a welfare station for African-American children at last made clean, unadulterated milk available to the city's poor of all races.

Almost immediately after the first welfare station opened, the medical services overshadowed its distribution of milk. Two afternoons each week, the volunteer physician-in-charge was available for office visits and house calls. For day-to-day operations, the association hired two women, a trained nurse to provide the majority of health services and a matron to care for equipment and clean. The nurse's duties very soon spread beyond physical examinations, with regular visits to homes, prenatal classes, "bacteriological examinations," and attendance upon women giving birth. In keeping with the association's view of its work as "almost entirely preventative," the station nurse also taught mothers to prepare clean, nutritious foods and to make children's clothes. Intended for patients aged three and under, the station clinic soon accepted older children as well. Families able to pay could purchase medicines at cost; others received prescriptions without charge.

These services were easy to tabulate and their results readily apparent. During 1913, the first year, the medical staff at the Trinity Park clinic treated 881 children. The nurse made 2,077 visits to homes, taught 37 expectant mothers in 17 classes at the station, attended 16 births, and herself treated 185 children. Within a year of the station's opening, the physicians reported better health and a decrease in infant mortality in the cotton mill area.[30] Although the demanding, varied duties seemed to drive nurses away after only a few months, the station continued to expand. In February 1915, dentists volunteered regularly at the first station, and the later infant welfare stations also added dental work to the medical care they provided.

As the city inaugurated health services, nurses at the infant welfare and milk stations cooperated with the public agencies as well as with other private organizations. In November 1914, the station nurse reported a case of measles to the city Board of Health, sent a patient to Saint Paul Hospital for surgery (provided free by the nuns), and employed a trained nurse for three nights to care for a sick child at home after the Baby Camp closed for the winter.[31] The association paid for treatments, including surgery, for one mother who had bad teeth, diseased tonsils, "female troubles," and crippling rheumatism. In July 1916, the city Health Department formally coordinated its efforts with the various private agencies and requested that the milk station nurses visit only certain designated areas in order to avoid duplicating the work of the public health nurses. In turn, the city nurses brought children to the clinics and, whenever possible, helped with their work.[32]

At times the clinics' staffs found themselves involved in general social work—reporting little boys for playing hooky, supplying clothes for schoolchildren, and distributing donated clothing to mothers and their newborn babies. By April 1915, the association, like the social workers at Neighborhood House, employed a teacher for regular domestic science classes at the station. The children's health problems, they had discovered, often resulted from lax housekeeping methods, particularly careless handling of food. In 1918, the Federated Charities, a new public office opened by the city government, assumed responsibility for the kindergartens and the day nurseries and assured them of a specified amount of dependable support. Private donors continued to provide additional funds, and both the Kindergarten Association and the Infant Welfare Association retained their own administrative staffs and boards of trustees.[33]

However hard their nurses and physicians worked, clinics could not handle all of children's health care needs through outpatient arrangements. During the hot months in Dallas, viral enteritis ("summer diarrhea") killed more infants by dehydration than all other illnesses combined. Children of indigent families were especially at risk, but Parkland, the general public hospital, lacked the facilities and staff to give sick babies specialized attention. In March 1913, seven nurses decided to establish a medical "camp" for infants and volunteered to care for the young patients. Like the social workers in Neighborhood House and the nurses at the infant welfare stations, they planned to teach the children's mothers the basic rules of good hygiene, as well as methods for sterilizing babies' bottles, keeping milk sanitary, and generally fighting flies and dirt.

The leader of the group was a public health nurse named May Forster Smith.[34] Often compared with Florence Nightingale because she was physically small, endlessly energetic, and completely devoted to her patients, May Smith was a native of South Carolina and a graduate of Cooper Hospital in Philadelphia. Immediate help in starting the Baby Camp came from her profession through the Dallas County Graduate Nurses Association. The Red Cross supplied four tents to be erected under shade trees on the grounds of Parkland Hospital, and two physicians donated their services to the children's hospital. The city Federation of Women's Clubs contributed money for supplies; individuals gave clothing, sheets, and other items needed by little children. Women from several clubs agreed to sew regularly for the seasonal hospital. When the Baby Camp closed in the fall, the nurses had cared for forty-eight babies.[35]

Impressed by the immediate need, the Dallas Federation of Women's Clubs offered to help search for better facilities. Appealing to the city for a permanent building, the Graduate Nurses Association promised two nurses for duty around the clock, while the federation pledged operating expenses. When city officials agreed, the federation donated fourteen hundred dollars of the money raised on Tag Day in 1914. The city hired an architect and paid building costs for the frame cottage he designed with a screened porch, a diet kitchen, bedrooms for nurses, and a bathroom.

Now dependent upon the combined support of city government and private donors, the Baby Camp was constructed on the Parkland grounds at a cost of fifteen thousand dollars. It opened on May 16, 1914, with facilities for forty patients up to the age of two years. Remaining open during World War I was a struggle, but in May 1919, May Smith found a private donor who gave one hundred thousand dollars to build a permanent children's hospital. Four years later, in 1923, the Bradford Memorial Hospital became an agency of the Community Chest, open to both private and indigent patients under age five, of any race or ethnic origin. Once again, an institution founded by women assumed a permanent place in the Dallas community.[36]

For safeguarding children's health, the single most widespread need was basic information about sanitation and nutrition. Each year, the state's Congress of Mothers sponsored Child Welfare Conferences. Hosted by the Dallas Council of Mothers and featuring experts who spoke on various aspects of child care, these events were part of a major attempt to raise the standards of cleanliness in private homes. Annual "Better Babies" contests at the State Fair gave prizes to the healthiest children from less privileged families, an apparently frivolous occasion that attracted publicity for the serious effort to educate mothers. In 1916, Dallas clubwomen observed "Baby Week," a program sponsored nationally by the General Federation of Women's Clubs to improve the health of young children, and two years later, the U.S. Children's Bureau sponsored a drive to "Save the Children." Grim statistics proved the need for such public attention: by 1916, twelve thousand babies died each year in Texas from improper care and inadequate feeding.[37]

The Dallas clubwomen's work to help children and families brought some degree of order and rationality into a city growing from 42,638 persons in 1900 to 92,104 in 1910 and 158,976 by 1920. People who remembered the earlier, more comprehensible world of small market towns and traditional rural communities, such as Dallas and Dallas County had been in the 1850s, must have found the new situation confusing and threatening, whatever the abundant opportunities it offered. Although the city's industrial workers were a relatively small, if sometimes vocal, segment of the population, since the 1870s newspapers frequently had published alarming stories about labor troubles and class conflict in other areas. Local concern for social order resembled the fear felt in large eastern and midwestern cities.

In bridging chasms of class and ethnicity, a "helping hand" was more effective than forceful suppression of rioting and violence. Clubwomen may have lacked appreciation for other cultures, but they believed in education as the means of self-improvement and in helping the poor raise their own standard of living.[38] The women hoped that lessons taught in the kindergartens, domestic science courses for mothers, and visits of social workers and welfare station nurses would serve as paths into a better life and eventually, assimilation into American culture. In extending the social responsibilities of privileged mothers beyond their own homes, the women's club projects held a significance beyond simply teaching children to wash their hands before meals or even providing free medical care: the clubwomen envisioned a social order characterized by compassion, however condescending their attitudes may too often have been.

The Progressive impulse toward "child saving" dominated the social agen-

cies established by the clubwomen, but their concerns also included adults, especially employed women. Mostly white, young, and single, many were newcomers to the city and barely able to earn a living wage. In 1910, the U.S. Bureau of
Labor published a report on the condition of women and children wage earners.
The study's author coined the term "women adrift" to describe females who
supported themselves and lived apart from their families.[39] As much as college-
educated members of the middle class, such workers in offices, department stores,
factories, and mills were "new women," and they made conservatives uneasy.
To the clubwomen in Dallas, the "business girls" were not so much threats
to the social order as they were other women's daughters, who needed safe
and comfortable places to live, and particularly meals and lodging they could
afford.

The cost of city living was easy to discern. In 1906, Baylor College of Medicine student Hallie Earle paid fifteen dollars a month for her room in a Dallas
boardinghouse and fifty cents a day for meals. Her total basic expenses were
around thirty dollars each month. She had to pay five dollars a cord for firewood
for her room, plus streetcar fares when her courses required observation of
medical procedures at Saint Paul Sanitarium. In addition, there were expenditures for books, supplies for classes, and occasional purchases of clothing.[40]

Hallie Earle could rely on her family in Waco, but many young women
were entirely self-supporting. In 1906, a stenographer in a law office did well to
begin at a salary of fifty dollars a month, while an "experienced ironer and
starcher" could wring only thirty-two dollars a month from her employer at a
steam laundry. In some offices, the wages for even experienced stenographers
began at twenty dollars a month. The best offers advertised in the *Morning News*
came from out-of-state firms looking for women to sell goods from their homes
at eighteen dollars per week and, for those who could travel through Dallas and
environs, twenty-one dollars a week, with expenses advanced. More than a decade later, these were still top salaries. Of the twenty-four women who applied
for rooms at the YWCA in April 1919, thirteen earned less than ten dollars a
week—too little even to afford rent as a boarder in a private home.[41]

However comfortable their own lives, clubwomen understood the ratio
between earnings and the cost of living. In May 1912, a Dallas resident spoke
on the topic "Women Wage Earners of Texas" at the annual meeting of the
Texas Federation of Women's Clubs' second district. Focusing her remarks on
working conditions, she reminded her middle-class audience that the purchased
clothing which they considered such "bargains" and which "emancipated" them
from the labor of home manufacture, was made from "the life's blood" of female factory workers. This speaker also cited the telephone exchanges, where
"intelligent, industrious girls [*sic*] work twelve hours each day, including Sunday, for starvation wages of $3.50 to $6.00 a week." The telephone companies

earned "large dividends" but paid "small wages, because they know necessity forces many girls to work at any price." The plight of temporary workers was even worse, she continued. Department stores hired young women for $2.50 a week during the Christmas rush, then laid them off after the holidays ended. By the following autumn, many were hospitalized with malnutrition. Calling for legal protection for employed women, she cited New Zealand's minimum wage law of 1894 and England's Trade Board Act of 1909.[42]

Reported in the *Morning News*, such information led to attempts by several women's organizations to ease the lives of female newcomers. In 1913, a committee of fifty WCTU members formed the Willard Hall Association and began searching for five hundred contributors to donate one dollar per month to support a home where "working girls" could live decently at reduced rates. Six years passed before Willard Memorial Hall opened on June 23, 1919, but early in 1916, the "Business Girls' Lodge" offered employed women affordable living quarters. Supported by the city and managed by the Dallas Federation of Women's Clubs, the lodge was located in a residence donated anonymously by a widow. With free meals for those who could not pay, this home also sheltered deserted wives, women whose husbands were hospitalized, and widows with young children. Later called the "Working Girls' Home" or "Woman's Industrial Home," the facility could house thirty-four women, as well as offer them employment in a sewing room. Their children stayed in the on-site day nursery, supervised by a volunteer from the Graduate Nurses Association.[43]

Religious organizations, too, supported safe and inexpensive accommodations for employed women. In 1915, the Catholic Ladies' Aid Society opened Saint Rita's Residential Club for single "Catholic girls working in Dallas and living away from home." With rooms for twenty residents, Saint Rita's offered a sewing class, a lecture series, and social events such as teas and "open house" receptions. By 1919, the Salvation Army was running a "Young Women's Hotel" for thirty-five guests; and in 1920, the Girls' Friendly Inn Society of Saint Matthew's Cathedral purchased a lot and opened a lodging house large enough for fifty-three women "who are earning a minimum wage." Residents paid five to fifteen dollars per month for rooms and five dollars per week for daily breakfasts and dinners. Whether supported by church groups or city funds, all these homes for employed women had matrons, curfews, house rules, and carefully worded qualifications for admission.[44] In a time of growing independence among young women, such restrictions drove all but those earning the lowest wages into the regular boardinghouses.

Of the institutions for employed women, the Young Women's Christian Association (YWCA) would have the longest life. About two years after the Girls' Co-Operative Home opened in 1899, it became the YWCA of Dallas under a charter from the State of Texas. In 1908, the YWCA was officially incorporated and affiliated with the national organization. With its twenty-two-member board including prominent clubwomen, the "Y" offered numerous services in addition to living accommodations. The cafeteria sold "balanced meals" for fifteen to seventeen cents and welcomed nonresidents at lunch. There were rooms for fifteen lodgers and a travelers' aid service by 1912. In an effort to thwart pimps and white slavers who were rumored to prey upon lone females, a representative met trains to "look after stranded girls" and help women passengers with transfers. In addition to a fully equipped gymnasium, the YWCA's education department offered a number of classes, including instruction in millinery and dressmaking, and in 1919 an "opportunity school" with courses designed to enable office workers to advance into better-paying positions with more responsibility.[45]

Founded in Boston in 1866, the YWCA was created to ease the entry of country dwellers into city life by providing for the "temporal, moral, and religious welfare of self-supporting women."[46] The organization soon became a major source of services for urban women. By March 1, 1913, the Dallas Y's gym classes enrolled 187, and the lunchroom committee reported serving 3,740 meals during the past month, as middle-class shoppers joined employed women for the noon meal. Before 1920, the YWCA thus became a women's community center, offering services unavailable elsewhere in the city. In response to the growing demand, the Y's board in 1919 launched a campaign to raise eight hundred thousand dollars to construct a new headquarters and a "Girls' Home" significantly larger than the original building.[47]

In addition to help with living expenses, clubwomen believed that female employees needed time to rest. With support from the Council of Mothers and individual donors, the Dallas Federation of Women's Clubs opened a camp in 1920 at Bachman's Dam, the city reservoir in northwestern Dallas. Providing a place where employed women could enjoy "a restful vacation . . . out of doors at a small charge," the camp was the vacation spot for "more than 500 [business] girls" during its first summer.[48]

Recognizing the limitations of private groups, in time some Dallas officials advocated regular municipal involvement in social problems. Adoption of the commission plan of city government in 1906 perhaps had improved efficiency in public business, but it had done little to increase elected officials' concern for social issues. While the city council usually cooperated with the clubwomen's requests, as a general rule male leaders tended to leave initiative to private groups. A different attitude appeared in the spring of 1915, when a newly elected mayor authorized the organization of a welfare department for the city.[49]

Patterned after the Board of Public Welfare pioneered in Kansas City in 1913, the Dallas Welfare Department had three divisions: an employment bureau, an aid department or social service office, and a committee for "censorship of commercialized amusements" with a separate board of appeals. In its first year of operation, 1916, the Welfare Department supported the Working Girls' Lodge (which by 1919 housed sixty women and their children) and ran a wood yard where unemployed men could work to pay for meals and lodging. The employment bureau found jobs for 108 women.[50] In yet another example of the combining of public and private resources, the United Charities administrative staff became the Welfare Department's social service office, and a city-funded school was opened to train social workers.

During the next year, the city further combined public and private means to create the Federated Charities Finance Association, the first effort in Dallas to organize a genuine system of aid. Informally affiliated with the Dallas Welfare Department, the Charities Association included eight nonsectarian private agencies then operating throughout the city: the United Charities, Infants Welfare and Milk Association, Baby Camp, Free Kindergarten Association, Dallas County Humane Society, Empty Stocking Crusade, Methodist Mission Lodging House, and Dallas Street and Newsboys Association. Later, Saint Matthew's Home for Children was added to the list. All but two, the Humane Society and United Charities, were programs founded and run by women, while women staffed and served as board members and officers for even those two.

Despite criticism elsewhere in the United States regarding the adequacy of organized charity, formal organization gave private groups a central source of community support, and this arrangement offered several advantages. By projecting an annual goal for fundraising, the Federated Charities (then the Welfare Council and later the Community Chest) insured member charities a stated amount of money each year. Freed at last from the vagaries of annual fundraising drives, each agency now could budget and depend upon being able to deliver specific services. While the funded agencies were freed from the distraction of having to seek contributions each year, businesses and individual citizens gave once instead of facing separate solicitations by all the good causes operating in Dallas. Furthermore, the Federated Charities expedited collections and disbursements with efficient bookkeeping and accounting methods.[51]

In 1917, a new city administration retained the Welfare Department but provided less support for aid and relief efforts. Equally serious, when community attention focused on the war effort after April 1917, people seemed to forget the needy at home. With city agencies neglected and faltering, social activist Elmer Scott chaired a meeting on July 7, 1917, to form the Civic Federation, an organization that would supplement public aid and serve as a clearinghouse for private efforts. With 7 women on the board of directors, 150 charter members represented both public and private welfare groups.[52] Benefiting from the past two decades of clubwomen's experience in operating social service agencies, the

Civic Federation was to become the leading voice for social concern in Dallas for almost forty years.

Founded to foster continuing education and public information, the Civic Federation became a center for social services at a time when public interest lagged in the concept of an integrated system of aid. Civic Federation case workers regularly visited the city's poor, then referred them to the appropriate public and private agencies. With determined leaders and dedicated volunteers, the private organization supplemented the city's official welfare department in championing the needs of the poor as a communitywide responsibility. According to founder Scott, the Civic Federation for many years was "the sole protagonist of a broad scheme of social reconstruction in Dallas."[53]

Whatever its degree of social concern, the public conscience rarely extended to African Americans. The city hired its first black social worker in 1918, but one woman could hardly manage to survey the assigned area. After 1918 as before, aid to the black poor remained mostly private, as neighbors and friends responded to whatever needs they encountered. In 1913, Claudia Lemmons moved two elderly women into a tiny shed behind her home, where she could manage their care. Two years later, Lemmons and four friends formed the Carnation Charity Club, only one example of the ways in which African-American women organized their customary systems of mutual aid. Club members pooled their dues to buy burial insurance for the women living in Lemmons' shed, then built a room for them onto her house. The group's work expanded quickly, as acquaintances and friends, as well as the city's black social worker, notified them of others who needed food, fuel, rent money, or medical attention. The women raised funds by charging fifteen cents a plate at chicken and catfish dinners, for which club members and white friends donated the food. With more than one hundred members by 1937, the club had helped over two thousand persons.[54]

By 1919–20, at least six such organizations operated in the black community, and, in almost every issue, the *Dallas Express* published notices of their regular meetings and reports of their projects. The Royal Arts Club, Corticelli Art Club, Ladies' Reading Club, and the Chautauqua divided time between their studies and the kinds of community work done by the Diamond Charity, Morning Star Charity, and Carnation Charity clubs. The Texas Federation of Colored Women's Clubs, founded in 1906, ran a settlement house in Dallas and collected goods for distribution to African Americans in need.[55]

The best efforts of private citizens and public offices still failed to reach everyone. Of all Dallas's residents, babies abandoned throughout the city were the most desperate, and their numbers rapidly outgrew the facilities available. Before 1918, the Child Welfare Department of the privately supported Dallas County Humane Society found women who could take the children into their homes. As the growing numbers of homeless infants overwhelmed these resources, the Humane Society's Child Welfare Director Emma Wylie Ballard suggested opening a home for such children.[56]

Born in Memphis and educated in private schools in Shreveport and Dallas, Emma Ballard enjoyed a comfortable life until widowhood left her with two young children to support. By 1918, she had worked for years with children in trouble, including those who came before the Dallas County Juvenile Court and those living in the local detention home. She also helped to found the state industrial home for delinquent girls at Elam, Texas. When the Humane Society approved her plan for a shelter, Ballard turned to the Council of Mothers. Women throughout the city donated used furniture, baby beds, and dishes, while merchants gave new items to equip the five-room cottage chosen to house the children. The Federation of Women's Clubs paid the first matron's salary and held a "sewing bee" to make clothing and linens.[57] Within two weeks the shelter was full, and the Humane Society had to rent a larger building.

During its first three years after opening on June 1, 1918, the shelter took in 542 children. A total of 178, or about one-third of those, died, but the rest were legally adopted or placed with relatives located by the Hope Cottage staff. After three years of cramped facilities and inadequate care that must have contributed to the high death rate, the shelter won promises of support from the Dallas Welfare Council. In August 1921, Hope Cottage emerged from the control of the Dallas County Humane Society to independent status as the Hope Cottage Association. Still facing a constant lack of adequate funds and "strong prejudice against the little population," the orphanage by this time housed around fifty children. Although the Ku Klux Klan was its largest donor during the 1920s, by the 1940s Hope Cottage sheltered and sought families to adopt African-American, as well as white, children.

In addition to their long-term support of social welfare agencies and institutions during the first two decades of the twentieth century, clubwomen in Dallas frequently aided victims of accidents and natural disasters. Despite its old-fashioned appearance, such aid now carried modern implications. In 1908, the women ignored ethnic and religious boundaries to collect money, boxes of food, and other supplies for the hundreds of families driven from their homes by major flooding along the Trinity River. For this kind of immediate, customary relief, as well as general charity and their permanent commitments, the women's organizations found imaginative ways to raise money.

In 1910, the Woman's Forum staged a water carnival with 150 clubwomen cast as sprites, naiads, nymphs, and fairies. Each fall, the Forum's chrysanthemum show and charity ball netted around two thousand dollars for an annual donation to the United Charities. Casual observers often have missed the serious purposes of such lighthearted occasions and failed to discern the importance of women's work in building community ties, at times beyond the city limits. Hardly was the Woman's Forum organized in 1906 before members were collecting donations for residents of San Francisco after the earthquake. In 1912, flood victims in Ohio received aid from the Dallas forum.[58]

With a renewal of social concern after the war, the city government reorganized the Federated Charities as the Dallas Welfare Council. Adding donor as well as recipient groups to its membership, the Welfare Council represented more private than public organizations. They included the Advertising League, the Chamber of Commerce, the Board of Public Welfare, the Civic Federation, and several men's service clubs (Lions, Rotary, Kiwanis, Mutual, University, and Automobile), as well as the Dallas Federation of Women's Clubs, the Woman's Forum, and the Dallas Council of Mothers. In addition, fifty-five citizens-at-large served on the advisory board.[59] Women's organizations, in other words, were integral to the city's developing system of relief and aid.

Through the institutions, organizations, and agencies they founded and ran, privileged white clubwomen touched the lives of thousands of individuals who were not members of their own families. In 1918, the September 15 issue of the *Dallas Survey,* the official publication of the Civic Federation, consisted of a list of the city's relief agencies.[60] The majority had been founded by women; virtually all were operated by females. Women ran three of the six free medical clinics and five of the seven health services that sent visiting nurses into neighborhoods and schools. Of the seven organizations included under the Federated Charities Finance Association—the United Charities, County Humane Society, Street and Newsboys' Club, Infants' Welfare and Milk Association, Baby Camp, Free Kindergarten Association, and Empty Stocking Crusade—women had founded the latter four and were officers, directors, and managers of the others.

Of the three homes for "unfortunate girls," women founded and ran two and were officers of the third. Needless to say, women ran the city's five settlement houses—the nonsectarian Neighborhood House, as well as two which were Methodist, one Presbyterian, and one Baptist. Women operated two of the three homes for the aged, all the day nurseries and free kindergartens, three of the five orphanages, three "rest camps," and all three boarding homes for employed women. Of all the community's efforts for charity, relief, benevolence, and caring in Dallas—both publicly and privately funded, offering long-term assistance and temporary aid—women had constructed by far the majority.

With their efforts to improve the lives of other people, white middle-class Dallas women were reaching farther into community life than at any previous time. The children's hospital, kindergartens and day nurseries, free medical and dental clinics, sources of clean milk, free classes and statewide conferences to provide instruction for mothers—such were the local products of the twin ideologies of domesticity and maternalism operating in conjunction with the Progressive crusade for "child saving." With their definitions of women's responsibility for personal relationships within their own homes, these doctrines also inspired women's concern for needs beyond the walls of their own particular houses. Women understood that the effects of city congestion bound residents in a community as closely as markets and trade conditions, that their own prosperity and leisure depended upon the labor of less privileged women in department stores and offices, factories and mills. Convinced of a "special" female nature and "superior moral sensibility," such women did not deny the destructive power of poverty and need, however narrowly middle-class their sense of values might be.

In a time when many—perhaps most—of the prosperous still blamed the poor for their own poverty, clubwomen helped children and their mothers first, and then entire families. Along with Saint Joseph's Orphanage and Mount Saint Michael, both run by Catholic nuns, three of the institutions founded by clubwomen for children before 1920 remained in operation during the 1990s: the Dallas Baby Camp (now part of Children's Medical Center), Hope Cottage, and the Dallas Free Kindergarten and Industrial Association (now Child Care Dallas). They join the Juliette Fowler Homes, Saint Paul Hospital, and the YWCA as permanent landmarks in the city's social-service skyline. Providing the key elements of concern, energy, and determination to enlarge the number and kinds of services available, women were primary agents in instituting the means of caring. Through these means, clubwomen expanded the community's response to those in need and established significant characteristics of modern urban life in Dallas.

Chapter Eight
Women's Political Culture and the Modern Service City

"Some say that she has overstepped her womanly prerogatives by going out beyond the home circle, but was it not for love of home and children that she was first prompted to do this work?"[1] As president of the Dallas Federation of Women's Clubs, Sarah Elizabeth Weaver wrote to the *Morning News* in 1906 in response to complaints that women were getting out of their "place." Although the matters then attracting women's concern—sanitation, health, safety, and children's well-being—were directly related to the domestic realm, in an urban setting they were community problems also. As such, they officially lay within the male arena of public affairs. Weaver's justification for women's "invasion" of that "male realm" was tactful, even diplomatic, but firm: "There is much more of the work of the world that women are doing that men have not the time to do." However circumspect her phrasing, the fact remained that women's solutions to social problems challenged the policies, political decisions, and concepts of government established by men.

By 1906, Dallas women were assuming new roles in public life. During the next decade, they would alter the city's physical structure and work to redefine governmental responsibilities at both state and local levels. Contrary to notions accepted for over a generation, women knew that the home was not separate from the rest of society, provided no one a haven from public policies, and afforded little, if any, protection against careless decision making or the failure of elected officials to come to terms with communitywide problems. Because conditions outside every urban home directly affected matters within it, any number of private, domestic concerns could be dealt with only as public issues. Meeting their familial duties in the city environment required women to participate in the decisions that determined numerous aspects of day-to-day living.

For newcomers to political life, the women were surprisingly effective.[2] Years before they could vote, they won passage of new city ordinances, persuaded city and county governments to create additional administrative positions, influenced changes in public policies, and got two women elected to public office. The leaders for these campaigns came from three organizations: the Dallas Federation of Women's Clubs, the Dallas Woman's Forum, and the Dallas Council of Mothers. Like their counterparts in major cities and small towns all over the United States, the clubwomen in Dallas worked to improve the health, safety—and morality—of urban dwellers. As the city was changing women's lives, so did women alter and shape the city.

Well before 1900, Dallas city government accepted limited responsibility for certain community services. The city provided police and fire protection in the 1870s and 1880s, paved streets and sidewalks, and installed open storm sewers, at least in the downtown area. Private companies handled other urban services, such as selling water, gas, and electric power to businesses and wealthier homeowners. Like most southerners, the city's elected leaders accepted the established order of things, and they greeted with incomprehension at best, and often outright hostility, the newfangled notions that the community should take responsibility for social functions traditionally centered in the home. The city supported a hospital used only by the indigent, a public health board with little authority, and, sporadically, a city chemist. In comparison with other, smaller Texas cities, Dallas was niggardly with its public schools.[3] As a general rule, matters not directly affecting the welfare of business fell under the category of "private."

In urging city officials to accept responsibility for personal and family needs that resulted from urban conditions, the women were inserting problems from the private realm of the home into public discussion. With such demands, they altered the boundaries of both terms, redefining private matters into public issues. Despite the support of progressive male leaders, many men's reactions ranged from outright criticism to simple "stonewalling." Neither response worked. As participants in the nationwide club movement, the Dallas women had a ready-made political agenda based on a coherent set of values, the ideals of domesticity and maternalism. Working through their voluntary associations, particularly the city and state Federations of Women's Clubs, they seemed effortlessly—indeed, instinctively—to refine the pressure-group strategies that would be useful as they developed a separate political culture.[4] Accepting the Progressive concept of more active, responsive government, the women helped to transform Dallas into a modern service city.[5]

The late 1890s and early 1900s perhaps seemed to be a good time to tackle social problems, for the Lone Star State enjoyed a reputation as forward-looking and progressive. The appearance was deceptive. However beneficial the ef-

Dallas in 1900. Courtesy Historic Photograph Collection, Dallas Public Library

fects of their policies, the intentions of Texas lawmakers were protective of traditional ways. The state constitution's restraints on political power grew out of white resentment of the Reconstruction government, not out of democratic convictions or concern about official corruption. Similarly, laws regulating the railroads and insurance companies resulted as much from distrust of "foreign" (that is, non-Texan), money and influence as from any populist impulse to protect ordinary people against the "interests."[6] Into this thicket of conservative, southern, and essentially agrarian attitudes came the urban clubwomen in Dallas—and in other Texas cities—confident and self-assured in their own judgment wherever home, health, and the well-being of families were concerned.

Women's political experience began with attempts to regulate children's employment in factories and mills, a local condition that could be improved only by state law. By 1900, twenty-eight states regulated children's wage work in some way, but because labor groups had taken up the issue in the 1870s and 1880s, child labor laws seemed radical to many voters. Nonetheless, after discussions by the Texas Federation of Women's Clubs, a group of women in Dallas launched a campaign against child labor in 1901, three years prior to organization of the National Child Labor Committee. With 2,842 wage earners employed in 177 small industries, Dallas was one of the two most industrialized cities in Texas. The 1900 census showed just under half of the city's laborers clustered in three kinds of work: manufacture of leather goods, printing and publishing, and foundry and machine tools production. The majority were scattered through "all other industries." Among the workers in this category was an undetermined number of children, most employed in the cotton mill.[7]

The leader of the campaign against child labor in Texas was Sudie Foster Roberts, who found her first supporters among the members of the Quaero Club, the literary group she had founded in 1892. A native of Fairfield, Texas, Roberts had moved with her family to Dallas in 1886. She was a graduate of Trinity University in San Antonio and, under the pen name "Ruth Carroll," wrote feature articles for the *Texas Farmer*. In 1901, when she was forty years old, her children were twelve and seven, within the age range of the youngsters employed in the mill. Her friends in the Quaero Club, much like the McKinney Avenue mothers, were educated women who soon would emerge as genteel activists in the city's social causes.[8]

Roberts formed a committee with the presidents of the Pierian Club and the Art Association. Using Alabama's recently enacted child labor law as their model, the three women wrote a bill for submission to the legislature, and the Texas Federation of Women's Clubs began a two-year campaign for its enactment. Considered a social evil by the privileged clubwomen, the employment of children increased the incomes of working-class families and lowered the labor costs of mill owners. The issue divided people along class and economic lines, and, although the measure passed the legislature in 1903, opponents weakened it to the point of uselessness. Twelve years later, in 1915, another round of intense campaigning by the state federation achieved a second law limiting child labor, as well as a statute for compulsory school attendance by all children aged eight through fourteen. As with the 1903 statute, the Dallas Cotton Mill and other Texas industries routinely evaded these regulations until 1933, when federal agencies began enforcing child labor laws nationwide.[9]

Perhaps not realizing how little effect their work against child labor would have, in 1903 Dallas clubwomen launched another statewide campaign on behalf of children, this one a drive to establish a juvenile justice system. This movement also grew out of a local problem too complex to handle at the local level. Alarmed by the growing numbers of young boys arrested for petty crimes as well as by the kids' pride in their exploits, in 1897 the city council passed an ordinance banning children from the streets at night unless accompanied by a parent or guardian. Abandoned and out of control, the scores of young boys who roamed the city had no homes, much less parents able to teach them proper behavior and provide moral guidance. These children hardly noticed so decorous a remedy as a city ordinance.[10]

Equally disturbing to the clubwomen, the legal system dealt with children by jailing them with adult offenders and sending them through regular court procedures. Reformers considered children's guilt, especially for minor offenses, to be different from adult crime and wanted Texas to adopt measures similar to programs for children recently implemented in Boston, St. Louis, and New York. The plan used in Colorado was especially appealing. Calling his purpose "child saving," Denver's Judge Ben Lindsey had created a separate system to try young offenders in special courts and then, upon conviction, send them to detention homes instead of to jail or reformatories. The youngsters went to school and reported to the court once a week.[11]

Launching the campaign for a juvenile justice system in 1903, Sarah Elizabeth Weaver made this the primary issue of her administration as president of the Dallas Federation of Women's Clubs. At the request of the County Judges and Commissioners' Association, Weaver and other leaders of the city federation collaborated with members of the state's judiciary to gather information about children in trouble and write a bill for presentation to the legislature. State Federation President Adella Turner, also a Dallas resident, appointed a special committee to continue the effort and herself served as an ex-officio member.

Passed in 1907, the juvenile justice law established separate procedures for minors, simply by granting to each county and district court the authority to sit as the juvenile court when hearing cases involving children.[12] This law was only the first step, and during the next decade Dallas women lobbied the legislature, circulated petitions among voters, and wrote letters to the governor and individual lawmakers asking for laws to provide funds for state training schools for boys and girls convicted in the new courts.[13]

Local implementation required the opening of a children's detention center, a natural project for the city's Federation of Women's Clubs. Having paid the first police matron's salary in 1906, the federation had also provided money to hire the first juvenile probation officer until 1910, when the city government added this expense to its budget. In 1913, the county commissioners established a temporary detention home and the federation donated three hundred dollars and such basic equipment as toothbrushes and linens. Intended to function as a children's jail, the home also accepted orphans and youngsters temporarily separated from their families.[14] A year later, in April 1914, clubwomen in the Dallas County Industrial Home Association opened a girls' correctional facility, to be supported, at least for the first year, by private donors.[15]

Just as women could not alleviate certain social conditions at the city level, they could not confine public school issues to one neighborhood. In 1905, a newly organized McKinney Avenue Mothers' Club allied with two other mothers' clubs to forestall dismissal of the school district's only music teacher. As in 1895–98, their actions had unanticipated political implications. By convincing the Board of Education to reverse its decision and renew the teacher's contract, the women directly influenced educational policy through the curriculum. Similarly, when the mothers' clubs persuaded the city to hire a sanitary inspector for the school system and to adopt new regulations for heating and ventilating the buildings, they were helping to shape policy decisions for the entire district, not merely for individual neighborhood schools.[16]

Also in 1905, the mothers' clubs in several neighborhood schools joined forces as the Mothers' Clubs Congress. Later changing their name to the Council of Mothers, this group hosted delegates from other cities and towns in 1909, when they met in Dallas to organize the Texas Congress of Mothers. The Congress became an advocacy group for children's well-being, not only working to improve the state's schools, but also distributing information about health, safety, and child care. Texas women thus joined the movement of "educated" or "scientific" motherhood and, well before 1920, secured a significant increase in publicly funded services for children.

Campaigns for child labor laws, a juvenile justice system, and improved schools reflected a national impulse that engaged men as well as women. Throughout the United States, the years between 1897 and 1920 were unprecedented for the number of institutions founded for children and the amount of legislation intended to serve their interests. In 1912, creation of the United States Children's Bureau seemed to institutionalize the social concern being focused on children. Charged with gathering and publishing information on education, health, and children's well-being, the bureau never had adequate funding. Too many Americans, and especially men in government, had trouble seeing children as a concern for the nation as a whole rather than only for the individual family.[17]

With more than a decade's experience in working to improve the lives of women and children, officers of the Dallas Federation of Women's Clubs decided in the summer of 1906 to found a new organization, the Dallas Woman's Forum. Planning to accommodate the women then on waiting lists to join the existing clubs, the forum's founders outlined courses of study in eight subject areas or departments: art, Bible and sacred history, music, philosophy and science, literature, household economics and pure food, civics and philanthropy, and current events. Two days after its founding, the Dallas Council of Mothers became the forum's ninth department.

A "department" club patterned after the Athenean Club of Kansas City, the forum ostensibly was another women's group devoted to culture and self-improvement, and certainly it served those purposes. Merely by its size, the forum achieved its founders' purpose of making the benefits and pleasures of club activity available to any woman who showed an interest. In addition, the Woman's Forum immediately provided its elite leaders with a wider base among the city's female population and thus a larger pool of talent, resources, and support for campaigns to improve the city's quality of life.

Elected the forum's first president, Adella Kelsey Turner led the new organization during its formative years. Born in 1856 in rural Texas near Marshall and orphaned at an early age, Turner grew up in the home of a music teacher in the small town of Jefferson. Soon after her marriage in 1879, she moved to Dallas, where two of her four sons died in early childhood. Her volunteer work began in 1886 with the founding of the Standard Club, which she later would head for two terms. Nothing in her background seemed especially conducive to the degree of activism she exhibited during her adult life.[18] Interested in virtually every community issue, from education and juvenile justice to the fine arts and civic beautification, Mrs. E. P. Turner (as she signed her name throughout her life) was among the founders and officers of so many civic organizations in Dallas that the initials "E. P." might have stood for "Everywhere Present."

In her inaugural address, Turner stressed the importance of club membership for women's self-development, but her plans reached far beyond personal and individual benefits. Promising to imitate the forum of the ancient Romans,

Adella Kelsey Turner, or as she signed herself throughout her life, Mrs. E. P. Turner,
in 1903, when she was president of the Dallas Federation of Women's Clubs.
Courtesy Historic Photograph Collection, Dallas Public Library

although not just in "cases in which only men were concerned," she intended for the organization to consider "every question that concerns the life of Dallas" in order to "study and correct wrongs and abuses wherever women's influence is needed." Above all, Turner insisted, women must seek "practical results" and not limit themselves to discussion of problems and issues. With almost three hundred members by the end of its first year, the forum constituted a substantial addition to the resources of the Dallas Federation of Women's Clubs.[19]

In August 1906, when the organization was barely five months old, Turner and the other forum officers waded into city politics. Because few matters reached as directly into home life as the quality of milk, food, and medicine, the women had little difficulty justifying their first major goal, passage of a pure food and drug ordinance for Dallas. About six weeks after President Theodore Roosevelt signed the Meat Inspection and Pure Food and Drug Acts, the forum's delegates began interviewing members of the city council about the food ordinance and the appointment of an official chemist.[20]

With this campaign, the women were pitting their judgment not only against male authority, but also against hundreds of small business owners. The problem of clean milk was not new. More than two decades earlier, in April 1884, editorials in the *Dallas Weekly Herald* had complained about the sale of impure milk, and not merely because of carelessness by producers. In order to have more to sell, farmers and dairymen often diluted milk with water, then added chalk to restore its appearance. Housewives could buy inspected milk in the regulated market on the first floor of City Hall, but supplies were limited.[21]

Composed entirely of mothers, the forum committee defined for the city standards of cleanliness equal to those in their own kitchens. Passed in December 1906, the pure food and drug ordinance included provisions for the city chemist to inspect all places where food and drink were sold; prohibited the sale of "unwholesome, adulterated" products; and prescribed penalties for violators. The new city law required metal seals on all containers for sale; demanded truthful labeling; forbade the slaughtering and sale of horses for food; established fines for Health Department employees who connived or assisted in violations; and listed specific methods for cleaning and sterilizing the implements, receptacles, and storage areas used to process milk.[22]

The law's strict provisions gave grocers, dairymen, druggists, and farmers an excuse to ask for a year's delay in enforcement. Pressure from the Woman's Forum and the Dallas Federation of Women's Clubs convinced the council to uphold the original plan; on January 1, 1907, Dallas's new pure food and drug ordinance went into effect. At the city's request, a committee of clubwomen worked to insure compliance and enforcement. As a result, numerous producers were arrested before the widespread practice of watering milk stopped.[23]

In this, as in subsequent incidents concerning reform issues, women and men tended to disagree about priorities, and the pure food and drug laws illustrated the crux of gendered politics. After the Dallas ordinance passed, *Morning News* columnist "Pauline Periwinkle" expressed the women's impatience, particularly regarding health and the safety of commercially processed food. Each year in the United States, she wrote, an estimated half-million children under the age of two died from "preservatives in milk and adulterated foods. Especially in matters municipal is woman's vote badly needed. . . . It wouldn't have taken a Congress of Mothers seventeen years to pass a Pure Food Law. Men have shut one eye and squinted so hard at commercial interests with the other that they see little else. The wonder is that doctors and undertakers and tombstone manufacturers don't join the grocers' lobby in defeating measures to injure their trade."[24]

Clubwomen elsewhere in the state followed Dallas's example and organized local campaigns on the issue. In November 1907, the Texas Federation of Women's Clubs appointed a committee to organize work for pure food and drug legislation for the entire state.[25] The drives for pure food and drug laws initiated a series of women's projects, all falling under the rubric of "municipal housekeeping." In Dallas, such measures served not so much to clean up behind "dirty" industry or careless manufacturers, or even to reform city government, as to supply residents with basic services that had never been established. During the first two decades of the twentieth century, the city more than tripled in size, as the population grew from nearly 43,000 persons in 1900 to almost 159,000 by 1920. Such growth seriously exacerbated old problems that city leaders had long neglected—waste disposal, for example, and the water supply, which rarely had been adequate and never really clean.

As women worked to acquire new city services and modernize older ones, their actions carried economic as well as political implications. Not only did their demands entail expenditures of tax money or special public bond issues for implementation, but also the women were challenging the opinions, decisions, and management of male leaders and officials. Numerous otherwise activist clubwomen had little interest in the right to vote and refused to work for the suffrage campaign, yet believed that they understood certain social problems and needs better than men.

For many years, Adella Turner's desire for the vote, for example, was lukewarm at best. In 1912, she explained, "Personally, [I] . . . do not care for the right of suffrage, but in a general way [I think] it would be a good thing because as the laws now stand women have no rights in Texas."[26] Five years later, after the United States' entry into World War I, she changed her mind, primarily because of the war: "I believe in equal suffrage because I believe in preparedness," she explained in December 1917. Still, she remained more a cultural or social than a political feminist. Turner expected the franchise to enable women to improve their pay and working conditions, and to experience "the development that comes when women are helped by women."[27]

While harboring few doubts that their values were good for society as a whole, club leaders like Turner were careful to retain the manners and standing of "ladies." Whatever their opinions on the issue of the vote, members of this generation were sure of themselves as women. The words *feminist* and *feminism* rarely appeared in the United States before 1913. Yet in expressing their concern for women and children and their belief in women's competence to decide important public issues, the clubwomen-reformers were assertive and confident enough to qualify as cultural, if not political, feminists.[28] Rarely hesitating to make their opinions known, even when they openly challenged law, government, and elected officials at every level, they nonetheless observed traditional rules of propriety.

Despite their initial condescension, the city's male leaders were the clubwomen's natural allies. Members of the same social class—the same social circles, even—the men in Dallas government often were related to the clubwomen by birth or marriage. They frequently agreed with the women and shared their inclinations to support the Progressive agenda. Predicting "a city without graft and almost without politics," a group of such businessmen and bankers in 1907 persuaded voters to accept a new charter for Dallas, one based on the commission plan of city government pioneered in Galveston. The city commission plan, supporters promised, would run according to the principles of business efficiency. Depriving minority citizens of representation because the commissioners were elected at large, this form of local government insured the control of leading businessmen over city affairs. Naming themselves the "Citizens' Association," these men dominated Dallas politics for over a decade, and their hand-picked candidates almost always won in city elections.[29]

Between 1907 and 1917, clubwomen persuaded the Citizens' Association, issue by issue, to accept an expanded role for government, one that reached beyond mere management of the city's physical development into matters of social welfare and enhanced services to residents, especially children. Before World War I, club officers often achieved their goals by using their own funds to start programs, including school lunches, visiting school nurses, the city's first police matron, and its first probation and truant officers. Within a short time, the Dallas City Council added these responsibilities to the city budget. As early as 1908, one city federation president bragged that the women's clubs "had the hearty cooperation, advice and financial aid of our City and County officials, and our progressive business men."[30] On a number of occasions, success for the women's program meant working to influence these influential men, who, once convinced, would take the issue to the voters.

In 1908, less than two years after their victory with the food and drug ordinance, activist clubwomen led their organizations into the most direct of political events, an election. Believing that they could improve Dallas public schools more rapidly with women on the Board of Education, officers of the mothers' club at the William B. Travis (formerly the McKinney Avenue) School gathered voters' signatures on petitions to add the names of two women to the list of candidates. Disagreement among city leaders produced two separate slates for the School Board, with Adella Turner and Ella Tucker among the nominees favored by the Citizens' Association. This support alone virtually insured their election.

Their own lack of the vote, interestingly enough, was irrelevant with regard to the right to hold public office, for the state constitution specified males or qualified electors only for two minor offices, both appointive.[31] Nonetheless, female candidates *per se* were controversial, and the campaign was lively. Opponents erroneously claimed that the election of women would be illegal, and they warned women would flock to the polls claiming the right to vote because women were running for office. Federation members countered that two women already had served, quite effectively, on school boards in the towns of Denison and Wills Point. Federation President Isadore Callaway further assured voters that women's only activity during the campaign would be distributing ten thousand cards advocating the two candidates, whose motto was simply: "The Welfare of the Child." Both women campaigned on the fact that they were mothers.[32]

Both, of course, also were distinguished for their civic work. For Adella Turner, club work was virtually a full-time career. Her female colleague, Ella Stephenson Tucker, would earn a national reputation with a lifelong crusade for fire safety, especially in the public schools. Tucker was among the few club leaders who had grown up in Dallas. For the mother of six children, four of whom were daughters, civic life began in 1897, when she helped to organize mothers' clubs in several public schools, and worked with the free kindergartens. In 1906, as president of the literary Friday Afternoon Club, she became a charter member of the Woman's Forum.

During her two years' service on the Board of Education, Tucker began to crusade for fire prevention, a cause that she continued to advocate as president of the Dallas Federation of Women's Clubs in 1911. In later years, her work for fire safety gained wide recognition, and she received numerous invitations to speak outside the state. Fire marshals and insurance agents wrote to express appreciation for her work, which had the practical result of reducing key rates for fire insurance in many Texas cities and towns.[33]

School board service seemed a reasonable extension of motherhood into public life. Seeking election was another matter, and the Dallas race in 1908 remains a study in how women tentatively stretched the rules of propriety and circumspectly claimed public spaces.[34] The federation's election workers went through the city to canvass voters and distribute literature in every "proper" ward—avoiding, that is, the areas where known brothels operated and, more than likely, African-American neighborhoods. When critics complained that "it did not look right in a Southern woman to take a prominent place," federation leaders reminded the public that in five southern states—Mississippi, Kentucky, Oklahoma, Louisiana, and Florida—women had certain limited rights regarding school matters.

With such strict scrutiny of their every move, the candidates took extra care to obey the rules of propriety. They could not, for example, "electioneer" at the polls, for federation members expressed dismay at the thought of so blatantly political an activity. Apparently neither woman ever spoke in her own behalf, except possibly at small, unpublicized private gatherings. Other clubwomen made statements in their favor to the newspapers, while men conducted much of the public campaign, speaking for the women at teas, receptions, and even at one meeting of the Council of Mothers. In lengthy letters and short personal statements to the *Morning News,* business leaders supported the women's election largely in the terms voiced by the women themselves.

Their high-minded focus on the issues of children's best interests enabled the women candidates and their supporters to deny partisanship. Within a strictly local race, political parties carried little or no significance, but the women made the absurd claim that, because "all good citizens stand for divorcement of school interests from politics," they were independent candidates and thus were not running *against* anyone.[35] This despite the fact that the Board of Education had only seven seats.

Of almost 13,000 eligible voters, 6,810 went to the polls. Adella Turner was elected handily, but Ella Tucker won by the slim margin of twenty-three votes.[36] With two of their number on the board, Dallas women secured their first elected representation in city government at any level. Once in office, neither of the new school trustees was shy, although both behaved with genteel reserve. During the first two years of their tenure, the women usually voted the same way, being on opposite sides of an issue on only two occasions. For every matter that resembled housework or homemaking, one or both could expect appointment to the investigating committee, although each, like the other board members, had assignments to standing committees. Turner was on the Finance Committee and the Committee on Supplies, Fuel, and Janitors; Tucker served on the Committee on Property and Repairs and chaired the Textbook Committee.[37]

Instead of the changes they had hoped to make, routine matters of operation dominated their terms in office. Ella Tucker did achieve one victory, long before the hazards of asbestos were known, with the board's vote to install fire-retardant deadeners in the floors of future schools.[38] Except for improving the school lunch menus, the two women achieved none of their special goals and certainly brought no sweeping changes to the school system. Indoor toilets, sanitary drinking fountains, safer fire escapes, and "fireproof" buildings would require more generous appropriations from the city.

Occupied with other issues or perhaps discouraged by Turner and Tucker's inability to effect significant changes, the Federation of Women's Clubs showed little interest in later school board races. In 1910, only about half as many voters went to the polls as in 1908, and both female candidates lost.[39] After 1910, the Socialist Party nominated female candidates—likely another reason for the federation's withdrawal. Already suspect for "violating" southern traditions, club leaders may well have decided to avoid every chance of becoming associated in people's minds with the Socialists. After 1915, antisuffragists throughout the United States regularly accused suffragists of being Socialists. With several of their members active in the Texas suffrage movement, the Dallas Federation leaders may have felt vulnerable to the charge. Perhaps they were reluctant to provide grounds for suspicion or to risk hurting either the campaign for the vote or their local reform efforts.[40] Nine years would pass before another woman served on the Board of Education in Dallas, and she was appointed in 1919 to complete a man's term.

Other civic projects—specifically, water filtration and the playground movement—kept the clubwomen busy. Like pure food and drug laws and election of women to the Board of Education, establishment of public playgrounds was a national trend sponsored by Progressives in the interest of children. The concept of public play parks originated in 1893, when Florence Kelley established the first playground at Hull House in Chicago. The idea gained momentum thirteen years later with the founding of the Playground Association of America. By 1910, eighty cities funded public playgrounds, with nearly one hundred others operating privately sponsored play parks. Equipped with slides, swings, and bars to climb, plus programs and activities planned and supervised by trained directors, the playgrounds gave children an alternative to the streets. If young boys used their energy in the play park, the reasoning went, they would be too tired for misdemeanors and destructive pranks.[41]

When the clubwomen began organizing their campaign for publicly supported playgrounds, the city owned only three parks. The oldest was City Park, developed during the 1880s on land acquired in 1876. Designed for picnics, walking, and carriage drives, this was a promenade park, a place to see and be seen—and to "Keep Off the Grass." The 147-acre Fair Park, purchased by the city in 1904, was the site each year of the annual Texas State Fair and Dallas Exposition. Complementing its exhibition halls and auditorium were baseball diamonds, driveways, walkways, and picnic grounds, none adequate for activities that appealed to children or working-class adults. The one play park in Dallas, the Kindergarten Play Lot, which first opened in March 1908, was only three-tenths of an acre in size. Although the Board of Education allowed the use of school grounds in the summer as public parks, no facilities existed for supervised activities and exercise, especially for disadvantaged children.[42]

Public interest in new parks encouraged the city to purchase four acres of land near the cotton mill, but the Dallas Federation met resistance to the idea of "teaching children to play." The only way to convince city government and the voters was to demonstrate the need. In February 1909, the federation hired a representative of the national Playground Association as a consultant for initial planning and a "publicity agent" to help arouse public interest. To attract children into the recreational program at the new Trinity Play Park, the mothers' clubs organized athletic contests in the schools and provided trophies for the winners. In March, the federation employed a male playground director and, soon afterward, a female assistant director.[43] Money came from several sources to pay their salaries and to purchase playground equipment for the four-acre park. A lecture by William Jennings Bryan earned $1,000, and the women raised $4,109 with the annual Tag Day collection. In addition, the federation's Empty Stocking and Juvenile Court committees diverted $1,800 from their own projects to boost the playground fund. In May, the city finalized purchase of land.[44]

Their work with the Trinity Play Park suggests that the clubwomen understood, at least to some degree, needs different from their own—in this case, the desire even among adults for sports and activity instead of decorous carriage drives and promenades. Success was immediate and easy to evaluate. In seven months, from March to September 1909, 4,905 persons visited the park; within one year—August 25, 1909, to August 25, 1910—more than 57,000 used the facility. Requesting that the federation retain its playground committee in an advisory capacity, the city government assumed responsibility for Trinity Park, including the salaries of its director and assistant. In 1913, the Park Board credited the park with "reducing crime and improving the moral condition of the Cotton Mill District." Concerned that young children were playing in busy streets, clubwomen in 1918 established a second play park about a mile north of downtown, in the neighborhood populated by immigrants from Mexico.[45] The Federation of Women's Clubs had introduced a new concept to Dallas, the public play park with recreational programs.

The playground movement provides perhaps the clearest example of how the women's clubs operated. Beginning a program with volunteer labor and small private donations, the women sought public support and funding only after the project was under way or the institution founded. They then gave control to city administrators, but often retained contact through an advisory committee. Overly sensitive to charges of "unwomanly" behavior, they hoped to avoid appearing "power hungry" or personally ambitious. Appearances aside, their methods had practical results. As volunteers, the clubwomen had limited time, money, and energy, and many of their endeavors were so large that any one of them could monopolize available resources, to the detriment—indeed, to the exclusion—of the others. By relinquishing each program as it became established, the federation could turn to other causes and in this way increase their contributions to Dallas, even though the ultimate result was the placing of their programs, and credit for their accomplishments, in male hands.

Perhaps most basic of the civic problems addressed by the clubwomen was the availability of clean water, an issue that carried implications for the health of everyone, not just one segment of the community. Although the Citizens' Association included husbands, brothers, and family friends of federation and forum officers, the men were not necessarily sympathetic when the women's plans entailed spending considerable amounts of money. Moreover, while Dallas male leaders were knowledgeable regarding business trends and economic issues, they retained a number of essentially rural assumptions—for example, that each family could make its own arrangements for water, fuel, and waste disposal. Although they understood how plentiful water benefited economic growth, they tended to accept very limited responsibility for the well-being of the public. Matters of health, in other words, lay within the private sphere, with each separate household.[46] Hence, in deciding to expand the city water system, the men saw no reason to install a purification plant.

From frontier days, water had been a chronic problem in Dallas. The situation became acute in 1908, when major flooding by the Trinity River swamped the entire system, making city government and citizens alike dependent for months on private suppliers and individual wells. With conditions complicated by a rapidly growing population, Dallas desperately needed a comprehensive, long-term plan.[47] Like pure foods and drugs, the need for clean water linked public policy and private well being in direct and undeniable ways.

The clubwomen's main concerns were the supply, its sources, and, particularly, the water's purity. In the women's view, city officials were projecting measures that at best were makeshift and inadequate. The water in the newest reservoir was, to be sure, far cleaner than that from the city's older sources. With only a few small towns and no large cities north and east of Dallas, the streams feeding this reservoir indeed were purer than those coming from the west. Still, city officials admitted, within the system, water from the new sources would mix with that in existing reservoirs. Despite the area's history of typhoid fever and vague, undiagnosed illnesses, the only plan for purification was to "doctor" the water with chemicals "when need became evident." In practical terms, this meant "treating" the water upon the occurrence of an epidemic directly traceable to the public water supply.[48]

Later, the clubwomen remembered the five-year campaign as a "long and sometimes bitter struggle." With speeches, letters to newspaper editors, petitions to the city government, and lobbying of the Citizens' Association, members and officers of the Dallas Federation labored to convince local officials of the need for filtration to purify the city's entire water supply. Most effective were their carefully researched reports on water systems and sanitation in other cities. Persistence won what the women came to consider their proudest victory. The city's first filtration plant opened on Turtle Creek Boulevard on May 14, 1913. For the first time ever, Dallas had a plentiful, purified supply of water.[49]

At once the federation began petitioning for a bond issue to raise money for a sewage disposal plant, a project in which they were only months ahead of the state. In 1913, the Texas legislature passed a law requiring cities with more than fifty thousand inhabitants to cease dumping raw sewage into the rivers and streams. With the opening of the sewage treatment plant in November 1914 and its upgrading in 1917, Dallas's basic sanitation system was completed.[50] The fact that, during these very years, male city leaders and officials were having trouble implementing a comprehensive plan for city improvements makes the women's success all the more striking. Business owners tended to equate the public good with the success of their own individual firms. Large-scale public projects that did not immediately benefit their personal interests must, they figured, somehow be helping someone else.[51]

In at least one respect, the drives to modernize the water and sewerage systems resembled the citywide Cleaner Dallas campaigns of 1899 and 1902 and the women's work for pure food and drug laws. All reflected a national "learning process," with people beginning to think of an entire city as a community and not as merely a collection of separate areas or neighborhoods. Such social issues as purified water and regulated foodstuffs arose during the waning years of the City Beautiful movement, as increasing numbers of Americans looked beyond the nation's rural traditions, with the myths of "rugged individualism" and romanticized self-sufficiency. These same years saw a trend toward city planning. "Thinking urban," to put it simply, involved learning to live with many other people within a limited space and, as a result, sharing problems as well as opportunities and cooperating on issues that affected everyone's interests. Perhaps because they empathized with less privileged women, particularly with regard to the duties of motherhood and the needs of children, clubwomen in many ways seemed able to grasp the terms of urban association more thoroughly, and sooner, than many men.[52]

Like the club leaders of the late 1880s and the 1890s, the women achieved impressive results with small numbers. Over twenty-six thousand adult white women lived in Dallas by 1910. Four years later, in 1914, the Federation of Women's Clubs had twenty-six member clubs that enrolled twelve hundred individuals, less than 5 percent of the city's white female population.[53] Led by perhaps twenty genuine (albeit proper and genteel) activists, the federation's membership tended to be more conservative than the officers and often less interested in improving urban life than in associating with the "right people." Still, they followed their leaders into the various social causes justified by motherhood, and they supported the opening of agencies and founding of institutions that, in a number of cases, have continued to widen public services for more than a century.

Running like a thread through fabric was the class consciousness that characterized the Progressive era everywhere in the United States. Clubwomen in Dallas realized the threat inherent in class differences and expressed their values in inclusive terms. As president of the Dallas Woman's Forum, Adella Turner spoke of a desire to achieve "true democracy of spirit [to] . . . bring together women from all walks of life." Turner never stated how far beyond her own elite circles she wished to reach, but she stressed the importance of clubs for widening women's world beyond the home, as well as for promoting the well-being of children. To be sure, for the female population in general, the metaphors of "womanhood" and "motherhood" spoke across class and ethnic lines as few other ideas could, to shared concerns and values if not to friendships and "sisterhood."[54]

On the other hand, the privileged women had learned, to some degree, to recognize and respect differences. Before World War I, the Dallas Federation of Women's Clubs included such organizations as the women's auxiliaries of the Dallas Letter Carriers and the Typographical Union, whose members came from the wage earning and lower middle classes. With their programs, the clubwomen continued to follow the philosophy of the Woman's Exchange, of "helping others help themselves." The founders of the Girls' Co-Operative Home and later of the YWCA hired instructors to help employed women upgrade their job skills, while Neighborhood House and the Infant Welfare Stations offered free classes in domestic science and child care. The clubwomen at least had advanced beyond "nice talks" on Sunday afternoons with tea and cake.

Race was another matter altogether. The clubwomen did not lack concern for African Americans, but they clearly felt unable—when or if they were so inclined—to defy the racial biases of their generation. Knowing well the feelings of their contemporaries, and perhaps unable emotionally to abandon teachings instilled during their own formative years, white women in Dallas kept their interracial work separate from other social causes. Individuals among them served, not altogether altruistically, on the board of a school for black girls that emphasized training for domestic service, the occupational category still employing the most women in Dallas. Other clubwomen opened, with demeaning restrictions, the infant stations to African-American babies. Tainted by prejudice, such cross-race efforts lacked the empathy applied across class and ethnic barriers.

Free medical clinics, monthly rummage sales, free kindergarten classes, and affordable day nurseries were essentially middle-class remedies, the expression of values that sought to patch up the most obvious of social problems without tackling fundamental, systemic causes that could threaten the structure of middle-class life. Sometimes accused of seeking to mold everyone in their own image, middle-class and elite clubwomen expressed—indeed, embodied—an ideal then so revered that few of their generation could imagine alternatives.[55] They aspired to lift the entire city, or at least its white residents, to conformity with their norms. However unrealistic for large numbers of women and families, the idealized images of domesticity and motherhood resonated across class and racial lines and retained much of their power in the coming century.

Whatever their degree of realism, the club projects resulted in long-term, beneficial effects on the community. With their research and consultations with experts, the clubwomen did much to raise the standards considered acceptable for public health and public institutions. The improved conditions that the middle- and upper-class mothers initially sought for their children in the McKinney Avenue School would, in time, characterize all the Dallas public schools. Similarly, such benefits as pure food and medicines, clean and plentiful water, and publicly funded recreation programs sooner or later reached throughout the city, and the weakest degree of their implementation surely constituted an improvement over earlier conditions.

As the concerns of mothers for home, family, and children defined the private issues that women pushed into the public arena, so did considerations of gender determine the evolution of women's political style.[56] The clubwomen skillfully employed the social techniques they knew best to develop effective political strategies and tactics that also were "appropriate." Adapting familiar and acceptable social forms to pressure-group methods, they turned receptions into occasions for lobbying government officials and teas into functions for recruiting supporters. The practice of asking for donations on busy street corners once a year on Tag Day resembled the mass approach necessary for petition drives and canvasses and, only a few years later, for telephone duty on election day.

Solutions for large-scale social problems meant redefining the prerogatives for allocating public funds, and such policies carried implications for the roles of government. In a community barely accustomed to paying for fire and police protection or even for schools, many of the women's causes not only required an expansion of tax-supported services and the public debt, but also the extension of public funding into areas traditionally either considered private or simply ignored.[57] The clubwomen wanted the government to address problems always before handled within families or perhaps by religious charities. When they insisted that elected officials accept responsibility for public health, women were rejecting the essentially rural outlook that prevailed in urban places in

Texas. In a larger sense, they also challenged the *laissez-faire* philosophy still followed by the nation's businessmen.[58] This, and not just disdain for their interests and judgment, undoubtedly created some of the resistance to women's goals. Demands to reconsider the responsibilities appropriate to government rarely have been welcomed.

Perhaps more than any other, the idea of *prevention* led to disagreements with conservatives in city and state government. Prevent disease and sickness with pure food regulations, milk inspections, purified water, adequate sewerage and garbage collection services; prevent death and injury with fire safety rules and safer construction of school buildings; prevent delinquency by keeping children occupied in parks and playground programs. Prevention required that money be spent before a problem developed and this was a concept too "advanced" even for many well-educated businessmen.

Alongside social and physical changes in Dallas, the women's most significant achievement was alteration of their own community roles. After the 1880s, the clubwomen shifted their primary attention from the needs of less advantaged women to focus on children's interests and in this way, coordinated the ideologies of domesticity and maternalism with the Progressive agenda of "child-saving." Projecting images of selflessness that served as protection from censure when they challenged policy decisions, they lobbied for new laws and requested public funds for innovative programs. This emergence of the clubwomen-housewives from an unlikely power base, the home, and their entry into public and political affairs brought a social change at least as radical as that caused by the growing numbers of women entering the paid labor force. Applied to matters of public concern, the duties of motherhood and the traditions of domesticity combined with urban conditions to inject new issues into the political arena and to infuse new values into public discourse, and the public culture. Moreover, they brought new participants—women—into politics and public life.

After 1912, the women's projects increasingly gained recognition, then came to be an accepted form of participation in community life. The invitation from the County Judges and Commissioners' Association to collaborate on writing the bill for the state's juvenile justice system was one expression of regard for the women's expertise. So were requests by city government that the federation retain its committees in advisory capacities to help city officials enforce the pure food and drug ordinance in 1907 and in 1910, to oversee administration of the play parks. In 1909–10, two women served on the city's first planning board. In contrast to the spontaneous, fill-in-the-gap nature of women's community participation during frontier times, by 1912 the clubwomen in Dallas found themselves increasingly accepted as participants in public life.[59]

During the early years of the twentieth century, clubwomen employed a cherished and meaningful complex of American symbols—family, motherhood, home—to alter the configuration of public values and thus to change the public culture. The means of this achievement was the network of female relationships formed within the voluntary associations organized by middle- and upper-class women, particularly the Dallas Federation of Women's Clubs, the Dallas Council of Mothers, and the Dallas Woman's Forum. For decades, the resulting city ordinances, state laws, administrative agencies, tax-supported services, and physical structures shaped and determined significant aspects of urban life.[60]

Chapter Nine
Suffragists and the City

"The club movement swept over the country like wildfire, and so was woman emancipated," observed Imogene Walker DeWitt in her history of the Thursday Morning Club.[1] A leader in Dallas women's organizations around the turn of the century, DeWitt wrote these words in 1942, but her assessment of the clubs was, if anything, too modest: the women's voluntary associations held historical significance for the entire community and not merely for half the population. Basic improvements in the city's infrastructure, major permanent institutions linking Dallas residents to the wider Anglo-European culture, organizations and agencies offering kinds of aid and assistance never before available, the entry of women into public life and politics, even the acquisition of a basic civil right for women—all resulted from the club movement, and all grew out of the conditions of urban life.

More than any other evidence, the local response to the campaign for the vote bore witness to the cordiality that existed between the clubwomen and the community. As a radical departure from age-old practice, as well as a challenge to the "separate spheres" ideology, the national drive for woman suffrage aroused resistance that ranged from heated argument to physical violence. In Dallas, the suffragists found their message at first merely tolerated and then accepted, a reaction similar to that experienced by club leaders when they first applied domestic standards and maternalist rhetoric to public issues.

In a sense, Dallas suffragists "cashed in on" the regard (if not always complete agreement) that both the city's elected leaders and a majority of the voters had extended to women activists in the clubs during the past fifteen years. By campaigning for the female school board candidates, appointing clubwomen to advisory committees and city commissions, and allocating tax money for programs initiated by the women, men had acknowledged clubwomen's strength within the public culture. For people assigned to a "sphere" separate from the recognized channels of community decision making, such influence itself was a major social achievement.[2]

Whatever community good will they may have inherited from the clubwomen, the suffragists forged their own ties with city residents, including professionals and business owners, elected officials and voters, employed women and the middle-class housewives who never joined the Dallas Equal Suffrage Association (DESA). After six years of participating in the public occasions and employing the symbolism that held significance for local popular culture, the suffragists won the city's endorsement in the state referendum of 1919, an election lost in the state as a whole.

The leaders and members of the DESA shared the social origins, as well as the social concerns, of the city's clubwomen. Founded in March 1913, DESA's forty-three charter members included daughters and nieces of the first generation of suffragists (1894–96), as well as veterans of the campaigns for water purification, child labor laws, the pure food and drug ordinance, publicly supported playgrounds, and the juvenile court system. Among them were the much-admired Mary Kittrell Craig, who still taught the literary class she had organized almost twenty years earlier, and Mattie Hightower Turner, who had held almost every local and state office in the WCTU and who helped to found the Texas Congress of Mothers in 1909. The experience of these older women was invaluable to the "college girls" and "young society matrons" whom the *Morning News* reported were the majority of DESA members.[3]

Unlike their mothers and aunts, who had (depending on the issue) pointedly ignored or explicitly denied the political implications of their programs, second-generation suffragists throughout Texas made no attempt to obscure the nature of their cause. Urged by a Democrat at the 1916 state party convention to "lift your skirts and step out of the dirty mire of politics never to return," one suffragist replied that the women intended instead "to lift our sleeves and houseclean these conventions until they are fit places for decent men as well as women."[4] In contrast to the clubwomen's highly praised (though informal and at times "behind-the-scenes") achievements in changing public policies, the suffragists in effect were advocating recognized roles for women, acknowledged and written into public life by law.

Their confidence derived as much from their own identities as from familiarity with the clubwomen's methods of achieving reform. The suffragist leaders in Dallas came from upper- and middle-class families, and most were native Texans or southerners. Their first president was a granddaughter of Sam Houston, Margaret Bell Houston Kaufman, who later won prizes for her poetry and wrote novels popular enough to be published in several languages. Her last book, *Cottonwoods Grow Tall* (1958), received critical praise as a work of literary merit. Her social status unquestioned, Kaufman was following in the footsteps of her aunt, Elizabeth Houston, an officer of the Texas Equal Rights Association in 1895.[5]

Subsequent leaders and officers also came from privileged families. DESA's second president, Texas Erwin Armstrong, graduated from Mary Hardin Baylor College in Belton, Texas, then married a Dallas banker. Widowed by 1914 and the mother of two children, she owned extensive property and thus had the financial means to devote full time to her two terms as suffragist leader.[6] In 1919, the year the Nineteenth Amendment was ratified, the DESA president was Nona Boren Mahoney. Her mother was a committed clubwoman who had held, among other offices, a place on the board of the Girls' Co-Operative Home. After the suffrage victory, Mahoney was active in the Texas Democratic Party, serving on

Margaret Bell Houston Kaufman, first president of the Dallas Equal Suffrage Association (1913), and her only child, Katherine, about 1910.
Sam Houston Memorial Museum, Huntsville, Tex.

the Administration Executive Committee in 1920 and chairing the state Executive Committee.[7] The DESA's competent, even canny, press secretary, Vernice Reppert, was one of the organization's most valuable members. Moving to Dallas from Kansas City around 1903, Reppert was a founder and charter member of the Woman's Forum. After the suffragist campaign, she studied law and joined her husband in active practice.[8]

Like the other suffragists, these DESA leaders were urbane and comfortable with city life, well able to use its assets for the benefit of their cause. Throughout the South, in fact, local campaigns for woman suffrage were one result of urbanization.[9] In 1910, seven Texas cities reported populations of 25,000 or more, and twenty towns listed between 5,000 and 25,000 people. With the population of Lone Star cities growing ten times faster than that of the countryside, by 1919 more than 30 percent of Texans lived in urban areas that were linked by the longest system of rail transportation in the South. By enabling leaders and officers to spread their message quickly, the railroads made it possible for Texas suffragists to build a statewide movement. The large cities provided hotel accommodations for meetings and conventions, as well as concentrations of voters to whom leaders could present programs and demonstrations.

Moreover, the cities became centers of campaigning and headquarters for the organizing of suffrage societies in the surrounding counties and regions. In 1914–15, the DESA leaders helped to start a dozenn suffrage groups in the small towns of Dallas County, more than in any other county in Texas.[10] Equally important was the background provided by clubwomen's experience in public life and in state and local politics, all acquired through the voluntary associations in large cities. Sharing the socioeconomic status and community esteem of the clubwomen, the suffragists were members of the civic-minded elite whose men were building the prosperous commercial economy and whose women had, among other things, recently won their campaigns for water purification and public play parks in Dallas.

Growing by 1917 to more than six hundred members and by 1919 adding several hundred more, the DESA's roster included the city's most prominent women. Among them were Sallie Griffis Meyer, president of the Dallas Art Association for seventeen years and co-author of the state's first child labor law; Alice Bryan Roberts, founder of the Saint Cecelia Club and sponsor of numerous local performances by nationally known musicians; Adella Turner and Ella Stephenson, the first two women elected to the Dallas Board of Education; Blanche Kahn Greenburg, founder of the Infant Welfare and Milk Stations; Ella Carruthers Porter, founder and for years president of the Texas Congress of Mothers; and Nettie Bailey Ford, editor of *Texas Motherhood Magazine*. Fannie Segur Foster, now sixty-one years of age, was a former officer of the city's first suffragist society of 1894–96; Isadore Callaway was the *Morning News* columnist "Pauline Periwinkle" and a veteran social activist. These and numerous other leaders devoted the majority of their time and energies to various civic and cultural concerns, but they lent their names and prestige to the campaign for the vote.

Like the club programs and reforms, the issue of woman suffrage engaged Dallas women at both state and national levels. The DESA's officers hosted two conventions of the Texas Equal Suffrage Association (TESA), in 1914 and again in 1916, and traveled to Austin numerous times to lobby lawmakers for suffrage bills.[11] In Dallas they sponsored nationally known speakers, such as Dr. Anna Howard Shaw, and hosted workshops and training courses led by organizers from the National American Woman Suffrage Association (NAWSA). Nona Boren Mahoney served the NAWSA as vice-president for Texas, and each year other Dallas officers, too, attended the NAWSA's annual meetings.

In 1916, three Dallas suffragists went to St. Louis during the Democratic convention that nominated Woodrow Wilson for his second term as president. They wore white dresses with yellow sashes and carried yellow parasols to stand in the "Golden Mile," the NAWSA demonstration in which women from every state in the Union silently lined both sides of the street along which the Democrats had to walk from their hotel to the convention hall. Forming a delegation that stretched for a full city block, the Texas suffragists had small yellow "Lone Stars" pinned to their dresses.[12]

While Dallas suffragists were drawing their city into yet another aspect of the wider national culture, they also were using local culture to translate a nationwide movement into a "hometown" message. Each October in Dallas, they hosted Suffrage Day at the State Fair of Texas, their best opportunity to reach a large, diverse audience. With attendance growing to more than one million by 1916, the fair has been called "historically . . . the city's single most important instrument in maintaining its position as the commercial and cultural center of North Texas."[13] Like other state and county fairs in the South and Midwest, the fair at Dallas played social and cultural, as well as commercial, roles. Business owners, farming families, schoolchildren, housewives, wage earners—everyone came to the fair, for the horse races, football games, art exhibitions, and musical performances, as well as for the livestock shows and household crafts competitions, demonstrations of new inventions in farm machinery, and, after 1900, displays of the latest-model automobiles.

In a time when few women traveled without male "protection," the State Fair offered particular advantages. With the railroad companies posting special low fares, women accompanied their families to Dallas, not only to view the performances and exhibitions, but also to pursue their own concerns and interests. The Texas Woman's Congress, the Texas Woman's Press Association, the

Texas Congress of Mothers, the state association of music clubs—these and other groups were organized during fair time in Dallas.

For the suffrage cause, the fair offered especially fine occasions for demonstrations, parades, and speeches by state and local leaders. Each year the suffragists rented space to set up a decorated booth to sell such "novelties" as pencils, playing cards, matchbooks, and small photographs of national suffrage leaders such as Susan B. Anthony and Anna Howard Shaw. In 1915, the suffragists rode in an automobile parade to the fairgrounds, then drove to several locations and spoke to the crowds from the open cars. The event was described by the *Morning News* as "the most unique . . . public speaking ever staged in Dallas."[14] "Suffrage Day" at the fair that year also was "Travelling Salesman's Day," and the suffragists dragooned hundreds of men into their campaign. According to the newspaper, "The ladies . . . have shown a diplomacy that would make England's Cabinet sick with envy in getting a 'Votes for Women' badge on every traveling salesman at the Fair . . . so the highways and byways are golden with the admonition of the cause."[15]

During the fair in 1916, the DESA hosted the annual luncheon following the state organization's board meeting. In the afternoon, the Dallas suffragists joined the TESA officers, who spoke to the crowds from automobiles parked at various places downtown. These occasions were their only open-air demonstrations.[16] Dallas voters, they knew, were too conservative to approve of the parades and rallies that were so successful in Galveston and Houston. However decorous their campaigning, the fair attracted more than one hundred thousand visitors each day and thus offered the best single opportunity for contact with people from all over North Texas.

In addition to events devoted specifically to suffrage, the DESA officers and leaders participated in social occasions held by other organizations. The suffragists stood in reception lines to greet ranchers' wives when the Cattlemen's Association met in Dallas and helped host the conventions of the state Congress of Mothers. For the 1916 Style Show Parade sponsored by several large department stores, the DESA members decorated a car with white and yellow flowers spelling "Vote for Women" and "Victory in 1917" along the sides.[17] All these activities were the sort they would have participated in even if they had not been campaigning for the vote. As news from the skilled Vernice Reppert, such occasions showed that the Dallas suffragists were within the "mainstream" of community life and were not the "unnatural" and "socialistic" women their opponents wished to depict.

During the decade after the clubwomen's drive for the city's pure food and drug ordinance of 1907, their frequent meetings with elected officials and their cooperation in communitywide programs led to an overt acceptance of women as participants in, and even leaders of, public life. With regard to issues related to the "female sphere," the clubwomen were major actors in defining the community's values—that is, the public culture. Usually subtle and exercised initially within middle- and upper-class social structures, their roles in the formulation of the public culture became highly visible during events that occurred in the winter and spring of 1916.[18]

Contemporaneous with woman suffrage, prohibition undoubtedly was the most volatile topic in Texas politics and the one most often classified, especially among the deeply religious, as a "mother's issue." Suffragists tended to sympathize with the "drys," though few of the DESA members were active in the prohibition movement. In 1915, the Texas attorney general won a major antitrust suit against the state's brewers, a victory that boosted "dry" hopes of political victory.[19] Within this climate of opinion, the Dallas Council of Mothers launched a campaign early in 1916 to ban alcoholic beverages from the State Fair. Justifying their position as beneficial to children, the women's efforts constituted an attempt to control an aspect of men's personal and public behavior.

The campaign originated in the mothers' club at the Travis (formerly the McKinney Avenue) Public School, the first Dallas women's organization to confront elected officials on matters of public interest. Now, with different leaders and membership (by 1916, the original McKinney Avenue mothers were officers and committee chairs in the major women's organizations, including the DESA), the Travis School Mothers' Club implemented the process of the initiative, first adopted as part of the 1906 city charter. After gathering enough signatures of registered voters to place the issue of State Fair beverages on the ballot for the upcoming city elections, officers of the Mothers' Council worked with the city attorney to draft a charter amendment that would exclude Fair Park from the Dallas saloon laws.[20]

Notwithstanding the widespread sympathy for prohibition and respect for their position in society as mothers, the women found themselves at odds with leading businessmen and local government officials. Not only were the mothers challenging a custom long accepted as a male privilege, but also they were threatening fair profits. If voters accepted the proposition, both the city and the Fair Board would lose money, as each collected a percentage of sales from the concessionaires who sold food and drink at the fair. In addition, tens of thousands of visitors from other areas in Texas would be disappointed to find themselves attending a "dry" State Fair. With support from the churches, the Anti-Saloon League, and the Dallas Pastors' Association, as well as the WCTU, the measure passed easily, even though it shared the ballot with candidates for the Board of Education and eight other city charter amendments.[21]

The campaign to "dry" the State Fair may have been a "woman's issue," but the United States' entry into World War I unquestionably involved the entire civilian population.[22] In the Dallas Patriotic Parade on April 10, 1917, the suffragists marched behind a banner promising "Men of America, We Will Do Our Share." Rejecting suggestions that the DESA disband because of the national emergency and donate its treasury to the war effort, the suffragists joined other city organizations in mobilization. The suffragists planted "Victory Gardens" and organized a Red Cross auxiliary to sew bandages and hospital gowns. They volunteered as chaperones in the canteen run by the Federation of Women's Clubs for soldiers stationed at Fort Dick, located on the fairgrounds in Dallas. As they listened to committee reports and discussed political tactics during their regular meetings, the suffragists knitted sweaters and socks for the Red Cross to pack for shipment to servicemen.[23]

Without slackening work for the vote, suffragist officers accepted leadership positions in the local war effort. The DESA Press Chairman Vernice Reppert became state chairman of the Woman's Liberty Loan Committee for the Eleventh Federal Reserve District. Former DESA President Texas Armstrong chaired the Dallas County Woman's War Savings Stamp Committee and led the organization of "thrift clubs," or war savings societies. Vice-president Nona Mahoney supervised the savings stamps booths throughout the city.[24] Such work kept them, as suffragists, in the public eye and enlarged their network of contacts. Nona Mahoney, for one, carried pamphlets and other suffrage literature everywhere she went, and she wrote to an Austin suffragist in 1918, "When suffrage is first, one works without hardly [sic] realizing it."[25]

Women's work in the war effort strengthened the suffragist arguments for the vote. Virtually everywhere in the United States, women filled vacancies left by men who volunteered for, or were drafted into, military service. The *Morning News* often published photographs of women in overalls working as machinists, laborers, and dope reclaimers for the railroads, and of women in long aprons operating linotype machinery for newspapers and print shops. In Dallas, women took jobs as elevator operators and streetcar conductors, as messengers for Western Union and operatives in the plant that manufactured cotton gins. Suffragists could now base their claims of female equality on women's actual behavior.

Even before the war, growth in the female labor force had changed minds about suffrage. Mary Kittrell Craig, for example, wrote a long letter to the *Morning News* in 1894 to state her belief that woman suffrage would undermine the family. Because mothers formed their sons' sense of morality, she argued, women ultimately were responsible for the condition of society. If women only used the power they already possessed, they could create a better world without encroaching upon the "masculine realm."[26] Nearly twenty years later, in 1913, Craig was a charter member of the DESA. She had come to see the vote as an appropriate response to changing times, as well as basic justice for women, especially widows and business owners, who paid taxes and obeyed "man-made laws."[27]

More dramatic than women's service on the home front was the fact that, by the time of the armistice in November 1918, 25,000 American women had served in some capacity in Europe—in army communications posts as telephone operators and secretaries; with the American Red Cross as doctors, nurses, and ambulance drivers; and in YWCA canteens. Refusing to give female personnel the official recognition of rank, the armed forces nonetheless eagerly recruited them, especially for medical service. In August 1918 alone, 118 Dallas nurses enlisted for military duty overseas.

Of the women serving in Europe, nearly six thousand were physicians. Among them was May Agness Hopkins.[28] A native of Austin, Hopkins was the only woman to graduate from the University of Texas School of Medicine in 1911. After an internship at the New England Hospital for Women and Children in Boston and a position as house physician in the Pennsylvania State Hospital in Warren, she began a pediatric practice in Dallas in 1912. Volunteering in 1918 to work with refugee children in France, she instead was assigned to the Smith College Relief Unit and sent to the town of Château-Thierry. There, on the banks of the Marne River about fifty miles from Paris, American troops had fought their first engagement of the war.

Working so close to the front lines that she was issued a helmet, Hopkins treated around one thousand battlefield casualties a day for several weeks. After commanding an evacuation of wounded men by river to the base hospital in Paris, she was transferred to the south of France, where she took charge of children's medicine in the thirteen departments bordering the Mediterranean. Several clinics and hospitals that she organized during the war were still in operation as late as 1939. With such experiences, she recalled many years later, "Dallas seemed a little tame."[29] After their military service in Europe, women physicians were popular speakers after the war and especially effective in appealing for donations to help pay the nation's war debt. Often appearing in full military uniform, which they now were allowed to wear, their wartime service lengthened the suffragists' list of reasons why women deserved the vote.

The success of the DESA's public relations strategy did not depend solely on the war effort or female employment. Perhaps the single most powerful popular symbol employed successfully by clubwomen and suffragists alike was that of motherhood. Indeed, the argument that mothers needed the vote to protect their homes and families lay just one logical step beyond the club leaders' frequent claims that their reforms would most benefit children. As Isadore Callaway observed in 1912 in her "Pauline Periwinkle" column, the ballot offered an efficient means of implementing goals. Many women, she wrote, had come to believe that "it would simplify matters for them could they influence legislation by a direct vote instead of by the indirect influence they are being all the time entreated [by male leaders] to exercise on this or that proposed measure."[30]

A "society" leader as well as a professional journalist and a pioneer in the city's club movement, Callaway understood how the women's work for social reforms over the years had come to take a great deal of time, even for women who were not employed outside their homes. Almost to a woman, the Dallas suffragists were housewives, not professional or employed women. While the suffragists appealed to the ideals of liberty, justice, and equality, to fairness in the labor force, and to women's contributions to the war effort, they more often invoked the values that ruled their own lives, families, and homes. When the *Dallas Times Herald* published a weekly series entitled "Why I Am a Suffragist," nearly two dozen DESA members wrote articles whose titles included "Political Dominance of Men Is an Evil to the Mothers," "There Is Need of the Mother Heart in Legislation," and "Women in Home Should Have Voice in Government." One woman stated simply, "When I Became a Mother, I Became a Suffragist."[31]

Such adept use of popular symbolism was matched by the suffragists' organizational skill, especially for two important events during the suffrage campaign. In February 1918, Dallas's member of the Texas House of Representatives, Barry Miller, promised that if the DESA could find five thousand local women to sign a petition endorsing suffrage, he would vote for pending legislation to enfranchise women in Texas primaries. After three days of planning, the suffragists, along with dozens of volunteers who were not DESA members, needed only four additional days to collect more than ten thousand names.[32] True to his word, Miller supported the bill giving Texas women partial suffrage, then accepted leadership of the suffrage caucus in the legislature and of the Dallas Men's Equal Suffrage Association.

In the summer of 1918, the deployment of skillfully organized volunteers was crucial to the drive to register female voters in time for the primary elections. Enacted by a margin too small to make it an emergency measure, the new law granting women the vote in state primaries would not take effect for ninety days after passage. This left only seventeen days before the voter registration deadline. The TESA officers and members laid aside all their other volunteer work in order to get as many women registered as possible. By July 14, thanks to the leadership of the city's suffragists, 16,809 of Dallas County's 33,000 women aged twenty-one and over were fully eligible to vote, more than in any other county in Texas.[33]

Not all women shared the triumph. When more than a hundred African-American women went to the courthouse to register, the sheriff in Dallas turned them away, and no whites of either sex protested. Like suffragists elsewhere in the South, the DESA's strategy regarding race was to ignore the issue unless forced to address it and then to be as indirect as possible about the eventuality of black women's voting. The summer of 1918 was a particularly shameful time to ignore the hopes of black citizens for full participation. African-American men had served the country in uniform, and African-American women had put in untold hours of volunteer effort on the home front.[34]

Despite the city's relatively small black population, tensions were high during and after the war, and a new militancy within the African-American community made itself felt in various ways. With four hundred members in March 1919, the city's chapter of the National Association for the Advancement of Colored People persuaded the Dallas government to discourage a touring drama company's presentation of *The Birth of a Nation*. The play, which glorified the Ku Klux Klan of post–Civil War times, was not performed. With more than one thousand members by June, the organization pressured the city's school board to build a new "colored" high school and to improve the elementary schools and the public parks in black neighborhoods. Frequent arguments and fights on the streetcars led the supervisor of public utilities to confer with police about designating separate cars for black and white passengers.[35]

Although other Texas cities, also, experienced racial tensions in 1918, black women registered to vote without incident in several cities, around five hundred in Houston alone. In Waxahachie, a small town about twenty miles south of Dallas, a judge advised the county tax collector to allow black women to register. In many places, however, African Americans were turned away as in Dallas, by sheriffs or other public officials. The black-owned *Dallas Express* encouraged black women to support woman suffrage, while the *Morning News* announced, "Negroes cannot vote in this primary election." And on election day, the official ballot had a pledge printed across the top: "I swear that I am a white Democrat."[36]

Politicians who failed to defend the rights of black women eagerly courted white suffragists and their organizing abilities. Immediately after passage of the primary law, a candidate for the U.S. Senate sought the women's help for his campaign, as did the Dallas County "Hobby for Governor" committee. The City Charter League invited women to a "mass meeting" to discuss proposed amendments to the city charter; on another occasion, political hopefuls gladly attended a "talk-fest" hosted by the DESA. Candidates for county judge, for example, wanted to explain their policies for the juvenile court and the county hospital, and their decisions about mothers' pensions. All these issues held particular interest for potential female voters.[37]

Ten months later, in May 1919, a statewide referendum to add a woman suffrage article to the Texas Constitution proved the DESA's success in communicating its message. Along with the Mothers' Council, the WCTU, women's church groups, and women's auxiliaries to fraternal organizations, the suffragists could claim the support of numerous male civic leaders, business owners, and professionals. Among these wealthy, well-educated men were the presidents of four banks, several judges, a number of physicians, and the owner of the country club.[38] Some backers, like Barry Miller, were converted conservative Democrats, but most tended to be progressive Democrats who believed that women would support the "right" laws and candidates. The progressive Democrats, in other words, saw woman suffrage as an immediate way to enlarge their constituency.

Woman suffrage had many female adherents who never joined the DESA. Wage-earning women had come to see that the right to vote would allow them to bring direct pressure on the state legislature for laws requiring better wages and improved working conditions. Each day during the voter registration period in 1918, a young social worker brought a dozen women operatives from the factories and mills to the courthouse to register.[39] Even very young women cared about the vote. Hazel Winterbauer, a teenager employed as a candy maker, was not a DESA member, but she wore a white dress and marched in the suffrage contingent in the Patriotic Parade in 1917. Another teenager, Lillie Day Birch, who later opened a printing business with her husband, argued with her father about women's rights and persuaded him to vote for suffrage in the referendum of May 1919.[40]

Along with political and civic leaders, employed women and young mothers, the city's business owners seemed to line up in the suffragist camp for the referendum. For several days before the election on May 24, movie theaters featured slide shows with arguments for suffrage. All Belo publications carried suffrage news, while the editors of two farmers' weeklies, *Farm and Ranch* (with circulation of over two hundred thousand) and the *Progressive Farmer* (with more than fifty-two thousand subscribers), promised a pro-suffrage article in every May issue.[41] The *Morning News* and its sister paper in Galveston ran a series of interviews with prominent local men who favored suffrage, as well as statements by such national figures as William Jennings Bryan, U. S. Secretary of War Newton D. Baker, and U. S. Secretary of Labor W. B. Wilson.

Commercial establishments, too, lent their support. "All the stores have a beautifully decorated suffrage window," Vernice Reppert wrote to the TESA President Minnie Fisher Cunningham. "All of our papers have front page boxed editorials favoring suffrage both today and tomorrow; all of the dry goods stores are mentioning suffrage in their ads and all for love."[42] Department stores provided space to set up suffrage "recruiting stations"; hotels and cafes added suffrage slogans to their menus; a printing company printed suffrage literature free of charge; a car sales company donated use of an automobile for county campaigning.[43]

However "elite" the DESA members and officers may have been, the support of merchants, business owners, and men's clubs (as well as women's "fraternal" societies) indicated the issue's appeal within the general population. With the assumption widespread that women voters would favor Prohibition, the suffragists gained strength among both Protestant and Catholic church leaders. At annual meetings in Dallas in 1917, both the Presbyterians and the Baptists endorsed woman suffrage. On the day before the referendum in 1919, Catholic Bishop Joseph P. Lynch issued a formal statement in the Dallas papers to express his personal hope that the suffrage amendment would pass.[44]

On May 24, suffrage leaders confidently predicted victory. The next day they learned that Dallas and Dallas County indeed had passed the state amendment by "substantial majorities," with 63 percent of the city and 60 percent of the county voters going for woman suffrage.[45] While suffragists earned direct credit for the success, demographic factors undoubtedly affected the results. Particularly in northern cities, large numbers of immigrant voters, many from conservative agrarian societies in Europe, helped to defeat woman suffrage. Such newcomers were few in Dallas. Nearly 80 percent of the city's population consisted of native-born whites, just under 71 percent with native-born parents. Despite a decade of increased immigration into Dallas by rural African Americans, black people comprised only 15.1 percent of the city's population, down from 19.6 percent ten years earlier.[46] In other areas of Texas, black voters opposed woman suffrage. Routinely barred from voting in the "white" elections in Dallas, they could not affect the city results.

Early returns announced victory for suffragists statewide, but this trend did not last. The woman suffrage amendment to the state constitution lost by more than fifty-five hundred votes; Prohibition won, without women's votes. The suffragists blamed "first paper" immigrants and the "alien vote" for their defeat, as well as heavy rains that kept voters from polls in many parts of the state. Some even found evidence of fraud and irregularities. Analysis of the returns, however, suggests that rural voters in North and East Texas were most responsible for the amendment's defeat.[47]

The suffragists did not wait long for better tidings. On June 4, less than two weeks after the Texas referendum, the federal suffrage amendment passed the U.S. Senate 56–24, by two votes more than the necessary two-thirds majority. Both Lone Star senators voted "Aye." On June 24, Texas became the ninth state to ratify the Nineteenth Amendment, by votes of 96–20 in the state house and 19–10 in the senate. The Lone Star State broke with the "solid South" and offset suffragist losses in the North.[48]

Of obvious importance for basic citizenship, the enactment of woman suffrage carried an additional significance for women's status. Because suffragists

Nona Boren Mahoney, last president of the Dallas Equal Suffrage Association
(1918–19), about 1922. Courtesy the children of Mary Boren Shamburger

skillfully employed maternalist rhetoric to muffle the individualism implied by
the right to vote, their victory suggested acceptance of the concept that women's
domestic values were valid principles for public policy.[49] Most people, women
and men alike, expected female voters to favor candidates and laws that would
protect home, family, children, employed women, and traditional morality. Thus,
the acceptance of woman suffrage implied public, formal recognition of the
importance to society of women's customary work. At the same time, the change
acknowledged their new social and community roles—albeit public roles dedicated to private, domestic concerns.

By 1919, the status quo included a significant degree of community visibility for women. Yet all too many women, as well as men, failed to comprehend

the extent of female participation in American public life and thus missed the real meaning of the suffrage victory. As Jill Conway has observed, even women leaders of national stature seem never to have freed themselves from accepted views and familiar images of "woman's special nature." Nor did most, apparently, ponder the meaning of full female citizenship in relation to the paradigm of the separate spheres.[50]

Dallas women, too, seemed not to understand the "different world" they had done so much to build. Oblivious to the blurring and in some ways the disappearance of the boundaries between public and private, many clung to the old perceptions of "nature" and the comfortable habits of gender. Especially serious was the way even women educators were much like the original Dallas County pioneers in terms of the goals they defined for their female students.

In 1913, Ela Hockaday opened what would become the city's most prestigious school for white girls.[51] With a strong program in the traditional liberal arts and emphasis on participation in sports, Hockaday intended to prepare her students to enter any college or university. With an independent personal life and a commitment to her profession, she began her career at eighteen and advanced rapidly to become principal of a public school in Sherman, Texas. Later, she taught biology in a college for several years. Disillusioned by 1911 by the effects of political bickering on education, she and a friend purchased a small farm in South Texas to work for two years as vegetable "farmerettes" before Hockaday opened the exclusive school in Dallas.

Hockaday hired a faculty with degrees from Smith, Wellesley, and Oxford; invited renowned speakers such as Gertrude Stein and Eleanor Roosevelt; taught her students to respect all faiths; collected antiques and china during her trips to Europe and the Near East; and gave legendary dinner parties at which she entertained city leaders as well as her students. But apparently she had little to say about racial or social justice, and she praised traditional values without seeming to notice their new applications. Whatever the opportunities opening for women and their newly won right to vote, she declared, "more important to all of them [is] woman's chief service, that of motherhood and homemaker." Instead of teaching her students that the long-accepted female roles gave them vital responsibilities for leadership in the community, she stressed the customary separation that assigned human lives to either "private" or "public."[52]

If old ways of thinking confined privileged young women to traditional lives, the segregated and discriminatory job market chained education for African Americans to the past. In February 1916, three white women, all club leaders in Dallas, served as board members to incorporate the Homemakers' Industrial and Trade School, an institution intended to "give instruction in all subjects necessary to make Negro women self-supporting." With the support of the mayor, the Mothers' Council, and the Board of Public Welfare, the all-white board of directors funded the school with private donations.[53]

Founded by Josie Briggs Hall, the organizer of the Dallas chapter of the Negro PTA, the school operated until 1928. "Homemaking is a science to be learned and not a drudgery to be dreaded," Hall's philosophy proclaimed, but students were not prepared solely to manage their own homes. Their training would also "help to solve the domestic service problem" in privileged households. Only grades one through six offered the standard academic curriculum. In the seventh through the twelfth grades, students took lessons in laundering, gardening, home economics, interior decoration, domestic sanitation and hygiene, fancy sewing, dressmaking, and personal hygiene. In a city with a growing number of clerical positions in businesses owned by blacks as well as whites, the school gave no courses in bookkeeping or accounting. Not even typing and shorthand were offered, much less college preparatory courses.

Instead, pupils received "practical training" along with classroom instruction: after classes each afternoon, they laundered their own clothing and bed linens. After finishing the washing and ironing, they had free time, unless the younger students needed care. Older pupils also raised a garden, and the vegetables they grew and canned helped to make the school self-supporting. With a faculty of three, all graduates of Prairie View Normal and Texas College in Tyler, the school awarded three hundred certificates during its first three years.

The Homemakers' School founder, Josie Briggs Hall, was deeply influenced by the race philosophy of Booker T. Washington. Perhaps the first black woman in Texas to publish her poetry, Hall resented the white stereotypes and the double standards under which African Americans labored. Still, she disapproved of woman suffrage and urged women to remain in their separate, domestic "sphere." The mother of five children, two of whom grew up to become professionals, Hall built a career for herself as an educator.[54]

The Southern Methodist University (SMU) administration and faculty also failed to prepare young women for community leadership. Opening classes in 1915, SMU was founded in 1910 by a special commission appointed at the Methodist Annual Conference. Initial enrollment balanced evenly between women and men, but from 1919 into the 1920s, the graduating classes were predominantly female, with men earning fewer than half the degrees conferred. At a time when coeducation was a matter of some controversy, SMU committed itself to an equal admissions policy for a practical reason: the tuition paid by women, especially "extension" students living in Dallas, was crucial to the institution's survival.[55]

The new university offered women scholarships and equal admission, but between 1915 and 1922, its annual bulletins included few role models. In 1915–

16, only four of the sixteen faculty members were women: two taught English, another education, and the fourth German and piano. As at many leading women's colleges, none of the women faculty held a degree beyond the bachelor's level. Male faculty were somewhat better qualified. Although only five held doctoral degrees in their fields, the rest had earned masters' degrees. In keeping with contemporary trends, SMU had a separate Department of Domestic Arts and Sciences, headed by a man in the School of Fine Arts. By 1917, the Department of Domestic Arts and Sciences had become the Home Economics Department, with academic courses required along with those in household crafts and home management.

Despite their generation's overwhelming orientation toward marriage and homemaking as bases of a lifestyle, very few SMU women majored in home economics: "We didn't go to college to learn how to do housework," one alumna remembered.[56] The earliest available data list 68 percent of the women graduates in the class of 1919 as earning degrees in English or modern languages. One majored in home economics, not because she planned to become a wife and mother and run her own home scientifically, but because she planned to teach or work with the new state and county programs for rural areas as a home demonstration agent. Most young women continued to see themselves primarily as future wives and mothers. They concentrated on academic subjects and earned bachelor's degrees that seemed to provide an appropriate "background" for a cultured, gracious, private life, not a foundation for careers or community participation and civic leadership.

The lasting results of the clubwomen's activities, the importance to everyday life of the domestic concerns they transformed into public issues, the profoundly political nature of their successes—none of these seemed to amend, much less dislodge, traditional concepts. Customary, familiar ideas and arrangements remained fixed—indeed, fossilized—in the minds of educators, college students, and the general public. People seemed able to comprehend society only as two "spheres," not as a multifaceted whole that allowed expression of human needs and abilities through numerous channels, among them the home and domestic life. To be sure, the success of the club and suffrage movements resulted to a large degree from the ways women used conservative ideas. Presenting themselves first as mothers and then as patriots, the suffragists turned a radical political demand into a "mainstream" issue within a rationale that allowed women, for that particular moment in historical time, real and effective leverage as arbiters of community values and standards for public behavior.

Yet, after only a short time in that mainstream, both club activists and suffragists allowed "their" issues to be subsumed within existing political mechanisms. Worse, they failed to maintain their identity as a separate constituency in Texas. The Women's Joint Legislative Council, organized in 1920 to coordinate the efforts of several major women's groups on behalf of women and children, had a remarkable record of achieving passage of the laws they sought. After 1927, this "Petticoat Lobby" disbanded because its member organizations wished to work separately.[57] Never again did Texas women muster the strength they displayed in the first seven years after achieving the vote.

The campaign for the ballot carried the clubwomen's activism to its logical conclusion. Women needed the vote, the suffragists argued, because it was just and right, but above all to protect the safety, health, and well-being of their families and homes. These were the very reasons the clubwomen cited for their involvement in public and political affairs. Most people, it seems, understood "families" and "homes" but ignored, if they ever understood, the significance of the ways in which, even before winning the vote, women integrated domestic standards and family values into the public culture. The suffragists' daughters would spend their lives, in a sense, testing their mothers' achievements. The suffragists' granddaughters, in the late 1960s, would reconceptualize the problems and begin to envision new solutions.

Conclusion

"This is a different world for woman from that our precious mothers knew, when they lived secluded lives and spoke in low tones awed by their 'Lords and Masters,'" wrote Imogene Walker DeWitt in her history of the Thursday Morning Club. "Now the influence of Woman is felt everywhere . . . from riveting the body of an airplane to the halls of state."[1] DeWitt was writing in 1942, but "woman's world" had changed decades earlier. Her mother's generation actually was not so timid as she remembered, while DeWitt and her contemporaries throughout the United States achieved unprecedented progress with regard to women's status. Shifting the boundaries of "public" and "private" and blurring the "separate spheres," women made their advances almost entirely in cities.

Within roughly eighty years from the time of its founding, Dallas developed through four identifiable stages to become a modern city. Always distinguished from the surrounding rural areas by its economy, Dallas by 1880 offered the financial and mercantile services and, before the turn of the century, the cultural experiences and social diversity characteristic of cities. To be sure, the pioneers of the 1850s established a genuinely urban culture, and, during the 1880s, railroads and freight wagon companies turned Dallas into a regional inland distribution center with the economic functioning of a modern commercial city. But only after 1900 could city leaders marshal the resources, whether public or private, to increase services to citizens, multiply opportunities for cultural expression, and protect the most vulnerable residents.

At every stage, women were active participants, whether incidentally in the unusual circumstances of the frontier or later in establishing the distinctive forms of urban living. Beginning in the late 1880s, middle- and upper-class women—virtually all of them married and mothers—worked to improve education and nurture the fine arts, and to alleviate, if not resolve, numerous social problems. Primarily through their initiative, Dallas acquired the agencies, institutions, and organizations to maintain standards for public health and safety, provide dependable assistance to those in need, and both preserve the cultural heritage and extend its expression in following generations. Many of the factors that classified Dallas as a modern city originated in efforts by women to improve life for families.

In that most fundamental of urban characteristics, the economy based upon trade and commerce, women labored at both the unseen, "private" domestic work that sustained the labor force and the more visible and "public" occupations of business ownership and wage employment. By 1920, work for upper- and middle-class wives consisted primarily of services and managerial tasks, changes dependent less on new products and appliances than on a family's ability to hire household help. Among blue-collar families, ever fewer women manufactured goods from raw materials they produced themselves, but higher standards of cleanliness absorbed their "freed" time. The female proportion of the Dallas paid labor force grew from around one-fifth in 1880 to more than one-fourth by 1920. At the same time, women spread throughout the city's economy in virtually every occupational category, including clerical and sales jobs, the professions, ownership of businesses, positions as officers in small family-owned firms, and all levels of management in large companies. Although as late as 1920 women in the newer kinds of work barely outnumbered those in jobs related to domestic skills, the growing female presence in the marketplace was as characteristic of the modern city as the variety of employment available there.

Less obvious but at least as important as the growth of employment were the other ways women participated in the public realm. Years before winning the vote, women developed unexpected expertise at influencing political decisions and altering social conditions, even to the point of affecting standards of acceptable behavior. While external developments dictated women's participation in the urban economy, their functioning in community life was autonomous and spontaneous.

One uniquely Anglo-American organization, the voluntary association, proved to be a flexible and highly effective device, both for generating routine social functions and for achieving social change. Forming new friendships through the ladies' aid, industrial, and benevolent societies in churches and synagogues, as well as the secular literary societies and study clubs, women also organized social occasions that fostered acquaintances among their families. Such events gave men, too, contacts beyond those developed through business and trade. With oyster suppers and "evening entertainments," benefit musicales and charity balls, women initiated the community patterns that came to be typical of urban places. Characterized by association at planned events rather than by spontaneous socializing at rural barn raisings and quilting bees, community in Dallas fragmented by 1880 into interest groups based on ethnicity, class, and religion. Individuals consciously chose membership in one or several groups, or none.

For a generation, women's organizations engaged in volunteer service that did as much as the developing urban economy to create the modern city. Unlike the church groups, with their consistently denominational focus, the study clubs very quickly turned their attention beyond merely personal interests and self-improvement to the opening of a privately funded "public" library and reading room, as well as such "village improvements" as planting shrubs around the courthouse. In their subsequent founding of permanent cultural institutions such as the Dallas Public Library and the Art Museum, the clubwomen provided evidence of a new division of civic labor by gender. First emerging in the 1880s and tacitly accepted during the 1890s, the first traces of this profound alteration in community duties appeared with the economic changes accompanying the railroads. The reversal in public gender roles occurred as men abandoned and women assumed responsibilities within the city's aesthetic life.

During these years, women also began to extend their customary obligations beyond traditional concepts of charity and benevolence. More than "taking care of our own" with seasonal or occasional "handouts," Dallas clubwomen initiated programs in health care for infants and children, and then for entire families. They sought, too, to "help others help themselves" with preschool education and, for mothers, training in child care, sanitation, hygiene, and nutrition. Reaching across class and ethnic (and later, racial) barriers, women founded and administered more than half the institutions, organizations, and agencies for public and private assistance in Dallas, whether secular or religious in character.

These pioneering efforts to establish a modern system of regular, dependable relief drew privileged middle- and upper-class women into political activism years before they won the right to vote. Clubwomen achieved the passage of city ordinances that improved health and safety, convinced the Dallas government to create administrative offices for problems affecting women and children, increased the number of city services for children, and succeeded in getting two club leaders elected to public office. With regard to issues clearly related to domestic affairs and the private realm, women found elected officials usually receptive to their views and cooperative in implementing stated goals. Men, also, tended to accept as domestic and female the values which women espoused, although they agreed more reluctantly that women's standards should be transposed from private into public life. The voluntary associations, themselves often classified as a primary characteristic of urban places, became the means by which female energy and expertise applied female values to change public policies and alter public values.

Even the suffrage campaign in Dallas grew out of the city's club movement. Surprisingly, the most useful measure of women's relationship to the city appeared during the campaign for woman suffrage. Like the clubwomen before them, the suffragists tapped a fund of deep public interest in domestic and familial concerns. Communicating their goals through symbols and events intimately linked to local and popular culture, the city's suffragists based their campaign on the rhetoric of motherhood, children, and the home. Benefiting from the clubwomen's consistent tact and diplomacy during the past twenty years, the suffragists won approval by both city and county voters of the woman suffrage amendment to the state constitution in a May 1919 referendum. This local victory suggests readiness by a majority of Dallas voters to extend formal, legal recognition to the significance of women's traditional work, as well as to newly developed public roles for women.

Always, the relationship of women with the city was reciprocal. The urban environment changed women's lives and work, presenting them with unprecedented opportunities, but also with living conditions that were often difficult and sometimes unacceptable. In turn, privileged women worked for improvements and reform, and in the process altered and shaped the physical and social conditions of living in an urban place.[2] Wealth generated by the urban economy's trade and commerce provided the leisure to address public concerns, to ponder and discuss issues and information received from women's organizations in other areas of Texas and the United States. The ease of intracity travel and communication fostered associations and friendships among female members of the ever-growing Dallas population, and such frequent contact encouraged women to share interests and concerns. Urban conveniences expedited the development of enduring relationships as privileged women identified first neighborhood, and then communitywide needs and problems and worked together to find remedies.

The women's efforts served more than immediate purposes. As mercantile and financial activities linked Dallas businesses to the national economy, the clubwomen's projects drew city residents beyond currently popular and commercial entertainment to participate in a wider cultural heritage. Joining several nationwide trends by affiliating with national associations and state federations, the clubwomen's social programs linked Dallas with major political and social movements.

At least as difficult as reaching their social and political goals was the fact that middle- and upper-class matrons had to circumvent and even transcend social expectations for their own lives. The ultimate result of their work to reform public policies and to affect official decisions was the redefinition of political issues, hardly an appropriate pursuit for southern ladies. As the clubwomen dealt with the conditions and problems of urban living, they forged age-old "female work" into new public roles. Through this transformation, they devel-

Elm Street, about 1910. Courtesy Historic Photograph Collection,
Dallas Public Library

oped new relationships with the community. Their achievement of an acceptable balance between propriety and conscience revealed an important aspect of the ways gender affected the building of city institutions and, through those institutions, the creation of urban life.

Perhaps most significant, women in Dallas, as throughout the nation, altered the boundaries of the "private, female sphere."[3] Through women's work in basic community functions and through their campaigns to improve living conditions, the aspects of human life customarily labeled "public" and "private" merged, overlapping and connecting through people's interactions and relationships into city life. In the economic system, through services as well as through producing, manufacturing, and processing goods; in founding major institutions to foster learning and the fine arts; in organizing an inclusive, dependable, citywide system of aid and relief; in politics, by setting priorities for public policy and for use of tax money to support facilities, agencies, and organizations that aided individuals—in all these arenas, women stretched and even distorted the accepted understanding of the terms *public* and *private*.

Erosion of the traditional delineations compromised, almost automatically, the customary separation of female and male "spheres." Just as, on the frontier, basic needs strained sex roles imposed by a patriarchal agricultural world, so did urban conditions challenge gender conventions, often less from necessity than with opportunity. The "separate spheres," each distinguished by its recipes

Main Street, about 1918. Historic Photograph Collection, Dallas Public Library

of responsibility and appropriateness for women or for men, meshed and blended in unforeseen ways and together, served the functions of building the city and creating urban life.

The record of women's work in Dallas challenges a fond American tradition, that the frontier held great benefits for women. Statistics alone allow little argument with David Potter's observation that cities offered women employment opportunities never available in rural areas.[4] For individuals, Potter was right, but as members of families, farmwomen benefited from their hard work and sacrifices during the period of early settlement. Aside from economic concerns, the frontier's "liberating" effects in Dallas County were temporary and shallow. Whatever their gains in familial wealth and status, female pioneers, like their men, aspired to recreate accustomed ways—to "return to normal." As soon as physical conditions allowed, women resumed their traditional "places" and reared their daughters to be southern ladies, not participants and leaders in community life.

In the context of urban living, the social results of industrialization proved less amenable to preferences and habits. The fundamental changes occurring after 1870 were rooted deeply in the economic base, with its unrivaled power to render age-old customs awkward at best and ultimately, obsolete. When fathers left urban homes for work each day, they altered forever the nature of family life and parental authority. When mothers no longer could grow food in the back-yard, they sought paid employment so as to contribute directly to the family's income or sent their daughters into the workforce. As the family relinquished traditional economic functions to the marketplace, it gained social advantages through the cooperative nature of urban life. In working to improve and expand the resources upon which urban families depended, women changed their own "place" in the community.

Armored against social criticism by an imagined moral superiority, yet shut out of the established dignity of the professions and the recognized authority of public offices, single and married women alike learned to wield power through the doctrines of domesticity and maternalism.[5] The result in Dallas was a contradiction of custom and tradition. Accompanying the institutions, organizations, agencies, and services never before available was a new status for women in the form of meaningful influence over what the community became; a voice in policy decisions and allocation of community resources; and acceptance as arbiters of values for community life and of standards for public behavior.

Cities, and not the frontier, emancipated American women. Often related to women's traditional roles, pressing urban problems drew matrons out of their homes into reform efforts, much as the growing, changing marketplace pulled single women into employment. As Dallas women and men divided and shared, contended and cooperated in the interests and concerns of urban life, the public and the private "spheres" overlapped in new ways, creating the forms of modern urban life.

Notes

Abbreviations

CAH   Center for American History, University of Texas Archives, Austin, Texas

DCD   Dallas City Directory

DFWC   Dallas Federation of Women's Clubs

DHS   Dallas Historical Society, Dallas, Texas

DMN   *Dallas Morning News*

DPL   Dallas Public Library, Dallas, Texas

GD 1878   *General Directory of the City of Dallas for 1878–1879* (Marshall, Tex.: Jennings Brothers, 1878)

GD 1880   *Morrison and Fourmy's General Directory of the City of Dallas for 1880–1881* (Dallas: Herald Printing Co., 1880)

GD 1883   *Morrison and Fourmy's General Directory of the City of Dallas, 1883–1884* (Dallas: Morrison and Fourmy, 1883)

GD 1885   *Morrison and Fourmy's General Directory of the City of Dallas, 1885–1886* (Galveston, Tex.: Morrison and Fourmy, 1885)

GD 1886   *Morrison and Fourmy's General Directory of the City of Dallas, 1886–1887* (Galveston, Tex.: Morrison and Fourmy, 1886)

GD 1888   *Morrison and Fourmy's General Directory of the City of Dallas, 1888–1889* (Galveston, Tex.: Morrison and Fourmy, 1888)

GD 1889   *Morrison and Fourmy's General Directory of the City of Dallas, 1889–1890* (Galveston, Tex.: Morrison and Fourmy, 1889)

GD 1891   *Morrison and Fourmy's General Directory of the City of Dallas, 1891–1892* (Galveston, Tex.: Morrison and Fourmy, 1891)

GD 1893   *Morrison and Fourmy's General Directory of the City of Dallas, 1893–1894* (Galveston, Tex.: Morrison and Fourmy, 1893)

GPO   U.S. Government Printing Office

SMU   Southern Methodist University, Dallas, Texas

TDCDPL   Texas/Dallas History Collection, Dallas Public Library

TFWC   Texas Federation of Women's Clubs

Introduction

1. Most accounts mention Charity Morris (Mrs. Mabel) Gilbert as the first white woman to live in Dallas County. For a few months in 1842, the Gilberts lived on the west side of the Trinity River, several miles south of Bryan's headright, before they left and built their home near the present town of Bonham. Many years passed before the site of the 1842 Gilbert homestead became part of Dallas. See John William Rogers, *The Lusty Texans of Dallas* (New York: E. P. Dutton, 1959), 31. Local historians accept Nov. 1841 as the founding date for Dallas, but sometimes they question the date when Margaret Beeman Bryan actually became the first female resident. One "old-timer" recalled that the Peters Colony agent performed the Bryans' wedding. Later, doubting its legality, they decided to make the eight-day trip by horseback to Bonham and repeat their vows before an ordained minister. Thus, Margaret Bryan may well have resided where Dallas would be several months earlier than her "official" wedding date of Feb. 1843. This account is in "Old Timers Recall Frontier Struggles at Meeting of Dallas County Pioneers," *Dallas Times Herald,* September 27, 1925.

2. Two books have influenced my definition of the stages of Dallas's growth: Henri Pirenne, *Medieval Cities: Their Origins and the Revival of Trade,* trans. Frank D. Halsey (Garden City, N.Y.: Doubleday/Anchor, 1925); and Lewis Mumford, *The City in History: Its Origins, Its Transformation, Its Prospects* (New York: Harcourt, Brace and World, 1961). Contrasts between merchants and farmers in Dallas County brought to mind Pirenne's discussion of the economic characteristics of early medieval towns. Mumford's study suggested the idea of distinguishing towns from cities through their respective functions, and his examination of other aspects of urban life proved useful for identifying the social and cultural elements that marked Dallas's progress from an agricultural village to a country market town and then a commercial city.

3. Size alone does not qualify a place as urban; see Louis Wirth's classic essay, "Urbanism as a Way of Life," *American Journal of Sociology* 44 (1938): 1–24, esp. 2, 5–6, 9–10. Mumford quotation in Mumford, *City in History,* 125; also see 93, 100, 259–88 (esp. 267, 271–73, 279–80), 283–86, 562–64, 571.

4. Jane Bock Guzmán, "Dallas Barrio Women of Power" (M.A. thesis, Univ. of North Texas, 1992); Gilbert Bailón, "Little Mexico: An Enduring Hub of Mexican Culture in Dallas" (senior paper, Univ. of Texas at Arlington, 1991), in Texas/Dallas History Collection, Dallas Public Library; Ethelyn Clara David, "Little Mexico: A Study of Horizontal and Vertical Mobility" (M.A. thesis, SMU, 1936).

5. For a definition of the "public culture," see Thomas Bender, "Wholes and Parts: The Need for Synthesis in American History," *Journal of American History* 73 (June 1986): 120–36, esp. 126–28, 130–33, 135. Perhaps the best statistically based evidence that women had political power before they gained the vote is in Theda Skocpol et al., "Women's Associations and the Enactment of Mothers' Pensions in the United States," *American Political Science Review* 87 (Sept. 1993): 686–701, esp. 687–89, 691, 694–97.

6. On women's building an "infrastructure of community," see Gerda Lerner, "Priorities and Challenges in Women's History Research," *Perspectives: American*

Historical Association Newsletter 26 (Apr. 1988): 17–20, esp. 20; and Robert V. Hine, *Community on the American Frontier: Separate but Not Alone* (Norman: Univ. of Oklahoma Press, 1980), 12–14.

7. E.g., see Kathryn Kish Sklar, "The Historical Foundations of Women's Power in the Creation of the American Welfare State, 1830–1930," in *Mothers of a New World: Maternalist Politics and the Origins of the Welfare State,* ed. Seth Koven and Sonya Michel (New York: Routledge, 1993), 43–93.

8. On the importance of local history, see Mary P. Ryan, "The Power of Women's Networks: A Case Study of Female Moral Reform in Antebellum America," *Feminist Studies* 5 (Spring 1979): 66–85; and Ryan's introduction to *Cradle of the Middle Class: The Family in Oneida County, New York, 1790–1865* (New York: Cambridge Univ. Press, 1981).

9. The classic study of domestic issues in politics is Paula Baker, "The Domestication of Politics: Women and American Political Society, 1780–1920," *American Historical Review* 89 (June 1984): 620–47.

10. On gender, see Joan Wallach Scott, *Gender and the Politics of History* (New York: Columbia Univ. Press, 1988), esp. 28–29; Louise A. Tilly, "Gender, Women's History, and Social History," *Social Science History* 13 (Winter 1989): 439–62, esp. 452; and Nancy F. Cott, *The Bonds of Womanhood: 'Woman's Sphere' in New England, 1780–1835* (New Haven, Conn.: Yale Univ. Press, 1977), esp. 125.

11. Along with Mumford's concept of urban functions, Eric Monkkonen's definition of the modern service city, offered in his *America Becomes Urban: The Development of U.S. Cities and Towns, 1780–1980* (Berkeley: Univ. of California Press, 1988), suggested the interpretive framework for chs. 7 and 8.

12. See Mary P. Ryan, "Gender and Public Access: Women's Politics in 19th-Century America," in *Habermas and the Public Sphere,* ed. Craig Calhoun (Cambridge, Mass.: MIT Press, 1992), 259–88, esp. 267, 271–73, 279–80, 283–86.

13. An example of the usual failure to identify and analyze any but superficial characteristics of social structures is Don H. Doyle, *New Men, New Cities, New South: Atlanta, Nashville, Charleston, Mobile, 1860–1910* (Chapel Hill: Univ. of North Carolina Press, 1990), 220–25. See Rogers, *Lusty Texans,* 180–81.

14. For discussion of the issues raised by separating human activities into private and public, see Diane Willen, "Women in the Public Sphere in Early Modern England: The Case of the Urban Working Poor," in *Gendered Domains: Rethinking Public and Private in Women's History,* ed. Dorothy O. Helly and Susan M. Reverby (Ithaca, N.Y.: Cornell Univ. Press, 1992), 183–98. Also see Michael H. Frisch, *Town into City: Springfield, Massachusetts, and the Meaning of Community, 1840–1880* (Cambridge, Mass.: Harvard Univ. Press, 1972), 48–49. For a provocative discussion of our continuing thralldom to the paradigm of separate spheres, see Judith A. McGaw, "No Passive Victims, No Separate Spheres: A Feminist Perspective on Technology's History," in *In Context: History and the History of Technology: Essays in Honor of Melvin Kranzberg,* ed. Stephen H. Cutcliffe and Robert C. Post, Research in Technology Studies Series, no. 1 (Bethlehem, Pa.: Lehigh Univ. Press; and London: Associated Univ. Presses, 1989), 175–78.

Chapter 1. Agricultural Village and County

1. Mercy Ann Mathis to My Dear Children, June 27, 1858, in Flora Mathis Papers, A3564, DHS.

2. "Old-Timers Recall Frontier Struggles"; Frank M. Cockrell, "A History of Early Dallas," photocopied and bound typescript, 1944, in TDCDPL, pp. 20–21, 30; Rogers, *Lusty Texans*, 19, 49, 52–53.

3. Ruth Myers Cooper, great-granddaughter of John and Emily Beeman, interview by author, handwritten notes, in author's possession, Dallas, Nov. 10, 1977. W. S. Adair, "For 84 Years Scott Beeman Has Lived Here" [memories of Scott Beeman], *DMN*, Oct. 11, 1925. See Rogers, *Lusty Texans*, 30–32; Ray A. Billington, *America's Frontier Heritage* (New York: Holt, Rinehart and Winston, 1966), 74.

4. Quoted in Rogers, *Lusty Texans*, 32.

5. W. S. Adair, "Great Road of Republic of Texas Started from Cabin of John Neely Bryan" [memories of Ed F. Bates], *DMN*, Sept. 10, 1922; Rogers, *Lusty Texans*, 24, 36–37. On the size of Dallas around 1844, John C. McCoy's handwritten autobiography, in Millicent Hume McCoy Papers, TDCDPL; and reminiscences of Mary Elizabeth Armstrong, *DMN*, Sept. 1, 1919.

6. W. S. Adair, "Pioneer Doctors Had a Hard Life" [memories of Dr. D. R. P. McDermett], *DMN*, July 3, 1921; John H. Cochran, *Dallas County: A Record of Its Pioneers and Progress* (Dallas: Arthur S. Mathis, 1928), 131–32. Regarding the limited services available in twentieth-century villages, see Monkkonen, *America Becomes Urban*, 47–48.

7. Catherine Jones (Mrs. George W.) James, "Seventy Years in the Garland, Dallas County, Texas, Area," unbound typescript, 1927, in Nicholson Memorial Library, Garland, Tex., p. 21; Frank M. Cockrell, "History of Early Dallas," 47.

8. W. S. Adair, "Dallas in 1847 Small Village on the Trinity" [memories of Addie Dye McDermett], *DMN*, June 21, 1925. I base my designation of Dallas as a village rather than a town, not upon size of population but rather upon the absence of urban functions, esp. the use of barter more often than money, and the lack of monetary services. On the definition of "town," see Pirenne, *Medieval Cities*, esp. 39–40.

9. For comparison with other frontiers, see Lawrence H. Larsen, *The Urban West at the End of the Frontier* (Lawrence: Regents Press of Kansas, 1978); Gunther Barth, *Instant Cities: Urbanization and the Rise of San Francisco and Denver* (New York: Oxford Univ. Press, 1975); Robert R. Dykstra, *The Cattle Towns: A Social History of the Kansas Cattle Trading Centers: Abilene, Ellsworth, Wichita, Dodge City, and Caldwell, 1867–1885* (New York: Atheneum, 1973); Kenneth W. Wheeler, *To Wear a City's Crown: The Beginnings of Urban Growth in Texas, 1836–1865* (Cambridge, Mass.: Harvard Univ. Press, 1968); Richard C. Wade, *The Urban Frontier: The Rise of Western Cities, 1790–1830* (Cambridge, Mass.: Harvard Univ. Press, 1959).

10. Sam Acheson, "Six Sisters in Love Field's Past," *DMN*, Dec. 16, 1968; *Notable Women of the Southwest: A Pictorial Biographical Encyclopedia of the Leading Women of Texas, New Mexico, Oklahoma, and Arizona* (Dallas: William T. Tandy, 1938), 66–67. On the importance of families in settling the frontier, see John Mack Faragher, *Women and Men on the Overland Trail* (New Haven, Conn.:

Yale Univ. Press, 1979), 33, 144; Julie Roy Jeffrey, *Frontier Women: The Trans-Mississippi West, 1840–1880* (New York: Hill and Wang, 1979), 76; Don H. Doyle, *The Social Order of a Frontier Community: Jacksonville, Illinois, 1825–1870* (Urbana: Univ. of Illinois, 1978), 12, 94–97, 115–18; Jack E. Eblen, "An Analysis of 19th-Century Frontier Populations," *Demography* 2 (1965): 399–413. On Dallas County pioneers, see Blaine T. Williams, "The Frontier Family: Demographic Fact and Historical Myth," in *Essays in the American West: The Walter Prescott Webb Memorial Lectures,* ed. Sandra L. Myres and Harold M. Hollingsworth (Austin: Univ. of Texas Press, 1968), 40–65, esp. 45.

11. On problems experienced by upper-class women on the East Texas frontier, see Joan E. Cashin, *A Family Venture: Men and Women on the Southern Frontier* (New York: Oxford Univ. Press, 1991), 106–107, 112.

12. [U.S. Census Office], *Seventh Census of the United States: 1850* [hereafter cited as *U.S. Census, 1850*] (Washington, D.C.: Robert Armstrong, Public Printer, 1853), 494, 501, 505; [U.S. Department of the Interior], *Population of the United States in 1860* (Washington, D.C.: Robert Armstrong, Public Printer, 1864) 4:472–73, 4:478–79.

13. For evaluation of home production in Dallas County, *U.S. Census, 1850,* 517, 518, 519; Rolla Milton Tryon, *Household Manufactures in the United States: 1640–1860* (Chicago, 1917; reprint, New York: Augustus M. Kelly, 1966), 243–44, 309, 310–11, 370–76, and 313n. On the home as the unit of production and its place within the trade-exchange economy, see Steven Hahn, "The 'Unmaking' of the Southern Yeomanry: The Transformation of the Georgia Upcountry, 1860–1890," in *The Countryside in the Age of Capitalistic Transformation: Essays in the Social History of Rural America,* ed. Steven Hahn and Jonathan Prude (Chapel Hill: Univ. of North Carolina Press, 1985), 179–203, esp. 181–83. On women's work elsewhere in the South, see Julia Cherry Spruill, *Women's Life and Work in the Southern Colonies* (New York: Russell and Russell/Atheneum, 1969), 80–81, 82–83. For comparison with other frontiers, see Everett Dick, *The Sod-House Frontier: A Social History of the Northern Plains from the Creation of Kansas and Nebraska to the Admission of the Dakotas* (Lincoln, Neb.: Johnson Publishing Co., 1954), 237–42.

14. John B. Billingsley, "From Missouri to Texas," typescript, A3637, DHS, pp. 5–6. Billingsley came through Dallas in Dec. 1843 or Jan. 1844 with his parents and five sisters. See Rogers, *Lusty Texans,* 32.

15. On Apr. 23, 1871, John M. McCoy wrote his parents that people in Dallas had been eating fresh vegetables for three weeks, and that farmers considered this to be a late season: in John M. McCoy, *When Dallas Became a City: Letters of John Milton McCoy, 1870–1881,* ed. Elizabeth York Enstam (Dallas: DHS, 1982), 35. On the importance of women's work on the frontier, see Faragher, *Women and Men,* 50–51, 59–61. Faragher's is the most thorough study of the kind and amount of work done by rural women and men in the 19th century.

16. The most complete list of garden vegetables grown in Dallas County is in Alice West Floyd, "Memories," *Elm Fork Echoes* 2 (Nov. 1974): 25; see also, John H. Cochran, *Dallas County,* 16, 30; and Isaac B. Webb, diary and small record book, in the Texas Collection, Fondren Library, SMU. Webb notes that he planted the

family's cabbages and red yams. Kalisk Wolski, *American Impressions,* trans. Marion Moore Coleman (Cheshire, Conn.: Cherry Hill Books, 1968), 182, describes the gardening techniques of Dallas County women. On women's food production on earlier southern frontiers, see Everett Dick, *The Dixie Frontier: A Comprehensive Picture of Southern Frontier Life Before the Civil War* (New York: Capricorn/Knopf, 1964), 288–90; and for wild foods, 287–91.

17. James, "Seventy Years," 3, 12–13. Packing butter in layers of salt to preserve it during the winter apparently was quite common during the 19th century: see Caroline Taylor, "Domestic Arts and Crafts in Illinois, 1800–1860," *Journal of the Illinois Historical Society* 33 (Sept. 1940): 296. And see Floyd, "Memories," 25. For most household tasks, methods on other frontiers resembled those in Dallas County; see Jo Ann Carrigan, "Nineteenth-Century Rural Self-Sufficiency: A Planter's and Housewife's 'Do-It-Yourself' Encyclopedia," *Arkansas Historical Society* 21 (1962): 132–45; Evadene A. Burris, "Keeping House on the Minnesota Frontier," *Minnesota History* 14 (Sept. 1933): 263–82.

18. Susan Anna Floyd Good to John J. Good, Dec. 22, 1861, in *Cannon Smoke: The Letters of Captain John J. Good, Good-Douglas Texas Battery, CSA,* comp. Lester Newton Fitzhugh (Hillsboro, Tex.: Hillsboro Junior College, 1971), 151–52.

19. As late as the 1930s, some women in Dallas continued to garden and raise livestock and fowl for food. Sadye Dupree (Mrs. Cleophus C.) Gee, interview by author, audio cassette and handwritten notes, in author's possession, Dallas, Feb. 10, 1987.

20. On snacks, Floyd, "Memories," 26. A study of farming and southern foods is Sam Bowers Hilliard, *Hog Meat and Hoecake: Food Supply in the Old South* (Carbondale: Southern Illinois Univ. Press, 1972). See Faragher, *Women and Men,* 52–53.

21. Anna Wideman Blair's memories in Kenneth Foree, "Flowers Bloomed for Fifty Years," *DMN,* Oct. 4, 1950; on use of punk, see Mattie Hord Crawford, "The Hord Home" [ca. 1922], manuscript essay, A231, DHS.

22. John H. Cochran, *Dallas County,* 53; Floyd, "Memories," 26; Kenneth Foree, "U.S. Golden Age She Sees as Now" [memories of Anna Wideman Blair], *DMN,* Jan. 18, 1951; Thomas and Rachel Haught Lumney, memories, in *Memorial and Biographical History of Dallas County, Texas* (Chicago: Lewis Publishing Co., 1892), 612. On the age-old importance of cloth making, see Elizabeth Wayland Barker, *Women's Work: The First 20,000 Years: Women, Cloth, and Society in Early Times* (New York: W. W. Norton, 1994). See Dick, *Dixie Frontier,* 283–85.

23. James, "Seventy Years," 21; Telitha Smith (Mrs. D. R. P.) McDermett, "Pages from My Life's Book," manuscript essay [1925], in Mrs. Paul C. Gerhard Papers, A4219, DHS.

24. James, "Seventy Years," 5–6, 11, 13; John H. Cochran, *Dallas County,* 53. Also see W. S. Adair, "Born in Dallas 77 Years Ago, and Still Here" [memories of John D. Beard], *DMN,* Apr. 18, 1926.

25. John H. Cochran, *Dallas County,* 53.

26. Telitha Smith (Mrs. D. R. P.) McDermett, "Pages from My Life"; Foree, "U.S. Golden Age." Philip Lindsley, *A History of Greater Dallas and Vicinity* (Chicago: Lewis Publishing Co., 1909) 1:50.

27. This average holds for two sets of figures: 1,231 children under age 15 and 318

women aged 20–40; and 1,151 children under age 20 and 387 women aged 20–50. Basic figures from *U.S. Census, 1850*, 494–95. Other Texas counties also had surprisingly small pioneer families. Among 1,850 families in Nueces County, the average had 4 children; of 896 families listed in the U.S. Census, only 12 had 10 or more; George M. Blackburn and Sherman L. Richards, "A Demographic History of the West: Nueces County, Texas, 1850," *Prologue* 4 (Spring 1972): 3–20. See Blaine T. Williams, "Frontier Family," 40–65; and Seymour V. Connor, "A Statistical Review of the Settlement of the Peters Colony, 1841–1848," *Southwestern Historical Quarterly* 57 (July 1953): 38–64.

28. Faragher, *Women and Men*, 57–59.

29. Ruth Myers Cooper, interview, Nov. 10, 1977. Mrs. Earl Freeman of Dallas provided genealogical information on the Gilberts.

30. George Jackson, *Sixty Years in Texas* (Quanah, Tex.: Peters Colony Historical Society, 1975), 35–36.

31. W. S. Adair, "Retired Fire Chief Came When Dallas Had 300 People," [memories of Thomas A. Myers], *DMN*, July 10, 1927; and W. S. Adair, "House Warming Was Aftermath of House Raising" [memories of Clint Tucker], *DMN*, Dec. 21, 1930. Charles F. Cretien, "Early Days in Dallas and Oak Cliff," bound typescript, 1963, in TDCDPL, p. 2; George Jackson, *Sixty Years*, 32–33. On the ubiquity of such activities, see Joan M. Jensen, "Cloth, Butter, and Boarders: Women's Household Production for the Market," *Review of Radical Political Economics* 12 (Summer 1980): 14–24, esp. 14–18.

32. Foree, "U.S. Golden Age"; James, "Seventy Years," 5–6.

33. James, "Seventy Years," 5, 19; Webb, diary; Foree, "Flowers Bloomed"; Faragher, *Women and Men*, 57.

34. Adair, "Pioneer Doctors Had a Hard Life"; W. S. Adair, "He Came Here When Dallas Was in Weeds" [memories of George W. Wood], *DMN*, June 5, 1927. Floyd, "Memories," 25, lists herbs; James, "Seventy Years," 2–3, lists wild medicinal plants, as does Mattie Jacoby Allen, "Cultural Patterns Attained in a Primitive Land [Dallas County, 1841–1853]," typescript [ca. 1937], A3724, DHS. On traditional herbal medicine, see Laurel Thatcher Ulrich, *A Midwife's Tale: The Life of Martha Ballard, Based on Her Diary, 1785–1812* (New York: Vintage, 1990), 48–52, 353–64.

35. Willie Flowers Carlisle, comp., "Old Cemeteries of Dallas County," bound typescript, 1946, in DPL. See Faragher, *Women and Men*, 57.

36. Ruth Myers Cooper, interview, Nov. 10, 1977; Foree, "U.S. Golden Age."

37. James, "Seventy Years," 5.

38. Foree, "U.S. Golden Age."

39. Ruth Myers Cooper, interview, Nov. 10, 1977; Frank M. Cockrell, "History of Early Dallas," 23; and Sue Merrifield Bryan's obituary, *DMN*, Jan. 7, 1945.

40. Catharine Coit to John Coit, Jan. 1, Feb. 4, and Feb. 11, 1865, all in Henry C. Coit Papers, A3577, Folder #68, DHS; memories of Anna Wideman Blair, in Stella Vinson Bryant, *Pioneers of Yesteryear: Pleasant Mound "Public" Cemetery and Memorial Park, 1848–1973* (Dallas: Pleasant Mound "Public" Cemetery Association, 1974), 78.

On 19th-century rural labor exchange networks, or the system of "swapping work," see John Mack Faragher, "Open-Country Community: Sugar Creek, Illinois, 1820–1850," in *The Countryside in the Age of Capitalistic Transformation: Essays in the Social History of Rural America*, ed. Steven Hahn and Jonathan Prude (Chapel Hill: Univ. of North Carolina Press, 1985), 233–58, esp. 245–46. On southerners' "habits of mutuality" within the "moral economy" of the pre-market economy, see Robert C. McMath, Jr., "Sandy Land and Hogs in the Timber: (Agri)cultural Origins of the Farmers' Alliance in Texas," in *The Countryside in the Age of Capitalistic Transformation: Essays in the Social History of Rural America*, ed. Steven Hahn and Jonathan Prude (Chapel Hill: Univ. of North Carolina Press, 1985), 205–29, esp. 207. Jonathan Prude, *The Coming of the Industrial Order: Town and Factory Life in Rural Massachusetts, 1810–1860* (New York: Cambridge Univ. Press, 1983), 8, mentions rural New England exchange networks. These are discussed at length in Michael Merrill, "Cash Is Good to Eat: Self-Sufficiency and Exchange in the Rural Economy of the United States," *Radical History Review* 17 (Winter 1977): 42–71.

41. Charles Barker to his mother, Jan. 23, 1853, and Aug. 10, 1859, both in Don Dreesen, "History of Oak Cliff," *Oak Cliff Dispatch-Journal*, May 6–June 1939, bound photocopy, in TDCDPL; *Dallas Herald*, Aug. 10, 1859. Also see J. W. Latimer, "The Wheat Region and Wheat Culture in Texas," in *Texas Almanac for 1859* (Galveston: *Galveston News*, 1859), 64–71. On farmers hauling flour and meal to trade for manufactured goods, W. S. Adair, "Dallas Was an Island in 1866" [memories of Clifton Scott], *DMN*, Sept. 3, 1922; W. S. Adair, "Prairie Chickens Were as Thick as Blackbirds" [memories of George W. Blair], *DMN*, June 8, 1924; George Jackson, *Sixty Years*, 16; W. S. Adair, "Time Was When There Was Not Three Hundred Dollars in Dallas" [memories of W. B. Taylor], *DMN*, Aug. 19, 1923. On the distinction between "exchange transactions" and "real market relations," see Hahn, "Unmaking of Southern Yeomanry," 179–203, esp. 197n 4.

42. On the self-sufficiency of southern farms, see Hahn, "Unmaking of Southern Yeomanry," 179–203, esp. 181, 183–84; and Gavin Wright, *The Political Economy of the Cotton South: Households, Markets, and Wealth in the 19th Century* (New York: W. W. Norton, 1978), 62–74, 164–76, although Wright never analyzes the actual production of foodstuffs. See Faragher, *Women and Men*, 215, regarding the economic independence of pioneers. Faragher cites Rodney C. Loehr, "Self-Sufficiency on the Farm," *Agriculture History* 26 (1952): 37–41; also see Faye E. Dudden, *Serving Women: Household Service in 19th-Century America* (Middletown, Conn.: Wesleyan Univ. Press, 1983), 248n 18.

43. Wolski, *American Impressions*, 191.

44. W. S. Adair, "Dallas Man Tells of Indian Fights" [memories of Henry C. Clark], *DMN*, June 10, 1923.

45. Foree, "Flowers Bloomed"; James, "Seventy Years," 4–5.

46. Floyd, "Memories," 24–27.

47. Ann Patton Malone, *Women on the Texas Frontier: A Cross-Cultural Perspective* (El Paso: Texas Western Press, 1983), 16–17; Forrest McDonald and Grady McWhiney, "The South from Self-Sufficiency to Peonage: An Interpretation," *American Historical Review* 85 (Dec. 1980): 1095–118, esp. 1104–107.

48. *U.S. Census, 1850*, 512.

49. Telitha Smith (Mrs. D. R. P.) McDermett, "The Old Hord Home," manuscript essay, ca. 1922, A231, DHS. Sam Acheson, *Dallas Yesterday,* ed. Lee Milazzo (Dallas: SMU Press, 1978), 27; on Mary Hord, *Memorial and Biographical History,* 158, 172.

50. Floyd, "Memories," 24; Webb, diary, Sept. 14, 1847, and Feb. 11, 1848; John H. Cochran, *Dallas County,* 49. For Rebecca Baker, [Office of the Census], Federal Manuscript Census for Texas, 1850, Dallas County, National Archives and Record Services microfilm, Series M32, Roll 910, p. 99: hereafter, Manuscript Census 1850, Dallas County.

51. On Sarah Gray, Mrs. Barry Miller, "Early Schools in Dallas," manuscript copy of address to DHS student program, November 27, 1941, A41209, DHS; and Evelyn Miller Crowell, "Portrait Sketch of Mamma," manuscript, 1959, DHS. Billington, *America's Frontier Heritage,* 74–81.

52. Webb, diary and small record book; Adolphus Werry, *History of the First Methodist Church* (Dallas: First Methodist Church, 1947), 32, 104. *Notable Women of the Southwest,* 66–67; Anna A. Cochran and Anna Brown Baker, "Memories Live On and On: The Story of the Stained Glass Windows in the Sanctuary of Cochran Chapel Methodist Church, 1856–1976," booklet, Cochran Chapel Methodist Church Archives, copy in author's possession, 1976; for a description of the first church building at Cochran Chapel, Elizabeth Cox Papers, A3643, DHS. See John H. Cochran, *Dallas County,* 17–18, 84; Rogers, *Lusty Texans,* 134; and Don H. Doyle, "Social Theory and New Communities in 19th-Century America," *Western Historical Quarterly* 8 (Apr. 1977): 159–60.

53. On the basic provisions for community and separate property classifications and the contrast between Spanish law and Anglo-American common law, Ocie Speer, *A Treatise on the Law of Marital Rights in Texas* (Rochester, N.Y.: Lawyers Co-Operative Publishing Co., 1916), 86–88, 92–96, 143; Loy M. Simpkins, ed., *Texas Family Law: Speer's Fifth Edition* (San Francisco: Lawyers Co-operative Publishing Co., 1975), 220–22 [Sec. 6:1–14:28], 557–61 [Sec. 15:1–34.8]. Also Kathleen Elizabeth Lazarou, "Concealed Under Petticoats: Married Women's Property and the Law of Texas, 1840–1980" (Ph.D. diss., Rice Univ., 1980). On women's rights under homestead exemption laws, Speer, *Treatise on Marital Rights,* 485–86; 546–48; Simpkins, *Texas Family Law,* 34–38, 63–80 [Sec. 35.1–End]. On Texas origins of the homestead exemption, see Paul Goodman, "The Emergence of Homestead Exemption in the United States: Accommodation and Resistance to the Market Revolution, 1840–1880," *Journal of American History* 80 (Sept. 1993): 470–98, esp. 470, 472, 477–78, 481, 482. On women's right to run for public office in Texas, Speer, *Treatise on Marital Rights,* 96–97; "Women Eligible for Most Offices in Texas," *DMN,* May 3, 1918; Terrence Stutz, "Town Fetes First Female Texas Mayor," *DMN,* July 25, 1993. James W. Paulsen has examined the later interpretation by the courts of the Texas Constitution of 1845 in "Women's Rights and the Antebellum Texas Supreme Court," a paper presented to the Texas State Historical Association meeting in Austin, February 29, 1996.

54. See Suzanne Lebsock, *The Free Women of Petersburg: Status and Culture in a Southern Town, 1784–1860* (New York: W. W. Norton, 1984), 26, for the reluctance of 19th-century southern women to remarry; on men's eagerness to remarry,

see Billington, *America's Frontier Heritage*, 215–16. Expressing the conventional wisdom, John H. Cochran, *Dallas County,* 84, comments that women, unlike men, would do anything to keep their families together.

55. Regarding the importance of marriage and family to both sexes, see Faragher, *Women and Men,* 156–59.

56. George Jackson, *Sixty Years,* 24–26; Mattie Jacoby Allen, "Cultural Patterns"; Adair, "House Warming"; Faragher, "Open-Country Community."

57. *Directory for the City of Dallas for the Year 1875,* arranged and prepared by F. E. Butterfield and C. M. Rundlett (Dallas: Butterfield and Rundlett, 1975) [hereafter cited as *DCD 1875*], 5.

58. Lindsley, *History of Greater Dallas,* 1:45.

59. W. S. Adair, "Education Came Hard to Pioneers" [memories of Judge J. F. Holmes], *DMN,* Nov. 6, 1927; Lindsley, *History of Greater Dallas,* 2:180–91; *Memorial and Biographical History,* 361–62, 509–10, 920. See Sherry L. Smith, "Single Women Homesteaders: The Perplexing Case of Elinor Pruitt Stewart," *Western Historical Quarterly* 22 (May 1991): 163–83; Paula M. Bauman, "Single Women Homesteaders in Wyoming, 1880–1930," *Annals of Wyoming* 58 (Spring 1968): 40–53; and Dick, *Sod-House Frontier,* 129–31. Regarding intermarriage among the pioneers, see, e.g., *Cannon Smoke:* John J. Good's wife, Susan Floyd Good, was related by marriage to four other Dallas County families. On the importance of such stable (and intermarried) families, see Richard S. Alcorn, "Leadership and Stability in Mid-19th-Century America: A Case Study of an Illinois Town," *Journal of American History* 61 (Dec. 1974): 685–702.

60. Regarding Dallas County women's being alone, see *Cannon Smoke,* v; Sarah Horton Cockrell Papers, A4340/A44963, DHS; and Frank M. Cockrell, "History of Early Dallas," 50. On changes in the traditional patriarchal family, see Ryan, *Cradle of Middle Class,* esp. 31–43; and Mary Ryan, *The Empire of the Mother: American Writing about Domesticity, 1830–1860* (New York: Haworth Press, 1982), esp. 18ff.

61. Dr. W. W. Hall, "Health of Farmers' Families," in U.S. Dept. of Agriculture, *Report of the Commissioner of Agriculture for the Year 1862* (Washington, D.C.: GPO, 1863), 462–70; and Faragher, *Women and Men,* 53–54, 62–64. On the economic importance of women's work, see William Cronon et al., "Women and the West: Rethinking the Western History Survey Course," *Western Historical Quarterly* 18 (July 1986): 272–73.

62. John H. Cochran, *Dallas County,* 83. George Jackson, *Sixty Years,* 35–36.

63. See Faragher, *Women and Men,* 51–53.

64. For the incident that gave rise to the Beemans' fears, James J. Beeman, "Memoirs," Dec. 24, 1886, photocopied typescript, in DHS; and Rogers, *Lusty Texans,* 31.

65. For similarities to other frontiers, see Glenda Riley, *The Female Frontier: A Comparative View of Women on the Prairie and the Plains* (Lawrence: Univ. Press of Kansas, 1988); and Wiley Britton, *Pioneer Life in Southwest Missouri* (Kansas City, Mo.: Smith-Grieves Co., 1929), esp. chs. 8 and 9. Chosen at random, descriptions of women's work in other preindustrial times, places, and cultures show striking similarities, regardless of the society's technological level. On women of the Kung Bushmen of the Kalahari, see Richard B. Lee, "What Hunters Do for a

Living, or, How to Make Out on Scarce Resources," in Richard B. Lee and Irven Devore, eds., *Man the Hunter* (Chicago: Aldine Publishing, 1966), 30–48; on Pawnee women of the Great Plains in the 1860s and before, see Gene Weltfish, *The Lost Universe: The Way of Life of the Pawnee* (New York: Ballantine Books, 1965); and on women in late medieval and Renaissance Europe, see Roland Bainton's essay "Katherine von Bora" in *Women of the Reformation in Germany and Italy* (Minneapolis, Minn.: Augsburg Publishing House, 1971), 23–45. Until manufacture and processing of basic goods were established in factories and mills, commercial production, also, lay in the producers' homes, organized through what now is known as the "domestic" or "putting-out" system of manufacture. However lucrative to the merchant-distributor, this arrangement provided necessary goods only in limited quantities, leaving most people to continue supplying their own needs.

66. David M. Potter, "American Women and the American Character," *Stetson Univ. Bulletin* 62 (Jan. 1962): 1–22, esp. 3–6.

Chapter 2. The Country Market Town

1. Jacquelyn Masur McElhaney, ed., "An Antebellum Chronicle: The Diary of Frances Killen Smith," pt. 1, "Girlhood in Dallas, 1857," *Legacies: A History Journal for Dallas and North Central Texas* vol. 1, no. 1 (Spring 1989): 33 (June 23 and 25, 1857). Gregg Cantrell, "Sam Houston and the Know-Nothings: A Reappraisal," *Southwestern Historical Quarterly* 96 (Jan. 1993): 327–44; T. R. Fehrenbach, *Lone Star: A History of Texas and the Texans* (New York: Collier, 1968), 333–35.

2. McElhaney, "Antebellum Chronicle," pt. 1, p. 33 (June 23 and 25, 1857). On American women's participation in public events during the antebellum years, see Mary P. Ryan, *Women in Public: Between Banners and Ballots, 1825–1880* (Baltimore, Md.: Johns Hopkins Univ. Press, 1990); and Virginia Gearhart Gray, "Activities of Southern Women: 1840–1860," *South Atlantic Quarterly* 27 (July 1928): 264–79, esp. 266–71.

3. Nancy McKinney Sayford, *The Latimer Legacy* (n.p.: privately published, 1995), 58, 60, 80–87: Genealogy Collection, Dallas Public Library. The late Joseph B. Latimer recalled that his father called James Wellington Latimer "Uncle Wake."

4. Rogers, *Lusty Texans,* 16, 42, 140. On the value of being a county seat, see Daniel J. Boorstin, *The Americans: The National Experience* (New York: Random House, 1965), 164–67. See Monkkonen, *America Becomes Urban,* on the nature of city charters (214–15) and on incorporation (xii–xiii, 4–5, 111–13).

5. Ads for all these businesses ran in the *Dallas Herald* during Feb.–July 1856, and for the exchange office, in the August and September issues. On 19th-century Texas banking, see Fehrenbach, *Lone Star,* 321–22. For discussion of development of the American middle class—the "middling sort" of the 1850s—in the 19th century, see Stuart M. Blumin, *The Emergence of the Middle Class: Social Experience in the American City, 1760–1900* (New York: Cambridge Univ. Press, 1989); and Cindy Sondik Aron, *Ladies and Gentlemen of the Civil Service: Middle-Class Workers in Victorian America* (New York: Oxford Univ. Press, 1987), esp. 14–17.

6. Regarding the economic base that defines urban life, see Pirenne, *Medieval Cities,* esp. 39–40, 73, 93–95, 98–99, 104, 107–108; and Max Weber, *The City,* trans. and ed. Don Martindale and Gertrude Neuwirth (New York: Free Press, 1958), esp. 49, 66. By 1850, trade and commerce, rather than farming, were the central economic activities in Dallas. As in 1850, U.S. Census reports of 1860 and 1870 failed to distinguish residents of Dallas proper from those of the county, but information about the town's population (see table 1) is available from other sources: *Texas Almanac for 1859,* 211; *Dallas Herald,* Dec. 5, 1860 (for U.S. Census figures); and "Census of the Town of Dallas, 1868," manuscript copy in DHS. Thanks to Jackie McElhaney for calling my attention to this last document. *Dallas Herald,* Nov. 19 and 26, 1870, for census report specific to Dallas; and editorial insert, "Census Report," in *Dallas City Directory and Reference Book, 1873–1874* [hereafter, *DCD 1873–74*] (Springfield, Mo.: Lawson and Edmondson, 1873).

7. *Dallas Herald,* Feb. 16 and Apr. 5, 1856. Frank M. Cockrell, "History of Early Dallas," 47; John H. Cochran, *Dallas County,* 281; Rogers, *Lusty Texans,* 131.

TABLE 1

POPULATION OF DALLAS

1858	430
1860	775
1868	1,299
1870	2,103
1873	7,036 (after arrival of both railroads)
1880	10,358 (U.S. Census)

Sources: *Texas Almanac for 1859,* 211; *Dallas Herald,* Dec. 5, 1860; "Census of the Town of Dallas, 1868," manuscript copy in DHS.

8. Frank M. Cockrell, "History of Early Dallas," 48–54; George H. Santerre, *Dallas' First Hundred Years, 1856–1956* (Dallas: Book Craft, 1955), 3.

9. *Dallas Herald,* Apr. 10, 1858; See Elizabeth York Enstam, "Opportunity versus Propriety: The Life and Career of Frontier Matriarch Sarah Horton Cockrell," *Frontiers* 6 (Fall 1981): 106–14. Also see Sam Acheson, *Dallas Yesterday,* 25, 116, 132.

10. *Dallas Herald,* Jan. 19, 1859; Frank M. Cockrell, "History of Early Dallas," 56–57. On the importance of hotels in antebellum cities, see Boorstin, *National Experience,* 134–47.

11. In 1861, one "old-timer" recalled, the ferry in dry weather was "two flat boats lashed together and reaching from bank to bank, really making a bridge, so that the ferry man had neither to paddle nor to pull in getting people across." W. S. Adair, "Orphaned on Way to Dallas Back in '61, Hill Is One of Three Living Here Ever Since" [memories of W. M. C. Hill], *DMN,* Oct. 24, 1926.

12. Copy of the petition against the bridge, Nov. 25, 1859, in Sarah Horton Cockrell

Papers, A4340/A44963, DHS. W. S. Adair, "Pioneers Balked at Toll Charges" [memories of T. R. Yeargan], *DMN,* Feb. 13, 1921; and W. S. Adair, "When a Toll Bridge Spanned the Trinity at Commerce Street" [memories of S. B. Scott], *DMN,* Dec. 31, 1922. On the speech to the legislature, Ruth Cockrell Wilson, interview by author, handwritten notes, in author's possession, Dallas, Sept. 18, 1977. The charter passed the Senate on Jan. 17 and the House on Feb. 7, 1860. A copy of the bridge charter, dated Feb. 9, 1860, is in Sarah Horton Cockrell Papers, A4340/A44963, DHS. In a last-minute maneuver, opponents attempted to attach an amendment allowing Dallas County three months to build a free bridge before construction of the toll bridge could begin. Like their petition against the charter, it failed. Frank M. Cockrell, "History of Early Dallas," 104–105.

13. *Dallas Herald,* Feb. 9, May 31, and Oct. 4, 1856.

14. Wolski, *American Impressions,* 180.

15. Ibid.

16. W. S. Adair, "Early Days in Dallas" [memories of C. E. Fretz], *DMN,* May 29, 1932; Wolski, *American Impressions,* 191.

17. Charles Barker to his brother, Jan. 23, 1853, in Dreesen, "History of Oak Cliff." For a list of prices in Dallas, John Larkin to Eleanor Hopkins, Jan. 18, 1856, in J. Lee Stambaugh Papers, A58115, DHS.

18. Telitha Smith (Mrs. D. R. P.) McDermett, "Pages from My Life"; Alice West Floyd, "Memories," *Elm Fork Echoes* 2 (Nov. 1974): 26. Ruth Myers Cooper, interview by author, handwritten notes, in author's possession, Dallas, Dec. 15, 1977.

19. *Dallas Herald,* May 25 and Nov. 2, 1859; Lindsley, *History of Greater Dallas,* 1:59–60.

20. *Dallas Herald,* June 1 and July 6, 1859.

21. Information about Maria Bingham is available in [Department of the Interior], Federal Manuscript Census for Texas, 1860, Dallas County, National Archives and Record Services, microfilm, Series M63, Roll 1292, p. 307; and [Department of the Interior], Federal Manuscript Census for Texas, 1870, Series M653, Roll 1581, p. 421: hereafter Manuscript Census 1870, Dallas County. And alphabetical listings in the city directories after 1873, and ads in *Dallas Herald,* esp. issues for Sept. 26, 1856; Jan. 27, Oct. 21, and Nov. 18, 1871; and Dec. 7, 1872.

22. On acceptance of women as teachers, see Kathryn Kish Sklar, *Catharine Beecher: A Study in American Domesticity* (New Haven, Conn.: Yale Univ. Press, 1973), esp. 113, 124–26, 129, 131, 151–59, 180–81; Polly Welts Kaufman, ed., *Women Teachers on the Frontier* (New Haven, Conn.: Yale Univ. Press, 1984), esp. xviii–xix, 2–3; and Anne Firor Scott, "The Ever-Widening Circle: The Diffusion of Feminist Values from the Troy Female Seminary, 1822–1872," in *Making the Invisible Woman Visible,* 64–88 (Urbana: Univ. of Illinois Press, 1984), and in *History of Education Quarterly* 19 (Spring 1979): 3–25.

23. Christie Anne Farnham, *The Education of the Southern Belle: Higher Education and Student Socialization in the Antebellum South* (New York: New York Univ. Press, 1994), esp. 15–17, 37, 49–50, 57, 67–82, 86–89, 91, 103, 111–18; and Steven M. Stowe, "The Not-So-Cloistered Academy: Elite Women's Education and Family Feeling in the Old South," in *The Web of Southern Social Relations: Women, Family, and Education,* ed. Walter J. Fraser et al. (Athens: Univ. of Geor-

gia Press, 1985), 90–106; and Eudora Ramsay Richardson, "The Case of the Women's Colleges in the South," *South Atlantic Quarterly* 29 (1930): 126–39.

24. E.g., Mary A. Mullen's advertisement, *Dallas Herald,* Sept. 21, 1859. On schools in the Masonic Hall, see *Dallas Herald,* Sept. 20, 1856.

25. E.g., ads for Mount Prairie High School, seven miles north of Dallas, and Pleasant View School, three miles east, both in *Dallas Herald,* Aug. 29, 1857; Independence Institute, *Dallas Herald,* Jan. 26, 1859; and Dallas Collegiate Institute, *Dallas Herald,* Aug. 29, 1857.

26. *Dallas Herald,* Aug. 3, Aug. 17, Sept. 21, and Sept. 24, 1859; *Texas Almanac for 1859,* 22.

27. *Dallas Herald,* June 29, 1859.

28. On the Methodist Church, *Memorial and Biographical History,* 319, 323; on Disciples of Christ, materials in the church archives, Central Christian Church, Dallas.

29. *Dallas Herald,* May 10 and July 12, 1856.

30. McElhaney, "Antebellum Chronicle," pt. 1, pp. 32 (June 4, 1857) and 35 (July 17, 1857).

31. *Dallas Herald,* Feb. 23, 1859; Jan. 25 and Apr. 25, 1860. Velma Irene Sandell, "The Effects of the Assimilation of the La Réunion Colonists on the Development of Dallas and Dallas County" (M.A. thesis, North Texas State Univ., 1986), 40.

32. On Juliette Peak, see Acheson, *Dallas Yesterday,* 375. For the tournament, *Dallas Herald,* Nov. 2, 1859; the dog fights, *Dallas Herald,* Sept. 11, 1859.

33. McElhaney, "Antebellum Chronicle," pt. 1, p. 33 (June 26, 1857).

34. On the actress, *Dallas Herald,* Sept. 11 and 21, 1859. On the circus, *Dallas Herald,* Oct. 13, 1859; and for another, McElhaney, "Antebellum Chronicle," pt. 1, p. 33 (June 12, 1857).

35. *Dallas Herald,* Feb. 9, 1856; Rogers, *Lusty Texans,* 134. On the role of voluntary associations in frontier towns, see Doyle, "Social Theory," 151–65, esp. 161–65; on their roles in urban life, see Richard D. Brown, "The Emergence of Urban Society in Rural Massachusetts, 1760–1830," *Journal of American History* 61 (June 1974): 29–51, esp. 30–31, 32, 38–39, 43, 45, 57; and Richard D. Brown, "The Emergence of Voluntary Associations in Massachusetts, 1760–1830," *Journal of Voluntary Action Research* 2 (Apr. 1973): 64–73.

36. For notices that new issues had arrived, *Dallas Herald,* May 24, June 26, July 5, July 26, and Sept. 20, 1856. Rogers, *Lusty Texans,* 134.

37. Farnham, *Education of Southern Belle,* 14. See Laura McCall, "'The Reign of Brute Force Is Now Over': A Content Analysis of *Godey's Lady's Book,* 1830–1860," *Journal of the Early Republic* 9 (Summer 1989): 217–36.

38. For a useful, succinct definition of domesticity, see Barbara Harris, *Beyond Her Sphere: Women and the Professions in American History* (Westport, Conn.: Greenwood Press, 1978). On the cross-class influence of domesticity, see Ruth M. Alexander, "'We Are Engaged as a Band of Sisters': Class and Domesticity in the Washington Temperance Movement, 1840–1850," *Journal of American History* 75 (Dec. 1988): 763–85; and Elizabeth Jameson, "Imperfect Union: Class and Gender in Cripple Creek, 1894–1904," in *Class, Sex, and the Woman Worker,* ed.

Milton Cantor and Bruce Laurie, 166–202 (Westport, Conn.: Greenwood Press, 1977), esp. 180–82. On societal expectations of antebellum wives, see Anne Firor Scott, *The Southern Lady: From Pedestal to Politics, 1830–1930* (Chicago: Univ. of Chicago Press, 1970), 4–79. On the influence of traditional rural community, see Jean E. Friedman, *The Enclosed Garden: Women and Community in the Evangelical South, 1830–1900* (Chapel Hill: Univ. of North Carolina Press, 1985). On domesticity on the 19th-century frontier, see Jeffrey, *Frontier Women*, 9–10; and June O. Underwood, "Western Women and True Womanhood: Culture and Symbol in History and Literature," *Great Plains Quarterly* 5 (Spring 1985): 93–106. On domesticity on the Texas frontier, see Jacquelin S. Reinier, "Concepts of Domesticity on the Southern Plains Agricultural Frontier, 1870–1920," in *At Home on the Range: Essays on the History of Western Social and Domestic Life,* ed. John R. Wunder (Westport, Conn.: Greenwood Press, 1985), 57–70.

39. E.g., Adair, "Early Days."

40. On changes in women's lives, see Gerda Lerner, "The Lady and the Mill Girl," in *The Majority Finds Its Past: Placing Women in History* (New York: Oxford Univ. Press, 1979), 23–24. See Mary P. Ryan, *Womanhood in America: From Colonial Times to the Present* (New York: New Viewpoints, 1975), 43, 165. On women's new authority in the home, see Ryan, *Cradle of Middle Class,* esp. 85, 101; and Ryan, *Empire of Mother,* 17–18, 45–48, 56–59, 118–19, 121–22.

41. McElhaney, "Antebellum Chronicle," pt. 1, pp. 29–35; Jacquelyn Masur McElhaney, ed., "An Antebellum Chronicle: The Diary of Frances Killen Smith," pt. 2, "Courtship and Marriage, 1857–1860," *Legacies: A History Journal for Dallas and North Central Texas* vol. 1, no. 2 (Fall 1989): 4–13.

42. McElhaney, "Antebellum Chronicle," pt. 2, p. 5 (Sept. 6 and Oct. 5, 1857).

43. W. S. Adair, "Saw Herds of Stock Driven Through City" [memories of George Cretien], *DMN,* Sept. 12, 1926.

44. Rogers, *Lusty Texans,* 131. *Cannon Smoke,* v. DCD *1875,* 6. U.S. Works Progress Administration, Texas Writers' Project, Dallas Unit, "Dallas Guide in History" (known as "WPA Guide"), American Guide Series, 1940, photocopy of bound typescript, 87–88, TDCDPL.

45. Telitha Smith (Mrs. D. R. P.) McDermett, "Pages from My Life"; Mattie Hord Crawford, "Hord Home."

46. *DMN,* May 5, 1959; John Henry Brown, *History of Dallas County, Texas, from 1837 to 1887* (Dallas: Milligan, Cornett and Farnham, 1887), 24; *Memorial and Biographical History,* 315. On the Latimer home, memories of Minerva Crutchfield Swindells, "Pioneer of Dallas Celebrates Birthday," *DMN,* Sept. 1, 1912.

47. McElhaney, "Antebellum Chronicle," pt. 1, pp. 32, 34 (May 19, June 4, July 2, 1857), and pt. 2, pp. 5–6 (Aug. 27, Sept. 4, Oct. 12, and Nov. 4, 1857; and Jan. 8, 1858). On the work done by upper-class southern women, see Anne Firor Scott, *Southern Lady,* 27–37.

48. On the exclusivism of fraternal organizations, see Mary Ann Clawson, *Constructing Brotherhood: Class, Gender, and Fraternalism* (Princeton, N.J.: Princeton Univ. Press, 1989); Robert V. Hine, *Community on Frontier,* 133; and Billington, *America's Frontier Heritage,* 97–98. Businessmen and wealthier farmers joined

the Masons, while those less prosperous joined the Odd Fellows, first organized in Dallas in 1854.

49. George Jackson, *Sixty Years,* 33. Such feelings of equality may have resulted, at least in part, from the lack of exclusive, segregated neighborhoods in Dallas; see Blumin, *Emergence of the Middle Class,* 231–40. On economic equality in the first generation on other frontiers, see Faragher, "Open-Country Community," 233–58, esp. 247.

50. Malone, *Women on the Texas Frontier,* 30; Eugene D. Genovese, "American Slaves and Their History," in *In Red and Black: Marxian Explorations in Southern and Afro-American History,* 102–28 (New York: Pantheon, 1969).

51. Minutes, Pleasant View Missionary Baptist Church, Aug. 16, 1863, Pleasant View Missionary Baptist Church Archives, Dallas.

52. *Dallas Herald,* Feb. 25, 1863.

53. John H. Cochran, *Dallas County,* 54.

54. For Dallas County slaveholders, none with more than twenty slaves, Dallas County Tax Rolls for 1860, DHS.

55. Lindsley, *History of Greater Dallas,* 1:64.

56. Kenneth Foree, "Dallas Gunners' Epic," *DMN,* Mar. 3, 1946. After the battle at Pea Ridge, Ark. (called Elk Horn or Elk Horn Tavern by Confederates), Union troops found this flag, never unfurled, lying on the ground; Good, *Cannon Smoke,* 172.

57. Sue Good to John J. Good, Sept. 22 and Dec. 22, 1861, in *Cannon Smoke,* 78, 152.

58. John H. Cochran, *Dallas County,* 87; Lindsley, *History of Greater Dallas,* 1:67; James L. Nichols, *The Confederate Quartermaster in the Trans-Mississippi* (Austin: Univ. of Texas Press, 1964), 19–21; Sandell, "Effects of Assimilation," 56, 80; "Pioneer of Dallas Celebrates Birthday," *DMN,* Sept. 1, 1912; and *Dallas Daily Times Herald,* Aug. 28, 1949.

59. *Dallas Herald,* Nov. 25 and Dec. 20, 1861; Nichols, *Confederate Quartermaster,* 19.

60. *Dallas Herald,* Sept. 11 and 18, 1861; Sue Good to John J. Good, Oct. 6, 1861, in *Cannon Smoke,* 91; also, in *Cannon Smoke:* Sue Good's letters of Sept. 22 (pp. 76–78); Sept. 30 (86–87); and Oct. 4 (88–90); and John J. Good to Sue Good, Oct. 26, 1861 (105). *Dallas Herald,* Sept. 18, 1861.

61. James, "Seventy Years," 11. See Anne Firor Scott, *Natural Allies: Women's Associations in American History* (Urbana: Univ. of Illinois Press, 1991), 68–72.

62. Sue Good to John J. Good, Sept. 22, 1861, in *Cannon Smoke,* 77 and n. 157. W. S. Adair, "Girl Heard Fire Alarm When Dallas Was Destroyed in Summer 1860" [memories of Sarah E. Morton], *DMN,* Aug. 27, 1922.

63. James, "Seventy Years," 11–13.

64. W. S. Adair, "Elm Street Once Trail in Brush" [memories of W. M. McCommas], *DMN,* Aug. 24, 1924. The term "living at home" meant producing the family's foods: Rebecca Sharpless, "Choices Amid Constraints: Cultural Continuity on Early-Twentieth-Century Central Texas Farms" (paper presented at annual meeting of Texas State Historical Association, Austin, Mar. 1, 1996).

65. *Dallas Herald,* Feb. 4 and Feb. 25, 1863; Minutes, Dallas County Commissioners Court, Book C, pp. 155, 156, 188, 197, in Dallas County Records Building.

66. Thomas H. Smith, "Conflict and Corruption: The Dallas Establishment vs. the Freedman's Bureau," *Legacies: A History Journal for Dallas and North Central Texas* vol. 1, no. 2 (Fall 1989): 24–30, esp. 25–27. Smith based his article on Records of the Assistant Commissioner for the State of Texas, U.S. Bureau of Refugees, Freedmen, and Abandoned Land, 1865–1869, National Archives Microfilm, in DPL; see esp. 30nn 5, 10, and 11.

67. Adair, "Dallas Was an Island in 1866."

68. Thomas H. Smith, "Conflict and Corruption," 25–26, 30nn 5, 6, and 7. On Freedmen's Schools in Dallas, Thomas H. Smith, "Conflict and Corruption," 26, has used the Records of the Superintendent of Education for the State of Texas, U.S. Bureau of Refugees, Freedmen and Abandoned Land, 1865–1867, National Archives Microfilm, in TDHDPL. See Barry A. Crouch and Larry Madaras, "Reconstructing Black Families: Perspectives from the Texas Freedman's Bureau Records," *Prologue* 18 (Summer 1986): 109–22, esp. 112–14; and William L. McDonald, *Dallas Rediscovered: A Photographic Chronicle of Urban Expansion, 1870–1925* (Dallas: DHS, 1978), 175–76, 179, 181.

69. On La Réunion, Victor Considerant, *Au Texas* (1854; reprint, Philadelphia: Porcupine Press, 1975); Rondel V. Davidson, "Victor Considerant and the Failure of La Réunion," *Southwestern Historical Quarterly* 76 (Jan. 1973): 277–96; George H. Santerre, *White Cliffs of Dallas: The Story of La Réunion, the Old French Colony* (Dallas: Book Craft, 1955), 53; Eloise Santerre, "Réunion" (M.A. thesis, SMU, 1936); Charles F. Cretien, "Early Days in Dallas," 3; Wolski, *American Impressions,* 173–83, 186–85. On assimilation of the "French colonists," see Sandell, "Effects of Assimilation," 28–43.

70. *Dallas Herald,* Dec. 5, 1860. On mobility in 19th-century Texas, see Susan Jackson, "Movin' On: Mobility Through Houston in the 1850s," *Southwestern Historical Quarterly* 81 (Jan. 1978): 251–82.

71. "Census of the Town of Dallas, 1868," in DHS; *Dallas Herald,* Nov. 19 and Nov. 26, 1870. See Alwyn Barr, "Black Migration into Southwestern Cities, 1865–1900," in *Essays on Southern History Written in Honor of Barnes F. Lathrop,* ed. Gary W. Gallagher, 5–38 (Austin: Univ. of Texas Press, 1980); Melvin J. Banks, "History," in *A Century of Faith, 1873–1973: A Short History of New Hope Baptist Church* (Dallas: New Hope Baptist Church, 1973), 11; special thanks to Mrs. Alvernon King Tripp for loaning her copy.

Chapter 3. Frontier *"Boom Town,"* Inland Distribution Center

1. Catharine Coit to William Coit, Sept. 10, 1873, in Henry C. Coit Papers, A3577, DHS.

2. Rogers, *Lusty Texans,* 125; William L. McDonald, *Dallas Rediscovered,* 21.

3. For the bridge charter, *Laws of the State of Texas* 6 (1870), ch. 27, pp. 545–47.

4. Frank M. Cockrell, "History of Early Dallas," 67–68.

5. John H. Cochran, *Dallas County,* 68.

6. *Dallas Weekly Herald,* Dec. 30, 1871; *DCD 1873–74,* 11. *Dallas Herald,* July 29, 1876; Dec. 8, 1877. On resistance to the tolls, Sarah Horton Cockrell Papers, A4340/A41355, DHS; Adair, "Pioneers Balked at Toll Charges"; W. S. Adair, "Tells Story of Dallas in Saloon Days" [memories of T. R. Best], *DMN,* Jan. 24, 1926; Frank M. Cockrell, "History of Early Dallas," 68–69.

7. John M. McCoy, *When Dallas Became a City,* 45, 64–66; S. G. Reed, *A History of the Texas Railroads* (Houston: St. Clair, 1960), 206, 209, 306, 361–63; and Rogers, *Lusty Texans,* 123–25.

8. W. S. Adair, "Times Were Wild in Young Dallas," *DMN,* Feb. 27, 1921; Adair, "Time Was When There Was Not Three Hundred Dollars"; W. S. Adair, "Wholesale Dry Goods Business in Dallas in Early Times" [memories of Maurice S. Levy], *DMN,* Jan. 1, 1922; Adair, "Early Days." Acheson, *Dallas Yesterday,* 132; William L. McDonald, *Dallas Rediscovered,* 21–23.

9. W. S. Adair, "Salesman Tells of Life 45 Years Ago" [memories of C. E. Dickson], *DMN,* Oct. 2, 1921; W. S. Adair, "Dallas Called Texas Wonder 50 Years Ago" [memories of Wood H. Ramsey], *DMN,* Oct. 4, 1925. On the hide trade, see John Stricklin Spratt, *The Road to Spindletop: Economic Change in Texas, 1875–1901* (Austin: Univ. of Texas Press, 1974), 27.

10. John T. Coit to William Coit, Mar. 17, 1871, noted that farmers were shifting to cotton from wheat; in Henry C. Coit Papers A3577. On economic factors in the growth of cities, see Robert F. Riefler, "Nineteenth-Century Urbanization Patterns in the United States," *Journal of Economic History* 39 (Dec. 1979), 478–508, esp. 963. See L. Tuffly Ellis, "The Revolutionizing of the Texas Cotton Trade, 1865–1885," *Southwestern Historical Quarterly* 73 (Apr. 1970): 478–508, esp. 503–504. On the Todd Mills, see Enstam, "Opportunity vs. Propriety," 106–14, esp. 107; William L. McDonald, *Dallas Rediscovered,* 20–21. On Dallas as a milling center, see Spratt, *Road to Spindletop,* 256.

11. W. S. Adair, "When Dallas Had 7054 Residents," *DMN,* May 1, 1921; Pat Jahns, *The Frontier World of Doc Holliday: Faro Dealer from Dallas to Deadwood* (Lincoln: Univ. of Nebraska Press, 1979), 49; Glenn G. Boyer, ed., *I Married Wyatt Earp: The Recollections of Josephine Sarah Marcus Earp* (Tucson: Univ. of Arizona Press, 1976), 55n 4 and 126n 7; and William L. McDonald, *Dallas Rediscovered,* 24, 26, 28–29.

12. The attitude of the general public may be seen in the sympathetic but patronizing tone of a *Dallas Herald* article, June 5, 1875, reporting the severe injuries of a badly beaten "variety girl." On the few opportunities available for local actresses, see Boyer, *I Married Wyatt Earp,* 18n 12.

13. On the depression's effects in Dallas, John M. McCoy to his mother, Feb. 14, 1875, in John M. McCoy, *When Dallas Became a City,* 131–32; and W. S. Adair, "Forty-six Years Ago in Dallas" [memories of Milton Hickox], *DMN,* Aug. 5, 1923. On nationwide effects, see Robert V. Bruce, *1877: Year of Violence* (Indianapolis: Bobbs-Merrill, 1959), 31; Robert H. Weibe, *The Search for Order, 1877–1920,* American Century Series (New York: Hill and Wang, 1967), 1, 7; Robert L. Heilbroner, *The Economic Transformation of America* (New York: Harcourt Brace Jovanovich, 1977), 106.

14. On rising crime and the "tramps," *Dallas Weekly Herald,* Aug. 15, 1874; Feb. 20, 1875; Sept. 30, 1876; Sept. 15, 1877; Jan. 22, 1878.

15. *Dallas Herald,* Jan. 16, 1875; John M. McCoy, *When Dallas Became a City,* 131.

16. Ads in the *Dallas Herald* and listings in the city directories, first published in 1873, are the only sources for dressmakers and milliners.

17. Marie L. Lamoreaux, "She Served Soup as 'Chaser' to Education," *Dallas Daily Times Herald,* Nov. 22, 1925.

18. Catharine Coit to her sister Sallie [Bunting Falconer], Jan. 22, 1872, in Henry C. Coit Papers A3577; Mary Louise Halbach, "Domesticity in the American South: Catharine Bunting Coit, 1837–1883" (M.A. thesis, Univ. of Texas at Dallas, 1982).

19. Halbach, "Domesticity"; and Coit to her sister Anna [Malloy], June 2, 1873, in Henry C. Coit Papers A3577.

20. Mrs. Barry Miller, "Early Schools in Dallas." All data about Lucinda Coughanour's Select School is from the *Dallas Herald:* e.g., June 25, 1870; Aug. 5 and Sept. 30, 1871; Aug. 11, 1875. See *DMN,* Oct. 1, 1935.

21. R. D. Coughanour's career, too, can be traced through his notices and professional cards in the *Dallas Herald* during the 1870s. On Mar. 3, 1871, John M. McCoy wrote to his parents that Dallas had about thirty-five lawyers, commenting, "Somebody is bound to starve"; in John M. McCoy, *When Dallas Became a City,* 57. On family use of women's earnings, see Tamara K. Hareven, "Modernization and Family History: Perspectives on Social Change," *Signs* 2 (1976): 200–201.

22. For advertisements of teachers, e.g., *Dallas Herald* issues for Aug. and Oct. 1870, and *GD 1878,* esp. 25–26.

23. Originally named the Dallas Female Institute, the college ran ads listing faculty, courses of study, and costs: *Dallas Herald,* Oct. 29, 1870; Sept. 12 and Sept. 26, 1874; Jan. 2 and Aug. 14, 1875. For news stories describing the school's spring examinations, *Dallas Herald,* June 1 and 14, 1877. Also see *To Give the Key of Knowledge: United Methodists and Education, 1784–1976* (Nashville: National Commission on United Methodist Higher Education, 1976), 13, 105, 165–66; and Mira Waller Ewin, "The Old Dallas Female College," *Southern Advocate,* July 4, 1935. A photocopy of Ewin's original manuscript is in DHS.

24. On Lawrence's Commercial College, *GD 1878,* 25 and advertisement between 120 and 121. On Male and Female High School, *Dallas Herald,* Oct. 29, 1870. See Acheson, *Dallas Yesterday,* 334. On final examinations in one local school, Cedar Springs Academy, *Dallas Herald,* July 13, 1872.

25. The sheriff's wife was Margaret I. (Mrs. James E.) Barkley; *Dallas Herald,* Apr. 30, 1870; Apr. 12, 1873; Dec. 4, 1875; Oct. 14 and Nov. 4, 1876. *DCD 1873–74* lists her as running a boardinghouse. The mayor's wife was Maria Hickman (Mrs. Henry S.) Ervay; John M. McCoy, *When Dallas Became a City,* 34, 44, 46, 68–69.

26. Simpkins, *Texas Family Law,* 595–99 [Sec. 15:1–34:8]. On women's legal rights in western states, see Mari J. Matsuda, "The West and the Legal Status of Women: Explanations of Frontier Feminism," *Journal of the West* 24 (Jan. 1985): 47–52.

27. Information about women's occupations is from surveys of DCDs during the 1870s.

28. Tabulation of data from Department of the Interior, Census Office, Federal Manuscript Census Records for Texas, 1880, Dallas County, National Archives and Record Services microfilm, Series T9, Roll 1299: hereafter Manuscript Census

1880, Dallas County. In 1880, 429 black women in Dallas were domestic servants, including laundresses, cooks, housekeepers, and maids; ten were hotel servants; and two were nurses. This census listed a total of 581 women in these occupations; they constituted 68.7 percent of the entire female labor force. On inaccuracies in the reporting of women's employment, see Nancy Folbre and Marjorie Abel, "Women's Work and Women's Households: Gender Bias in the U.S. Census," *Social Research* 56 (Autumn 1989): 545–69.

29. Information about African-American families is from a tabulation of data from the Manuscript census 1870, Dallas County. See Shepard Krech III, "Black Family Organization in the 19th Century: An Ethnological Perspective," *Journal of Interdisciplinary History* 12 (Winter 1982):429–52, esp. 431–32 and n. 5; James Smallwood, "Emancipation and the Black Family: A Case Study in Texas," *Social Science Quarterly* 47 (Mar. 1977): 849–57; Herbert G. Gutman, "Persistent Myths about the Afro-American Family," *Journal of Interdisciplinary History* 6 (1975): 181–220; and Frank F. Furstenberg, Jr., Theodore Hershberg, and John Modell, "The Origins of the Female-Headed Black Family: The Impact of the Urban Experience," *Journal of Interdisciplinary History* 6 (1975): 221–33.

30. *DMN*, Sept. 25, 1923. For other accounts of former slaves who in the 1870s paid for their homes with washing and ironing, *DMN*, Aug. 28, 1949; and C. A. Keating, *Keatings and Forbes Families and Reminiscences of C. A. Keating: A.D. 1758–1920* (Dallas: Privately published, 1920), 172. See William L. McDonald, *Dallas Rediscovered*, 179, 181.

31. On laundresses, *Dallas Herald*, July 9, 1870; Thomas H. Smith, "Blacks in Dallas: From Slavery to Freedom," *Heritage News* 10 (Spring 1985): 18–22, esp. 22.

32. The male/female ratio was calculated from data from the 1873 special census of Dallas, insert in *DCD 1873–74*. Unless otherwise stated, information about the boardinghouses is from DCDs for 1873–74, 1875, and 1878–79.

33. On meals in one Dallas boardinghouse, Mary Alice Peele McCoy to her parents-in-law, Feb. 12, 1874, in John M. McCoy, *When Dallas Became a City*, 126. Aurelia Cockrell Gray described the boardinghouse in Groesbeck, Tex., where she lived soon after her marriage, in letters to her mother, June 5 and June 12, 1871, in Monroe F. Cockrell, ed., "Sarah Horton Cockrell in Early Dallas," photocopied and bound typescript, 1961, in Genealogy Collection, DPL. Boarding remained important well into the 20th century, past the frontier period in Texas and elsewhere; see Jensen, "Cloth, Butter and Boarders," 14–24, esp. 18–21.

34. Grace Deatherage (Mrs. Paul) Taylor, interview by author, handwritten notes, in author's possession, Dallas, July 28, 1977. John M. McCoy to his parents, Dec. 6, 1870 (p. 17), and Apr. 23, 1871 (34); and John M. McCoy to Addie McCoy, Dec. 19, 1871 (46), all in John M. McCoy, *When Dallas Became a City*. See Susan Strasser, *Never Done: A History of American Housework* (New York: Pantheon, 1982), 148, 154, 155; John Modell and Tamara K. Hareven, "Urbanization and the Malleable Household: An Examination of Boarding and Lodging in American Families," *Journal of Marriage and the Family* 35 (Aug. 1973): 470–75, 477–78.

35. John H. Cochran, *Dallas County*, 53–54. In Dallas, Mary Alice McCoy, e.g., raised livestock and bees in her backyard: Cora M. Taggart to her grandmother, Oct. 7, 1877 (p. 141), and John M. McCoy to his mother, Nov. 19, 1877 (143), both

in John M. McCoy, *When Dallas Became a City*. On Jan. 17, 1884, the *Dallas Herald* reported that a woman in town was "hooked" by her cow, although she was not seriously wounded. In older cities, such as Providence, R.I.; Springfield, Mass.; New York City; and Washington, D.C., livestock frequently escaped from their backyard pens. See Monkkonen, *America Becomes Urban*, 40–41 and 252–53n 11.

36. James, "Seventy Years," 16. In *Dallas Herald*, Sept. 24, 1870, H. G. Bohny advertised for butter, eggs, and lard for his bakery and C. C. Jennings for foodstuffs for the Crutchfield House dining room. On garden vegetables, *GD 1880*, 15; John M. McCoy to his parents, Apr. 23, 1871, in John M. McCoy, *When Dallas Became a City*, 34; Jensen, "Cloth, Butter and Boarders."

37. Adair, "Saw Herds of Stock"; Adair, "Early Days"; Adair, "Retired Fire Chief."

38. John M. McCoy to Mary Alice Peele, June 10, 1872 (p. 113); John M. McCoy to his parents, Mar. 26, 1871 (34); John M. McCoy to his parents, n.d. (21) and Dec. 1870 (17), all in John M. McCoy, *When Dallas Became a City*.

39. Unless otherwise stated, data on Ursuline Academy is from "The Annals," Archives of the Ursuline Residence, Dallas. Elizabeth York Enstam, "The 'Adventurous Ursulines': Unlikely Pioneers to a Texas Boom Town," *Heritage News* 12 (Summer 1987): 7–11.

40. *Dallas Herald*, Aug. 27, 1874.

41. *DCD 1875*, 20.

42. The only study of the Dallas water system is M. E. Bolding with Erie H. Bolding, *Origin and Growth of the Dallas Water Utilities* (Temple, Tex.: Privately published, 1981), esp. 9, 11–12, 18–20, 21, in TDCDPL. Adair, "Times Were Wild"; *DCD 1875*, 9.

43. Marie Louise Giles, "Early History of Medicine in Dallas, 1841–1900" (M.S. thesis, Univ. of Texas, Austin, 1951), 130–32, 185–88.

44. Henrietta McCoy Taggart to her parents, Aug. 1, 1877, in John M. McCoy, *When Dallas Became a City*, 136.

45. Taggart to her parents, Nov. 25, 1877 (p. 143), and Feb. 17 and Mar. 1, 1878 (147–50), in John M. McCoy, *When Dallas Became a City*.

46. On the McCoys' arrival in Dallas, John M. McCoy, *When Dallas Became a City*, 159. On family functioning during rural-to-urban migration, see Sally Griffen and Clyde Griffen, "Family and Business in a Small City: Poughkeepsie, New York, 1850–1880," in *Family and Kin in Urban Communities, 1700–1930*, ed. Tamara K. Hareven (New York: New Viewpoints, 1977), 144–63; see Hareven's introductory comments, 2–3, 8, 10, and 13n 4, in the same volume. See also Hareven, "Modernization and Family History," 195–97.

47. Doc Miller, interviews by author, audio cassette, in author's possession, Dallas, Sept. 5 and Sept. 7, 1990.

48. *DCD 1875*. This sample consisted of listings under the letters A–G. Of 193 listings, 41 percent showed business owners and professionals residing in the buildings where they earned their livings. For examples of merchant families who lived in the same buildings where their businesses were, see Adair, "Early Days"; William L. McDonald, *Dallas Rediscovered*, 18.

49. William L. McDonald, *Dallas Rediscovered*, 87, 103–104, 108.

50. On class as segregated experience, see Blumin, *Emergence of the Middle Class,* 231–40.

51. Banks, "History," 11–12. William L. McDonald, *Dallas Rediscovered,* 175, 179; Barr, "Black Migration," 15–38; *African-American Families and Settlements of Dallas: On the Inside Looking Out: Exhibition, Family Memoirs, Personality Profiles and Community Essays,* ed. BDR Editorial Board (Dallas: Black Dallas Remembered, Inc., 1990), 1:23.

52. On several of the European ethnic groups who arrived in the 1870s, see Valentine J. Belfiglio, "Early Settlers in Dallas: A New Life with Old Values," *Heritage News* 10 (Winter 1985–86): 4–7; and special issue on immigrants to Dallas: *Heritage News* 10 (Spring 1985). On how frontier communities dealt with immigration, see Alcorn, "Leadership and Stability," 685–702; Doyle, "Social Theory," 151–65. On the modern city's "nonsharing cultures," see Monkkonen, *America Becomes Urban,* 92–93.

53. William L. McDonald, *Dallas Rediscovered,* 13, 18.

54. On the city ordinances, *Dallas Herald,* June 15, 1872; John M. McCoy, *When Dallas Became a City,* 74–76.

55. On the volunteer fire company, *GD 1878,* 20–21; Acheson, *Dallas Yesterday,* 325. On the street railways, Adair, "Forty-Six Years Ago"; on city service personnel, Adair, "Times Were Wild." See Larsen, *Urban West,* 58, 73, 84, 87.

56. Lindsley, *History of Greater Dallas,* 1:109. John M. McCoy to his parents, May 11, 1873, in John M. McCoy, *When Dallas Became a City,* 104; W. S. Adair, "Kidd Springs Land Open in Early Days" [memories of Wilber M. Kidd], *DMN,* Sept. 21, 1924.

57. *DCD 1873–74,* 14.

58. W. S. Adair, "Dallas' First 'Opera House' Opened in 1873," *DMN,* Mar. 4, 1923; W. S. Adair, "Dallas Has Seen the Time When Food Was To Be Had for Asking," *DMN,* Oct. 23, 1921.

59. *Dallas Herald,* May 18, 1878; Lindsley, *History of Greater Dallas,* 1:111.

60. *Dallas Herald,* Dec. 18, 1875; Jan. 15, 1876. See Elisabeth Griffith, *In Her Own Right: The Life of Elizabeth Cady Stanton* (New York: Oxford Univ. Press, 1984), 165.

61. *Dallas Herald,* Dec. 18, 1875; Mar. 18, 1876.

62. Sarah Cockrell to Aurelia Cockrell, Aug. 28, Oct. 16, Oct. 27, Nov. 12, Nov. 17, and Nov. 28, 1870; and Sept. 3 and Sept. 4, 1871: all in Monroe F. Cockrell, "Sarah Horton Cockrell in Early Dallas."

63. Sarah Cockrell to R. B. Fulkerson, Aug. 28 and Sept. 2, 1870; Sarah Cockrell to Aurelia Cockrell, Aug. 6, Aug. 18, and Oct. 27, 1870: all in Monroe F. Cockrell, "Sarah Horton Cockrell in Early Dallas." Frank M. Cockrell, "History of Early Dallas," 37–38.

64. *Dallas Herald,* Oct. 14, 1876. The editor had visited at random 16 businesses owned and operated by women. Fifteen were dressmaking and millinery shops, the other a mattress manufacturing firm whose owner employed "some six to ten women," as well as her son. With his estimate of 1,500, the editor may well have been somewhat dazzled by the employed women, for, in a population of more than 10,000, the census lists only 838 women of both races working for wages. Tabulations of data from manuscript census 1880, Dallas County. On the other

hand, before 1910 (and, some scholars say, afterwards, too) the census takers tended to ignore all but the most obviously employed women, although they recorded roughly twice as many as the DCDs. On problems with the decennial U.S. censuses, see Valerie Kincaide Oppenheimer, *The Female Labor Force in the United States: Demographic and Economic Factors Governing Its Growth and Changing Conditions,* Population Monograph Series, Number 5 (Westport, Conn.: Greenwood Press, 1970), 151; Robert W. Smuts, "The Female Labor Force: A Case Study in the Interpretation of Historical Statistics," *Journal of the American Statistical Association* 55 (Mar. 1960): 71–79.

65. Sarah Horton Cockrell Papers, A4340/A43301, DHS. John M. McCoy, *A Brief History of the First Presbyterian Church, Dallas* (Dallas: Session of the First Presbyterian Church, 1914).

66. Lucinda (Mrs. W. L.) Williams, *Golden Years: An Autobiography* (Dallas: Baptist Standard Publishing Co., 1921), 85ff.; Mary Carter Toomey, "Woman's Influence Shown Behind 'Every Fine Thing'" [memories of Lucinda (Mrs. W. L.) Williams], *DMN,* Jan. 26, 1930; and Leon McBeth, *The First Baptist Church of Dallas: Centennial History, 1868–1968* (Grand Rapids, Mich.: Zondervan, 1968), esp. 19–20, 25–26, 28, 29, 33, 35, 45, 49, 67–68.

67. Donald G. Mathews, *Religion in the Old South* (Chicago: Univ. of Chicago Press, 1977), 47, 67–79, 89–91, 101–103, 112–17, esp. 110; Ryan, *Cradle of Middle Class,* 52–54; Werry, *History of First Methodist,* 32, 51, 104.

68. Constitution of the Ladies' Industrial Society of the First Presbyterian Church of Dallas, Texas, 1876, in Archives, First Presbyterian Church, Dallas. Mrs. Gross R. Scruggs, comp., "Ladies' Industrial Society of the First Presbyterian Church, Dallas, Texas," minutes and clippings from the society's scrapbook, in Mrs. J. W. Blake Papers, A6040, DHS; and *Dallas Herald,* May 6, 1876. John M. McCoy, *First Presbyterian Church;* Werry, *History of First Methodist,* 38, 52–53, 124–25; and McBeth, *First Baptist Church,* 67. Also W[oman's] M[issionary] U[nion] History of the First Baptist Church, Dallas, Texas (Dallas: Woman's Missionary Union, [1953]), p. 7, in DPL.

69. Jan. 22, 1876.

70. John H. Cochran, *Dallas County,* 141–45; George Jackson, *Sixty Years,* 33.

Chapter 4. The Young Commercial City

1. On women's organizations in the 1880s, *GD 1880,* 43, 47; *GD 1885,* 50–53; and *GD 1889,* 53, 55, 56–57. On the roles of clubs and societies in new communities, see Walter S. Glazer, "Participation and Power: Voluntary Associations and the Functional Organization in Cincinnati in 1840," *Historical Methods Newsletter* 5 (Sept. 1972): 151–68, esp. 165–66, and 168n 24. On the boundaries and definitions of the public and the private, see Sara Evans, "Women's History and Political Theory: Toward a Feminist Approach to Public Life," in *Visible Women: New Essays on American Activism,* ed. Nancy A. Hewitt and Suzanne Lebsock (Urbana: Univ. of Illinois Press, 1993), 119–39, esp. 121–30.

2. McBeth, *First Baptist Church,* 350–52.

3. Patricia R. Hill, *The World Their Household: The American Woman's Home*

Mission Movement and Cultural Transformation, 1870–1920 (Ann Arbor: Univ. of Michigan Press, 1985), esp. 3–8, 13–14, 23–24, 40–41, 83–84, 102, 108–109, and 195n1; John Patrick McDowell, *The Social Gospel in the South: The Woman's Home Mission Movement in the Methodist Episcopal Church, South, 1886–1939* (Baton Rouge: Louisiana State Univ. Press, 1982), 9–11; and Joan Jacob Brumberg, "Zenanas and Girlless Villages: The Ethnology of American Evangelical Women, 1870–1910," *Journal of American History* 69 (Sept. 1982): 350–52.

4. On organizing the Dallas Union, *Union Signal*, Aug. 27, 1885, CAH; and *DMN*, Feb. 9, June 9, July 12, 1886. On newsboys' home, *DMN*, Feb. 1, 1893; on "rest cottage" at State Fair, *DMN*, Sept. 9, 1895; on "working girls' home," *DMN*, Apr. 16, 1913. Jacquelyn Masur McElhaney, "Childhood in Dallas, 1870–1900" (M.A. thesis, SMU, 1962), 51–52; *Dallas Daily Times Herald*, Jan. 27, 1893; *DMN*, Apr. 16, 1913. In 1917–18, the Dallas unions sold 560 subscriptions to this publication, which implies a good deal more sympathy for WCTU goals than membership figures in DCD might indicate; see *Texas White Ribbon*, May 1914 and Feb. 1920, copy in Rockwell Brothers Papers, CAH. Thanks to Judith N. McArthur for these notes. On political work by the Texas WCTU, Judith N. McArthur, "Motherhood and Reform in the New South: Texas Women during the Progressive Era" (Ph.D. diss., Univ. of Texas at Austin, 1992), esp. ch. 1. On history of national WCTU, see Ruth Bordin, *Woman and Temperance: The Quest for Power and Liberty, 1873–1900* (Philadelphia: Temple Univ. Press, 1982). On the Texas organization, May Harper Baines, *A Story of Texas White Ribboners* (N.p.: N.p., 1935), 23. On WCTU's influence on American women's public roles, see Jack S. Blocker, Jr., "Separate Paths: Suffragists and the Women's Temperance Crusade," *Signs* 10 (Spring 1985): 460–76, esp. 464, 471–72, 475.

5. On the socioeconomic characteristics of the clubwomen, see Patricia R. Hill, *World Their Household*, 55–56; on the different inclinations of different groups of women, see Nancy A. Hewitt, *Women's Activism and Social Change: Rochester, New York, 1822–1872* (Ithaca, N.Y.: Cornell Univ. Press, 1984), esp. 22–23; and Karen J. Blair, *The Clubwoman as Feminist: True Womanhood Redefined, 1868–1914* (New York: Holmes and Meier, 1980), 63–64.

6. On American women's clubs through the 19th century, see Karen J. Blair, *Clubwoman as Feminist*, 7–13, 21–25, 50, 52–55, 57–58, 61, 62. On southern women's clubs, see Anne Firor Scott, "The 'New Woman' in the New South," in *Making the Invisible*, 216–17, 219, and in *South Atlantic Quarterly* 61 (Autumn 1962): 471–82; and Anne Firor Scott, *Southern Lady*, 150–63. On the Auto-Biological Society of Galveston, "Pauline Periwinkle" column, *DMN*, Oct. 18, 1897.

7. Minutes, Pearl Street Reading Club, in John Henry Brown Papers, CAH.

8. *Dallas Weekly Herald*, June 2, 1881; on public library, *GD 1885*, 64; *GD 1889*, 58.

9. A private party with musical performances by guests is described in *DMN*, Mar. 17, 1886. On the founding of the Musicale, *DMN*, July 27, 1919. For descriptions of regular Musicale meetings, *DMN*, Nov. 24 and Dec. 8, 1890; May 22, 1902; and Jan. 11, 1907; and several unidentified, undated clippings, probably from the "society" publication *Beau Monde*, in Mrs. Jules Schneider Scrapbook, A3872, DHS.

10. *Dallas Times Herald* Aug. 28, 1949; *DMN*, Feb. 28, 1939; and Oct. 1, 1924;

Who's Who of the Womanhood of Texas (Fort Worth: TFWC, 1923), 140. On the Bernhardt feud, see A. C. Greene, *A Place Called Dallas: The Pioneering Years of a Continuing Metropolis* (Dallas: Dallas County Heritage Society, 1975), 61. In 1879, when he first came to Dallas, Jules Schneider was president of Schneider and Davis Wholesale Grocery Co. and of Consolidated Street Railway Co. By 1882, he was president of the Dallas Gas and Fuel Co.; by 1895, he also was vice-president of the City National Bank: Acheson, *Dallas Yesterday*, 334, 370–71.

11. Constitution and By-laws, and Minutes 1892, Dallas Shakespeare Club, in DHS; on the club's founding, *DMN*, Jan. 29, 1886. Standard Club Record Book and Scrapbook, A6250, DHS. Megan Seaholm, "Earnest Women: The White Woman's Club Movement in Progressive Era Texas, 1880–1920" (Ph.D. diss., Rice Univ., 1988), pt. 1, pp. 208–11; Michael V. Hazel, "Dallas Women's Clubs: Vehicles for Change," *Heritage News* 11, no. 1 (Spring 1986): 18–21.

12. On the Chautauqua Literary and Scientific Club (later Pierian Club), *Dallas Social Directory, 1900–1901,* comp. Mrs. Ora Adams (Dallas: John P. Worley, 1900), 43–44; Pierian Club Yearbook, 1903–1904, in DHS. On the Quaero Club, *DMN*, Oct. 30, 1935; *Red Book of Dallas, 1895–96* (Dallas: Holland Brothers Publishing, 1895; reprint, A. H. Belo Corp., 1966), 26–27; and *Social Directory, 1900–1901,* 46–47. Mrs. E. A. DeWitt, "History of the Browning Study Club," typescript pamphlet [ca. 1942], in DHS, p. 2.

13. Leon Harris, *Merchant Princes: An Intimate History of Jewish Families Who Built Great Department Stores* (New York: Harper and Row, 1979), 157–66, esp. 165; William L. McDonald, *Dallas Rediscovered*, 107–109. On the paper dolls, Hazel McCarley Winterbauer, interview by author, handwritten notes, in author's possession, Dallas, Mar. 29, 1978.

14. *DMN*, Nov. 2, 4, and 7, 1898. On raising money for Baptist orphanage, *DMN*, Oct. 16, 1893; on the Woman's Home, unidentified clipping in Schneider Scrapbook, A3872, DHS. See Ruthe Winegarten and Cathy Schechter, *Deep in the Heart: The Lives and Legends of Texas Jews: A Photographic History* (Austin: Eakin Press, 1990), 51.

15. On the appearance of a social elite in new cities and towns, see Wade, *Urban Frontier*, 203, 207–209. William L. McDonald, *Dallas Rediscovered*, 39.

16. For contrast, see Elizabeth Hayes Turner's discussion of the elite in the older port city of Galveston in, "Women, Religion, and Reform in Galveston, 1880–1920," in *Urban Texas: Politics and Development*, ed. Char Miller and Heywood T. Sanders (College Station: Texas A&M Univ. Press, 1990), 77–79. On the importance of a "core" of stable families in a frontier community, see Doyle, "Social Theory," 151–65; Alcorn, "Leadership and Stability," 685–702.

17. For definition of "middle class," see Blumin, *Emergence of the Middle Class*, esp. 231–32, 247, 249; and Stuart M. Blumin, "The Hypothesis of Middle-Class Formation in 19th-Century America: A Critique and Some Proposals," *American Historical Review* 90 (Apr. 1985): 299–338, esp. 311–12. The presence of a middle class long has been recognized as one of the basic characteristics of an urban place. In Europe, the earliest middle class consisted of merchants who developed the trade and commerce that distinguished the towns emerging within the feudal system; see Pirenne, *Medieval Cities*, 93–119. On streets forbidden to Dallas "la-

dies," Rogers, *Lusty Texans,* 140, 145. Carolyn Bruchen, in "Manners and Morals: Women and Etiquette of the City, 1825–1860," a paper presented to the Fourth Southern Conference on Women's History, Charleston, S.C., June 14, 1997, has examined the development of a special etiquette for "ladies" to use in navigating the shoals of urban public spaces.

18. On women's roles in creating the middle class, see Blumin, *Emergence of the Middle Class,* 237–38; Ryan, *Cradle of Middle Class.* On women's roles in creating middle-class "sensibility" and lifestyle, see Elaine S. Abelson, *When Ladies Go A-Thieving: Middle-Class Shoplifters in the Victorian Department Store* (New York: Oxford Univ. Press, 1989); and Karen Halttunen, *Confidence Men and Painted Women: A Study of Middle-Class Culture in America, 1830–1870* (New Haven, Conn.: Yale Univ. Press, 1982). William L. McDonald, *Dallas Rediscovered,* chs. 4–7, includes photographs and descriptions of the homes over which the middle- and upper-class matrons presided. On the etiquette of "calling," *Red Book of Dallas, 1895–96,* 5, 7, 9.

19. On southerners' slow pace in developing a "women's culture," see Friedman, *Enclosed Garden.* Also see Hareven, "Modernization and Family History," 198–200.

20. Hareven, in the introduction to her *Family and Kin,* 6, notes that many who were new to city life retained "previous traditions" in family economic matters. Similarly, some immigrants neglected (or were unable) to develop ways to take advantage of urban living.

21. On the presence of a "women's culture" in Galveston, Elizabeth Hayes Turner, "Women, Religion, and Reform," 86.

22. On the importance of a "coherent internal social structure" for a city's development, see David R. Johnson, "Frugal and Sparing: Interest Groups, Politics, and City Building in San Antonio, 1870–85," in Char Miller and Sanders, *Urban Texas,* 34–36. On women's prominence in establishing "social network and infrastructures," see Lerner, "The Challenge of Women's History," *Majority Finds Its Past,* esp. 179. The concept of "women's culture" is, like domesticity and the "cult of true womanhood," an interpretive cornerstone of U.S. women's history. For basic definitions of the concept, see Linda K. Kerber, "Separate Spheres, Female Worlds, Woman's Place: The Rhetoric of Women's History," *Journal of American History* 75 (June 1988): 9–39, esp. 14–18; and Carol Lasser, "'Let Us Be Sisters Forever': The Sororal Model of 19th-Century Female Friendship," *Signs* 14 (Autumn 1988): 158–81. On the sentiments of "sisterhood," see Carroll Smith-Rosenberg, "The Female World of Love and Ritual: Relations Between Women in 19th-Century America" in *Disorderly Conduct: Visions of Gender in Victorian America* (New York: Oxford Univ. Press, 1985), 53–76; Keith E. Melder, *Beginnings of Sisterhood: The American Woman's Rights Movement* (New York: Schocken Books, 1977), esp. 30–48; Cott, *Bonds of Womanhood,* esp. ch. 1. See Carolyn Forrey, "The New Woman Revisited," *Women's Studies* 2 (1974): 37–56.

23. For formation of new communities, see Robert V. Hine, *Community on Frontier,* esp. 18, 22, 25–31. For a succinct discussion of major sociological theories regarding community in urban places, see Ira Katznelson, "Reflections on Space and the City," in *Power, Culture, and the City: Essays on New York City,* ed. John

Hull Mollenkopf (New York: Russell Sage Foundation, 1988), 285–300, esp. 299.

24. On the concept of "cultural spheres" in American cities after 1870, see Neil Harris, *Cultural Excursions: Marketing Appetites and Cultural Tastes in Modern America* (Chicago: Univ. of Chicago Press, 1990), 24. On historical changes in community, see Thomas Bender, *Community and Social Change in America* (New Brunswick, N.J.: Rutgers Univ. Press, 1978), esp. 6–10; Roland L. Warren, *The Community in America* (Lanham, Md.: Univ. Press of America, 1978).

25. On May 22, 1884, the *Dallas Weekly Herald* published a total of 13 cases for the week; on May 4, 1886, the *DMN* listed 5 for the previous day. For a study of one city, see Elaine Tyler May, *Great Expectations: Marriage and Divorce in Post-Victorian America* (Chicago: Univ. of Chicago Press, 1980), esp. ch. 2. On increased divorce nationwide, see William L. O'Neill, *Divorce in the Progressive Era* (New Haven, Conn.: Yale Univ. Press, 1967). On the suicides, *Dallas Weekly Herald,* Jan. 5, 1881, and Jan. 12, 1882; *DMN,* Oct. 9, 1885, and July 12, 1886.

26. *GD 1888,* 2–3, 4. On housing shortage, *Dallas Weekly Herald,* Feb. 1882 issues and esp. Mar. 15, 1883; on "tramps," *Dallas Weekly Herald,* Nov. 13, 1884; on city ordinances to deal with the problems, McElhaney, "Childhood in Dallas," 47.

27. McElhaney, "Childhood in Dallas," 48–50, 53–54.

28. Ibid. On programs elsewhere, see Michael B. Katz, *In the Shadow of the Poorhouse: A Social History of Welfare in America* (New York: Basic Books, 1986), 51–52.

29. *Dallas Daily Times Herald,* Jan. 27, 1893.

30. *Dallas Weekly Herald,* Nov. 17, 1881; June 29, 1882; Apr. 5, 1883; June 11 and Nov. 21, 1885; Mar. 12, 1886.

31. Minutes, Dallas German Ladies Aid Society, in TDCDPL. *Dallas Clubwoman* 2 (Oct. 16, 1909): 3, in DHS. Regarding ethnic diversity, special issue of *Heritage News* 10, no. 1 (Spring 1985); and Valentine J. Belfiglio, "Early Italian Settlers in Dallas: A New Life with Old Values," *Heritage News* 10, no. 4 (Winter 1985–86): 4–7. On Buckner Home, *DMN,* Jan. 1, 1907.

32. McElhaney, "Childhood in Dallas," 39, 24–43.

33. William Mumford to the Lady Managers of the Charity Ball, Mar. 13, 1886, in Mrs. E. H. Cary Papers, A5743, DHS; *DMN,* Mar. 2, 10 and 11, 1886.

34. *DMN,* Mar. 17 and 29, 1886.

35. Numerous clippings about the Woman's Home are in the Schneider Scrapbook, A3872, DHS. *DMN,* Aug. 17 and Sept. 8, 1886; Jan. 9, Aug. 8, and Aug. 30, 1895; Nov. 22, 1901. Schneider Scrapbook also includes clippings describing Ladies' Musicale fundraising recitals. On the home's officers, *GD 1893.* McElhaney, "Childhood in Dallas," 40.

36. *Dallas Times Herald,* June 2, 1891; Jan. 18, 1897; May 29, 1898; Feb. 3, 1899; *DMN,* Apr. 23 and Oct. 4, 1894; Jan. 3, Feb. 16, and Mar. 7, 1895; Jan. 5, 1900; Dec. 4, 1901. Thanks to Jackie McElhaney for calling my attention to these sources. *GD 1893,* 68; *Memorial and Biographical History,* 305; Lindsley, *History of Greater Dallas,* 1:201.

37. *Round Table* 1 (May 1889): 15, 18, in TDCDPL; and *GD 1888,* 55.

38. *GD 1889*, 60, 102. "The Woman's Exchange of Texas, Austin, Texas," pamphlet, n.d., in CAH. See Lucy M. Salmon, "The Woman's Exchange: Charity or Business?" *Forum* 13 (1892): 394–406; Sheila M. Rothman, *Woman's Proper Place: A History of Changing Ideals and Practices, 1870 to the Present* (New York: Basic Books, 1978), 86–87. On Aug. 7, 1919, a second Woman's Exchange opened in Dallas: *DMN*, Aug. 3, 1919.

39. Acheson, *Dallas Yesterday*, 374–76; *Christian Courier*, June 27, 1889; documents and misc. news clippings in the Juliette Fowler Homes Archives, Dallas. Also *GD 1893*, 68.

40. For the original, classic definition of domesticity and "true womanhood," see Barbara Welter, "The Cult of True Womanhood: 1800–1860," in *Dimity Convictions: American Women in the 19th Century* (Athens, Ohio: Ohio Univ. Press, 1976), 21–41.

41. On women's organization memberships in the 1880s, *GD 1880*, 43, 47, and *GD 1889*, 53, 55, 56–57.

42. Dallas County Tax Rolls for 1880, in DPL. See Pirenne, *Medieval Cities*, esp. 39–40, 73, 93–95, 98–99, 104, 107–108.

43. By 1890, total bank clearings were eight times larger than in 1887, as seven banks prospered alongside thirty investment agencies and eight building and loan companies. *GD 1891*, 6; *GD 1889*, 4. On building and loan associations, *GD 1886*, 49. See Spratt, *Road to Spindletop*, 10, 127–33; Avery Luvere Carlson, *A Monetary and Banking History of Texas: From the Mexican Regime to the Present Day, 1821–1929* (Fort Worth: Fort Worth National Bank, 1930), esp. 10, 21–39.

44. Department of the Interior, Census Office, *Report on Manufacturing Industries in the U.S. at the 11th Census: 1890* [hereafter *11th U.S. Census, 1890*], vol. 2, pt. 2: *Statistics of Cities* (Washington, D.C.: GPO, 1895), 174, 176. Also U.S. Dept. of Commerce and Labor, Bureau of the Census, *Abstract of the 12th Census of the United States* (Washington, D.C.: GPO, 1902), 353; and U.S. Dept. of Commerce and Labor, Bureau of the Census, *Census Reports*, vol. 8, *12th Census of the United States, 1900* [hereafter *12th U.S. Census, 1900*]: *Manufactures*, pt. 2: *States and Territories* (Washington, D.C.: GPO, 1902), 876–77. Also *GD 1880*, 10–20; Spratt, *Road to Spindletop*, 254, 268; and William L. McDonald, *Dallas Rediscovered*, 21, 23.

45. "Dallas, Dallas County, Texas," in *Miscellaneous Documents of the House of Representatives for the 2d Session of the 47th Congress, 1882–83*, pt. 19 (Washington, D.C.: GPO, 1885): 311–14. The classic definition of the commercial basis for cities is Pirenne, *Medieval Cities*. William L. McDonald, *Dallas Rediscovered*, 23, 30, 76; and Ronald L. Davis and Harry D. Holmes, "Introduction—Studies in Western Urbanization," *Journal of the West* 13 (July 1974): 1–5.

46. Tabulation, not sampling, from Manuscript Census 1880, Dallas County; and survey of *GD 1880*. Almost 30 percent of all employed African-American women in Dallas were married, but of the wage-earning white women, only 16 percent were married. For comparison with other southern areas, see Elyce Rotella, *From Home to Office: United States Women at Work, 1870–1930*, Studies in American History and Culture, no. 2 (Ann Arbor, Mich.: UMI Research Press, 1981), 11.

On conditions under which women worked, see U.S. Bureau of Labor, *4th Annual Report of the Commissioner of Labor, 1888* (Washington, D.C.: GPO, 1889). On patterns of women's employment in western cities such as Denver, Kansas City, and San Francisco, see Joan M. Jensen and Darlis A. Miller, "The Gentle Tamers Revisited: New Approaches to the History of Women in the American West," *Pacific Historical Review* 49 (May 1980): 211.

47. In 1880, of 23 dressmakers, 5 were shop owners who hired 11 dressmakers, and 7 others "took in" sewing at home. Of the 120 listed in 1890, 12 were shop owners, 73 were hired by the shops and large dry goods stores, and 75 were self-employed. Dressmakers and milliners increased from 23 in 1880 to 120 by 1889–90, boardinghouse keepers from 11 in 1880 to 94 in 1889–90. Unless stated, these occupations were listed in DCDs for 1883–84, 1886–87, 1889–90, and in Manuscript Census 1880, Dallas County. On the contrast between Dallas women's jobs and those elsewhere, see Rotella, *Home to Office*, 65, 103. Women elsewhere in the U.S., too, benefited from increasing specialization within occupations that were related to housework and therefore socially acceptable; see Alice Kessler-Harris, *Out to Work: A History of Wage-Earning Women in the United States* (New York: Oxford Univ. Press, 1982), esp. 141. Since a federal manuscript census is lacking for 1890, the DCDs are the only sources available for tracking change in women's employment between 1880 and 1890. As a general rule, the DCD for any given year identified only about half the total number of employed women, and its listings concentrated upon employees and owners of commercial establishments rather than those in domestic service.

48. Tabulations from Manuscript Census 1880, Dallas County. For the census years after 1865, the numbers of employed black women elevated the percentages of women in the southern labor force, making the figures similar to those for industrialized cities of the North; see Claudia Goldin, "Female Labor Force Participation: The Origin of Black and White Differences, 1870–1880," *Journal of Economic History* 37 (Mar. 1977): 87–112.

49. *GD 1889*, 259, 311.

50. On teachers in the city's public schools, Minutes, Board of Education, City of Dallas, 1:2, 1:18, 1:153; *GD 1880*, 37; *GD 1883*, 65–66. Walter J. E. Schiebel, *Education in Dallas: Ninety-wo Years of History, 1874–1966* (Dallas: Dallas Independent School District, 1966), 2–6.

51. The student population grew from 1,457 in 1884 to 2,930 in 1889, and the number of teachers rose from 23 to 51; *Mayor's Message and Annual Reports of City Offices of the City of Dallas, Texas, for the Fiscal Year Ending Apr. 15, 1889* (Dallas: City Council, 1889), 12, in TDCDPL. According to *GD 1889*, 49–50, 10 males and 46 females taught in the public schools. *Dallas Weekly Herald*, Aug. 17, 1882; *GD 1889*, 3, 49–50.

52. *GD 1880*, 38; *GD 1889*, 52–66.

53. For listings of the St. Mary's faculty, *GD 1889*, 33, and *GD 1891*, 58–59. Oak Cliff College for Young Ladies, *Bulletin 1892*, A6097, DHS; *GD 1889*, 51; *GD 1893*, 55–56; *Memorial and Biographical History*, 325–26.

54. McElhaney, "Childhood in Dallas," 28–31, 33, and 142nn 80 and 90.

55. Tabulations from data in *GD 1886, GD 1889.*

56. *11th U.S. Census, 1890, Manufacturing Industries,* pt. 2: *Statistics of Cities,* 176. On the cotton mill, *GD 1889,* 62; tabulations are from total listings in *GD 1889.* Andrew Morrison, *The Industries of Dallas: Her Relations as a Center of Trade, Manufacturing Establishments and Business Houses* (Galveston: Metropolitan Publishing Co., 1887), in Mrs. Howard Cox Papers, A44152, DHS.

57. *GD 1889,* 112.

58. On Julia E. Burnett, Pumps, Gas, Water and Steam Fittings, *GD 1886,* 96; Marguerite A. Archinard, president, East Dallas Bank, *GD 1889,* 84; Rosaline E. Hanks, Hanks and Hanks Furniture, *GD 1889,* 246–47; Isabella McLeod, Dallas Stone Quarry, *GD 1889,* 349; Nancy P. Patterson, Patterson and Stevenson Drug Store, *GD 1889,* 393.

59. For photographs, see William L. McDonald, *Dallas Rediscovered,* 34, 40–41, 42 (#31), 44–45, 50–51. On the depression, W. S. Adair, "Panic Times Found Dallas Without Cash" [memories of A. F. Slater], *DMN,* Sept. 9, 1928.

60. *Dallas Weekly Herald,* Nov. 29, 1883; *DMN,* Nov. 10, Nov. 20, and Nov. 17, 1885; Mar. 8, 1886.

61. Quotation, *Dallas Weekly Herald,* Apr. 3, 1884; on roaming livestock, *DMN,* May 31 and July 5, 1883; Oct. 20, 1885; Apr. 28 and May 15, 1886.

62. "The Annals," Archives, Ursuline Residence, Dallas.

63. Ettie Fulkerson Cockrell, Diary, in Archives, Dallas County Heritage Society. See Foree, "U.S. Golden Age." Anna Wideman Blair drove a wagon along a regular route through Dallas residential neighborhoods to sell chickens for 25 cents each and eggs for 5 cents a dozen to housewives.

64. *GD 1880,* 15.

65. For Sarah Cockrell's transactions involving land, Dallas County Deed Records 1880–89, Dallas County Records Building; Probate Records, TDCDPL; Sarah Horton Cockrell Papers, A4340 (1880s) and A4340/A472, DHS; and map in Sarah Horton Cockrell Probate Records. Evaluation of real property in Dallas, 1892, in *GD 1891,* 5–6. On the Cockrell Building, William L. McDonald, *Dallas Rediscovered,* 36, 52, and, on the "Addition," 104.

66. Sarah Horton Cockrell Papers, A5549, DHS; obituary, *DMN,* Apr. 27, 1892. Demonstrating Cockrell's "unostentatious charity," her grandson found, among her personal papers, "hundreds" of "IOUs" from members of both races for various sums of money, grocery orders, and firewood. Only a few were marked "paid." Monroe F. Cockrell, "Destiny in Dallas: A Study," typescript, 1958, TDHDPL, p. 20.

67. On the classic sociological theories of urbanism, see Katznelson, "Reflections on Space and the City," 285–300, esp. 290–92, 296–98.

   Regarding the nature of a city, see Mumford, *City in History,* esp. 125, 458. On urban characteristics, Richard D. Brown, "Emergence of Urban Society," esp. 30–31, 32, 38–39, 43, 45, 57. See Richard D. Brown, "Emergence of Voluntary Associations," 64–73.

Chapter 5. Women and the Urban Economy

1. *DMN*, Apr. 29, 1895.
2. See tables 2–5. Even census data provide little more than estimates of women's employment; see Folbre and Abel, "Women's Work," 545–60.

TABLE 2

FEMALES WHO WERE EMPLOYED

(PERCENT OF TOTAL POPULATION)

	1880[1]	1890	1900[1]	1910[2]	1920[1]
Dallas	27.0	—	26.12	29.4	36.2
Texas	12.4	14.2	15.5	21.1	15.7
U.S.	14.7	17.4	18.8	23.4	21.1

Notes:

1. 16 and over
2. 15 and over

Sources:

Calculations for Dallas came from:

Manuscript census for Texas, 1880, Dallas County, National Archives and Records Service microfilm, Series T9, Roll 1299; Manuscript census for Texas, 1900, Dallas County, National Archives and Records Service microfilm, Series T623, Roll 1625; U.S. Bureau of the Census, *12th Census of the United States, 1900: Population*, pt. 2 (Washington, D.C.: GPO, 1902), 127; U.S. Bureau of the Census, *13th Census of the U.S., 1910*, vol. 4: *Occupation Statistics*, 221, 223, 225; U.S. Bureau of the Census, *14th Census of the U.S., 1920*, vol. 3: *Population*, 1015, and vol. 4: *Occupations*, 340, 367–68, 459, 692, 801, 803.

Calculations for Texas came from:

U.S. Bureau of the Census, *13th Census of the U.S., 1910*, vol. 4: *Occupation Statistics*, 37; U.S. Bureau of the Census, *14th Census of the U.S., 1920*, vol. 4: *Occupations*, 364.

Calculations for U.S. came from:

U.S. Bureau of the Census, *Statistics of the Population of the U.S.: 10th Census, 1880* (Washington, D.C.: GPO, 1883), 712; U.S. Bureau of the Census, *14th Census of the U.S., 1920*, vol. 2: *Population*: 462–534; and vol. 4: *Occupations*: 32, 802–87. And see *Statistics of Women at Work*, supervised by Joseph A. Hill (Washington, D.C.: GPO, 1907), 131.

For discussion of the problems involved in working with the decennial U.S. censuses, see Nancy Folbre and Marjorie Abel, "Women's Work and Women's Households: Gender Bias in the U.S. Census," *Social Research* 56 (Autumn 1989): 545–69; Valerie Kincaide Oppenheimer, *The Female Labor Force in the United States: Demographic and Economic Factors Governing Its Growth and Changing Conditions*, Population Monograph Series, no. 5 (Westport, Conn.: Greenwood Press, 1970), 151; and Robert W. Smuts, "The Female Labor Force: A Case Study in the Interpretation of Historical Statistics," *Journal of the American Statistical Association* 55 (March 1960): 71–79.

TABLE 3
WOMEN IN DALLAS LABOR FORCE
(PERCENT OF TOTAL DALLAS LABOR FORCE)

1880	1890	1900	1910	1920
20.5[1]	—	24.4[1]	25.4[2]	28.1[2]

Notes:

   1. Age 16 and over

   2. Age 15 and over

Sources:

Manuscript census for Dallas County, 1880 and 1900; U.S. Bureau of the Census, *12th Census of the United States, 1900: Population,* vol. 2, pt. 2 (Washington, D.C.: GPO, 1902), 127; U.S. Bureau of the Census, *13th Census of the U.S., 1910,* vol. 4: *Occupation Statistics,* 221, 223, 225; U.S. Bureau of the Census, *14th Census of the U.S., 1920,* vol. 3: *Population,* 1015, and vol. 4: *Occupations,* 340, 367–68, 459, 692, 801, 803.

TABLE 4
EMPLOYED WOMEN, BY MARITAL STATUS
(PERCENT OF ALL WOMEN)

	1880	1890	1900	1910	1920
Dallas					
Single[1]	42.4[2]	—	40.5[2]	46.5[2]	58.3[3]
Married	13.0[3]		5.6[3]	10.9[3]	19.5[3]
United States					
Single[1]	—	37.7[3]	40.5[3]	46.5[3]	46.4[3]
Married	—	4.6[3]	5.6[3]	10.7[3]	9.0[3]

Notes:

   1. Divorced, widowed, never married

   2. Age 16 and over

   3. Age 15 and over

Sources:

Manuscript census for Dallas County, 1880 and 1900; U.S. Bureau of the Census, *Statistics of the Population of the U.S.: 10th Census, 1880* (Washington, D.C.: GPO, 1883), 712; U.S. Bureau of the Census, *12th Census of the United States, 1900: Population,* pt. 2 (Washington, D.C.: GPO, 1902), 127; U.S. Bureau of the Census, *13th Census of the U.S., 1910,* vol. 4: *Occupation Statistics,* 221, 223, 225; U.S. Bureau of the Census, *14th Census of the U.S., 1920,* vol. 2: *Population:* 462–534; vol. 3: *Population,* 1015; vol. 4: *Occupations,* 32, 340, 367–68, 459, 692, 801, 802–87, 803. Also see *Statistics of Women at Work,* supervised by Joseph A. Hill (Washington, D.C.: GPO, 1907), 131.

TABLE 5

PERCENT OF MARRIED WOMEN IN TOTAL DALLAS FEMALE LABOR FORCE

1880	1890	1900	1910	1920
24.2	—	21.4	—	31.6

Sources:

Manuscript census for Dallas County, 1880 and 1900; U.S. Bureau of the Census, *12th Census of the United States, 1900: Population*, pt. 2 (Washington, D.C.: GPO, 1902), 127; U.S. Bureau of the Census, *13th Census of the U.S., 1910*, vol. 4: *Occupation Statistics*, 221, 223, 225; U.S. Bureau of the Census, *14th Census of the U.S., 1920*, vol. 3: *Population*, 1015, and vol. 4: *Occupations*, 340, 367–68, 459, 692, 801, 803.

3. See table 6 for comparative data on female employment for the U.S., Texas, and major Texas cities.

TABLE 6

FEMALE EMPLOYMENT
U.S., TEXAS, AND MAJOR TEXAS CITIES

	Women Employed (Percent of All Women)		Female Labor Force (Percent of Entire Labor Force)	
	(ages 16 & above)	(ages 15 & above)	(ages 16 & above)	(ages 15 & above)
	1910	1920	1910	1920
U.S.	23.4	21.2	21.2	20.5
Texas	21.1	15.7	24.1	17.7
Austin	26.2	22.0	30.0	31.0
Dallas	29.4	36.2	25.4	28.1
Fort Worth	24.8	28.9	20.2	21.1
Galveston	31.7	22.4	25.1	22.1
Houston	31.8	33.3	26.7	27.0
San Antonio	25.3	29.0	24.8	24.2

Note:

The declines for Texas and the U.S. resulted from the fact that in 1910, but not in 1920, census takers had explicit instructions to include as "Employed" rural women who regularly worked without pay on family farms. See Oppenheimer, *Female Labor Force*, 151.

Sources:

U.S. figures are from "Facts About Working Women," *Women's Bureau Bulletin*, no. 46 (Washington, D.C.: GPO, 1925), 4, cited in Louise Michele Newman, ed., *Men's Ideas, Women's Realities: Popular Science, 1870–1915* (New York: Pergamon, 1985), 251. For Texas and selected cities, figures are from U.S. Department of Commerce, Bureau of the Census, *13th Census of the U.S., 1910*: vol. 4: *Occupation Statistics*, 211, 232, 233, 269, 520–22; and from U.S. Department of Commerce, Bureau of the Census, *14th Census of the U.S., 1920*: vol. 3: *Population: Composition and Characteristics of the Population by States* (Washington, D.C.: GPO, 1923), 985, 1015; and vol. 4: *Population: Occupations*, 315, 364, 466, 467, 468, 470, 839.

4. See table 3. *Dallas City Directory for 1920* (Dallas: John F. Worley and Co., 1920), 6–7 (hereafter *DCD 1920*), estimated the value of Dallas's retail business at $250 million and the wholesale trade at nearly $350 million. This profile of the industries and manufacturing plants is from a tabulation of firms listed in the index of *DCD 1920.* Also *DMN,* Mar. 17, 1918; Aug. 3, 1919. On "suitability" as a factor in women's employment, see Martha Norby Fraundorf, "The Labor Force Participation of Turn-of-the-Century Married Women," *Journal of Economic History* 39 (June 1979): 401–18; Louise A. Tilly and Joan Wallach Scott, *Women, Work, and Family* (New York: Holt Rinehart Winston, 1978). On other, unquantifiable influences on women's employment, see Maurine Weiner Greenwald, "Working-Class Feminism and the Family Wage Ideal: The Seattle Debate on Married Women's Right to Work, 1914–1920," *Journal of American History* 76 (June 1989): 118–49; Kessler-Harris, *Out to Work,* 135–37.

5. "Vareta Pinkston Gulley," in *Family Business in Dallas: A Matter of Values,* ed. Pam Lange and Mindie Lazarus-Black (Dallas: Dallas Public Library, 1982), 70–71.

6. For tabulation, not surveys, of African-American dressmakers: Manuscript census for Texas, 1900, Dallas County, National Archives and Record Services microfilm, Series T623, Roll 1625; and U.S. Dept. of Commerce, Bureau of the Census, *14th Census of the U.S., 1920* [hereafter *14th U.S. Census, 1920*], vol. 4: *Occupations* (Washington, D.C.: GPO, 1923), 803, 1093. Calculations for dressmakers are from data in the Manuscript Census 1880, Dallas County; and *10th U.S. Census,* 1880, 712; and U.S. Dept. of Commerce, Bureau of the Census, *13th Census of the U.S., 1910* [hereafter, *13th U.S. Census, 1910*], vol. 4: *Occupation Statistics* (Washington, D.C.: GPO, 1913), 221, 223, 225; and *14th U.S. Census, 1920:* vol. 2: *General Report and Analytical Tables,* 1268, and vol. 4: *Occupations,* 820–21, 1092. Also Helen L. Sumner, *History of Women in Industry in the U.S.,* pt. 9: *Report on the Condition of Woman and Child Wage-Earners in the U.S.,* Sen. Doc. 645, 61st Cong., 2d sess. (Washington, D.C.: GPO, 1910): 42–43, 87–88. See Kessler-Harris, *Out to Work,* 28–29, 120; and Ruth Schwartz Cowan, *More Work for Mother: The Ironies of Household Technology, from the Open Hearth to the Microwave* (New York: Basic Books, 1983), 74–75.

7. Manuscript census 1880, Dallas County; *14th U.S. Census, 1920,* vol. 3: *Population,* 1015, and vol. 4: *Occupations,* 820–21; and surveys of DCDs, 1880 and 1920.

8. Descriptive information from surveys of DCDs for 1900, 1910, 1920; statistics from *14th U.S. Census, 1920,* vol. 4: *Occupations:* 164, 820, 1092, 1093. On Julia Shamburger, Esther Shamburger Davis, interview by author, handwritten notes, in author's possession, Dallas, Aug. 29, 1984.

9. *Black Presence in Dallas: Historic Black Dallasites,* comp. Sadye Gee, ed. Darnell Williams (Dallas: Museum of African-American Life and Culture, 1987), 59, 109.

10. In 1880, Dallas had a self-employed laundress for every 37.1 persons, or approx. every 6.6 households; by 1920, 1 for every 76 persons or every 14.8 households. In 1880, Dallas had 1 domestic servant for every 38.5 residents or for each 6.6 dwellings; by 1920, 1 for every 50.5 residents or every 9.9 dwellings. Manuscript census 1880, Dallas County; and *10th U.S. Census, 1880, 712;* and *14th U.S.*

Census, 1920, vol. 2: *Population,* 1268, 1271; and vol. 4: *Occupations,* 820–21. Also see Joseph A. Hill, *Women in Gainful Employment,* Census Monograph no. 9 (Washington, D.C.: GPO, 1929), 36; and Kessler-Harris, *Out to Work,* 113, 345.

11. *14th U.S. Census, 1920,* vol. 4: *Occupations,* 1093. Also see Goldin, "Female Labor Force Participation," 87–112. On the Dallas black population, see tables 7–12.

TABLE 7
EMPLOYED DALLAS AFRICAN-AMERICAN WOMEN
(PERCENT OF ALL DALLAS AFRICAN-AMERICAN WOMEN)

1880	1890	1900	1910	1920
76.3[1]	—	65.0[1]	—	59.9[2]

Notes:
1. Age 16 and over
2. Age 15 and over

Sources:
Manuscript census for Texas, 1880, Dallas County, National Archives and Record Services microfilm, Series T9, Roll 1299; Manuscript census for Texas, 1900, Dallas County, National Archives and Record Services microfilm, Series T623, Roll 1625; U.S. Bureau of the Census, *14th Census of the U.S., 1920,* vol. 4: *Occupations,* 459.

TABLE 8
EMPLOYED DALLAS AFRICAN-AMERICAN WOMEN WHO WERE MARRIED
(PERCENT OF ALL EMPLOYED DALLAS AFRICAN-AMERICAN WOMEN)

1880	1890	1900	1910	1920
29.8[1]	—	63.0[1]	—	51.3[2]

Notes:
1. Age 16 and over
2. Age 15 and over

Sources:
U.S. Bureau of the Census, *14th Census of the U.S., 1920,* vol. 4: *Occupations,* 459.

TABLE 9
MARRIED DALLAS AFRICAN-AMERICAN WOMEN WHO WERE EMPLOYED
(PERCENT OF ALL MARRIED DALLAS AFRICAN-AMERICAN WOMEN)

1880	1890	1900	1910	1920
58.2[1]	—	39.0[1]	—	54.0[2]

Notes:
1. Age 16 and over

TABLE 9 NOTES (CONTINUED)
2. Age 15 and over

Sources:
U.S. Bureau of the Census, *14th Census of the U.S., 1920*, vol. 4: *Occupations*, 459.

TABLE 10
AFRICAN AMERICANS IN DALLAS FEMALE LABOR FORCE
(PERCENT OF TOTAL DALLAS FEMALE LABOR FORCE)

1880	1890	1900	1910	1920
60.8[1]	—	55.6[1]	—	27.6[2]

Notes:
1. Age 16 and over
2. Age 15 and over

Sources:
U.S. Bureau of the Census, *14th Census of the U.S., 1920*, vol. 4: *Occupations*, 459.

TABLE 11
AFRICAN AMERICANS AMONG DALLAS EMPLOYED MARRIED WOMEN
(PERCENT OF ALL DALLAS EMPLOYED MARRIED WOMEN)

1880	1890	1900	1910	1920
74.9[1]	—	64.0[1]	—	44.8[2]

Notes:
1. Age 16 and over
2. Age 15 and over

Sources:
U.S. Bureau of the Census, *14th Census of the U.S., 1920*, vol. 4: *Occupations*, 459.

TABLE 12
AFRICAN AMERICANS IN DALLAS POPULATION
(PERCENT OF TOTAL DALLAS POPULATION)

1880	1890	1900	1910	1920
18.6	20.7	21.2	19.6	15.1

Note:
Includes all age groups

Sources:
U.S. Bureau of the Census, *14th Census of the U.S., 1920*, vol. 4: *Occupations*, 459.

12. All information about women's employment in the department stores is from surveys of DCDs for the years stated. See Cowan, *More Work*, 80–81.

13. Sumner, *History of Women in Industry,* 212–21. On the shifting of gender definitions in printing, see Ava Baron, "The Masculinization of Production: The Gendering of Work and Skill in U.S. Newsprinting, 1850–1920," in Helly and Reverby, *Gendered Domains,* 277–88.

14. On Fitzgerald, Elizabeth Brooks, *Prominent Women of Texas* (Akron, Ohio: Werner Co., 1896), 129–30; *DMN,* Oct. 14, 1910; Rogers, *Lusty Texans,* 180; Acheson, *Dallas Yesterday,* 202–204. Information about Ford has been gleaned piecemeal from censuses and city directories. Joan L. Dobson, "Literature for All Tastes: Magazines Published in Dallas," *Heritage News* 12 (Winter 1987–88): 4–7, 10.

15. Jacquelyn Masur McElhaney, *Pauline Periwinkle and Progressive Reform in Dallas* (College Station: Texas A&M Univ. Press, forthcoming). Jackie McElhaney, "Pauline Periwinkle: Crusading Columnist," *Heritage News* 10 (Summer 1985): 15–18; Acheson, *Dallas Yesterday,* 204–206.

16. All information on women business owners is from surveys of DCDs for the years stated.

17. All information about L. Engers and Co. is from DCDs, 1886–1915.

18. Information from DCDs for the years cited; "Things Home Women May Do," *DMN,* Apr. 2, 1913, praising the occupations individual housewives had created for themselves.

19. See tables 7–11. Unless stated, all information about the occupations of African-American women is from surveys of DCDs for years stated; from the *14th U.S. Census, 1920,* vol. 4: *Occupations,* 1092–93; and from *Dallas Express,* July 5, 1919; Jan. 17 and Apr. 10, 1920. On Feb. 15 and Oct. 4, 1919, the *Express* also published articles about openings with the federal government for stenographers and typists; on Feb. 8, 1919, about jobs available for women in Pittsburgh; and on Mar. 15, 1919, a notice that the Dickson Orphanage in Gilmer, Tex., needed a stenographer and a music teacher.

20. Stanley Marcus, *Minding the Store: A Memoir* (New York: Signet/New American Library, 1975), 1–4, 7, 11, 16, 21, 43–44, 75, 87–88, 103; and Leon Harris, *Merchant Princes,* 161–66.

21. Speer, *Treatise on Marital Rights,* 140–41, 163, 235, 292–93, 323–39, 330–32, 368–70. Also see Simpkins, *Texas Family Law,* 597–98 [Sec. 15:1–34.8]; Lazarou, "Concealed Under Petticoats," 170–72.

22. In 1910, 298 stenographers were men; in 1920, 285; from *13th U.S. Census, 1910,* vol. 3: *Population, Nebraska-Wyoming,* 225; and *14th U.S. Census, 1920,* vol. 4: *Occupations:* 1093. On national trends, see Sharon Hartman Strom, *Beyond the Typewriter: Gender, Class, and the Origins of Modern American Office Work, 1900–1930* (Urbana: Univ. of Illinois Press, 1992), 172–226.

23. Samplings of *DMN* classified ads, Mar.–Apr. and Sept.–Oct. 1920.

24. Unless stated, all information about women's occupations in government agencies and private organizations is from surveys of DCDs for years stated. See Rotella, *Home to Office,* 61, 65, 97–99, 103–108.

25. J. Howard Ardrey Papers, A3938, DHS; and Rex V. Lentz, "A History of Banking in Dallas," unpublished manuscript, ca. 1940, in Mrs. Rex V. Lentz Papers, A7435, DHS. On Dallas before 1910, see Char Miller and David R. Johnson, "The Rise of Urban Texas," in Char Miller and Sanders, *Urban Texas,* 16–23, and James

Howard, *Big D Is for Dallas: Chapters in the 20th-Century History of Dallas* (Austin: Privately published, 1957), 53, 56, 62.

26. *14th U.S. Census, 1920,* vol. 4: *Occupations:* 821, 1093. On the employment of middle- and working-class daughters, see Strom, *Beyond the Typewriter,* 273–313, 314–66. On the greater likelihood that daughters would stay in school during their teen years, see David Tyack and Elizabeth Hansot, *Learning Together: A History of Coeducation in American Public Schools* (New Haven, Conn.: Yale Univ. Press for the Russell Sage Foundation, 1990), 126–27, 143–45, 170–79. See Kessler-Harris, *Out to Work,* 27, 113, 119; Elyce J. Rotella, "Women's Labor Force Participation and the Decline of the Family Economy in the United States," *Explorations in Economic History* 17 (Apr. 1980): 95–117, esp. 99–100, 101–102, 109; Claudia Goldin, "Household and Market Production of Families in a Late-19th-Century American City," *Explorations in Economic History* 16 (1979): 119, 124–28; and Claudia Goldin, "The Changing Economic Role of Women: A Quantitative Approach," *Journal of Interdisciplinary History* 13 (Spring 1983): 720–21.

27. Strom, *Beyond the Typewriter,* 15–62; Rothman, *Woman's Proper Place,* 49. Also see Oppenheimer, *Female Labor Force,* 151; Kessler-Harris, *Out to Work,* 61, 128, 135–39.

28. For comparison with other cities in the South and elsewhere in the U.S., see tables 13 and 14.

The categories of domestic service and office/clerical positions drew different segments of the female population, in terms of age, education, and race. The decline in domestic servants was due in part to the proportionate decrease in the black population as a whole in Dallas, but at the same time department stores and other businesses offered increasing numbers of jobs considered suitable for black women. In addition, the city's African-American middle class was growing, and numerous matrons were able to leave the job market for full-time work in their own homes. See tables 9–12.

TABLE 13

CHANGES IN EMPLOYMENT PROFILE, DALLAS

a. Women Over Age 15, by Employment Category
(Percent of All Dallas Women Employed)

	1900	1910	1920
Manufacturing	19.0	14.0	11.0
Trade	6.0	14.0	12.0
Transportation	6.0	3.0	6.0
Professional Service	8.0	9.8	9.3
Domestic Service	61.0	55.0	35.0
Clerical (office only)	5.6	10.7	26.4

b. Men Over Age 15, by Employment Category
(Percent of All Dallas Men Employed)

	1900	1910	1920
Manufacturing	25.0	31.2	30.4
Trade	23.0	26.4	25.8
Transportation	10.7	10.2	11.4
Professional Service	7.0	8.0	8.0
Domestic Service	24.0	12.0	8.4
Clerical (office only)	8.3	10.9	14.1

c. All Labor Force Over Age 15, by Employment Category
(Percent of Entire Dallas Labor Force)

	1900	1910	1920
Manufacturing	24.0	27.0	25.0
Trade	34.0	22.0	22.0
Transportation	6.0	8.0	10.0
Professional Service	7.0	7.0	6.0
Domestic Service	33.0	23.0	16.0
Clerical (office only)	7.6	9.0	16.0

Sources:

Manuscript census for Texas, 1900, Dallas County, National Archives and Record Services microfilm, Series T623, Roll 1625; *1910 Census*, vol. 4: Population: *Occupations*, 221, 223, 224; U.S. *14th Census of the U.S., 1920*, vol. 4: *Occupations*, 150, 152, 154, 156, 158, 160, 162, 164, 166.

TABLE 14
PROFILE OF FEMALE EMPLOYMENT IN 1920:
AVERAGES FOR SELECTED CITIES WITH POPULATIONS OVER 100,000
(PERCENT OF TOTAL FEMALE POPULATION)

Four Texas Cities:

	Manufac.	Domestic Services	Prof. Services	Transp.	Trade	Clerical
Dallas	11.0	35.0	9.3	6.0	12.0	26.4
Fort Worth	13.9	37.6	10.2	5.3	10.0	22.4
Houston	12.0	46.5	9.3	3.9	11.5	19.8
San Antonio	16.0	63.0	14.0	3.6	12.1	26.0

Selected Cities in Four United States Regions:

	Manufac.	Domestic Services	Prof. Services	Transp.	Trade	Clerical
South	16.4	49.6	8.3	2.4	7.6	15.6
Northeast	21.2	24.6	10.0	3.1	10.3	26.4

Selected Cities in Four United States Regions:

	Manufac.	Domestic Services	Prof. Services	Transp.	Trade	Clerical
Midwest	19.0	23.2	11.3	3.9	11.4	30.0
West	15.0	25.9	15.7	4.3	12.9	26.0

Note:

Selected cities included for regional averages are:

South: Atlanta, Norfolk, Richmond, Memphis, New Orleans, Birmingham.

Northeast: Boston, Hartford, New York, Philadelphia, Pittsburgh, Syracuse.

Midwest: Chicago; Des Moines; Indianapolis; Kansas City, Mo.; Omaha; Toledo.

West: Denver, Los Angeles, Portland, Oregon, Salt Lake City, San Francisco, Seattle.

Sources:

U.S. Bureau of the Census, *14th Census of the U.S.*, *1920*, vol. 4: *Occupations:* 809–67.

29. Except as stated, all information on women managers is from a survey of *DCD* 1920.

30. Except as stated, all information on stenographers is from surveys of DCDs for years stated. Also see Leslie Woodcock Tentler, *Wage-Earning Women: Industrial Work and Family Life in the United States, 1900–1930* (New York: Oxford Univ. Press, 1982), 89–93, 107–109.

31. Kenneth Foree, "Fighters' Blood Is in Her Veins" [memories of Helen Viglini], *DMN*, Apr. 25, 1938. On other female attorneys, *DMN*, Oct. 28, 1914.

32. Except as stated, all information on women in the professions is from DCDs for years stated.

33. *Yearbook and 67 Years* (Dallas: Oak Cliff Christian Church, 1957), 56, 59–60, 64. Carrie Bryant Chasteen, interview by William Martin Smith, typescript, Aug. 9, 1966, in Oak Cliff Christian Church archives, Dallas. Also *DMN*, June 16, 1929.

34. *DMN*, Mar. 17, 1918; Aug. 3, 1919.

35. Quotation in *DMN*, Dec. 3, 1918. *DMN*, May 7 and May 31, 1917; Aug. 18, Sept. 20, and Oct. 9, 1918.

36. Quotation in *DMN*, Nov. 12, 1918. *DMN*, Aug. 7, Aug. 11, Aug. 16, Sept. 10, Sept. 12, Sept. 19, and Sept. 24, 1918.

37. Kessler-Harris, *Out to Work*, 116, 224, and Maurine Weiner Greenwald, *Women, War, and Work: The Impact of World War I on Women Workers in the United States* (Westport, Conn.: Greenwood Press, 1980), 4, 13, 23, 25, 26; Rotella, *Home to Office*, 11.

38. *DMN*, Jan. 11, 1920.

39. Quotation in *DMN*, Feb. 20, 1919; and *DMN*, Feb. 23, 1919.

40. On the YWCA "opportunity school," *DMN*, Apr. 20, May 4, July 7, July 19, and Aug. 3, 1919.

41. On the advertising league, see "Uplifting the 'Ad' Business," *Dallas* 6 (Apr. 1927): 29; *DMN*, Mar. 29, 1919. On business and professional women, *DMN*, July 3 and Oct. 9, 1918, and July 7 and July 11, 1919. Information about the nurses is from DCD club listings and from Minutes, DFWC, 1917, in TDCDPL.

42. See table 15. *14th U.S. Census, 1920,* vol. 4: *Occupations:* 820; Joseph A. Hill, *Women in Gainful Occupations,* 109. Attempts to distinguish between women employed in "new" occupations and those related to traditional homemaking create problems with the U.S. Census categories. Dressmakers and seamstresses not in factories could be running their own shops, sewing for department stores, employed by other dressmakers, or taking orders in freelance arrangements in their own homes. The census enumerators almost always failed to indicate the specific conditions of such work. Cooks frequently were listed as general servants, and more than one housewife got lumped with "housekeepers," a paid occupation.

TABLE 15

CATEGORIES OF DALLAS WOMEN'S OCCUPATIONS

a. Occupations Related to Traditional Household Tasks

	1880	1900	1920
Total Employed	838[1]	4,322[1]	21,772[2]
Sewing Trades (dressmakers, milliners, seamstresses, tailoresses not in factories)	82	557	917
Teachers	22	295	990
Boardinghouse Keepers (includes hotels, rented rooms)	23	286	535
Nurses	5	98	462
Midwives (and untrained nurses)	—	3	315
Domestic Servants (includes private homes, hotels, service institutions, waitresses, cooks)	296	1,369	3,485
Laundresses (independent)	280	914	2,093
Laundry Employees	—	34	531
Retail Dealers (includes grocers, restaurant and cafe	—	8	180

TABLE 15 CONTINUED

CATEGORIES OF DALLAS WOMEN'S OCCUPATIONS

a. Occupations Related to Traditional Household Tasks

	1880	1900	1920
owners, merchants, florists, drug store owners, confectioners)			
Personal Services (includes manicurists, barbers, hairdressers, masseuses)	—	13	185
Percent of Employed[3]	85	84.3	45

b. Occupations Unrelated to Traditional Household Tasks

	1880	1900	1920
Sales Personnel (includes clerks in stores)	11	129	2,196
Stenographers (includes typists)	—	178	2,962
Clerical	—	17	1,827
Bookkeepers (also cashiers and accountants)	—	37	960
Telephone Operators (and telegraph)	—	53	1,244
Factory Workers (includes operatives)	—	131	1,909
Percent of Employed[3]	1	13	51

Notes:

1. Age 16 and over
2. Age 10 and over
3. The figures in this table do not account for 100 percent of Dallas employed women for any of the three years, because the table omits occupations in which women were, in effect, "tokens." These include medicine, photography, printing and proofreading, even editors and writers, as well as those classified only as "works" or "laborer." Furthermore, some figures mentioned in the text came from city directories, which cannot be correlated with U.S. Census data.

Sources:

Tabulations, not surveys, of the U.S. Bureau of the Census, Manuscript censuses for Texas, 1880 and 1900, Dallas County; U.S. Bureau of the Census, *14th Census of the United States . . . 1920*, vol. 4: *Occupations* (Washington, D.C.: GPO, 1923), 152–60.

43. See tables 4, 8, 9, and 11. Also, Manuscript census 1880, Dallas County; *14th U.S. Census, 1920,* vol. 4: *Occupations:* 367–68, 459, 692, 801. See Goldin, "Changing Economic Roles of Women," 714–15, 723, 732.

44. *14th U.S. Census, 1920,* vol. 4: *Occupations:* 459, 1093. See Goldin, "Female Labor Force Participation."

45. Tabulations of data from Manuscript census 1880, Dallas County; Manuscript census for Texas, 1900, Dallas County; *13th U.S. Census, 1910,* vol. 3: *Abstract:* 96, 656; and *14th U.S. Census, 1920,* vol. 3: *Population:* 1015, and vol. 4: *Occupations, 367–68, 801.* On "factors . . . [that] make the female labor market unique," see Janice Fanning Madden, *The Economics of Sex Discrimination* (Lexington, Mass.: D.C. Heath, 1973).

46. Information about black women's employment is from a survey of *DCD 1920,* as well as *14th U.S. Census, 1920,* vol. 4: *Occupations,* 367–68, 801.

47. In "Waging War on 'Loose Living Hotels . . . and Cheap Soda Water Joints': Urban Development and the Criminalization of Working-Women in Public Space," a paper presented at the Fourth Southern Conference on Women's History, Charleston, S.C., June 14, 1997, Georgina Hickey has examined the social anxiety toward employed single women in Atlanta early in the twentieth century. Copy in author's possession. Joanne J. Meyerowitz, *Women Adrift: Independent Wage Earners in Chicago, 1880–1930* (Chicago: Univ. of Chicago Press, 1988).

48. On gender- and sex-neutral occupations, see Strom, *Beyond the Typewriter,* 231–34, 274, 357–58, 378–84; Kessler-Harris, *Out to Work,* 28–29, 78, 120. See Edward Gross, "Plus Ça Change . . . ? The Sexual Structure of Occupations Over Time," *Social Problems* 16 (1968): 198–209. On the lingering influence of gender on employment, see Alice Kessler-Harris, *A Woman's Wage: Historical Meanings and Social Consequences* (Lexington: Univ. Press of Kentucky, 1990), 57–80, esp. 62.

49. Aside from applications of political theory to housework, Marxist scholars have done a great deal of valuable research and provocative analysis of work in the home as production. Regarding this literature, see Helly and Reverby, *Gendered Domains,* esp. 10–11. Also see Terry Fee, "Domestic Labor: An Analysis of Housework and Its Relation to the Production Process," *Review of Radical Political Economics* 8 (Spring 1976): 1–8; and Margaret Benston, "The Political Economy of Women's Liberation," *Monthly Review* 21 (Sept. 1969): 13–27.

50. On the relationship of the home to society, see Cowan, *More Work,* 6–7; and Strasser's introduction to her book, *Never Done,* xiii. The compilers of the 1900 census returns also commented on the importance of housework: U.S. Dept. of Commerce and Labor, Bureau of the Census, *Supplementary Analysis and Derivative Tables: 1900* (Washington, D.C.: GPO, 1906), 439. See Gerda Lerner, "Just a Housewife," in *Majority Finds Its Past,* esp. 137–40. On the "official" devaluation of housework after 1910, see Folbre and Abel, "Women's Work," 547, 557. For a lyrical description of housework as "making life," Willa Cather, *Shadows on the Rock* (New York: A. A. Knopf, 1960), 197–98.

The single most important influence on my interpretation of housework as basic to the city's economy is John B. Leeds, *The Household Budget, with a Spe-*

cial Inquiry into the Amount and Value of Household Work (Philadelphia: Privately published, 1917). Leeds argues (20–23) that the housewife does not become a consumer by the act of purchasing goods, but only by the acts of using them—eating meals, burning oil in the lamps, wearing clothes, etc. By separating purchase from use, Leeds calls attention to the fact that purchased goods—foodstuffs, for example—require at least some final processing or preparation before they are usable, while other items, such as clothing, require constant maintenance. Leeds also argues that, as the means of acquisition, purchasing is part of modern production. The final steps of processing are part of the manufacture and production of the goods for consumption, and they occur (even today, in the late 20th century) in the home (11, 20, 22, 26 passim). Leeds understands service work to be an integral part of the production process, whether in the home or the marketplace. When these final stages of processing and preparation—these services—are done for pay, they become part of the market economy. Otherwise, they remain within the use economy of the home. (The phrase "use economy of the home" is mine, not Leeds's.) McGaw, in "No Passive Victims," 172–91, esp. 183n 7, discusses home manufacture for wages, (also called "piece work") under contract with a manufacturer, as completing the goods made by factories and mills. A case could be made, however, that the maintenance of goods is completion of their processing and thus also a part of their manufacture.

51. Scholars have defined the terms of work done in the home in several ways. Arleen Liebowitz, "Women's Work in the Home," in *Sex, Discrimination, and the Division of Labor,* ed. Cynthia B. Lloyd (New York: Columbia Univ. Press, 1975), 223–43, esp. 224, sees household production as production of commodities but does not consider that production to include services. To Rotella, in *Home to Office,* 43, 101, the term "family economy" means the pooling of wages, not household production of goods or services for household use. For Robert W. Smuts, *Women and Work in America* (New York: Columbia Univ. Press, 1959), 11–17, "home production" means earning money at home.

52. Regarding unpaved streets and the lack of conveniences in black neighborhoods, *Dallas Express,* Jan. 18 and Oct. 11, 1919; on the lack of water and sewerage systems, gas and electric power, Mar. 27, 1919; for directions for cleaning gas stoves, Feb. 28, 1920. Streets in the area of the original Freedmantown were paved by 1913; William L. McDonald, *Dallas Rediscovered,* 181.

53. Gee, interview, Feb. 10, 1987.

54. Information about the work methods of turn-of-the-century housewives came from Hazel McCarley Winterbauer, interviews by author, handwritten notes, in author's possession, Dallas, Apr. 4 and May 22, 1985; Winterbauer, interview, Mar. 29, 1978; and Alvernon King Tripp, interview by author, handwritten notes, in author's possession, Dallas, Nov. 9, 1978. During the 1890s and early 1900s, Anna Wideman Blair had a "regular route" through Dallas, selling eggs for 5 cents a dozen, chickens for 25 cents apiece, and turkeys at $1 each: Foree, "U.S. Golden Age."

55. For memory of the "poor" mother, Ruth Ellen Clower (Mrs. John L.) Eddy, interview by author, handwritten notes, in author's possession, Dallas, May 1, 1978.

56. See table 16.

TABLE 16

AVERAGE COST PER FAMILY FOR VARIOUS ARTICLES
OF FOOD CONSUMED IN THE SOUTH CENTRAL STATES, 1901

Fresh Beef	$ 37.84
Salt Beef	.33
Fresh hog products*	15.60
Salt hog products*	28.09
Other meat	1.40
Poultry*	5.93
Fish	3.95
Eggs*	13.20
Milk*	12.25
Butter*	21.74
Cheese*	3.36
Lard*	14.31
Tea	2.69
Coffee	12.22
Sugar	15.70
Molasses	2.93
Flour and meal	22.68
Bread*	9.55
Rice	3.70
Potatoes*	11.54
Other Vegetables*	16.62
Fruit*	11.52
Vinegar, pickles, etc.*	4.41
Other foods*	21.12
Total	$292.68
Total value of goods likely produced by Dallas housewives	$176.73
Adjusted to typical southern diet	$232.10

Notes:

1. Asterisk denotes food that southern women grew and processed.
2. For problems in evaluating late-twentieth-century housework, see Rae Andre, *Homemakers: The Forgotten Workers* (Chicago: University of Chicago, 1981), esp. p. 5; William H. Gauger, "Household Work: Can We Add It to the GNP?" *Journal of Home Economics* 65 (Oct. 1973): 12–15; John Kenneth Galbraith, "The Economics of the American Housewife," *Atlantic Monthly* (Aug. 1973): 78–83. For a survey of earlier work on the value of housework, see Nona Glazer-Melbin, "Housework," *Signs* 1 (Summer 1976): 905–20.

Source:
Cost of Living and Retail Prices of Food: 18th Annual Report of the Commission on Labor, 1903, Document 23, 1903 (Washington, D.C.: GPO, 1904), 71, 81.

57. On southerners' diets, see Hilliard, *Hog Meat,* 37–44, 47–51.

58. Leon Harris, *Merchant Princes,* 163.

59. Winterbauer, interview, Mar. 29, 1978.

60. Cowan, *More Work,* 43–45. Strasser, *Never Done,* 6, gives a list of "modern conveniences" available to turn-of-the-century housewives. Leeds, *Household Budget,* 79–82.

61. Grace Deatherage Taylor, interview, July 28, 1977; May Cole's journal, A7781, DHS. On hired household help as a badge of middle-class status, see Dudden, *Serving Women,* 108–10, 112–13.

62. On increased productivity of the housewife, see Cowan, *More Work,* 99–101.

63. Tripp, interview, Nov. 9, 1978.

64. For one estimate of the length of the housewife's work day in 1900–1920 and of her increased productivity, Leeds, *Household Budget,* 68–73. Also see Cowan, *More Work,* 99–101, 158–59; and Marion Woodbury, "Time Required for Housework in a Family of Five With Small Children," *Journal of Home Economics* 10 (1918): 226–30.

65. On relationship of a mother's education to the amount of time she spent with her children, see Liebowitz, "Women's Work," 223–43, esp. 224.

66. See table 4.

Chapter 6. City of Women

A portion of this chapter has been published in Elizabeth York Enstam, "They Called It 'Motherhood': Dallas Women and Public Life," in *Hidden Histories of Women in the New South,* ed. Virginia Bernhard, Betty Brandon, Elizabeth Fox-Genovese, Theda Perdue, and Elizabeth H. Turner, 71–105 (Columbia: Univ. of Missouri Press, 1994). This material is republished here by permission of the Univ. of Missouri Press.

1. Quoted in "Texas: Texas Federation of Women's Clubs," in Jennie June (Mrs. J. C.) Croly, *History of the Woman's Club Movement in America* (New York: Henry G. Allen and Co., 1898), 1097.

2. *DMN,* July 5, 1896. See Carroll Smith-Rosenberg, "Bourgeois Discourse and the Progressive Era: An Introduction," in *Disorderly Conduct,* esp. 176; and Carroll Smith-Rosenberg, "The New Woman as Androgyne: Social Disorder and Gender Crisis, 1870–1936," in *Disorderly Conduct,* 245–96; Karen J. Blair, *Clubwoman as Feminist,* 98–99.

3. For a provocative treatment of the public-private dichotomy in the "separate spheres" paradigm, see Evans, "Women's History and Political Theory," 121–30.

4. *DMN,* May 1, May 10, and May 22, 1893. "Minutes of the First Session of the Texas Equal Rights Association, May 10, 1893," Texas Equal Rights Association Scrapbook, in Jane Y. McCallum Papers, Austin History Center, Austin Public Library, Austin, Tex.; reprinted in *Citizens at Last: The Woman Suffrage Movement in Texas,* ed. Ruthe Winegarten and Judith N. McArthur (Austin: Ellen C. Temple, 1987), 87–93. See A. Elizabeth Taylor, "The Woman Suffrage Movement in Texas," in *Citizens at Last,* 12–48, esp. 16–18, and in *Journal of Southern*

History 27, no. 2 (May 1951): 194–215. On pre-1890 southern suffragists, see Anne Firor Scott, *Southern Lady,* 165–76.

5. Interview with suffrage leaders the evening before the first meeting of the Texas Equal Rights Association, *DMN,* May 10, 1893.

6. On woman suffrage in Texas in 1868 and 1875, *Citizens at Last,* 56–61, 65–71.

7. Eleanor Flexner, *Century of Struggle: The Woman's Rights Movement in the U.S.* (New York: Atheneum, 1974), 159–62, 216–20, 222.

8. *DMN,* Mar. 14, Apr. 11, Apr. 23, and June 7, 1894, for Trumbull's remarks before the Texas Equal Rights Association convention in Fort Worth; June 9, 1894, for her work organizing new societies. Also *Dallas Daily Times Herald,* May 9, 1894; *Dallas Times Herald,* Feb. 3, 1979.

9. For reports of the regular meetings, *DMN,* May 9, May 21, June 19, Sept. 2, and Nov. 25, 1894; Jan. 6, Jan. 12, Feb. 17, Mar. 3, Mar. 17, Apr. 6, and Apr. 14, 1895. On women's claiming public spaces, see Kerber, "Separate Spheres," 36; and Sarah Deutsch, "Learning to Talk More Like a Man: Boston Women's Class-Bridging Organizations, 1870–1940," *American Historical Review* 97 (Apr. 1992): 379–484, esp. 390.

10. E.g., *DMN,* Mar. 17, Apr. 28, Sept. 9, Sept. 16, Sept. 23, and Sept. 30, 1894; Sept. 16, Sept. 26, and Sept. 29, 1895.

11. "House Joint Resolution No. 29 to Amend Section 2 of Article 6 of the Constitution of the State of Texas, 29 Mar. 1895," in Texas State Library; reprinted in *Citizens at Last,* 113–14.

12. *DMN,* June 9 and Nov. 4, 1892; June 13, June 19, and Oct. 8, 1894. A. Elizabeth Taylor, "Woman Suffrage," 21–33.

13. For reports of the last meetings and activities of the Texas Equal Rights Association, *DMN,* June 7, June 8, Oct. 13, Oct. 22, and Oct. 23, 1896. For news reports of the political parties, the Spiritualists, and the Freethinkers, *DMN,* July 3, Aug. 18, Aug. 29, Aug. 30, and Sept. 2, 1894; Oct. 1 and Oct. 7, 1895; and A. Elizabeth Taylor, "Woman Suffrage," 21.

14. For accounts of early meetings, *DMN,* June 18, June 25, July 8, and July 10, 1893. On program at State Fair, *DMN,* Oct. 23, 1893. Fannie Mae Hughes, "History of the Texas Woman's Press Association," pamphlet (Huntsville, 1935), in CAH. On the association's 25th anniversary, *DMN,* May 8, 1918.

15. On pre-1868 women's groups, see Barbara J. Berg, *The Remembered Gate: Origins of American Feminism: The Woman and the City, 1800–1860* (New York: Oxford Univ. Press, 1078); and Melder, *Beginnings of Sisterhood,* esp. 49–76, ch. 4. On origins of the Woman's Congress, see Ruth Bordin, *Frances Willard: A Biography* (Chapel Hill: Univ. of North Carolina Press, 1986), 70–71; and see Karen J. Blair, *Clubwoman as Feminist,* 23–24, 32–33, 39, 61–62.

16. Anne Firor Scott, "New Woman," 216–17, 219; and Anne Firor Scott, *Southern Lady,* 150–63. See also Marjorie Stratford Mendenhall, "Southern Women of a 'Lost Generation,'" *South Atlantic Quarterly* 33 (Oct. 1934): 337, 350–51; Julia Magruder, "The Typical Woman of the New South," *Harper's Bazaar* 33 (Nov. 3, 1900): 1685–87; Julia Magruder, "Club Life in the South," *Arena* 6 (1892): 374–78.

17. On organization of the congress by the Texas Woman's Press Association, *DMN,* Oct. 22 and Oct. 24, 1893; special train fares, *DMN,* Oct. 27, 1893; definition of

their purposes, *DMN*, Oct. 6, 1895. On the first year's complete program, *DMN*, Oct. 23, 1893; text of Trumbull's paper, in *DMN*, Oct. 29, 1893. Stella F. Christian, ed. and comp., *The History of the TFWC* (Houston: TFWC, 1919), 6. Christian is right in stating that the Texas Woman's Congress changed its name in 1894, but she errs in claiming that the group first met that year.

18. *DMN*, Oct. 10, 1897.

19. Christian, *History of TFWC*, 5–8, 12–15. Belle Smith and Adella (Mrs. E. P.) Turner represented the Dallas Standard Club; Susan (Mrs. J. C.) Ardrey and Sallie (Mrs. George K.) Meyer, the Pierian Club; Kate Scurry Terrell, the Shakespeare Club; and Pearl B. (Mrs. A. P.) Carey, the Current Events Club; ibid., 18–19. An early history of women's clubs in Texas is in *DMN*, Nov. 22, 1903. The Woman's Congress, later the Council of Women of Texas, met during the State Fair; *DMN*, Oct. 6, Oct. 28, and Oct. 13, 1894; Oct. 21, 1896; Oct. 18, 1897.

20. Karen J. Blair, *Clubwoman as Feminist*, 108–14. Martha E. D. White, "The Work of the Woman's Club," *Atlantic Monthly* 93 (May 1904): 615. With 275,000 members by 1904, the General Federation grew steadily and by 1914 had 48 state federations, 6,000 clubs, and 1,000,000 members. *General Federation of Women's Clubs Magazine*, Mar. 1914, published these statistics on its title page; e.g., this issue, in Mrs. Percy Pennybacker Papers, CAH. See Carl N. Degler, *At Odds: Women and the Family in America from the Revolution to the Present* (New York: Oxford Univ. Press, 1980), esp. ch. 13, "The World Is Only a Large Home."

21. Christian, *History of TFWC*, 12.

22. Minutes, DFWC, Dec. 2, 1917, in TDCDPL. *DMN*, Jan. 27, 1902, and Oct. 30, 1938; White, "Work of the Woman's Club," 615, 618–19, 620. *History of the DFWC, 1898–1936* (Dallas: DFWC, 1936), 16. Also Hazel, "Dallas Women's Clubs," 18–21.

23. For mention of one former library, see *Dallas Times Herald*, Feb. 5, 1956; on the series of meetings in 1894, *DMN*, Apr. 22, Apr. 23, Apr. 30, May 7, and May 21. On the Clionian and Fin de Siècle Clubs, the Chautauqua Circle, and the Theosophical Reading Class, *DMN*, Apr. 23, 1894.

24. Minutes, Board of Trustees, DPL, 1899–1935, esp. Mar. 1, Mar. 30, Apr. 26, June 15, and Sept. 19, 1899, in TDCDPL. *DMN*, Mar. 12 and Sept. 19, 1899. Also Larry Grove, *DPL: The First 75 Years* (Dallas: DPL, 1977), esp. 15–22, 25, 28, 33–37, 40, 52–53; and *History of DFWC*, 8, 15, 17.

25. Minutes, Library Board, Dec. 8, 1904, for books sent to the boys' club at Neighborhood House, and Feb. 14, 1907, for a similar arrangement at Methodist Wesley House.

26. Minutes, Library Board, Apr. 12, 1906 (p. 126); June 7, 1906 (130–31); Oct. 2, 1906 (132–33); Feb. 14, 1907 (140); June 13, 1907 (144); June 9, 1908 (147).

27. Heidi Gale Stein, "The DPL's Association with Andrew Carnegie's Library Philanthropy" (professional paper, North Texas State Univ., 1987), TDCDPL, 19–20, 23–29.

28. Journal of the Art Students' League, 1893–94, in John Henry Brown Papers, CAH; and *DMN*, Feb. 3, 1893. Random copies of *Round Table* are in TDCDPL. Geraldine Propper Cristol, "The History of the Dallas Museum of Fine Arts" (M.A. thesis, SMU, 1970), 5–6, 9–11; Jerry Bywaters, *Seventy-Five Years of Art in Dal-*

las: *The History of the Dallas Art Association and the Dallas Museum of Fine Arts* (Dallas: Dallas Museum of Fine Arts, 1978). *Dallas Times Herald,* Sept. 7 and Sept. 13, 1903. Also Hazel, "Dallas Women's Clubs," 20; and Michael V. Hazel, "Art for the People: Dallas' First Public Gallery," *Heritage News* 9 (Fall 1984): 4–8, 14.

29. Mrs. W. L. Crawford Papers, A3694, DHS. *Dallas Weekly Herald,* June 5, 1884. North Texas Female College, Sherman, Tex., *Catalogue, Session of 1893–1894,* in SMU Archives, p. 15. On exhibitions at Crawford Gallery even after the Dallas Museum of Art opened, *DMN,* June 1, 1913; Oct. 26, 1914; May 12 and May 19, 1918. *Notable Women of the Southwest,* 79; *Who's Who in Womanhood,* 47, 187; and Rogers, *Lusty Texans,* 249.

30. On founding of Public School Art League, unidentified booklet [hereafter "PTA History"] on history of the Dallas City Council of PTAs [1970s?], photocopy supplied by Archives, Dallas City Council of Parent-Teacher Associations, p. 2, in author's possession. See Cristol, "Museum," 12.

31. *DMN,* Nov. 9, 1901; Cristol, "Museum," 9–12, 17–19, 20–25, 28. See Grove, *DPL,* 37.

32. Cristol, "Museum," 19, 28–32; *DMN,* Dec. 24, 1932; and Hazel, "Dallas Women's Clubs," 20. Women also founded art museums in Cincinnati and Indianapolis; see Blake McKelvey, *The Urbanization of America [1860–1915]* (New Brunswick, N.J.: Rutgers Univ. Press, 1963), 208–209, 210–11. On attempts to enlarge audiences for late-nineteenth-century museums and libraries, see Neil Harris, *Cultural Excursions,* 17–18, 21–22, 23.

33. *Dallas Weekly Herald,* Jan. 2, 1874, and Feb. 14, 1875; Acheson, *Dallas Yesterday,* 211–13, 218, 221. *Dallas Directory for 1900* [hereafter *DCD 1900*] (Dallas: John F. Worley Directory Co., 1900), 49–50; *Directory of Greater Dallas, 1910* [hereafter *DCD 1910*] (Dallas: John F. Worley Printing Co., 1910), 56–58; and *Dallas City Directory for 1920* (Dallas: John F. Worley and Co., 1920), 45–49, include bands, orchestras, and choruses in the sections on clubs and societies. For occasions when music clubs and societies brought major performers to Dallas, *DMN,* May 1, 1912; Apr. 6, 1913; Oct. 6, 1915.

34. Lindsley, *History of Greater Dallas,* 2:389, 2:391. *DMN,* Jan. 4, 1907; Oct. 30, 1928. Wednesday Morning Choral Club Handbook (vertical file), in TDCDPL. A women's Beethoven Club also met during the 1890s: *DMN,* Jan. 10, 1895. By 1902, the Amphion Club gave regular recitals: *DMN,* May 27, 1902. *The Blue Book of Dallas: A Social and Club Directory, 1909* (Dallas: The South Publishing Co., 1909), 64.

35. *DMN,* Oct. 20, 1899; Acheson, *Dallas Yesterday,* 211–13; Rogers, *Lusty Texans,* 230–33; *DCD 1900,* 165; and obituary, in *Dallas Daily Times Herald,* Mar. 6, 1952.

36. St. Cecelia Club, *Yearbook,* 1902, 1903, and 1904; and *Blue Book of Dallas* (Dallas: John F. Worley, 1909), 59, both in TDCDPL. *DMN,* Sept. 23, 1895; Jan. 4, 1907; *Dallas Times Herald,* Aug. 28, 1949. For similar music clubs in Memphis, Louisville, Cleveland, Columbus, Grand Rapids, and elsewhere, see John Warren, "The Women Who Are Making a Musical America," *Delineator* 76 (Sept. 1910): 164, 210.

37. Rogers, *Lusty Texans,* 230–33.

38. Mrs. Jules Schneider Scrapbook, 1892–1905, DHS, contains numerous unidentified clippings about meetings of the Derthick Musical and Literary Club. *The Dallas Social Directory, 1900–1901,* comp. Ora Adams (Dallas: John F. Worley, 1900), 57, 65–66; and Michael V. Hazel, "The Dallas Symphony Club: Inaugurating a Musical Tradition," *Heritage News* 11 (Fall 1986): 8–10, 14. William H. Greenburg, "Autobiographical Sketch," unbound typescript, ca. 1948, p. 15; original in the American Jewish Archives, Cincinnati, Ohio; copy available in the Jewish Community Center Archives, Dallas. Thanks to archivist Fannie Zelcer, Cincinnati. Ellen Persons Bourland, "History of the Dallas Symphony Orchestra: 1900–1980" (M.A. thesis, SMU, 1981), 1–2, 7–8, 10, 15, 26, 31.

39. For comments by the store owners, *DMN,* Jan. 12, 1902. On contrast between arts supporters in Dallas and elsewhere, see Helen Lefkowitz Horowitz, *Culture in the City: Cultural Philanthropy in Chicago from the 1880s to 1917* (Lexington: Univ. of Kentucky Press, 1976).

40. *DMN,* Jan. 15, 1906. Regarding men of the 1850s and their response to the Masonic bell, McElhaney, ed., "Antebellum Chronicle," pt. 2, p. 12 (Feb. 16, 1860) and pp. 12–13 (Feb. 27, 1860).

41. On women's early charity work, see Berg, *Remembered Gate,* 145–51; Ryan, *Womanhood in America,* 128–31. On United Charities, see *DMN,* Oct. 1, 1925; McElhaney, "Childhood in Dallas," 63–65. Along with its private contributions, United Charities received annual donations from Dallas County and the City of Dallas: Minutes, Commissioners' Court, 17:187. *Dallas Daily Times Herald,* Feb. 18 and Mar. 10, 1895. Other Texas cities joined the trend toward organized charities: *Charities: The Official Organ of the Charity Organization Society of the City of New York* 14 (May 5, 1906): 701. The 1893–97 depression caused many cities to reassess their relief policies: see Katz, *Shadow of Poorhouse,* 147–49.

42. On conditions in the city hospital first opened in 1872, *DMN,* Aug. 11, 1889; on the opening of Parkland Memorial Hospital and an outline of the history of the city hospital since 1874, *DMN,* May 19 and May 20, 1894.

43. Public Relations file, St. Paul Hospital, Dallas, includes news clippings, essays in typescript, and pamphlets and brochures. The order was founded in France in 1633 by St. Vincent de Paul. Mother Seton's community in Maryland joined the Sisters of Charity in 1850, nearly 30 years after her death.

44. The first nursing school in Texas was established at Galveston's John Sealy Hospital in 1890. Before 1900, young nuns trained by observing and working with the older sisters.

45. *DMN,* Mar. 15, 1899; Jan. 12, 1902. The Home for Aged Women was listed in DCDs through the year 1907, and through 1920 in journals of annual councils of the diocese; in Archives, Episcopal Diocese of Dallas. And see David M. Dean, *Breaking Trail: Hudson Stuck of Texas and Alaska* (Athens, Ohio: Ohio Univ. Press, 1988), 31–32.

46. Archives, Episcopal Diocese of Dallas, have materials on St. Matthew's Home for Children; see esp. the letter from Hudson Stuck, dean of St. Matthew's Cathedral, to Mrs. Alloa Butler, Apr. 25, 1910.

47. On the opening and dedication of Sheltering Arms, *Dallas Daily Times Herald,*

Feb. 17, 1893; *DMN,* Apr. 16 and June 6, 1895; and *King's Messenger,* Apr. 1896, in Bridwell Library, Perkins School of Theology, SMU. Also *History of Woman's Work, North Texas Conference, Methodist Episcopal Church, South* (N.p.: History Committee, Woman's Missionary Society, North Texas Conference, 1929), 77, 129–32. On Virginia K. Johnson's life, *DMN,* July 21, 1934; and Elizabeth York Enstam, "Virginia K. Johnson: A Second Chance for the 'Wayward,'" *Heritage News* 10 (Summer 1985): 6–8, 14. On the national rescue movement, see McDowell, *Social Gospel,* 118–21; Ruth Rosen, *The Lost Sisterhood: Prostitution in America, 1900–1819* (Baltimore, Md.: The Johns Hopkins Univ. Press, 1982), 7–13.

48. Information on black women's employment is from tabulations, not sampling, of data in Manuscript Census 1880, Dallas County; Manuscript Census 1900, Dallas County. On the growing African-American middle class, Mamie L. McKnight, ed., *First African-American Families of Dallas: Creative Survival: Exhibition and Family History Memoirs* (Dallas: Black Dallas Remembered Steering Committee, 1987) 1:68, 73, 77, 90, 99, 103; and *African-American Families and Settlements,* 2:23–25, 96.

49. *DMN,* Mar. 27, 1893. Jennifer L. Pettit has investigated the relationships between African-American values and class identification in "Class, Consumerism, and Club Work: Racializing, Genderizing, and Politicizing Socioeconomic Identity," a paper presented at the Fourth Conference in Women's History, Charleston, S.C., June 12, 1997, copy in author's possession.

50. Archives, Julia C. Frazier Elementary School, Dallas: on loan to DHS, 1977–78; and Howard Univ. Office of Alumni Affairs. Gee, interview, Feb. 10, 1987.

51. On the men's literary group, *DMN,* Mar. 16, 1893; on the clubs, *DMN,* May 5, 1895, and *African-American Families and Settlements,* 2:25. On YMCA, *DMN,* Mar. 2, 1902; on WCTU, *DMN,* May 4, 1902. On black women's early literary societies, see Anne Firor Scott, *Natural Allies,* 112. Regarding their community work elsewhere, see Kathleen C. Berkeley, "'Colored Ladies Also Contributed': Black Women's Activities, from Benevolence to Social Welfare" in *Web of Southern Social Relations: Women, Family, and Education,* ed. Walter J. Fraser, Jr.; R. Frank Saunders, Jr.; and Jon L. Wakelyn (Athens: Univ. of Georgia Press, 1985), 181–203; Gerda Lerner, "Community Work of Black Club Women" in *Majority Finds Its Past,* 86–88. On the Texas Federation of Colored Women's Clubs, see Elizabeth L. Davis, *Lifting as They Climb: The National Association of Colored Women* (1933; reprint, Ann Arbor: University Microfilms International, 1971), 397–98.

52. U.S. Department of Commerce, Bureau of the Census, *Historical Statistics of the U.S.: Colonial Times to 1970,* pt. 1 (Washington, D.C.: U.S. Bureau of the Census, 1975), Series B5–10, p. 49; Series B67–98, p. 54. Louise Michele Newman, ed., *Men's Ideas, Women's Realities: Popular Science, 1870–1915* (New York: Pergamon Press, 1985), 106–108, 114–15. Donald R. Rindfuss, "Changing Patterns of Fertility in the South: A Social-Demographic Examination," *Social Forces* 57 (Dec. 1978): 621–35, notes that until 1945 the South had the highest fertility rates in the nation. Fertility rates in this section may have been slowed by the Civil War and Reconstruction, not by urbanization and the improvements in education

and living standards that affected the birth rate elsewhere. See Linda Gordon, *Woman's Body, Woman's Right: A Social History of Birth Control in America* (New York: Grossman-Viking, 1976), 48–49. See Carroll Smith-Rosenberg, "The Abortion Movement and the AMA, 1850–1880" in *Disorderly Conduct,* 224; Hareven, *Family and Kin,* 5, 14n 14. Richard A. Easterlin, "Factors in the Decline of Farm Family Fertility in the United States; Some Preliminary Research Results," *Journal of American History* 63 (Dec. 1976): 600–614, suggests several explanations but concludes only that scholars have inadequate data. See also Robert V. Wells, "Demographic Change and the Life Cycle of American Families," *Journal of Interdisciplinary History* 2 (Autumn 1971): 273–82.

53. U.S. Census Bureau, *Historical Statistics,* 47; Series B107–115, p. 55; Series B116–125; Series B126–135, p. 56; and Series B193–200, p. 63. See Robert V. Wells, "Women's Lives Transformed: Demographic and Family Patterns in America, 1600–1970," in *Women of America,* ed. Mary Beth Norton and Carol Berkin (Boston: Houghton Mifflin, 1979), 16–33; Daniel Scott Smith, "Family Limitation, Sexual Control, and Domestic Feminism in Victorian America" in *Clio's Consciousness Raised: New Perspectives on the History of Women,* ed. Mary S. Hartman and Lois Banner (New York: Harper Colophon, 1974), 119–36.

54. U.S. Census Bureau, *Historical Statistics,* Series F71–97 and F98–124, p. 231; Series F210–215, p. 238; Series F250–261, p. 240; and F287–296, p. 242. On rapid growth of national wealth between 1870 and 1910, see David Morgan, *Suffragists and Democrats: The Politics of Woman Suffrage in America* (East Lansing: Michigan State Univ. Press, 1972), 69.

55. The enrolled girls were 51.2 percent of African Americans aged 5–14, 51.5 percent of whites; and for boys, 48.2 percent of African Americans and 50.8 percent of whites. *12th U.S. Census, 1900: Population,* vol. 2, pt. 2, pp. 386, 388, 390, 392, 394, 396. *DMN,* June 1 and June 6, 1900; McElhaney, "Childhood in Dallas," 33–35.

56. For statistics on women's secondary and higher education, see Newman, *Men's Ideas,* 62–63. For number, sex, and race of those enrolled in the Dallas schools in 1900, see *12th U.S. Census, 1900: Population,* vol. 2, pt. 2, pp. 386, 388, 390, 392, 394, 396. See Barbara M. Solomon, *In the Company of Educated Women: A History of Women and Higher Education in America* (New Haven, Conn.: Yale Univ. Press, 1985), 123.

57. On the qualifications of women faculty members in the women's colleges, see Rothman, *Woman's Proper Place,* 39; and Christine Ladd Franklin, "The Education of Women in the Southern States," in *Woman's Work in America,* ed. Annie Nathan Meyer (1891; reprint, New York: Arno Press, 1972), 89–106 and 437. Information about St. Mary's, as both institute and college, is from: Archives, Episcopal Diocese of Dallas, including college catalogs and yearbooks; undated, typewritten memories of Bishop Alexander C. Garrett; and Gerald Grattan Moore, *The Diocese of Dallas, 1895–1952* (Dallas: St. Matthew's Cathedral, 1952), esp. 11–12, 24. Also *DMN,* Sept. 1, 1941; *Directory of Greater Dallas, 1910,* 84. Elizabeth York Enstam, "St. Mary's College: A Modern Education for Women," *Heritage News* 11 (Fall 1986): 11–14; Acheson, *Dallas Yesterday,* 249–52. St. Mary's closed in 1930: *Dallas Times Herald,* Feb. 5, 1956.

58. On the Vassar program and the controversy over academic training for women, see Maxine Seller, "G. Stanley Hall and Edward Thorndike on the Education of Women: Theory and Policy in the Progressive Era," *Educational Studies* 11 (1981): 365–74; and Rothman, *Woman's Proper Place*, 26–39, 41–42. On the American fashion of frail, sickly women, see Lois W. Banner, *American Beauty* (New York: Knopf, 1983), 45–65. On exercise as a popular movement, see Banner, *American Beauty*, 139–46. On the concept of "vigorous femininity," see Rothman, *Woman's Proper Place*, 32–37.

59. Karen J. Blair, *Clubwoman as Feminist*, 68–69; White, "Work of the Woman's Club," 614; and Anne Firor Scott, "Women's Voluntary Associations in the Forming of American Society," in *Making the Invisible*, 279–94. See other works by Anne Firor Scott: "Old Wives' Tales," in *Making the Invisible*, 330–31; "Woman's Place Is in the History Books," in *Making the Invisible*, 368–70; "On Seeing and Not Seeing," *Journal of American History* 71 (June 1984): 7–21, esp. 18, 20; and *Southern Lady*, 135–41.

60. *DMN*, Dec. 24, 1932; Cristol, "Museum," 28–32; and Hazel, "Dallas Women's Clubs," 20.

61. Mrs. W. L. Williams, *Golden Years: Autobiography* (Dallas: Baptist Standard Publishing Co., 1921), 114, 117–18. See Anne Firor Scott, *Southern Lady*, 135–41. The Woman's Missionary Union was formed in 1888 as an auxiliary to the Southern Baptist Convention. On missionary societies and the skills needed in public life, see Patricia R. Hill, *World Their Household*, 14, 78–79, 83–84, 108–109.

62. On the concept of "women's culture," see Kerber, "Separate Spheres," esp. 14–18. See Anne Firor Scott, "New Woman," 216–17. In 1901, the Dallas Women's Alliance of the First Unitarian Church was holding monthly drills in parliamentary procedure, and by 1907 so was the Dallas Woman's Forum. On voluntary associations as a "means to order," see Glazer, "Participation and Power," esp. 165–66, 168n 24.

63. "PTA History," 1–2. For examples of the Public School Art League's work, *DMN*, Nov. 9, 1901, and Jan. 12, 1902. On the league's work for the Dallas Art Museum, Cristol, "Museum," 10–12.

64. "PTA History," 2. "Dallas Mothers' Council Comes of Age" [memories of Olivia Allen Dealey], *DMN*, June 22, 1930.

65. On politics as more than elections and on women's political culture, see Paula Baker, "Domestication of Politics," 620–47, esp. 621–22, 624–25; and Susan Bourque and Jean Grosshaltz, "Politics as an Unnatural Practice: Political Science Looks at Female Participation," *Politics and Society* 4 (1974): 225–66, esp. 258–59.

66. *Galveston Morning News*, Apr. 10, 1883. On Olivia Dealey's work with the Public School Art League, *DMN*, Jan. 12, 1902; on her work with the Standard Club and the DFWC Parks and Playground Committee, *DMN*, July 19, 1908; Oct. 30, 1928; June 22, 1930. On her work with the DFWC Juvenile Court Committee, *Dallas Clubwoman*, Nov. 7, 1908, DHS. Obituary, *DMN*, Jan. 29, 1960; and *History of DFWC*, 45. Henry Camp Harris, Sr., "Dallas: Acorn Planters of Yesterday, 1864–1924," pamphlet [1966], p. 17, in DeGolyer Library, SMU; and Ernest Sharpe, *G. B. Dealey of the Dallas News* (New York: Henry Holt and Co., 1955), 26, 38, 148.

67. On Dallas women reformers, see Hazel, "Dallas Women's Clubs," 18–21. Judith N. McArthur, *Creating the New Woman: The Rise of the Southern Women's Progressive Movement in Texas* (Urbana: Univ. of Illinois Press, forthcoming, Spring 1998). The narrow definition of politics as involving only public office, voting, and elections has contributed to neglect of women's pre-1920 political history: see Maureen A. Flanagan, "Gender and Urban Political Reform: The City Club and the Woman's City Club of Chicago in the Progressive Era," *American Historical Review* 95 (Oct. 1990): 1032–50, esp. 1033–34, 1046, 1050; and Nancy F. Cott, "What's in a Name? The Limits of 'Social Feminism'; or, Expanding the Vocabulary of Women's History," *Journal of American History* 76 (Dec. 1989): 809–29, esp. 820–23. See Ryan, *Women in Public,* 174, for women's "reconstruction of the public" in American cities, which by 1880 "had become a wide open arena of political contention."

Chapter 7. City of Mothers

Portions of this chapter were first published as "The Forgotten Frontier: Dallas Women and Social Caring," *Legacies: A History Journal for Dallas and North Central Texas* vol. 1, no. 1 (Spring 1989): 20–28, and are republished by permission.

1. Kenneth Foree, "Patron Saint," *DMN,* Apr. 20, 1947.
2. "Pauline Periwinkle" column, *DMN,* Feb. 12, 1912. On the ways women's groups "created new civic space in which women used their new knowledge and power to expand state responsibility," see Kathryn Kish Sklar, "Two Political Cultures in the Progressive Era: The National Consumers' League and the American Association for Labor Legislation," in *U.S. History as Women's History: New Feminist Essays,* ed. Linda K. Kerber, Alice Kessler-Harris, and Kathryn Kish Sklar (Chapel Hill: Univ. of North Carolina Press, 1995), 36–62, esp. 41, 45–46, 47.
3. On the concept of the public culture, see Bender, "Wholes and Parts," 126–27, 130–32, 135.
4. *DMN,* Mar. 6, 1918; May 31, 1919; and June 7, 1925; and *Dallas Times Herald,* Aug. 28, 1949. *Dallas Weekly Herald,* June 9, 1881.
5. Minutes, Dallas German Ladies Aid Society, in TDCDPL, esp. June 5, Sept. 4, Oct. 2, and Nov. 6, 1918; Dec. 3, 1919.
6. Minutes, Commissioners Court, 8:289, 8:465, 8:534, 10:133, 10:191, 10:180, 10:377, 13:154, 13:582, 15:43, 15:51, 15:129, 15:169. Debbie Mauldin Cottrell, "The County Poor Farm System in Texas," *Southwestern Historical Quarterly* 93 (Oct. 1989): 169–90, esp. 170, 173, 178. On conditions at the Dallas County Poor Farm, *DMN,* Mar. 23 and Mar. 26, 1908. On the history of the poorhouse/poor farm as an American institution, see Katz, *Shadow of Poorhouse,* all of pt. 1, esp. 32.
7. *DMN,* Sept. 7, 1919.
8. Tripp, interview, Nov. 9, 1978. McElhaney, "Childhood in Dallas," 58–62; *Dallas Daily Times Herald,* Sept. 8, 1891.
9. On cities' responses to the depression, see Katz, *Shadow of Poorhouse,* 148–50.
10. On Progressivism, see Leroy Ashby, *Saving the Waifs: Reformers and Dependent*

Children, 1890–1917 (Philadelphia: Temple Univ. Press, 1984), 8–9; John White-clay Chambers's preface to *The Tyranny of Change: America in the Progressive Era, 1900–1917* (New York: St. Martin's Press, 1980), pp. v–vii; and Rothman, *Woman's Proper Place,* 107–20. On southern Progressives, see Anne Firor Scott, "A Progressive Wind from the South, 1906–1913," *Journal of Southern History* 29 (Feb. 1963): 53–70; Dewey W. Grantham, *Southern Progressivism: The Reconciliation of Progress and Tradition* (Knoxville: Univ. of Tennessee Press, 1983); and Lewis L. Gould, *Progressives and Prohibitionists: Texas Democrats in the Wilson Era* (Austin: Univ. of Texas Press, 1973).

11. Regarding the day nurseries and their founders' reluctance to appear to encourage mothers' employment, see Sonya Michel, "The Limits of Maternalism: Policies Toward American Wage-Earning Mothers During the Progressive Era," in *Mothers of a New World: Maternalist Policies and the Origins of Welfare States,* ed. Seth Koven and Sonya Michel, (New York: Routledge, 1993), 277–391.

12. For the history of the kindergartens, Mary I. Wood, *The History of the General Federation of Women's Clubs for the First 22 Years of Its Organization* (New York: General Federation of Women's Clubs, 1912), 167; and Seaholm, "Earnest Women," pt. 1, p. 131 and 176n 161. By 1904, clubwomen in various Texas cities and towns operated a total of 58 free kindergartens.

13. Mrs. J. C. Roberts to Anna Pennybacker, June 24, 1902, in TFWC Papers, Blagg-Huey Library, Texas Woman's Univ.; and Jacquelyn Masur McElhaney, "The Only Clean, Bright Spot They Know," *Heritage News* 11 (Fall 1986): 19–22. On the first campaign for a child labor law in Texas, see ch. 8 below. For kindergartens opened in Dallas, "A Plain Talk about the Kindergarten and a Report of the Work in Dallas of the Dallas Free Kindergarten and Training Association" [ca. 1914], in DHS. Mary King Drew, *A History of the Kindergarten Movement in Texas, from 1886 to 1942* (Dallas: N.p., [ca. 1942]), 8–10, 12–15, 18–22; McElhaney, "Clean, Bright Spot." "Report of the Dallas Free Kindergarten and Industrial Association, 1903–1904," esp. 7; and "Dallas Free Kindergarten Training School and Industrial Association, 1909–1910": both pamphlets in TDCDPL. *Dallas Times Herald,* Apr. 18, May 4, May 9, and June 8, 1897; Aug. 21, 1899; Oct. 21, 1901. *Dallas Daily Times Herald,* Jan. 30 and Feb. 22, 1900; May 26, 1901. For the history of the kindergarten movement nationwide, see Rothman, *Woman's Proper Place,* 99.

14. Minutes Book, Dallas Free Kindergarten, Training School, and Industrial Association, Jan. 1910–Jan. 1911, entries for Oct. 13 and Nov. 10, 1910 (pp. 65, 74), in DHS.

15. Ibid., Jan. 12, 1911 (p. 83).

16. Sara M. Evans, *Born for Liberty: A History of Women in America* (New York: Free Press, 1989), 147–50, 163–64; James Leibz, *A History of Social Welfare and Social Work in the United States* (New York: Columbia Univ. Press, 1978), 121–35, 180–83.

17. "Pauline Periwinkle" on Jane Addams and Hull House, *DMN,* Oct. 5, 1903. On founding of Neighborhood House, *DMN,* Sept. 30, 1917, and Mrs. Morris Liebman Papers, A3653, DHS. "Report, Free Kindergarten Association, 1903–1904," 8; and "Kindergarten Association, 1909–1910," 31–35. On Neighbor-

hood House's work, *Dallas Clubwoman,* July 4, 1908, in DHS. On Neighborhood House's services, see Robert A. Woods and Albert J. Kennedy, eds., *Handbook of Settlements* (New York: Russell Sage Foundation, 1911; reprint, New York: Arno Press and *New York Times,* 1970), 294; and Mrs. Warren L. Ross, "History of the Dallas [First Unitarian Church] Women's Alliance," pamphlet, 1968, p. 16, First Unitarian Church, Dallas; and copy in author's possession. For a general history of the settlement house movement, see Allen F. Davis, *Spearheads for Reform: The Social Settlements and the Progressive Movement, 1890–1914* (New York: Oxford Univ. Press, 1967).

18. The first Tag Day was in Feb. 1908: *History of DFWC,* 75. Receipts were audited by the Chamber of Commerce, signed by its president and secretary, sent to the city commissioner for finance, then published; *DMN,* June 19, 1911. The collection netted a tidy sum each year: $4,200 in 1908; $3,917 in 1909; $4,000 in 1910: *Dallas Clubwoman,* Mar. 6, 1909; Mar. 12, 1910.

19. Unidentified clipping, ca. 1917, in Mrs. Morris Liebman Papers, A3653, DHS.

20. *DMN,* Jan. 12, 1919.

21. On both Wesley Chapel and Wesley House, *DMN,* Jan. 1, 1907; *King's Messenger* Jan. 1913, 4; May 1913, 4; Nov. 1913, 2; Apr. 1914, 5; *History of Woman's Work, North Texas,* 28, 30, 86–88. See McDowell, *Social Gospel,* 62–64; McKelvey, *Urbanization of America,* ch. 11.

22. On "child-saving," see Katz, *Shadow of Poorhouse,* 114–15. On perhaps the earliest origins of the cult of motherhood, via the direct influence of Scottish thinkers on American social ideas, see Rosemarie Zagarri, "Morals, Manners, and the Republican Mother," *American Quarterly* 44 (June 1992): 192–215, esp. 203–207, 209. On "scientific motherhood," see Rothman, *Woman's Proper Place,* 97–132. See ch. 8 below.

23. Molly Ladd-Taylor, "Hull House Goes to Washington: Women and the Children's Bureau," in *Gender, Class, Race, and Reform in the Progressive Era,* ed. Noralee Frankel and Nancy S. Dye, 110–26 (Lexington: Univ. Press of Kentucky, 1991); and Linda Gordon, "Putting Children First: Women, Maternalism, and Welfare in the Early Twentieth Century," in Kerber, Kessler-Harris, and Sklar, *U.S. History as Women's History,* 71.

24. "PTA History," 4–5. *DMN,* Oct. 3, Oct. 4, and Oct. 10, 1909; Martha Lavinia Hunter, *A Quarter of a Century: History of the Dallas Woman's Forum* (Dallas: Dallas Woman's Forum, 1932), 10; *Club Woman's Argosy* 6 (Dec. 1909), 29, copy in Mrs. Percy Pennybacker Papers, CAH. On mothers' clubs nationwide, see Rothman, *Woman's Proper Place,* 103–104.

25. The Sisters of St. Mary of Namur opened Our Lady of Good Counsel School in 1903; the Sisters of Divine Providence opened St. Joseph's Academy for German Catholic children in 1905. On St. Joseph's Orphanage, see: undated, unidentified news clippings, and the "Remark Book," the journal of the Dunne Memorial Home for Boys, 1917–56, esp. pp. 279–83; all in Archives, Order of the Incarnate Word, St. Joseph's Center, Dallas. I thank Sister Laura Magowan, Dallas, and Sister Rita Pendergast, archivist, Incarnate Word Generalate, San Antonio, for history of the orphanage.

26. News clippings, brochure for a nonsectarian fundraising drive in 1921, and hand-

written memories of Sister Mary Eudes Tims, who came to Dallas in 1919 and died in 1977: all in Archives, Sisters of Our Lady of Charity, Mount St. Michael Home and School, Dallas. Special thanks to Sister Gabriel and Sister Saint Anthony. *Dallas Clubwoman,* Dec. 5, 1908; *Texas Catholic,* Nov. 12, 1960. Regarding the numbers of American children in various kinds of institutions, see Ashby, *Saving the Waifs,* xi.

27. Unless stated, information about the infant welfare and milk stations is from Folders F-A-2 and F-B-3, Archives, Child Care Dallas.

28. On Greenburg's club work, John Simons, ed., *Who's Who in American Jewry.* (New York: National News Association, 1939), 3:388. On services to children as a means for women's entry into public life, see Ashby, *Saving the Waifs,* 80–82.

29. Minutes, Directors Meeting, Dallas Infant Welfare and Milk Association, Apr. 29, 1915, F-B-3, Archives, Child Care Dallas. Trinity Play Park is treated below. In 1924, the Infant Welfare and Milk Association merged with the Dallas Free Kindergarten Association. For almost two more decades, the new organization ran its own small welfare system, with the free kindergartens, the day nurseries, and the various services available in the medical and dental clinics at the infant welfare and milk stations. All these services were supported by the Community Chest after 1921. In 1925, the kindergarten teachers' training school became part of SMU's Department of Education.

30. On the success of neighborhood clinics in northern cities before 1920 and their destruction by physicians in the late 1920s, see Katz, *Shadow of Poorhouse,* 137–45.

31. The Baby Camp was a children's hospital first opened in 1913.

32. On organization of the city's Department of Health, *DMN,* Jan. 1, 1916.

33. *DMN,* Jan. 1, Jan. 13, and Dec. 5, 1916.

34. Michael V. Hazel, "May Smith and the Dallas Baby Camp," *Heritage News* 10 (Summer 1985): 19–25.

35. *DMN,* Mar. 5, 1913. On opening ceremonies of Baby Camp, *DMN,* May 16, 1913; and Hunter, *Quarter of a Century,* 38.

36. By Jan. 1, 1930, the Bradford Memorial Hospital for Babies could accommodate 60 children; in 1948, Bradford Memorial joined two other children's hospitals to become the present Children's Medical Center of Dallas.

37. For Texas infant mortality figures, *DMN,* Feb. 23, 1916. On the annual Child Welfare Conferences sponsored by the Council of Mothers, *DMN,* Oct. 3, 10, 11, and 17, 1915; Feb. 13, 15, 17, 18, 22, 23, and Feb. 27, 1916. On the annual Better Babies Contest at the State Fair, *DMN,* Oct. 1, 19, 24, 25, 27, and 29, 1914; and Oct. 22, 1915. On the "Save the Children" drive, *DMN,* July 3 and 4, 1918. Random copies of *Texas Motherhood Magazine* are in various depositories in Texas, such as CAH and DPL; a complete run exists at the Medical College of Pennsylvania in Philadelphia. See Ladd-Taylor, "Hull House," 112–17, on ways children's issues enabled women to cross class and ethnic lines.

38. See Anne Firor Scott, *Natural Allies,* 4. On the problems of poverty and class conflict in northern cities, see McKelvey, *Urbanization of America,* ch. 10, pp. 143–55.

39. Meyerowitz, *Women Adrift,* xvii, xix, 46–55, 65–66, 68. And see Folbre and Abel, "Women's Work," 561.

40. Hallie Earle to her mother, Mar. 11 and Oct. 17, 1906, and an undated letter, all in Earle Graves Family Papers, 4A56, Texas Collection, Baylor Univ., Waco, Tex.

41. Wage/salary listings from "Help Wanted, Female" classified ads in *DMN*, Oct. 1906 and Apr. 1919.

42. *DMN*, May 20, 1912.

43. On Willard Hall, *DMN*, May 25, June 23, and July 25, 1913, and June 23, 1919. On the city-funded home, *DMN*, Jan. 9, Feb. 2, Feb. 21, and Feb. 23, 1916.

44. On St. Rita's, *DMN*, Dec. 29, 1918, and Aug. 16, 1919; on the Salvation Army's Girls' Hotel, *DMN*, May 4 and May 11, 1919; on the Girls' Friendly Inn, *Journal of the 25th Annual Council of the Protestant Episcopal Church in the Diocese of Dallas*, May 30–June 1, 1920, pp. 45–46; and *Journal of the 27th Council of the Protestant Episcopal Church in the Diocese of Dallas*, 1922, pp. 40–41. On women's objections to such homes, see Meyerowitz, *Women Adrift*, 79–84, 86–91.

45. "Dateline YWCA of Metropolitan Dallas," YWCA Archives, courtesy of Nancy Goebel; "YWCA, Dallas, Texas, 1908–1945," pamphlet, CAH; and *DMN*, Jan. 25, 1902; Oct. 12, 1909; Feb. 14, 1916; Jan. 12, Jan. 17, Jan. 18, Jan. 22, and Jan. 23, 1919. On the "opportunity school," *DMN*, Apr. 20, May 4, July 7, July 19, and Aug. 3, 1919. Also *Dallas Times Herald*, Aug. 28, 1949; and Elizabeth Hayes Turner, "Issues of Protection and Class: Galveston Women in the Progressive Era" (paper presented at Women and Texas History Conference, Austin, Oct. 6, 1990; copy in author's possession).

46. Anne Firor Scott, *Natural Allies*, 104–10; Meyerowitz, *Women Adrift*, 46; Rothman, *Woman's Proper Place*, 74; Frances Helen Mains and Grace Louchs Elliott, *From Deep Roots: The Story of the YWCA's Religious Dimensions* (New York: National Board of YWCA of USA, 1974), 12, on English origins of the Y; and Elizabeth Dodge Huntington Clarke, *The Joy of Service* (New York: National Board of YWCA, 1979).

47. *DMN*, Mar. 1, 1913; July 4, July 6, and Aug. 13, 1918; Aug. 10, 1919.

48. Minutes, DFWC, May 6, 1919, p. 2; and Oct. 1920, p. 2, in TDCDPL. *DMN*, Mar. 25, July 12, and July 13, 1919.

49. On adoption of commission plan of city government, see ch. 8 below. Minutes, City of Dallas, 12:486 (June 16, 1915); and 12:544 (May 1, 1916). Mayor Henry Lindsley's administration passed several new city ordinances related to health and safety, all recorded in Minutes, City of Dallas: clearing and cutting weeds, 12:507 (June 25, 1915); removal of dead trees and partially burned buildings, 12:566 (July 14, 1915); licensing of milk producers and sellers, 12:617 (Aug. 2, 1915). Elmer Scott, *Eighty-Eight Eventful Years: Being the Intimate Story of Elmer Scott in Industry and the Humanities and of the Civic Federation of Dallas Over a Third of a Century* (Dallas: Civic Federation of Dallas, 1954), 14–17, 32–39; also *DMN*, Apr. 21, 1954. See Katz, *Shadow of Poorhouse*, 152–56.

50. *DMN*, Jan. 1 and Feb. 23, 1916. *History of DFWC*, 76–78; *DMN*, Aug. 13 and Sept. 11, 1919. Men staying in the city-supported mission had to obey various regulations, including a curfew and general oversight of their activities.

51. In 1909, a representative of the Russell Sage Foundation spoke to the mayor and city council on the value of organizing the city's charities according to the best business and accounting methods: *DMN*, Dec. 23, 1909. On long-term effects—

not all of them positive—of federated charities and esp. the Community Chests, see Katz, *Shadow of Poorhouse*, 156–57; and Leibz, *History of Social Welfare*, 111–27.

52. *DMN*, July 18, 1917; *Dallas Times Herald*, Mar. 10, 1959; Elmer Scott, *Eighty-Eight Eventful Years*, 40.

53. Elmer Scott obituary, *DMN*, Apr. 21, 1954.

54. Kenneth Foree, "Tan Dorcas," *DMN*, June 20, 1946. On forms of benevolence among black and Latin residents elsewhere, see Nancy A. Hewitt, "Politicizing Domesticity: Anglo, Black, and Latin Women in Tampa's Progressive Movements," in Frankel and Dye, *Gender, Class, Race, and Reform*, 24–41.

55. On the African-American city welfare worker, *Dallas Express*, July 5, 1919; and Feb. 14 and May 10, 1920. On the Texas Federation of Colored Women's Clubs, *Dallas Express*, May 3, Nov. 22, and Dec. 6, 1919; and Elizabeth L. Davis, *Lifting as They Climb*, 397–98. On other clubs, *Dallas Express*, Sept. 13, 1919 (Chautauqua); Jan. 25, 1919 (Royal Arts Club); May 10, 1919 (Diamond Charity Club); Sept. 6, 1919 (Morning Star Charity Club); Mar. 6, 1920 (Corticelli Art Club); Apr. 10, 1920 (Ladies' Reading Club). On forms of benevolence among black women, see Darlene Clark Hine, "'We Specialize in the Wholly Impossible': The Philanthropic Work of Black Women" in *Lady Bountiful Revisited: Women, Philanthropy, and Power*, ed. Kathleen D. McCarthy (New Brunswick, N.J.: Rutgers Univ. Press, 1990), 70–93; and Gerda Lerner, "Community Work of Black Club Women" in *Majority Finds Its Past*, 83–93, and in *Journal of Negro History* 59 (Apr. 1974): 158–67.

56. *DMN*, July 9, 1922, and brochure published by Hope Cottage in the Hope Cottage Archives. *Who's Who of Womanhood of Texas*, 11, 183. Minutes, Commissioners Court, 17:166 (July 17, 1919), and 17:561 (Jan. 6, 1921).

57. *DMN*, Mar. 12, 1913, and Oct. 30, 1938.

58. Hunter, *Quarter of a Century*, 3, 16, 28–29, 33, 38; Also Lindsley, *History of Greater Dallas*, 2:392–93.

59. Unidentified clipping in Civic Federation file, TDCDPL; and see *DMN*, Jan. 1 and Apr. 2, 1916. For published reports of welfare work in Dallas, *DMN*, Mar. 9, 1913; Jan. 13, Jan. 20, Jan. 21, Jan. 22, Jan. 29, and Feb. 3, 1916; Feb. 2, 1917; and Oct. 21, 1918. In 1923, the Welfare Council was superseded by the Community Chest.

60. Entire issue, *Dallas Survey: A Journal of Social Work* 2 (Sept. 15, 1918): available TDCDPL. See Anne Firor Scott, *Natural Allies*, 178–80.

Chapter 8. Women's Political Culture and the Modern Service City

Portions of this chapter have been published in Elizabeth York Enstam, "They Called It 'Motherhood': Dallas Women and Public Life," in *Hidden Histories of Women in the New South*, ed. Virginia Bernhard, Betty Brandon, Elizabeth Fox-Genovese, Theda Perdue, and Elizabeth H. Turner, 71–95 (Columbia: Univ. of Missouri Press, 1994). This material is republished here by permission of the Univ. of Missouri Press.

1. *DMN,* Jan. 15, 1906; *History of DFWC,* 30–35.

2. On women's pre-suffrage political effectiveness, see Suzanne Lebsock, "Women and American Politics, 1880–1920," in *Women, Politics, and Change,* ed. Louise Tilly and Patricia Gurin (New York: Russell Sage Foundation, 1990), esp. 30. For a statistical assessment of women's ability to alter public policies before 1920, see Skocpol et al., "Women's Associations," 686–701, esp. 687–88, 691, 694–96. On women's fundamental roles in altering governmental responsibilities, see Maureen A. Flanagan, "The City Profitable, the City Livable: Environmental Policy, Gender, and Power in Chicago in the 1910s," *Journal of Urban History* 22 (Jan. 1996): 163–90, esp. 165–67, 172–76, 178–81; and Sklar, "Historical Foundations," 43–93; esp. see 44–46 for Sklar's definition of the issue. See Paula Baker, "Domestication of Politics," 620–47.

3. In the mid-1880s, Galveston spent $40,000 a year on public education, Houston $30,000, and San Antonio $32,000, compared to Dallas's $2,500. Even after they began receiving $20,000 a year from state funds, Dallas schools had less money than those in the other major Texas cities. See McElhaney, "Childhood in Dallas," 22, 28–31, 142nn 80 and 90.

4. For the earliest examination of women's political culture, see Paula Baker, "Domestication of Politics." See Jacquelyn Dowd Hall, "Partial Truths: Writing Southern Women's Histories," in *Southern Women: Histories and Identities,* ed. Virginia Bernhard, Elizabeth Fox-Genovese, Theda Perdue, and Betty Brandon (Columbia: Univ. of Missouri Press, 1992), 11–29.

5. On the concept of the modern service city, see Monkkonen, *America Becomes Urban,* esp. 6, 130, 157, 215, 218–22.

6. Gould, *Progressives and Prohibitionists,* 25–26, 36–40, 285–88.

7. *13th U.S. Census, 1910,* vol. 9: *Manufactures 1909,* 1214. See U.S. Dept. of Commerce and Labor, Bureau of the Census, *Occupations at the 12th Census,* Special Reports (Washington, D.C.: GPO, 1904): 437, 439.

8. Obituary, in *DMN,* Mar. 8, 1924. On the child labor law, see Mrs. J. C. Roberts to Mrs. [Percy V.] Pennybacker, May 26, June 24, and Oct. 3, 1902, all in TFWC Papers, Blagg-Huey Library, Texas Woman's Univ., Denton; and *DMN,* Jan. 12, Feb. 10, and May 1, 1902. On Ruth Carroll, see "Pauline Periwinkle" column, *DMN,* Oct. 4, 1897; and *Texas Farmer,* Oct. 7, 1899. Thanks to Tonia Carlisle, archivist, Texas State Library, for locating this citation. See Christian, *History of TFWC,* 86–87, 135–36, 311.

9. In 1902–1903, Hudson Stuck, dean of St. Matthew's Cathedral, acted more or less as the women's "front man": see Roberts's letters, cited above, and Stuck's own comments in *DMN,* Feb. 10, 1902. See Judith N. McArthur, "Saving the Children: The Women's Crusade Against Child Labor, 1902–1918" in *Women and Texas History: Selected Essays,* ed. Fane Downs and Nancy Baker Jones (Austin: Texas State Historical Association, 1993), 57–71. Nationwide, the issue created rifts among women along class lines: see Ladd-Taylor, "Hull House," 110–26, esp. 115–21. On enforcement, see *DMN,* Sept. 26, 1918; Apr. 2 and Aug. 27, 1919; and Ruth A. Allen, *East Texas Lumber Workers: An Economic and Social Picture, 1870–1950* (Austin: Univ. of Texas Press, 1961), 44, 61–65. See Katz, *Shadow of Poorhouse,* 130–34.

10. *Dallas Times Herald*, May 26, 1897; McElhaney, "Childhood in Dallas," 55–58.

11. *DMN*, Feb. 2, 1903; and Oct. 30, 1938; and see Ashby, *Saving the Waifs*, 4.

12. For juvenile justice law, see *General Laws of the State of Texas Passed at the Regular Session of the 30th Legislature . . . Jan. 8, 1907 . . . [to] Apr. 12, 1907* (Austin: von Boeckmann-Jones Co., Printers, 1907), 135–41. *DMN*, June 29 and July 2, 1906; Oct. 30, 1938. *History of DFWC*, 11, 33; Dallas Woman's Forum, *Yearbook, 1907–1908*, in Archives, Dallas Woman's Forum, p. 31; Hunter, *Quarter of a Century*, 13; Christian, *History of TFWC*, 134, 143, 187–88, 219–20, 243. Also see Janet Schmelzer, "Thomas M. Campbell: Progressive Governor of Texas," *Red River Valley Historical Review* 3 (Fall 1978): 52–63; Katz, *Shadow of Poorhouse*, 134–37; and Susan Tiffin, *In Whose Best Interest?: Child Welfare Reform in the Progressive Era* (Westport, Conn.: Greenwood Press, 1982), 215–29.

13. On the Girls' Training School, *DMN*, Oct. 17, 1914; Christian, *History of TFWC*, 208–10, 219–20; "The Girls' Training School," *Club Woman's Argosy* 6 (Dec. 1909), 3: available in the Pennybacker Papers.

14. *DMN*, Feb. 26, 1906; Feb. 16, 1914. On work for the detention home, *Dallas Clubwoman*, July 19, Nov. 7, Nov. 21, and Dec. 5, 1908; Jan. 16 and Jan. 23, 1909; and *History of DFWC*, 11, 32, 37, 52.

15. *DMN*, Feb. 5, 1914.

16. "PTA History," 3, 5, 8, 9, 11, 12. On mothers' clubs' continued vigilance regarding school conditions, *DMN*, May 16, 1912; *Dallas Times Herald*, Feb. 5, 1956.

17. Tiffin, *In Whose Best Interest?*, 215; Ashby, *Saving the Waifs*, 13.

18. *DMN*, June 8, 1938. Diana Church, "Mrs. E. P. Turner: Clubwoman, Reformer, Community Builder," *Heritage News* 10 (Summer 1985): 9–14.

19. Dallas Woman's Forum, *Yearbook, 1907–1908*, 30–31, 34; Edna Frances Wesson, "Through the First 21 Years with the Dallas Woman's Forum," typescript; *Yearbook, 1910–1911*, 14–15; and *Yearbook, 1911–1912*, 16–19; all in Archives, Dallas Woman's Forum. Hunter, *Quarter of a Century*, 1–2, 4–6, 11; and Helen M. Winslow, "The Story of the Woman's Club Movement," *New England Magazine* 38 (July 1908): 543–57.

20. Dallas Woman's Forum, *Yearbook, 1907–1908*, 31; Hunter, *Quarter of a Century*, 3–4.

21. *Dallas Weekly Herald*, Apr. 3, 1884; M. E. Bolding with Erie H. Bolding, *Origin and Growth*, 23.

22. Minutes, Dallas City Council, vol. 32 (1906): for city chemist, Aug. 14 (p. 214) and Sept. 11 (248). On pure food and drug ordinance, Nov. 7 (315); Nov. 13 (331–32); Dec. 11 (371); and Jan. 22, 1907 (419). See also Ordinance Records, City of Dallas, 19:177–81, 19:231, 19:609; *Dallas Clubwoman*, Jan. 23, 1909.

23. *DMN*, Jan. 1, Jan. 3, Feb. 2, Feb. 3, and Feb. 7, 1907. *History of DFWC*, 37, includes names of the members of the Federation committee appointed at the city's request to help with enforcement. Dallas Woman's Forum, *Yearbook, 1907–1908*, 31; Hunter, *Quarter of a Century*, 4, 44, 46. Lindsley, *History of Greater Dallas*, 2:302. Minutes, City of Dallas, vol. 32 (1906): for the Board of Health, Sept. 25 (p. 261); Oct. 4 (275); Oct. 9 (298). Ordinance Records, 13:459, 19:177–81, 19:231, 19:609. "Report of the City Chemist," *Annual Reports of the City of*

Dallas, 1906–1907 (Dallas, 1907), 131–40, in DPL. See Elizabeth Hayes Turner, "Women, Religion, and Reform," 75–95.

24. *DMN,* Feb. 11, 1907. On the ways women's stands on civic issues diverged from men's, see Flanagan, "Gender and Urban Political Reform," 1032–33. On ways even men in commission governments preferred to spend public money, see Bradley Rice, *Progressive Cities: The Commission Government Movement in America, 1901–1920* (Austin: Univ. of Texas Press), 69–70, 86.

25. *History of DFWC,* 39. On how such vital issues have been neglected by historians, see Anne Firor Scott, *Natural Allies,* 157–58.

26. *DMN,* May 2, 1912.

27. *Dallas Times Herald,* Dec. 30, 1917.

28. On the origins of the term *feminism,* see Nancy F. Cott, *The Grounding of Modern Feminism* (New Haven, Conn.: Yale Univ. Press, 1987), 14–15, 289n 4. For definitions and explanations of "cultural feminism," see Cott, "What's in a Name?" esp. 815, 826; Josephine Donovan, *Feminist Theory: The Intellectual Traditions of American Feminism* (New York: Holmes and Meier, 1980), 31–60. And see Karen J. Blair, *Clubwoman as Feminist,* 5: Blair discusses the politicizing of "domestic feminism," but she differs from other scholars on this subject in using this term instead of "cultural feminism." Also see Cott, *Grounding,* 16, 19; and Ellen DuBois et al., "Politics and Culture in Women's History: A Symposium," *Feminist Studies* 6 (Spring 1980): 26–64.

29. Having lost dominance in the 1917 city elections, the Citizens' Association resumed its "behind-the-scenes" leadership in 1931, as the Citizens' Charter Association; see Acheson, *Dallas Yesterday,* 165–68, 170–77, 188–90. See Rice, *Progressive Cities,* 15, 25, 28, 30–33, 63–66, 76, 88–91; and David Hammack, "Problems of Power in the Historical Study of Cities, 1800–1960," *American Historical Review* 83 (Apr. 1978): 323–49. For the ways urbanization required more efficient and better organized city administration, see Katz, *Shadow of Poorhouse,* 152–54.

30. Ella (Mrs. P. P.) Tucker to President, TFWC, Apr. 3–5, 1911, in Records, DFWC, in TDCDPL; and "PTA History," 7, 9. Regarding clubwomen's alliances with male leaders, see Deutsch, "Learning to Talk," 379–404, esp. 391.

31. *DMN,* May 3, 1918.

32. On the nineteenth-century ideology of motherhood, see Ryan, *Empire of Mother,* esp. 8, 17–18, 46–47, 51, 56–59; and Ryan, *Cradle of Middle Class,* 27–32, 85, 89–91. On development of women's political culture in the U.S., see Sklar, "Historical Foundations," 43–93, esp. 60–69; and Paula Baker, "Domestication of Politics." See Hall, "Partial Truths," 22–23.

33. *DMN,* Oct. 30, 1938; Apr. 14, 1941; *Who's Who of Womanhood,* 167, 204.

34. On women and public spaces, see Deutsch, "Learning to Talk," 390; and Kerber, "Separate Spheres," 36.

35. On the events and rhetoric of the 1908 school board race, see *DMN,* 1908, as follows: getting names on the ballot, and the man who withdrew from the race to work for Adella Kelsey (Mrs. E. P.) Turner, Mar. 23; not "electioneering" at the polls and the "non-political" and "non-competitive" nature of the race, Mar. 25 and 26, Apr. 6; distributing campaign literature in the "proper wards," Mar. 26,

28, and 29; refusing "special favors," Mar. 31; prejudice against southern women in "prominent places," Apr. 4; men supporting the women candidates, Mar. 29 and 31, Apr. 4; election returns, Apr. 8 and 9. Also Mar. 28 and 29, Apr. 5 and 6. On the notion that women's "special nature" lifted all their endeavors "above politics," see Paula Baker, "Domestication," 631.

36. *DMN*, Mar. 25 and 26, and Apr. 6, 1908; Michael V. Hazel, "A Mother's Touch: The First Two Women Elected to the Dallas School Board," *Heritage News* 12 (Spring 1987): 9–12.

37. Minutes, Dallas Board of Education, May 4, June 3, Aug. 12, Aug. 29, Sept. 22, Oct. 19, and Dec. 14, 1908; Jan. 18, Feb. 19, June 30, and July 12, 1909.

38. Minutes, Dallas Board of Education, June 30, 1909; *History of DFWC*, 5, 61–68.

39. Hazel, "Mother's Touch," 12.

40. On later school board elections, see *DMN*, Apr. 2, 1912; Apr. 3, 1914; Apr. 5, 1916. In 1918, two women ran as PTA candidates, but both lost: *DMN*, Feb. 2, 1918.

41. On the campaign for parks and playgrounds, see McElhaney, "Pauline Periwinkle," 16. On the uses of parks by different segments of the urban population, see Roy Rosenzweig, "Middle-Class Parks and Working-Class Play: The Struggle Over Recreational Space in Worcester, Massachusetts, 1870–1910," *Radical History Review* 21 (Fall 1979): 31–46. For a history of parks and playgrounds, see Maury Klein and Harvey A. Kantor, *Prisoners of Progress: American Industrial Cities, 1850–1920* (New York: Macmillan, 1976), 401–402.

42. Harry Jebsen, Jr.; Robert M. Newton; and Patricia R. Hogan, *Centennial History of the Dallas, Texas, Park System, 1876–1976* (Lubbock, Tex.: Texas Tech Univ. Press, 1976), 4–13, 36, 91, 133, 217–18, 220–21, 227.

43. City of Dallas, *Report for the Year 1914–1915 of the Park Board of the City of Dallas* (Dallas: City of Dallas, 1915), 7, 14–15, 51–52; and City of Dallas, "A City Plan for Dallas: Report of the Park Board [1911]," Feb. 21, 1913, pamphlet: both in TDCDPL. *DMN*, Feb. 16, 1914; *History of DFWC*, 8–9, 48–52, 57–58.

44. *History of DFWC*, 49, 57–58; *DMN*, Oct. 30, 1938.

45. *DMN*, Jan. 1, 1916. *History of DFWC*, 58; and Jebsen, Newton, and Hogan, *Centennial of Dallas Park System*, 226–27, 232. On DFWC members in an advisory capacity concerning parks and playgrounds, *DMN*, May 10, 1912. On the park for Mexican children, *DMN*, Nov. 10, 1918.

46. On the sources of Dallas water, M. E. Bolding with Erie H. Bolding, *Origin and Growth*, 11–12, 18–20, 21, 33, 48, 56–59, 65–68, 71–72, 73–74, 92. On the economic impact of water and waste disposal systems, see Stuart Galishoff, "Triumph and Failure: The American Response to the Urban Water Supply Problems, 1860–1923," in *Pollution and Reform in American Cities, 1870–1920*, ed. Martin V. Melosi, 35–57 (Austin: Univ. of Texas Press, 1980); and Joel A. Tarr et al., "The Development and Impact of Urban Wastewater Technology: Changing Concepts of Water Quality Control, 1850–1930," in Melosi, *Pollution and Reform in American Cities*, 59–82. See Melosi, "Environmental Crisis in the City: The Relationship Between Industrialization and Urban Pollution," in Melosi, *Pollution and Reform in American Cities*, 3–31. On how clubwomen challenged men's attitudes, altered the definition of "political" issues, and so widened the functions of

government and its responsibilities to people, see Paula Baker, "Domestication," 641; Deutsch, "Learning to Talk," 390.

47. M. E. Bolding with Erie H. Bolding, *Origin and Growth,* 56–57.

48. *DMN,* Dec. 8, 1909; *History of DFWC,* 6–7, 56–65. Galishoff, "Triumph and Failure," 36–38.

49. *History of DFWC,* 1–2, 56–60, 65. *Dallas Clubwoman,* Nov. 7 and Dec. 5, 1908; Apr. 10, 1909; Mar. 12, 1910.

50. *DMN,* Dec. 8, 1909 and Oct. 30, 1938; M. E. Bolding with Erie H. Bolding, *Origin and Growth,* 56–57, 71–75, 92.

51. On attitudes of Dallas business owners and leaders toward communitywide projects, and esp. for comprehensive city planning, see William H. Wilson, *The City Beautiful Movement* (Baltimore, Md.: Johns Hopkins Univ. Press, 1989), ch. 12, esp. 256, 272–73, 275.

52. William H. Wilson, *City Beautiful;* Donald A. Krueckerberg, ed., *Introduction to Planning History in the U.S.* (New Brunswick, N.J.: Rutgers Univ. Press for Center for Urban Policy Research, 1983), esp. 3–6; Jon A. Peterson, "The City Beautiful Movement: Forgotten Origins and Lost Meanings," in Krueckerberg, *Introduction to Planning History,* 40–57, esp. 41–53; and A. F. Davis, "Playgrounds, Housing, and City Planning," in Krueckerberg, *Introduction to Planning History,* 73–87, esp. 83–85. For the American mythos of "the West" with regard to the rural-urban difference, and on gendered politics, see Arnaldo Testi, "The Gender of Reform Politics: Theodore Roosevelt and the Culture of Masculinity," *Journal of American History* 81 (Mar. 1995): 1509–33, esp. 1512, 1522–24, 1530–31; for a more literary view, see Jane Tompkins, *West of Everything: The Inner Life of Westerns* (New York: Oxford Univ. Press, 1992).

53. *Texas Club Woman,* Apr. 27, 1914; thanks to Judith N. McArthur for this source, available in the Pennybacker Papers.

54. On the issue of social control, see Eileen Boris, "Reconstructing the 'Family': Women, Progressive Reform, and the Problem of Social Control," in Frankel and Dye, *Gender, Class, Race, and Reform,* 73–86, esp. 74, 78, 82.

55. Wesson, "Through the First 21 Years"; Dallas Woman's Forum, *Yearbook, 1910–1911,* 15. See Katz, *Shadow of Poorhouse,* 123–24, on U.S. class conflict, 1880–1917. On agreement among women concerning concepts of womanhood and motherhood, see Paula Baker, "Domestication," 633, 640. On cross-class efforts in Texas, Elizabeth Hayes Turner, "Issues of Protection and Class."

56. On how women altered the definition of political issues, see Deutsch, "Learning to Talk," 390; Paula Baker, "Domestication," 641. And see Monkkonen, *America Becomes Urban,* 93–95, 101–102, 106–10, 145–46, 213, 215, 230, 309nn 13 and 14; and Ashby, *Saving the Waifs,* 10.

57. Michael McGerr, "Political Style and Women's Power, 1830–1930," *Journal of American History* 77 (Dec. 1990): 804–85. On how women changed American society, see Anne Firor Scott, *Natural Allies,* 175–77. On the home as a base of power, see Glenna Matthews, *"Just a Housewife": The Rise and Fall of Domesticity in America* (New York: Oxford Univ. Press, 1987), 64–71, 75–91.

58. On male-female differences regarding the role of local government in achieving an acceptable urban environment, see Flanagan, "City Profitable," 165–67, 173–74.

59. On problems with distinctions between public and private, see Nancy F. Cott, "Giving Character to Our Whole Civil Polity: Marriage and the Public Order in the Late 19th Century," in Kerber, Kessler-Harris, and Sklar, *U.S. History as Women's History,* 107–21, esp. 109–10, 114–15.

60. On the public culture and the city, see Thomas Bender, "Metropolitan Life and the Making of Public Culture," in Mollenkopf, *Power, Culture, and Place,* 261–71. See Katznelson, "Reflections on Space and the City," 285–300, esp. 299.

Chapter 9. Suffragists and the City

1. Mrs. E. A. DeWitt, "The History of the Thursday Morning Study Club," typescript [ca. 1942], A4457-Msb, DHS, p. 3.

2. For women on city advisory committees, see *DMN,* May 26, 1910. On the clubwomen's sense of the men's cooperation, see Ella (Mrs. P. P.) Tucker to President, TFWC, Apr. 3–5, 1911, in DFWC Records, in TDCDPL. On clubwomen's alliances with male leaders, see Deutsch, "Learning to Talk," 379–404, esp. 391.

3. *DMN,* Mar. 13 and 16, 1913. On Craig, Mrs. M. K. Craig, "Pioneer Southern Woman Tells Why She Became a Suffragist," *Dallas Times Herald,* June 10, 1917; Elizabeth Brooks, *Prominent Women of Texas* (Akron, Ohio: Werner Co., 1896), 151–52; and Acheson, *Dallas Yesterday,* 209–11. On Turner, Mrs. John S. Turner, "Transformation of the Home due to Modern Industrialization," *Dallas Times Herald,* July 29, 1917; Sinclair Moreland, *The Texas Women's Hall of Fame* (Austin: Biographical Press, 1917), 26–28; and Baines, *Story of Texas White Ribboners,* 46–48. *Dallas Times Herald,* July 29, 1917.

4. Quotation in Jane Y. McCallum, "Activities of Women in Texas Politics," in *Texas Democracy: A Centennial History of Politics and Personalities of the Democratic Party, 1836–1936,* ed. Frank Adams (Austin: Democratic Historical Association, 1937) 1:469–70. On the clubwomen's initial reluctance to admit their involvement in politics, see Enstam, "They Called It 'Motherhood'," 71–105.

5. *Houston Chronicle,* June 24, 1966; obituary, *Dallas Times Herald,* July 15, 1966; *Fort Worth Star-Telegram,* Aug. 14, 1932, vertical file, CAH; review of *Cottonwoods Grow Tall, New York Times,* Nov. 23, 1958; Florence Elberta Barns, *Texas Writers of Today* (Dallas: Tardy Publishing Co., 1935), 244; and *The Handbook of Texas* (Austin: Texas State Historical Association, 1961), 3:407.

6. On Armstrong, *DMN,* Mar. 7, 1960. Marguerite Davis to Minnie Fisher Cunningham, Jan. 7, 1916; Cunningham to Texas Erwin Armstrong, Feb. 17 and Sept. 26, 1917: both in McCallum Papers. Davis to Cunningham, Mar. 5, 1917, in Minnie Fisher Cunningham Papers, Houston Metropolitan Research Center, Houston Public Library.

7. Vernice Reppert to Cunningham, May 30, 1917; and Nona Boren Mahoney to Jesse Daniel (Mrs. Roger P.) Ames, Oct. 22, 1918, both in Jane Y. McCallum Papers; *Fort Worth Record,* June 27, 1920, clipping in the Jesse Daniel Ames Papers, DHS; and obituary in *DMN,* Mar. 23, 1926.

8. Reppert to Cunningham, May 18, 1919, in Cunningham Papers; *DMN,* May 18, 1919; *History of DFWC,* 47–55.

9. Elizabeth Hayes Turner discusses the significance of urbanization for women's

organizations in "Women Progressives and the Origins of Local Suffrage Societies in Texas," paper presented at meeting of Houston Area Southern Historians, Oct. 1991: copy in author's possession. See Gould, *Progressives and Prohibitionists,* 29, 249–50.

10. A. Elizabeth Taylor, "Woman Suffrage," 30n 50.

11. On the 1914 Texas Equal Suffrage Association convention, *DMN,* Apr. 8–10, 1914. On the 1916 meeting, *DMN,* May 10–13, 1916; and Helen D. Moore to Nona Boren Mahoney, May 4, 1916, in McCallum Papers.

12. *DMN,* June 12 and June 13, 1916; June 15, 1919; and McCallum, "Activities of Women," 470.

13. William L. McDonald, *Dallas Rediscovered,* 231.

14. *DMN,* Oct. 24, 1915.

15. On other activities at State Fair, Edith H. League to Armstrong, Oct. 17, 1917; Reppert to Annette Finnigan, Aug. 2, 1914; Armstrong to Cunningham, Aug. 9, 1914; and Hattie D. M. Wallie to Nona Boren Mahoney, July 17, 1914, all in McCallum Papers. And *DMN,* Oct. 23 and 24, 1913; Oct. 1, 27, 28, and 29, 1914; Oct. 7, 1915.

16. *DMN,* Oct. 23, 1915; Oct. 23 and 24, 1916.

17. *DMN,* Feb. 23, 1916. On the Cattlemen's Association reception, see *DMN,* Mar. 1 and 9, 1919.

18. On the public culture, see Bender, "Wholes and Parts," 120–36, esp. 126–28, 130–31, 135.

19. *The Brewers and Texas Politics* (San Antonio: Anti-Saloon League of San Antonio, 1916), all legal papers, including evidence and depositions, of the suit. On the original association of woman suffrage and prohibition in the public mind, McCallum, "Activities of Women," 467. On temperance movement as an attack on male privilege, see Blocker, "Separate Paths," 463–64, 466, 469, 471, 472.

20. *DMN,* Jan. 25, 26, 27, and 29; Feb. 8 and 15, 1916.

21. *DMN,* Jan. 21, 28, and 30; Feb. 1 and 11; Apr. 2, 4, and 5, 1916.

22. Any electoral victory for Prohibitionists alarmed the suffragists, who feared that the Prohibitionists might lose interest in woman suffrage if they decided they could win without women's votes: Reppert to Cunningham, Dec. 13, 1918, in McCallum Papers.

23. On the Patriotic Parade, *DMN,* Apr. 10 and 11, 1917. On Dallas suffragists and support for the U.S. government, Mrs. David M. Munro to Cunningham, Apr. 8, 1917, in McCallum Papers; for the DESA's other war work, Katherine Jalonick to Cunningham, Dec. 3, 1917; Reppert to Cunningham, May 7, 1917; and Reppert to Cunningham, n.d., all in the Cunningham Papers; *DMN,* May 1, 3, 5, and 24, 1917; *DMN,* Nov. 15 and 20, 1917.

24. Reppert to Cunningham, June 7 and Nov. 30, 1917; and n.d., all in McCallum Papers; *DMN,* June 7 and Oct. 4, 1917; Mar. 17 and 29, May 9 and 12, 1918.

25. Mahoney to Ames, Oct. 22, 1918, in McCallum Papers.

26. *DMN,* Apr. 22, 1894.

27. *DMN,* June 10, 1917.

28. *DMN,* May 7 and 31, 1917; Aug. 18 and Sept. 20, 1918. On the various kinds of

women's war service, *DMN*, Mar. 24 and May 26, 1918; Jan. 28 and Mar. 14, 1919. On women physicians, *DMN*, Apr. 13, May 12, 14, 17, and 19, 1919; *Texas Democrat,* May 1919, in A. Caswell Ellis Papers, CAH; *Dallas Times Herald,* Feb. 7 and 10, 1918; May 1, 1919. On American women physicians in Europe, see Ellen S. More, "'A Certain Restless Ambition': Women Physicians and World War I," *American Quarterly* 41 (Dec. 1989): 636–60; and see Ida Clyde Clarke, *American Women and the World War* (New York: D. Appleton, 1918).

29. *DMN*, May 7 and 31, 1917; Aug. 18 and Sept. 20, 1918. *YWCA War Work Bulletin,* no. 51 (Dec. 6, 1918), DHS. *DMN,* Aug. 5 and Sept. 26, 1918; quotation in *DMN*, Apr. 8, 1956; Shirley Kreasan Krieg, *The History of Zeta Tau Alpha, 1898–1928* (N.p.: Zeta Tau Alpha, 1939) 1:416–30. Thanks to the anonymous Texas A&M Univ. Press reviewer for providing this source. Obituary, *DMN,* May 31, 1972; *American Medical Directory: A Register of Physicians* (Chicago: Press of the American Medical Association, 1931), 1527; and *American Medical Directory: A Register of Physicians* (Chicago: Press of the American Medical Association, 1958), 1197.

30. *DMN*, Feb. 12, 1912. See Judith Papachristou, "Women's Suffrage Movement: New Research and New Perspectives," *OAH Newsletter* 14 (Aug. 1986): 6–8.

31. E.g., *Dallas Times Herald,* June 10 and 24, July 22, Aug. 2, Sept. 2, and Dec. 30, 1917. See Ellen Carol DuBois, "Outgrowing the Compact of the Fathers: Equal Rights, Woman Suffrage, and the U.S. Constitution, 1820–1878," *Journal of American History* 74 (Dec. 1987): 836–62, esp. 851.

32. On events of the petition drive, Reppert to Cunningham, Nov. 19, 1917, in McCallum Papers; *DMN,* Mar. 5–10 and 12, 1918; *Dallas Times Herald,* Mar. 12, 1918.

33. On the registration drive, *DMN,* June 28, July 2, 3, 10, 11, 13, and 14, 1918; and *Dallas Times Herald,* July 14, 1918. Suffragists exceeded their goal of 15,000 registered women but fell far short of the number of registered male voters, 26,723. On the political skill of the TESA leader, see Judith N. McArthur, "Minnie Fisher Cunningham's Backdoor Lobby in Texas: Political Maneuvering in a One-Party State," in *One Woman, One Vote: Rediscovering the Woman Suffrage Movement,* ed. Marjorie Spruill Wheeler (Troutdale, Ore.: New Sage Press, 1995), 315–32. Judith N. McArthur, "Cracking the Solid South: Texas as a Case Study," paper presented to the Third Annual American Heritage Center Symposium: Women in Public Life, University of Wyoming, Laramie, Sept. 1994; copy in author's possession.

34. On the black women turned away, see *DMN,* July 9, 1918. On how other southern suffragists dealt with the issue of race, see Suzanne Lebsock, "Woman Suffrage and White Supremacy: A Virginia Case Study," in Hewitt and Lebsock, *Visible Women,* 62–100, esp. 64–65, 70, 75–79.

35. On the NAACP, *Dallas Express,* Mar. 1 and 15, and June 21, 1919; on conflicts with whites on streetcars, *Dallas Express,* Mar. 15, July 12, and Oct. 4, 1919.

36. *Dallas Express,* Oct. 18 and 25, 1919; Mar. 6, 1920; *DMN,* July 9 and 27, 1918; quotation, July 21, 1918. On black women in Houston, *DMN,* July 10, 1918. On black women in Waxahachie, (Judge) G. C. Groce to M. M. Crane, July 9, 1918, in Martin McNulty Crane Papers, CAH. On black women and suffrage, see Flexner,

Century of Struggle, 189–92; Paula Giddings, *When and Where I Enter: The Impact of Black Women on Race and Sex in America* (New York: Bantam, 1984), 116–31.

37. *DMN,* May 26, 1918; Walter J. Crawford to M. M. Crane, May 8, 1918, in Crane Papers. Politicians statewide agreed that William Hobby won the 1918 gubernatorial election because of women's votes: Crane to Reppert, July 19, 1918, in Crane Papers; *DMN,* July 25 and 29, Aug. 4, 1918. And see Gould, *Progressives and Prohibitionists,* 245.

38. List of DESA's male supporters, in Reppert to Cunningham, n.d., Cunningham Papers. Among them were State Sen. M. M. Crane; Thomas B. Love, a well-known supporter of Woodrow Wilson; U.S. Rep. Hatton Sumners; Cesar Lombardi, manager of A. H. Belo and Co.; and Dallas Mayor Henry D. Lindsley. All were lifelong Democrats with sympathy for certain aspects of the Progressive Party's agenda.

39. *DMN,* July 11, 1918.

40. Winterbauer, interview, Mar. 29, 1978; Lillie Day Birch, interview by author, handwritten notes, in author's possession, Dallas, May 22, 1984.

41. Reppert to Cunningham, May 7, 1919, in Cunningham Papers; *DMN,* May 11, 14, and 23, 1919; *Dallas Times Herald,* May 23, 1919.

42. Reppert to Cunningham, May 23, 1919, in Cunningham Papers.

43. *DMN,* May 31, 1919.

44. On the Presbyterians, Reppert to Cunningham, May 20, 1917 [the date of this letter is incorrect; the measure passed on May 25, 1917]; and Cunningham to Katherine Jalonick, Aug. 11, 1917; both in Cunningham Papers. *DMN,* May 25 and 26, 1917. On the Baptists, *DMN,* May 18 and Nov. 11, 1917; May 16, 1918. On Bishop Lynch, Reppert to Cunningham, May 19 and 22, 1919, both in Cunningham Papers. On Bishop Lynch's remarks against woman suffrage six years earlier, *DMN,* June 12, 1913.

45. *DMN,* May 24, 25, 26, 28, and 29, 1919. *Dallas Times Herald,* May 25, 1919; *Houston Chronicle,* May 27, 1919. For statewide results by county, *Citizens at Last,* 189–92. The woman suffrage amendment won in Houston–Harris County with almost 54 percent of the vote and in Austin with 53 percent, but it lost in Travis County with 49 percent. The issue lost in Galveston with 34 percent and in San Antonio with 40 percent, but it won in El Paso with 58 percent and in both Fort Worth and Tarrant County with 51 percent. The suffragists lost Waco but won Beaumont and Brownsville. Cities and towns tended to favor woman suffrage, if by a small average percentage; on May 28, the *Fort Worth Record* reported that 388 urban areas together gave the suffrage amendment 52 percent of their votes. Also see *DMN* and *Dallas Times Herald* for May 25 and 26, 1919, and *Fort Worth Record,* June 3, 1919.

46. *14th U.S. Census, 1920,* vol. 3: *Population: Composition and Characteristics . . . by States:* 1015; and vol. 4: *Occupations, by States:* 150, 152, 154, 156, 158, 160, 162, 164, 166. Also *DCD 1900,* 667–68; and *DCD 1920,* 49. On changes in the Dallas labor force, *Occupations at the 12th Census,* 437, 439; *13th U.S. Census, 1910,* vol. 4: *Occupations, by States:* 221, 223, 225. On new immigrants nationwide and the issue of woman suffrage, see Eileen L. McDonagh and H. Douglas

Price, "Woman Suffrage in the Progressive Era: Patterns of Opposition and Support in Referenda Voting, 1910–1918," *American Political Science Review* 79 (June 1985): 415–35.

47. Regarding analysis of the results according to the actual vote, *Houston Chronicle*, May 29, 1919. Texas was one of eight states allowing immigrants to vote after merely applying for citizenship. In 1919, not only could newcomers from rural Mexico vote, but so could those from Germany, whom the suffragists on occasion called "the enemy aliens." On Texas suffragists' explanations of their loss statewide, see *Citizens at Last,* 188–89; for their suspicion of election fraud, *Dallas Times Herald,* May 29, 1919.

48. *DMN*, May 29, June 5, 25, 27, 28, and 29, 1919; Reppert to Cunningham, n.d. [before June 27, 1919], in McCallum Papers; Cunningham to Carrie Chapman Catt, July 2, 1919, in Winegarten and McArthur, *Citizens at Last,* 193–95; and see A. Elizabeth Taylor, "Woman Suffrage," 46–47. On the ratification process through the Texas legislature, Willie D. Bowles, "The History of the Woman Suffrage Movement in Texas" (M.A. thesis, Univ. of Texas at Austin, 1939), 107. And see Gould, *Progressives and Prohibitionists,* 254–66.

49. On expression of domestic values as public policy, see Sklar, "Historical Foundations," 43–93.

50. Jill Conway, "Women Reformers and American Culture, 1870–1930," *Journal of Social History* 5 (1971–72): 164–77, esp. 174.

51. Ruth J. Kyle, interview by author, handwritten notes, in author's possession, Dallas, June 12, 1978. Hortense Landauer Sanger, "The Road Already Traveled: Hockaday, 1913–1964," *Hockaday* 49 (June 1964): 3–6; *Hockaday Four-Cast* 1 (Dec. 4, 1961); and typewritten memoirs by Ela Hockaday's former students, all in Archives, Hockaday School, Dallas; *The New Handbook of Texas* (Austin: Texas State Historical Association, 1996) 3:643–44.

52. *Hockaday, 1913–1938: The Alumni* [sic] *Association Observes the School's 25th Anniversary* (Dallas: Hockaday Alumnae Association, 1938), 6.

53. *Dallas Express,* Feb. 15, 1919; Mar. 8, 1920; *DMN,* Mar. 15, 1919. On the purposes of the school, *Dallas Express,* Nov. 11, 1920.

54. Ruthe Winegarten, *Black Texas Women: 150 Years of Trial and Triumph* (Austin: Univ. of Texas Press, 1995), 77, 106, 143–44, 194; and Paul M. Lucko, "Josie Briggs Hall," in *New Handbook of Texas,* 3:415.

55. Information about SMU is from the SMU bulletins, 1915–22, and printed programs for graduation exercises, 1919–21, all in University Archives, SMU.

56. Mildred Miles (Mrs. Percy C.) Fewel (School of Liberal Arts, Class of 1921), interview by author, handwritten notes, in author's possession, Dallas, Apr. 18, 1988.

57. On the Women's Joint Legislative Council, also known as the "Petticoat Lobby," McCallum, "Activities of Women," and *Citizens at Last,* 221–30.

Conclusion

1. Mrs. E. A. DeWitt, "The History of the Thursday Morning Study Club," typed manuscript [circa 1942], A4457-Msb, DHS, p. 3.

2. On the significance of urbanization for women's organizations, Turner, "Women Progressives and the Origins of Local Suffrage Societies." See Gould, *Progressives and Prohibitionists,* 29, 149–50.

3. See Ryan, "Gender and Public Access," 259–88, esp. 272–74, 279–80, 283–86; Evans, "Women's History and Political Theory," 119–39; and introduction to Helly and Reverby, *Gendered Domains,* esp. 13. For definitions of the "public" and the "private" and their relationship to the city, see Hans Paul Bahrdt, "Public Activity and Private Activity as Basic Forms of City Association," in *Perspectives on the American Community,* ed. Roland L. Warren (Chicago: Rand McNally, 1966), 68–85.

4. Potter, "American Women," 1–22.

5. Single women, too, could use maternalist principles and rhetoric to achieve goals in social reform; Judith N. McArthur, "Eleanor Brackenridge: The San Antonio Community and Beyond," paper presented at meeting of Texas State Historical Association, Lubbock, Tex., Mar. 3, 1989; copy in author's possession.

Bibliography

I. *Primary Sources*

A. MANUSCRIPTS

Allen, Mattie Jacoby. "Cultural Patterns Attained in a Primitive Land." Typescript, ca. 1937. Dallas Historical Society.

"The Annals." Ursuline Archives, Ursuline Residence, Dallas.

Ardrey, J. Howard. Papers. Dallas Historical Society.

Billingsley, John B. "From Missouri to Texas." Typescript, [Dec. 1843–Jan. 1844.] A3637. Dallas Historical Society.

Brown, John Henry. Papers. Center for American History, University of Texas Archives, Austin.

Carlisle, Willie Flowers, comp. "Old Cemeteries of Dallas County." Typescript, 1946. Texas/Dallas Collection, Dallas Public Library.

Cary, Mrs. E. H. Papers. Dallas Historical Society.

Cockrell, Ettie Fulkerson. Diary. Dallas County Heritage Society.

Cockrell, Monroe F. "Destiny in Dallas: A Study." Typescript, 1958. Texas/Dallas Collection, Dallas Public Library.

Cockrell, Monroe F., ed. "Sarah Horton Cockrell in Early Dallas." Letters. Photocopied and bound typescript, 1961. Genealogy Collection, Dallas Public Library.

Cockrell, Sarah Horton. Papers. Dallas Historical Society.

Coit, Catharine. Letters. In Henry C. Coit Papers. Dallas Historical Society.

Coit, Henry C. Papers. Dallas Historical Society.

"Constitution of the Ladies Industrial Society of the First Presbyterian Church of Dallas, Texas." 1876. First Presbyterian Church Archives, Dallas.

Cox, Mrs. Howard. Papers. Dallas Historical Society.

Crane, Martin McNulty. Papers. Center for American History, University of Texas Archives, Austin.

Crawford, Katherine Lamar (Mrs. W. L.). Papers. Dallas Historical Society.

Crawford, Mattie Hord. "The Hord Home." Manuscript essay, 1922. A231. Dallas Historical Society.

Cretien, Charles F. "Early Days in Dallas and Oak Cliff." Typescript, 1963. Texas/Dallas Collection, Dallas Public Library.

Cunningham, Minnie Fisher. Papers. Houston Metropolitan Research Center, Houston Public Library.

Dallas Federation of Women's Clubs. Papers. Texas/Dallas Collection, Dallas Public Library.

Dallas Free Kindergarten and Industrial Association. Reports, 1903–1904; 1909–1910. Texas/Dallas Collection, Dallas Public Library.

Dallas Free Kindergarten, Training School, and Industrial Association. Minutes Book, 1910–1911. Dallas Historical Society.

Dallas German Ladies' Aid Society. Minutes. Texas/Dallas Collection, Dallas Public Library.

Dallas Public Library. Board of Trustees. Minutes, 1899–1935. Texas/Dallas Collection, Dallas Public Library.

Dallas Shakespeare Club. Papers. Dallas Historical Society.

Dallas Standard Club. Papers. Dallas Historical Society.

Dallas Woman's Forum. Yearbooks and typed historical essays. Dallas Woman's Forum Archives.

Dealey, George Bannerman. Papers. Dallas Historical Society.

DeWitt, Mrs. E. A. "History of the Browning Study Club." Pamphlet. Typescript, ca. 1942. Dallas Historical Society.

———. "The History of the Thursday Morning Study Club." Typescript, ca. 1942. Dallas Historical Society.

Earle-Graves Family. Papers. Texas Collection, Baylor University, Waco, Texas.

Ellis, A. Caswell. Papers. Center for American History, University of Texas Archives, Austin.

Frazier, Julia C. Frazier Elementary School Archives, Dallas.

Greenburg, William H. "Autobiographical Sketch." Unbound typescript, ca. 1948. Original in American Jewish Archives, Cincinnati, Ohio. Copy in Jewish Community Center Archives, Dallas.

[History of Dallas City Council of Parent-Teacher Associations.] Unidentified booklet, ca. 1970s. Dallas City Council of PTAs Archives.

Hockaday School. Papers. Hockaday School Archives, Dallas.

Hughes, Fannie Mae. "History of the Texas Woman's Press Association." Pamphlet. Huntsville, 1935. Center for American History, University of Texas Archives.

Infants' Welfare and Milk Stations. Papers. Child Care Dallas Archives.

James, Catherine Jones (Mrs. George W.). "Seventy Years in the Garland, Dallas County, Texas, Area." Unbound typescript, 1927. Nicholson Memorial Library, Garland, Texas.

Journals of the Annual Councils, Protestant Episcopal Church in the Diocese of Dallas. Dallas: Protestant Episcopal Diocese of Dallas, 1881–1930. Archives, St. Matthew's Cathedral, Dallas.

Juliette Fowler Home. Fowler Home Archives, Dallas.

Lenz, Mrs. Rex V. Papers. Dallas Historical Society.

Lenz, Rex V. "A History of Banking in Dallas." Manuscript, ca. 1940. Mrs. Rex V. Lenz Papers, Dallas Historical Society.

Liebman, Mrs. Morris. Papers. Dallas Historical Society.

McCallum, Jane Y. Papers. Austin History Center, Austin Public Library. Austin, Tex.

McCoy, Millicent Hume. Papers. Texas/Dallas Collection, Dallas Public Library.

McDermett, Telitha Smith (Mrs. D. R. P.). "The Old Hord Home." Ca. 1922. Dallas Historical Society.

———. "Pages from My Life's Book." Manuscript, ca. 1925. Mrs. Paul C. Gerhard Papers, Dallas Historical Society.

Mathis, Flora. Papers. Dallas Historical Society.

"Memoirs of James J. Beeman, Written December 24, 1886." Photocopied typescript. Dallas Historical Society.

Miller, Evelyn Crowell. "Portrait Sketch of Mamma." Manuscript, 1959. Dallas Historical Society.

Miller, Minnie (Mrs. Barry). "Early Schools in Dallas," Address to Dallas Historical Society Student Program, November 29, 1941. Dallas Historical Society.

Mount St. Michael Home and School. Papers. Sisters of Our Lady of Charity Archives, Dallas.

Pennybacker, Mrs. Percy. Papers. Center for American History, University of Texas Archives, Austin.

Pleasant View Missionary Baptist Church. Minutes. Pleasant View Missionary Baptist Church Archives, Dallas.

"Remark Book" [Journal of the Dunne Memorial Home for Boys, 1917–1956]. Order of the Incarnate Word Archives, St. Joseph's Center, Dallas.

St. Cecelia Club. Yearbooks. Texas/Dallas Collection, Dallas Public Library.

St. Mary's College. Episcopal Diocese of Dallas Archives, St. Matthew's Cathedral.

St. Paul Hospital. Public Relations File. St. Paul Hospital, Dallas.

Schneider, Mrs. Jules. Scrapbook. Dallas Historical Society.

Scruggs, Mrs. Gross R., comp. "Ladies Industrial Society of the First Presbyterian Church, Dallas, Texas." Minutes and clippings from the society's scrapbook. In Mrs. J. W. Blake Papers, A6040, Dallas Historical Society.

[Special] Census [taken by the City of] Dallas, 1868. Dallas Historical Society.

Stambaugh, J. Lee. Papers. Dallas Historical Society.

Texas Federation of Women's Clubs. Papers. Blagg-Huey Library, Texas Woman's University, Denton.

Webb, Isaac B. Diary and small record book. Texas Collection, Fondren Library, Southern Methodist University, Dallas.

"The Woman's Exchange of Texas, Austin, Texas." Pamphlet, n.d. Center for American History, University of Texas Archives, Austin.

Young Women's Christian Association. Papers. YWCA of Metropolitan Dallas Archives.

B. PUBLISHED PRIMARY SOURCES

Adair, W. S. "Born in Dallas 77 Years Ago, and Still Here." Memories of John D. Beard. *Dallas Morning News,* April 18, 1926.

———. "Dallas Called Texas Wonder 50 Years Ago." Memories of Wood H. Ramsey. *Dallas Morning News,* October 4, 1925.

———. "Dallas in 1847 Small Village on the Trinity." Memories of Addie Dye McDermett. *Dallas Morning News,* June 21, 1925.

———. "Dallas Man Tells of Indian Fights." Memories of Henry C. Clark. *Dallas Morning News,* June 10, 1923.

————. "Dallas Was an Island in 1866." Memories of Clifton Scott. *Dallas Morning News,* September 3, 1922.

————. "Early Days in Dallas." Memories of C. E. Fretz. *Dallas Morning News,* May 29, 1932.

————. "Education Came Hard to Pioneers." Memories of Judge J. F. Holmes. *Dallas Morning News,* November 6, 1927.

————. "Elm Street Once Trail in Brush." Memories of W. M. McCommas. *Dallas Morning News,* August 24, 1924.

————. "For 84 Years Scott Beeman Has Lived Here." Memories of Scott Beeman. *Dallas Morning News,* October 11, 1925.

————. "Forty-six Years Ago in Dallas." Memories of Milton Hickox. *Dallas Morning News,* August 5, 1923.

————. "Girl Heard Fire Alarm When Dallas Was Destroyed in Summer 1860." Memories of Sarah E. Morton. *Dallas Morning News,* August 17, 1922.

————. "Great Road of Republic of Texas Started from Cabin of John Neely Bryan." Memories of Ed F. Bates. *Dallas Morning News,* September 10, 1922.

————. "He Came Here When Dallas Was in Weeds." Memories of George W. Wood. *Dallas Morning News,* June 5, 1927.

————. "Kidd Springs Land Open in Early Days." Memories of Wilber M. Kidd. *Dallas Morning News,* September 21, 1924.

————. "Orphaned on Way to Dallas Back in '61, Hill Is One of Three Living Here Ever Since." Memories of W. M. C. Hill. *Dallas Morning News,* October 24, 1926.

————. "Panic Times Found Dallas Without Cash." Memories of A. F. Slater. *Dallas Morning News,* September 9, 1928.

————. "Pioneer Doctors Had a Hard Life." Memories of D. R. P. McDermett. *Dallas Morning News,* July 3, 1921.

————. "Pioneers Balked at Toll Charges." Memories of T. R. Yeargan. *Dallas Morning News,* February 13, 1921.

————. "Prairie Chickens Were as Thick as Blackbirds." Memories of George W. Blair. *Dallas Morning News,* June 8, 1924.

————. "Retired Fire Chief Came When Dallas Had 300 People." Memories of Thomas A. Myers. *Dallas Morning News,* July 10, 1927.

————. "Salesman Tells of Life 45 Years Ago." Memories of C. E. Dickson. *Dallas Morning News,* October 2, 1921.

————. "Saw Herds of Stock Driven Through Town." Memories of George Cretien. *Dallas Morning News,* September 12, 1926.

————. "Tells Story of Dallas in Saloon Days." Memories of T. R. Best. *Dallas Morning News,* January 24, 1926.

————. "Time Was When There Was Not Three Hundred Dollars in Dallas." Memories of W. B. Taylor. *Dallas Morning News,* August 19, 1923.

————. "When a Toll Bridge Spanned the Trinity at Commerce Street." Memories of S. B. Scott. *Dallas Morning News,* December 31, 1922.

————. "Wholesale Dry Goods Business in Dallas in Early Times." Memories of Maurice S. Levy. *Dallas Morning News,* August 21, 1923.

Armstrong, Mary Elizabeth. "Reminiscences." *Dallas Morning News,* September 1, 1919.

Boyer, Glenn G., ed. *I Married Wyatt Earp: The Recollections of Josephine Sarah Marcus Earp*. Tucson: University of Arizona Press, 1976.

The Brewers and Texas Politics. San Antonio: Anti-Saloon League of San Antonio, 1916.

Bryant, Stella Vincent. *Pioneers of Yesteryear: Pleasant Mound "Public" Cemetery and Memorial Park, 1848–1973*. Dallas: Pleasant Mount "Public" Cemetery Association, 1974.

Craig, Mrs. M. K. "Pioneer Southern Woman Tells Why She Became Suffragist." *Dallas Times Herald*, June 10, 1917.

Floyd, Alice West. "Memories." *Elm Fork Echoes* 2 (November 1974).

Foree, Kenneth. "Fighters' Blood Is in Her Veins." Memories of Helen Viglini. *Dallas Morning News*, April 25, 1938.

———. "Flowers Bloomed for Fifty Years." Memories of Anna Wideman Blair. *Dallas Morning News*, October 4, 1950.

———. "U.S. Golden Age She Sees as Now." Memories of Anna Wideman Blair. *Dallas Morning News*, January 18, 1951.

Good, John J. *Cannon Smoke: The Letters of Captain John J. Good, Good-Douglas Texas Battery, CSA*. Compiled by Lester Newton Fitzhugh. Hillsboro, Texas: Hillsboro Junior College, 1971.

Greenwood, Jane L. "The Dallas Mothers' Council Comes of Age." Memories of Olivia Allen Dealey. *Dallas Morning News*, June 22, 1930.

Jackson, George. *Sixty Years in Texas*. Quanah, Texas: Peters Colony Historical Society, 1975.

Keating, C. A. *Keatings and Forbes Families and Reminiscences of C. A. Keating, A.D. 1758–1920*. Dallas: Privately published, 1920.

Lamoreaux, Marie L. "She Served Soup as 'Chaser' to Education." [Memories of Dallas in the 1870s]. *Dallas Daily Times Herald*, November 22, 1925.

Latimer, J. W. "The Wheat Region and Wheat Culture in Texas." In *The Texas Almanac for 1859*, pp. 64–71. Galveston: *Galveston News*, 1859.

McCoy, John Milton. *When Dallas Became a City: Letters of John Milton McCoy, 1870–1881*. Edited by Elizabeth York Enstam. Dallas: Dallas Historical Society, 1982.

McElhaney, Jacquelyn Masur, ed. "An Antebellum Chronicle: The Diary of Frances Killen Smith." 2 parts. *Legacies: A History Journal for Dallas and North Central Texas*, vol. 1, no. 1 (Spring 1989) and vol. 1, no. 2 (Fall 1989).

Memorial and Biographical History of Dallas County, Texas. Chicago: Lewis Publishing Company, 1892.

Scott, Elmer. *Eighty-Eight Eventful Years: Being the Intimate Story of Elmer Scott in Industry and the Humanities and of the Civic Federation of Dallas Over a Third of a Century*. Dallas: Civic Federation of Dallas, 1954.

Swindells, Minerva Crutchfield. "Pioneer of Dallas Celebrates Birthday." [Memories of Dallas in the 1850s and 1860s]. *Dallas Morning News*, September 1, 1912.

Toomy, May Carter. "Woman's Influence Behind 'Every Fine Thing.'" Memories of Lucinda (Mrs. W. L.) Williams. *Dallas Morning News*, January 26, 1930.

Turner, Mrs. John S. "Transformation of the Home Due to Modern Industrialization." *Dallas Times Herald*, July 20, 1917.

Williams, Lucinda (Mrs. W. L.). *Golden Years: An Autobiography*. Dallas: Baptist Standard Publishing Company, 1921.

Wolski, Kalisk. *American Impressions.* Translated by Marion Moore Coleman. Cheshire, Conn.: Cherry Hill Books, 1968.

C. DIRECTORIES

The Blue Book of Dallas: A Social and Club Directory, 1909. Dallas: South Publishing Company, 1909.

Butterfield, F. E., and C. M. Rundlett. *Directory for the City of Dallas for the Year 1875.* Dallas: Butterfield and Rundlett, 1875.

Dallas City Directory for 1920. Dallas: John F. Worley and Company, 1920.

Dallas Directory for 1900. Dallas: John F. Worley Directory Company, 1900.

Dallas Social Directory, 1900–1901. Compiled by Mrs. Ora Adams. Dallas: John F. Worley, 1900.

Directory of Greater Dallas, 1910. Dallas: John F. Worley Printing Company, 1910.

General Directory of the City of Dallas for 1878–1879. Compiled by C. D. Morrison and Company. Marshall, Tex.: Jennings Brothers, 1878.

Lawson's and Edmondson's Dallas City Directory and Reference Book including a complete Society, Statistical, and Business Directory for 1873–74. Springfield, Mo.: The Mission Patriot Book and Job Printing House, 1873.

Morrison & Fourmy's General Directory of the City of Dallas for 1880–81. Dallas: Herald Printing, 1880.

Morrison & Fourmy's General Directory of the City of Dallas, 1883–84. Dallas: Morrison & Fourmy, 1883.

Morrison & Fourmy's General Directory of the City of Dallas, 1885–86. Galveston: Morrison & Fourmy, 1885.

Morrison & Fourmy's General Directory of the City of Dallas, 1886–87. Galveston: Morrison & Fourmy, 1886.

Morrison & Fourmy's General Directory of the City of Dallas, 1888–89. Galveston: Morrison & Fourmy, 1888.

Morrison & Fourmy's General Directory of the City of Dallas, 1889–90. Galveston: Morrison & Fourmy, 1889.

Morrison & Fourmy's General Directory of the City of Dallas, 1891–1892. Galveston: Morrison & Fourmy, 1891.

Morrison & Fourmy's General Directory of the City of Dallas, 1893–94. Galveston: Morrison & Fourmy, 1893.

Red Book of Dallas, 1895–96. Dallas: Holland Brothers Publishing, 1895, Reprint, Dallas: A. H. Belo Corporation, 1966.

D. NEWSPAPERS AND PERIODICALS

Dallas Clubwoman. Dallas Historical Society.

Dallas Daily Times Herald

Dallas Evening Journal

Dallas Express

Dallas Herald

Dallas Morning News

Dallas Survey: A Journal of Social Work. Texas/Dallas Collection, Dallas Public Library.

Dallas Times Herald

Dallas Weekly Herald
Fort Worth Star-Telegram
Fort Worth Record
Houston Chronicle
King's Messenger. Bridwell Library, Perkins School of Theology, Southern Methodist University, Dallas.
New York Times
Round Table. Texas/Dallas Collection, Dallas Public Library.
Texas Motherhood Magazine. Selected issues. Center for American History, University of Texas Archives; Texas/Dallas Collection, Dallas Public Library.

E. UNITED STATES CENSUS DOCUMENTS (IN CHRONOLOGICAL ORDER)

Manuscript Census Records for Texas. National Archives and Records Services microfilm. Dallas County, 1850: Series M32, Roll 910; 1860: Series M653, Roll 1292; 1870: Series M653, Roll 1581; 1880: Series T9, Roll 1299; 1900: Series T623, Roll 1625.

[U.S. Census Office] *Seventh Census of the United States: 1850.* Washington, D.C.: Robert Armstrong, Public Printer, 1853.

[U.S. Department of the Interior] *Population of the United States in 1860.* Washington, D.C.: Robert Armstrong, Public Printer, 1864.

Hall, W. W. "Health of Farmers' Families." In *Report of the Commissioner of Agriculture for the Year 1862*, pp. 462–70. Washington, D.C.: Government Printing Office, 1863.

U.S. Department of the Interior, Bureau of the Census. *Statistics of the Population of the United States: Tenth Census, 1880.* Washington, D.C.: Government Printing Office, 1883.

"Dallas, Dallas County, Texas." *Miscellaneous Documents of the House of Representatives, for the Second Session of the Forty-Seventh Congress, 1882–83.* Part 19. Washington, D.C.: Government Printing Office, 1885.

U.S. Bureau of Labor. *Fourth Annual Report of the Commissioner of Labor, 1888.* Washington, D.C.: Government Printing Office, 1889.

U.S. Department of the Interior, Census Office. *Report on Manufacturing Industries in the United States at the Eleventh Census: 1890, part 2: Statistics of Cities.* Washington, D.C.: Government Printing Office, 1895.

U.S. Department of Commerce and Labor, Bureau of the Census. *Abstract of the Twelfth Census of the United States.* Washington, D.C.: Government Printing Office, 1902.

U.S. Department of Commerce and Labor, Bureau of the Census. *Twelfth Census of the United States, 1900, volume 8: Manufactures, part 2: States and Territories.* Washington, D.C.: Government Printing Office, 1902.

U.S. Department of Commerce and Labor, Bureau of the Census. *Supplementary Analysis and Derivative Tables: 1900.* Washington, D.C.: Government Printing Office, 1906.

U.S. Department of Commerce, Bureau of the Census. *Thirteenth Census of the United States, 1910, volume 3: Population Nebraska-Wyoming;* and volume 4: *Occupation Statistics.* Washington, D.C.: Government Printing Office, 1913.

U.S. Department of Commerce, Bureau of the Census. *Fourteenth Census of the United*

States, 1920, volume 2: *General Report and Analytical Tables;* volume 3: *Population: Composition and Characteristics of the Population by States;* volume 4: *Population: Occupations.* Washington, D.C.: Government Printing Office, 1923.

Hill, Joseph A. *Women in Gainful Employment.* Census Monograph no. 9. Washington, D.C.: Government Printing Office, 1929.

U.S. Department of Commerce, Bureau of the Census. *Historical Statistics of the United States: Colonial Times to 1970.* 2 parts. Washington, D.C.: Government Printing Office, 1975.

F. OTHER GOVERNMENT DOCUMENTS

City of Dallas. *Annual Reports of the City of Dallas, 1906–1907.* Dallas: City of Dallas, 1907. Texas/Dallas Collection, Dallas Public Library.

City of Dallas. *A Plan for Dallas: Report of the Park Board [1911].* Prepared by George E. Kessler, Landscape Architect of St. Louis and Kansas City. February 21, 1913. Texas/Dallas Collection, Dallas Public Library.

City of Dallas. *Mayor's Message and Annual Reports of City Offices of the City of Dallas, Texas, for the Fiscal Year Ending April 15, 1889.* Dallas: City Council, 1889. Texas/Dallas Collection, Dallas Public Library.

City of Dallas. Board of Education. Minutes, 1880–95. Dallas Independent School District.

City of Dallas. City Council. Minutes. Office of the City Secretary.

City of Dallas. Ordinance Records. Office of the City Secretary.

City of Dallas. *Report for the Year 1914–1915 of the Park Board of the City of Dallas.* Dallas: City of Dallas, 1915. Texas/Dallas Collection, Dallas Public Library.

Dallas County. Commissioners' Court. Minutes. Dallas County Records Building.

Dallas County. Deed Records, 1880–1990. Dallas County Records Building.

Dallas County. Probate Records. Texas/Dallas Collection, Dallas Public Library.

Dallas County. Tax Rolls, 1846–1910. Reel #1 (1846–77). Texas/Dallas Collection, Dallas Public Library.

General Laws of the State of Texas, Passed at the Regular Session of the Thirtieth Legislature. Austin: Von Boeckmann–Jones Company, Printers, 1907. Dallas County Law Library.

Sumner, Helen L. *History of Women in Industry in the United States,* vol. 9: *Report on the Condition of Woman and Child Wage-Earners in the United States.* Senate Document No. 645. 61st Congress, Second Session. Washington, D.C.: Government Printing Office, 1910.

G. INTERVIEWS

Birch, Lily Day Inman. Dallas, May 22, 1984.

Eddy, Ruth Ellen Clower (Mrs. John L.). Dallas, May 1, 1978.

Cooper, Ruth Myers. Dallas, November 10, 1977; December 15, 1977.

Dupree, Sadye (Mrs. Cleophus C.). Dallas, February 10, 1987.

Fewel, Mildred Miles (Mrs. Percy C.). Dallas, April 18, 1988.

Kyle, Ruth J. Dallas, June 12, 1978.

Miller, Doc. Dallas, September 5 and 7, 1990.

Shamburger, Esther Davis. Dallas, August 29, 1984.

Taylor, Grace Deatherage (Mrs. Paul). Dallas, July 28, 1977.

Tripp, Alvernon King. Dallas, November 9, 1978.

Wilson, Ruth Cockrell. Dallas, September 18, 1977.

Winterbauer, Hazel McCarley. Dallas, March 29, 1978.

II. Secondary Works

A. BOOKS

A Century of Faith: A Short History of New Hope Baptist Church. Dallas: New Hope Baptist Church, 1973.

Abelson, Elaine S. *When Ladies Go A-Thieving: Middle-Class Shoplifters in the Victorian Department Store*. New York: Oxford University Press, 1989.

Acheson, Sam. *Dallas Yesterday*. Edited by Lee Milazzo. Dallas: Southern Methodist University Press, 1977.

Adams, Frank, ed. *Texas Democracy: A Centennial History of Politics and Personalities of the Democratic Party, 1836–1936*. Austin: Democratic Historical Association, 1937. 2 volumes.

African-American Families and Settlements of Dallas: On the Inside Looking Out: Exhibition, Family Memoirs, Personality Profiles, and Community Essays. Edited by Editorial Board, Black Dallas Remembered. Dallas: Black Dallas Remembered, Inc., 1990.

Allen, Ruth A. *East Texas Lumber Workers: An Economic and Social Picture, 1870–1950*. Austin: University of Texas Press, 1961.

Aron, Cindy Sondik. *Ladies and Gentlemen of the Civil Service: Middle-Class Workers in Victorian America*. New York: Oxford University Press, 1987.

Ashby, Leroy. *Saving the Waifs: Reformers and Dependent Children, 1890–1917*. Philadelphia: Temple University Press, 1984.

Baines, May Harper. *A Story of Texas White Ribboners*. N.p.: N.p., 1935.

Bainton, Roland. *Women of the Reformation in France and Germany*. Minneapolis, Minn.: Augsburg Publishing House, 1971.

Banner, Lois. *American Beauty*. New York: Knopf, 1983.

Barker, Elizabeth Wayland. *Women's Work: The First 20,000 Years: Women, Cloth, and Society in Early Times*. New York: W. W. Norton, 1994.

Barns, Florence Elberta. *Texas Writers of Today*. Dallas: Tardy Publishing Company, 1935.

Barth, Gunter. *Instant Cities: Urbanization and the Rise of San Francisco and Denver*. New York: Oxford University Press, 1975.

Bender, Thomas. *Community and Social Change in America*. New Brunswick, N.J.: Rutgers University Press, 1978.

Berg, Barbara J. *The Remembered Gate: Origins of American Feminism, The Woman and the City, 1800–1860*. New York: Oxford University Press, 1978.

Bernhard, Virginia; Betty Brandon; Elizabeth Fox-Genovese; Theda Perdue; and Elizabeth H. Turner, eds. *Hidden Histories of Women in the New South*. Columbia: University of Missouri Press, 1994.

Bernhard, Virginia; Elizabeth Fox-Genovese; Theda Perdue; and Betty Brandon, eds. *South-*

ern Women: Histories and Identities. Columbia: University of Missouri Press, 1992.

Billington, Ray A. *America's Frontier Heritage.* New York: Holt, Rinehart and Winston, 1966.

Black Presence in Dallas: Historic Black Dallasites. Compiled by Sadye Gee. Edited by Darnell Williams. Dallas: Museum of African-American Life and Culture, 1987.

Blair, Karen J. *The Clubwoman as Feminist: True Womanhood Redefined, 1868–1914.* New York: Holmes and Meier, 1980.

Blumin, Stuart M. *The Emergence of the Middle Class: Social Experience in the American City, 1760–1900.* New York: Cambridge University Press, 1989.

Bolding, M. E., with Erie H. Bolding. *Origin and Growth of the Dallas Water Utilities.* Temple, Tex.: Privately published, 1981.

Boorstin, Daniel. *The Americans: The National Experience.* New York: Random House, 1965.

Bordin, Ruth. *Frances Willard: A Biography.* Chapel Hill: University of North Carolina Press, 1986.

———. *Woman and Temperance: The Quest for Power and Liberty, 1873–1900.* Philadelphia: Temple University Press, 1982.

Britton, Wiley. *Pioneer Life in Southwest Missouri.* Kansas City, Mo.: Smith-Grieves Company, 1929.

Brooks, Elizabeth. *Prominent Women of Texas.* Akron, Ohio: Werner Company, 1896.

Brown, John Henry. *History of Dallas County, Texas, from 1837 to 1887.* Dallas: Milligan Cornett and Farnham, 1887.

Bruce, Robert V. *1877: Year of Violence.* Indianapolis: Bobbs-Merrill, 1959.

Calhoun, Craig, ed. *Habermas and the Public Sphere.* Cambridge, Mass.: MIT Press, 1992.

Cantor, Milton, and Bruce Laurie, eds. *Class, Sex, and the Woman Worker.* Westport, Conn.: Greenwood Press, 1977.

Carlson, Avery Luvere. *A Monetary and Banking History of Texas: From the Mexican Regime to the Present Day, 1821–1929.* Fort Worth: Fort Worth National Bank, 1930.

Cashin, Joan E. *A Family Venture: Men and Women on the Southern Frontier.* New York: Oxford University Press, 1991.

Chambers, John Whiteclay. *The Tyranny of Change: America in the Progressive Era, 1900–1917.* New York: St. Martin's Press, 1980.

Christian, Stella F., ed. and comp. *The History of the Texas Federation of Women's Clubs.* Houston: Texas Federation of Women's Clubs, 1919.

Clarke, Elizabeth Dodge Huntington. *The Joy of Service.* New York: National Board of the YWCA, 1979.

Clarke, Ida Clyde. *American Women and the World War.* New York: D. Appleton, 1918.

Clawson, Mary Ann. *Constructing Brotherhood: Class, Gender, and Fraternalism.* Princeton, N.J.: Princeton University Press, 1989.

Cochran, John H. *Dallas County: A Record of Its Pioneers and Progress.* Dallas: Arthur S. Mathis, 1928.

Considerant, Victor. *Au Texas.* 1854; reprint, Philadelphia: Porcupine Press, 1975.

Cott, Nancy F. *The Bonds of Womanhood: "Woman's Sphere" in New England, 1780–1835.* New Haven, Conn.: Yale University Press, 1977.

———. *The Grounding of Modern Feminism.* New Haven, Conn.: Yale University Press, 1987.

Cowan, Ruth Schwartz. *More Work for Mother: The Ironies of Household Technology from the Open Hearth to the Microwave*. New York: Basic Books, 1983.

Croly, Jennie June (Mrs. J. C.). *History of the Woman's Club Movement in America*. New York: Henry G. Allen and Company, 1898.

Cutliffe, Stephen H., and Robert C. Post, eds., *In Context: History and the History of Technology: Essays in Honor of Melvin Kranzberg*. Research in Technology Studies, no. 1. Bethlehem, Pa.: Lehigh University Press; and London and Toronto: Associated University Presses, 1989.

Davis, Allen F. *Spearheads for Reform: The Social Settlements and the Progressive Movement, 1890–1914*. New York: Oxford University Press, 1967.

Davis, Elizabeth L. *Lifting as They Climb: The National Association of Colored Women*. 1933; reprint, Ann Arbor: University Microfilms International, 1971.

Dean, David. *Breaking Trail: Hudson Stuck of Texas and Alaska*. Athens, Ohio: Ohio University Press, 1988.

Degler, Carl N. *At Odds: Women and the Family in America, from the Revolution to the Present*. New York: Oxford University Press, 1980.

Dick, Everett. *The Dixie Frontier: A Comprehensive Picture of Frontier Life Before the Civil War*. New York: Capricorn/Knopf, 1964.

———. *The Sod-House Frontier: A Social History of the Northern Plains from the Creation of Kansas and Nebraska to the Admission of the Dakotas*. Lincoln, Neb.: Johnson Publishing Company, 1954.

Donovan, Josephine. *Feminist Theory: The Intellectual Traditions of American Feminism*. New York: Holmes and Meier, 1980.

Downs, Fane, and Nancy Baker Jones, eds. *Women and Texas History*. Austin: Texas State Historical Association, 1993.

Doyle, Don H. *New Men, New Cities, New South: Atlanta, Nashville, Charleston, Mobile, 1860–1910*. Chapel Hill: University of North Carolina Press, 1990.

———. *The Social Order of a Frontier Community: Jacksonville, Illinois, 1825–1870*. Urbana: University of Illinois, 1978.

Drew, Mary King. *A History of the Kindergarten Movement in Texas, From 1886 to 1942*. Dallas: N.p., [ca. 1942].

Dudden, Faye. *Serving Women: Household Service in Nineteenth-Century America*. Middletown, Conn.: Wesleyan University Press, 1983.

Dykstra, Robert R. *The Cattle Towns: A Social History of the Kansas Cattle Trading Centers: Abilene, Ellsworth, Wichita, Dodge City, and Caldwell, 1876 to 1885*. New York: Atheneum, 1973.

Elliott, Grace Louchs. *From Deep Roots: The Story of the YWCA's Religious Dimensions*. New York: National Board of the YWCA of the USA, 1974.

Evans, Sara M. *Born for Liberty: A History of Women in America*. New York: Free Press, 1989.

Faragher, John Mack. *Women and Men on the Overland Trail*. New Haven, Conn.: Yale University Press, 1979.

Farnham, Christie Anne. *The Education of the Southern Belle: Higher Education and Student Socialization in the Antebellum South*. New York: New York University Press, 1994.

Fehrenbach, T. R. *Lone Star: A History of Texas and the Texans*. New York: Collier, 1968.

McKnight, Mamie L., ed. *First African-American Families of Dallas: Creative Survival: Exhibition and Family History Memoirs.* Dallas: Black Dallas Remembered Steering Committee, 1987.

Flexner, Eleanor. *Century of Struggle: The Woman's Rights Movement in the United States.* New York: Atheneum, 1974.

Frankel, Noralee, and Nancy S. Dye, eds. *Gender, Class, Race, and Reform in the Progressive Era.* Lexington: University Press of Kentucky, 1991.

Fraser, Walter J.; R. Frank Sanders, Jr.; and Jon L. Wakelyn, eds. *The Web of Southern Social Relations: Women, Family, and Education.* Athens: University of Georgia Press, 1985.

Friedman, Jean E. *The Enclosed Garden: Women and Community in the Evangelical South, 1839–1900.* Chapel Hill: University of North Carolina Press, 1985.

Frisch, Michael H. *Town into City: Springfield, Massachusetts, and the Meaning of Community, 1840–1880.* Cambridge, Mass.: Harvard University Press, 1972.

Gallagher, Gary W., ed. *Essays on Southern History Written in Honor of Barnes F. Lathrop.* Austin: University of Texas Press, 1890.

Genovese, Eugene D. *In Red and Black: Marxian Explorations in Southern and Afro-American History.* New York: Pantheon, 1969.

Gordon, Linda. *Woman's Body, Woman's Right: A Social History of Birth Control in America.* New York: Grossman-Viking, 1976.

Gould, Lewis L. *Progressives and Prohibitionists: Texas Democrats in the Wilson Era.* Austin: University of Texas Press, 1973.

Grantham, Dewey W. *Southern Progressivism: The Reconciliation of Progress and Tradition.* Knoxville: University of Tennessee Press, 1983.

Greene, A. C. *A Place Called Dallas: The Pioneering Years of a Continuing Metropolis.* Dallas: Dallas County Heritage Society, 1975.

Greenwald, Maurine Weiner. *Women, War, and Work: The Impact of World War I on Women Workers in the United States.* Westport, Conn.: Greenwood Press, 1980.

Griffith, Elisabeth. *In Her Own Right: The Life of Elizabeth Cady Stanton.* New York: Oxford University Press, 1984.

Grove, Larry. *Dallas Public Library: The First 75 Years.* Dallas: Dallas Public Library, 1977.

Hahn, Steven, and Jonathan Prude, eds. *The Countryside in the Age of Capitalistic Transformation: Essays in the Social History of Rural America.* Chapel Hill: University of North Carolina Press, 1985.

Halttunen, Karen. *Confidence Men and Painted Women: A Study of Middle-Class Culture in America, 1830–1870.* New Haven, Conn.: Yale University Press, 1982.

Hareven, Tamara K., ed. *Family and Kin in Urban Communities, 1700–1930.* New York: New Viewpoints, 1977.

Harris, Barbara. *Beyond Her Sphere: Women and the Professions in American History.* Westport, Conn.: Greenwood Press, 1978.

Harris, Leon. *Merchant Princes: An Intimate History of Jewish Families Who Built Great Department Stores.* New York: Harper and Row, 1979.

Harris, Neil. *Cultural Excursions: Marketing Appetites and Cultural Tastes in Modern America.* Chicago: University of Chicago Press, 1990.

Hartman, Mary, and Lois Banner, eds. *Clio's Consciousness Raised: New Perspectives on the History of Women.* New York: Harper Colophon, 1974.

Heilbroner, Robert L. *The Economic Transformation of America*. New York: Harcourt Brace Jovanovich, 1977.

Helly, Dorothy O., and Susan M. Reverby, eds. *Gendered Domains: Rethinking Public and Private in Women's History*. Ithaca, N.Y.: Cornell University Press, 1992.

Hewitt, Nancy A. *Women's Activism and Social Change: Rochester, New York, 1822–1872*. Ithaca, N.Y.: Cornell University Press, 1984.

Hewitt, Nancy A., and Suzanne Lebsock, eds. *Visible Women: New Essays on American Activism*. Urbana: University of Illinois Press, 1993.

Hill, Patricia R. *The World Their Household: The American Woman's Home Mission Movement and Cultural Transformation, 1870–1920*. Ann Arbor: University of Michigan Press, 1985.

Hilliard, Sam Bowers. *Hog Meat and Hoecake: Food Supply in the Old South*. Carbondale: Southern Illinois University Press, 1972.

Hine, Robert V. *Community on the American Frontier: Separate but Not Alone*. Norman: University of Oklahoma Press, 1980

History of the Dallas Federation of Women's Clubs, 1898–1936. Dallas: Dallas Federation of Women's Clubs, 1936.

History of Women's Work, North Texas Conference, Methodist Episcopal Church, South. N.p.: History Committee, Woman's Missionary Society, North Texas Conference, 1929.

Horowitz, Helen Lefkowitz. *Culture in the City: Cultural Philanthropy in Chicago from the 1800s to 1917*. Lexington: University of Kentucky Press, 1976.

Howard, James. *Big D Is for Dallas: Chapters in the Twentieth-Century History of Dallas*. Austin: Privately published, 1957.

Hunter, Martha Lavinia. *A Quarter of a Century: History of the Dallas Woman's Forum*. Dallas: Dallas Woman's Forum, 1932.

Jahns, Pat. *The Frontier World of Doc Holliday: Faro Dealer from Dallas to Deadwood*. Lincoln: University of Nebraska Press, 1979.

Jebsen, Harry, Jr.; Robert M. Newton; and Patricia R. Hogan. *Centennial History of the Dallas, Texas, Park System, 1876–1976*. Lubbock: Texas Tech University Press, 1976.

Jeffrey, Julie Roy. *Frontier Women: The Trans-Mississippi West, 1840–1880*. New York: Hill and Wang, 1979.

Katz, Michael B. *In the Shadow of the Poorhouse: A Social History of Welfare in America*. New York: Basic Books, 1986.

Kaufman, Polly Welts, ed. *Women Teachers on the Frontier*. New Haven, Conn.: Yale University Press, 1984.

Kerber, Linda; Alice Kessler-Harris; and Kathryn Kish Sklar, eds. *U.S. History as Women's History: New Feminist Essays*. Chapel Hill: University of North Carolina Press, 1995.

Kessler-Harris, Alice. *Out To Work: A History of Wage-Earning Women in the United States*. New York: Oxford University Press, 1982.

———. *A Woman's Wage: Historical Meanings and Social Consequences*. Lexington: University Press of Kentucky, 1990.

Klein, Maury, and Harvey A. Kantor. *Prisoners of Progress: American Industrial Cities, 1850–1920*. New York: Macmillan, 1976.

Koven, Seth, and Sonya Michel, eds. *Mothers of a New World: Maternalist Politics and the Origins of the Welfare State*. New York: Routledge, 1993.

Krueckerberg, Donald A., ed. *Introduction to Planning History in the United States*. New Brunswick, N.J.: Rutgers University Press for Center for Urban Policy Research, 1983.

Lange, Pam, and Mindie Lazarus-Black, eds. *Family Business in Dallas: A Matter of Values*. Dallas: Dallas Public Library, 1982.

Larsen, Lawrence H. *The Urban West at the End of the Frontier*. Lawrence: Regents Press of Kansas, 1978.

Lebsock, Suzanne. *The Free Women of Petersburg: Status and Culture in a Southern Town, 1784–1860*. New York: W. W. Norton, 1984.

Lee, Richard B., and Irven Devore, eds. *Man the Hunter*. Chicago: Aldine Publishing, 1966.

Leeds, John B. *The Household Budget with a Special Inquiry into the Amount and Value of Household Work*. Philadelphia: Privately published, 1917.

Leibz, James. *A History of Social Welfare and Social Work in the United States*. New York: Columbia University Press, 1978.

Lerner, Gerda. *The Majority Finds Its Past: Placing Women in History*. New York: Oxford University Press, 1979.

Lindsley, Philip. *A History of Greater Dallas and Vicinity*. Chicago: Lewis Publishing Company, 1909. 2 volumes.

Lloyd, Cynthia B., ed. *Sex, Discrimination, and the Division of Labor*. New York: Columbia University Press, 1975.

McArthur, Judith N. *Creating the New Woman: The Rise of the Southern Women's Progressive Movement in Texas*. Urbana: University of Illinois Press, forthcoming.

McBeth, Leon. *The First Baptist Church of Dallas: Centennial History, 1868–1968*. Grand Rapids, Mich.: Zondervan, 1968.

McCoy, John Milton. *A Brief History of the First Presbyterian Church, Dallas*. Dallas: Session of the First Presbyterian Church, 1914.

McDonald, William L. *Dallas Rediscovered: A Photographic Chronicle of Urban Expansion, 1870–1925*. Dallas: Dallas Historical Society, 1978.

McDowell, John Patrick. *The Social Gospel in the South: The Woman's Home Mission Movement in the Methodist Episcopal Church, South, 1886–1939*. Baton Rouge: Louisiana State University Press, 1982.

McKelvey, Blake. *The Urbanization of America [1860–1915]*. New Brunswick, N.J.: Rutgers University Press, 1963.

Madden, Janice Fanning. *The Economics of Sex Discrimination*. Lexington, Mass.: D. C. Heath, 1973.

Malone, Ann Patton. *Women on the Texas Frontier: A Cross-Cultural Perspective*. El Paso: Texas Western Press, 1983.

Marcus, Stanley. *Minding the Store: A Memoir*. New York: Signet/New American Library, 1975.

Mathews, Donald G. *Religion in the Old South*. Chicago: University of Chicago Press, 1977.

Matthews, Glenna. *"Just A Housewife": The Rise and Fall of Domesticity in America*. New York: Oxford University Press, 1987.

May, Elaine Tyler. *Great Expectations: Marriage and Divorce in Post-Victorian America.* Chicago: University of Chicago Press, 1980.

Melder, Keith E. *Beginnings of Sisterhood: The American Woman's Rights Movement.* New York: Schocken Books, 1977.

Melosi, Martin V., ed. *Pollution and Reform in American Cities, 1870–1920.* Austin: University of Texas Press, 1980.

Meyer, Annie Nathan, ed. *Woman's Work in America.* 1891; reprint, New York: Arno Press, 1972.

Meyerowitz, Joanne J. *Women Adrift: Independent Wage Earners in Chicago, 1880–1930.* Chicago: University of Chicago Press, 1988.

Miller, Char, and Heywood T. Sanders, eds. *Urban Texas: Politics and Development.* College Station: Texas A&M University Press, 1990.

Mollenkopf, John Hull, ed. *Power, Culture, and Place: Essays on New York City.* New York: Russell Sage Foundation, 1988.

Monkkonen, Eric. *American Becomes Urban: The Development of U.S. Cities and Towns, 1780–1980.* Berkeley: University of California Press, 1988.

Moore, Gerald Grattan. *The Diocese of Dallas, 1895–1952.* Dallas: St. Matthew's Cathedral, 1952.

Moreland, Sinclair. *The Texas Women's Hall of Fame.* Austin: Biographical Press, 1917.

Morgan, David. *Suffragists and Democrats: The Politics of Woman Suffrage in America.* East Lansing: Michigan State University Press, 1972.

Morrison, Andrew. *The Industries of Dallas: Her Relations as a Center of Trade, Manufacturing Establishments, and Business Houses.* Galveston: Metropolitan Publishing Company, 1887. Copy in Mrs. Howard Cox Papers, Dallas Historical Society.

Mumford, Lewis. *The City in History: Its Origins, Its Transformation, Its Prospects.* New York: Harcourt, Brace and World, 1961.

Myres, Sandra L., and Harold M. Hollingsworth, eds. *Essays in the American West: The Walter Prescott Webb Memorial Lectures.* Austin: University of Texas Press, 1968.

Newman, Louise Michele, ed. *Men's Ideas/Women's Realities: Popular Science, 1870–1915.* New York: Pergamon, 1985.

Nichols, James L. *The Confederate Quartermaster in the Trans-Mississippi.* Austin: University of Texas Press, 1964.

Norton, Mary Beth, and Carol Berkin, eds. *Women of America.* Boston: Houghton Mifflin, 1979.

Notable Women of the Southwest: A Pictorial Biographical Encyclopedia of the Leading Women of Texas, New Mexico, Oklahoma, and Arizona. Dallas: William T. Tandy, 1938.

O'Neill, William L. *Divorce in the Progressive Era.* New Haven, Conn.: Yale University Press, 1967.

Oppenheimer, Valerie Kincaide. *The Female Labor Force in the United States: Demographic and Economic Factors Governing Its Growth and Changing Conditions.* Population Monograph Series, no. 5. Westport, Conn.: Greenwood Press, 1970.

Pérez, Joan Jenkins. *New Handbook of Texas.* Austin: Texas State Historical Association, 1996. 5 volumes.

Pirenne, Henri. *Medieval Cities: Their Origins and the Revival of Trade.* Trans. Frank D. Halsey. Garden City, N.Y.: Doubleday/Anchor.

Reed, S. G. *A History of the Texas Railroads*. Houston: St. Clair Press, 1960.

Rice, Bradley. *Progressive Cities: The Commission Government Movement in America, 1901–1920*. Austin: University of Texas Press, 1977.

Riley, Glenda. *The Female Frontier: A Comparative View of Women on the Prairie and the Plains*. Lawrence: University Press of Kansas, 1988.

Rogers, John Williams. *The Lusty Texans of Dallas*. New York: E. P. Dutton, 1959.

Rotella, Elyce. *From Home to Office: United States Women at Work, 1870–1930*. Studies in American History and Culture, no. 25. Ann Arbor: UMI Research Press, 1981.

Rosen, Ruth. *The Lost Sisterhood: Prostitution in America, 1900–1919*. Baltimore, Md.: Johns Hopkins University Press, 1982.

Rothman, Sheila. *Woman's Proper Place: A History of Changing Ideals and Practices, 1870 to the Present*. New York: Basic Books, 1978.

Ryan, Mary P. *Cradle of the Middle Class: The Family in Oneida County, New York, 1790–1865*. New York: Cambridge University Press, 1981.

———. *The Empire of the Mother: American Writing About Domesticity, 1830–1860*. New York: Haworth Press, 1982.

———. *Womanhood in America: From Colonial Times to the Present*. New York: New Viewpoints, 1975.

———. *Women in Public: Between Banners and Ballots, 1825–1880*. Baltimore. Md.: Johns Hopkins University Press, 1990.

Santerre, George H. *Dallas' First Hundred Years, 1856–1956*. Dallas: Book Craft, 1955.

———. *White Cliffs of Dallas: The Story of La Réunion, the Old French Colony*. Dallas: Book Craft, 1955.

Schiebel, Walter J. E. *Education in Dallas: Ninety-Two Years of History, 1874–1966*. Dallas: Dallas Independent School District, 1966.

Schlissel, Lillian; Vicki L. Ruiz; and Janice Monk, eds. *Western Women: Their Land, Their Lives*. Albuquerque: University of New Mexico Press, 1988.

Scott, Anne Firor. *Making the Invisible Woman Visible*. Urbana: University of Illinois Press, 1984.

———. *Natural Allies: Women's Associations in American History*. Urbana: University of Illinois Press, 1991.

———. *The Southern Lady: From Pedestal to Politics, 1830–1930*. Chicago: University of Chicago Press, 1970.

Scott, Joan Wallach. *Gender and the Politics of History*. New York: Columbia University Press, 1988.

Sharpe, Ernest. *G. B. Dealey of the Dallas News*. New York: Henry Holt and Company, 1955.

Simons, John, ed. *Who's Who in American Jewry*. New York: National News Association, Inc., 1939. 3 volumes.

Simpkins, Loy M., ed. *Texas Family Law: Speer's Fifth Edition*. San Francisco, Calif.: Lawyers Co-operative Publishing Company, 1975. 5 volumes.

Sklar, Kathryn Kish. *Catharine Beecher: A Study in American Domesticity*. New Haven, Conn.: Yale University Press, 1973.

Smith-Rosenberg, Carroll. *Disorderly Conduct: Visions of Gender in Victorian America*. New York: Oxford University Press, 1986.

Smuts, Robert W. *Women and Work in America*. New York: Columbia University Press, 1959.

Solomon, Barbara M. *In the Company of Educated Women: A History of Women and Higher Education in America*. New Haven, Conn.: Yale University Press, 1985.

Speer, Ocie. *A Treatise on the Law of Marital Rights in Texas*. Rochester, N.Y.: Lawyers Co-Operative Publishing Company, 1916.

Spratt, John Stricklin. *The Road to Spindletop: Economic Change in Texas, 1875–1901*. Austin: University of Texas Press, 1974.

Spruill, Julia Cherry. *Women's Life and Work in the Southern Colonies*. New York: Russell and Russell/Atheneum, 1969.

Strasser, Susan. *Never Done: A History of American Housework*. New York: Pantheon, 1982.

Strom, Sharon Hartman. *Beyond the Typewriter: Gender, Class, and the Origins of Modern American Office Work, 1900–1930*. Urbana: University of Illinois Press, 1992.

Tentler, Leslie Woodcock. *Wage-Earning Women: Industrial Work and Family Life in the United States, 1900–1930*. New York: Oxford University Press, 1982.

Thompkins, Jane. *West of Everything: The Inner Life of Westerns*. New York: Oxford University Press, 1992.

Tiffin, Susan. *In Whose Best Interest? Child Welfare Reform in the Progressive Era*. Westport, Conn.: Greenwood Press, 1982.

Tilly, Louise A., and Joan W. Scott. *Women, Work, and Family*. New York: Holt, Rinehart Winston, 1978.

To Give the Key of Knowledge: United Methodists and Education, 1784–1976. Nashville: National Commission of United Methodist Higher Education, 1976.

Tryon, Rolla Milton. *Household Manufactures in the United States: 1640–1860*. Chicago, 1917; Reprint, New York: Augustus M. Kelly, 1966.

Tyack, David, and Elizabeth Hansot. *Learning Together: A History of Coeducation in American Public Schools*. New Haven, Conn.: Yale University Press for the Russell Sage Foundation, 1990.

Ulrich, Laurel Thatcher. *A Midwife's Tale: The Life of Martha Ballard, Based on Her Diary, 1785–1812*. New York: Vintage, 1990.

Wade, Richard C. *The Urban Frontier: The Rise of Western Cities, 1790–1830*. Cambridge, Mass.: Harvard University Press, 1959.

Warren, Roland L. *The Community in America*. Chicago: Rand McNally, 1966; and Lanham, Md.: University Press of America, 1978.

Weber, Max. *The City*. Translated and edited by Don Martindale and Gertrude Neuwirth. New York: Free Press, 1958.

Weibe, Robert H. *The Search for Order, 1877–1920*. American Century Series. New York: Hill and Wang, 1967.

Welter, Barbara. *Dimity Convictions: American Women in the Nineteenth Century*. Athens, Ohio: Ohio University Press, 1976.

Weltfish, Gene. *The Lost Universe: The Way of Life of the Pawnee*. New York: Ballantine Books, 1965.

Werry, Adolphus. *History of the First Methodist Church*. Dallas: First Methodist Church, 1947.

Wheeler, Kenneth W. *To Wear a City's Crown: The Beginnings of Urban Growth in Texas, 1836–1865*. Cambridge, Mass.: Harvard University Press, 1968.

Wheeler, Marjorie Spruill, ed. *One Woman, One Vote: Rediscovering the Woman Suffrage Movement*. Troutdale, Ore.: New Sage Press, 1995.

Wilson, William H. *The City Beautiful Movement*. Baltimore, Md.: Johns Hopkins University Press, 1989.

Winegarten, Ruthe. *Black Texas Women: 150 Years of Trial and Triumph*. Austin: University of Texas Press, 1995.

Winegarten, Ruthe, and Cathy Schechter. *Deep in the Heart: The Lives and Legends of Texas Jews: A Photographic History*. Austin: Eakin Press, 1990.

Winegarten, Ruthe, and Judith N. McArthur, eds. *Citizens at Last: The Woman Suffrage Movement in Texas*. Austin: Ellen C. Temple, 1987.

Who's Who of the Womanhood of Texas. Fort Worth: Texas Federation of Women's Clubs, 1923.

W[oman's] M[issionary] U[nion] History of the First Baptist Church, Dallas, Texas. Dallas: Woman's Missionary Union, [1953].

Wood, Mary I. *The History of the General Federation of Women's Clubs for the First Twenty-Two Years of Its Organization*. New York: General Federation of Women's Clubs, 1912.

Woods, Robert A., and Albert J. Kennedy, eds. *Handbook of Settlements*. New York: Russell Sage Foundation, 1911; Reprint, New York: Arno Press and *New York Times*, 1970.

Wright, Gavin. *The Political Economy of the Cotton South: Households, Markets, and Wealth in the Nineteenth Century*. New York: W. W. Norton, 1978.

Wunder, John R., ed. *At Home on the Range: Essays on the History of Western Social and Domestic Life*. Westport, Conn.: Greenwood Press, 1985.

Yearbook and 67 Years. Dallas: Oak Cliff Christian Church, 1957.

B. ARTICLES

Alcorn, Richard S. "Leadership and Stability in Mid-Nineteenth-Century America: A Case Study of an Illinois Town." *Journal of American History* 61 (Dec. 1974): 685–702.

Alexander, Ruth. "'We Are Engaged as a Band of Sisters': Class and Domesticity in the Washington Temperance Movement, 1840–1850." *Journal of American History* 75 (Dec. 1988): 763–85.

Baker, Paula. "The Domestication of Politics: Women and American Political Society, 1780–1920." *American Historical Review* 89 (June 1984): 620–46.

Bauman, Paula M. "Single Women Homesteaders in Wyoming, 1880–1930." *Annals of Wyoming* 58 (Spring 1968): 40–53.

Belfiglio, Valentine J. "Early Italian Settlers in Dallas: A New Life with Old Values." *Heritage News* 10 (Winter 1985–1986): 4–7.

Bender, Thomas. "Wholes and Parts: The Need for Synthesis in American History." *Journal of American History* 73 (June 1986): 120–36.

Benston, Margaret. "The Political Economy of Women's Liberation." *Monthly Review* 21 (Sept. 1969): 13–27.

Blackborn, George M., and Sherman L. Richards. "A Demographic History of the West: Nueces County, Texas, 1850." *Prologue* 4 (Spring 1972): 3–20.

Blocker, Jack S., Jr. "Separate Paths: Suffragists and the Women's Temperance Crusade." *Signs* 10 (Spring 1958): 460–75.

Blumin, Stuart M. "The Hypothesis of Middle-Class Formation in Nineteenth-Century America: A Critique and Some Proposals." *American Historical Review* 90 (Apr. 1985): 299–338.

Bourque, Susan, and Jean Grosshaltz. "Politics as an Unnatural Practice: Political Science Looks at Female Participation." *Politics and Society* 4 (1974): 225–66.

Brown, Richard D. "The Emergence of Urban Society in Rural Massachusetts, 1760–1820." *Journal of American History* 61 (June 1974): 29–51.

———. "The Emergence of Voluntary Associations in Massachusetts, 1760–1830." *Journal of Voluntary Action Research* 2 (Apr. 1973): 64–73.

Brumberg, Joan Jacob. "Zenanas and Girlless Villages: The Ethnology of American Evangelical Women, 1870–1910." *Journal of American History* 69 (Sept. 1982): 347–71.

Burris, Evadene A. "Keeping House on the Minnesota Frontier." *Minnesota History* 14 (Sept. 1933): 263–82.

Cantrell, Gregg. "Sam Houston and the Know-Nothings: A Reappraisal." *Southwestern Historical Quarterly* 96 (Jan. 1993): 327–44.

Carrigan, Jo Ann. "Nineteenth-Century Rural Self-Sufficiency: A Planter's and Housewife's 'Do-It-Yourself' Encyclopedia." *Arkansas Historical Society* 21 (1972): 132–45.

Church, Diana. "Mrs. E. P. Turner: Clubwoman, Reformer, Community Builder." *Heritage News* 10 (Summer 1985): 9–14.

Connor, Seymour V. "A Statistical Review of the Settlement of the Peters Colony, 1841–1848." *Southwestern Historical Quarterly* 57 (July 1953): 38–64.

Conway, Jill. "Women Reformers and American Culture, 1870–1930." *Journal of Social History* 5 (1971–72): 164–77.

Cott, Nancy F. "What's in a Name? The Limits of 'Social Feminism'; or, Expanding the Vocabulary of Women's History." *Journal of American History* 76 (Dec. 1989): 809–29.

Cottrell, Debbie Mauldin. "The County Poor Farm System in Texas." *Southwestern Historical Quarterly* 93 (Oct. 1989): 169–90.

Cronon, William, et al. "Women and the West: Rethinking the Western History Survey Course." *Western Historical Quarterly* 18 (July 1986): 272–73.

Crouch, Barry A., and Larry Madaras. "Reconstructing Black Families: Perspectives from the Texas Freedman's Bureau Records." *Prologue* 18 (Summer 1986): 109–22.

Davidson, Rondel V. "Victor Considerant and the Failure of La Réunion." *Southwestern Historical Quarterly* 76 (Jan. 1973): 277–96.

Davis, Ronald L., and Harry D. Holmes. "Introduction: Studies in Western Urbanization." *Journal of the West* 13 (July 1974): 1–5.

Deutsch, Sarah. "Learning to Talk More Like a Man: Boston Women's Class-Bridging Organizations, 1870–1940." *American Historical Review* 97 (Apr. 1992): 379–484.

Dobson, Joan L. "Literature for All Tastes: Magazines Published in Dallas." *Heritage News* 12 (Winter 1987–88): 4–7, 10.

Doyle, Don Harrison. "Social Theory and New Communities in Nineteenth-Century America." *Western Historical Quarterly* 8 (Apr. 1977): 151–65.

Dreeson, Don. "History of Oak Cliff." *Oak Cliff Dispatch-Journal,* May 6–June 1939. Photocopy. Texas/Dallas Collection, Dallas Public Library.

DuBois, Ellen Carol. "Outgrowing the Compact of the Fathers: Equal Rights, Woman Suffrage, and the United States Constitution, 1820–1878." *Journal of American History* 74 (Dec. 1987): 836–62.

Easterlin, Richard A. "Factors in the Decline of Farm Family Fertility in the United States: Some Preliminary Research Results." *Journal of American History* 63 (Dec. 1976): 600–614.

Eblen, Jack E. "An Analysis of Nineteenth-Century Frontier Populations." *Demography* 2 (1965): 399–413.

Ellis, Tuffly. "The Revolutionizing of the Texas Cotton Trade, 1865–1885." *Southwestern Historical Quarterly* 73 (Apr. 1970): 478–508.

Enstam, Elizabeth York. "The 'Adventurous Ursulines': Unlikely Pioneers to a Texas Boom Town." *Heritage News* 12 (Summer 1987): 7–11.

———. "Opportunity versus Propriety: The Life and Career of Frontier Matriarch Sarah Horton Cockrell." *Frontiers* 6 (Fall 1982): 106–14.

———. "St. Mary's College: A Modern Education for Women." *Heritage News* 11 (Fall 1986): 11–14.

———. "Virginia K. Johnson: A Second Chance for the 'Wayward.'" *Heritage News* 10 (Summer 1985): 6–8.

Erwin, Mira Waller. "The Old Dallas Female College." *Southern Advocate,* July 4, 1935. Photocopy of manuscript, Dallas Historical Society.

Fee, Terry. "Domestic Labor: An Analysis of Housework and Its Relation to the Production Process." *Review of Radical Political Economics* 8 (Spring 1976): 1–8.

Flanagan, Maureen A. "The City Profitable, The City Livable: Environmental Policy, Gender, and Power in Chicago in the 1920s." *Journal of Urban History* 22 (Jan. 1996): 163–90.

———. "Gender and Urban Political Reform: The City Club and the Woman's City Club of Chicago in the Progressive Era." *American Historical Review* 95 (Oct. 1990): 1032–50.

Folbre, Nancy, and Marjorie Abel. "Women's Work and Women's Households: Gender Bias in the U.S. Census." *Social Research* 56 (Autumn 1989): 545–60.

Foree, Kenneth. "Dallas Gunners' Epic." *Dallas Morning News,* March 3, 1946.

———. "Patron Saint." Story of Sister Brendan, Order of St. Vincent de Paul. *Dallas Morning News,* Apr. 20, 1947.

———. "Tan Dorcas." Story of Claudia Lemmons and African-American charity. *Dallas Morning News,* June 20, 1946.

Forrey, Carolyn. "The New Woman Revisited." *Women's Studies* 2 (1974): 37–56.

Frauendorf, Martha Norby. "The Labor Force Participation of Turn-of-the-Century Married Women." *Journal of Economic History* 39 (June 1979): 401–81.

Furstenberg, Frank F., Jr.; Theodore Hershberg; and John Modell. "The Origins of the Female-Headed Black Family: The Impact of the Urban Experience." *Journal of Interdisciplinary History* 6 (1975): 221–33.

Glazer, Walter S. "Participation and Power: Voluntary Associations and the Functional Organization in Cincinnati in 1840." *Historical Methods Newsletter* 5 (Sept. 1972): 151–68.

Goldin, Claudia. "The Changing Economic Role of Women: A Quantitative Approach." *Journal of Interdisciplinary History* 13 (Spring 1983): 707–33.

———. "Female Labor Force Participation: The Origin of Black and White Differences, 1870–1880." *Journal of Economic History* 37 (Mar. 1977): 87–112.

———. "Household and Market Production of Families in a Late Nineteenth-Century American City." *Explorations in Economic History* 16 (April 1979): 111–31.

Goodman, Paul. "The Emergence of Homestead Exemption in the United States: Accommodation and Resistance to the Market Revolution, 1840–1880." *Journal of American History* 80 (Sept. 1993): 470–98.

Gray, Virginia Gearhart. "Activities of Southern Women: 1840–1860." *South Atlantic Quarterly* 27 (July 1928): 264–79.

Greenwald, Maurine Weiner. "Working-Class Feminism and the Family Wage Ideal: The Seattle Debate on Married Women's Right to Work, 1914–1920." *Journal of American History* 76 (June 1989): 118–49.

Gross, Edward. "Plus Ça Change . . . ? The Sexual Structure of Occupations Over Time." *Social Problems* 16 (1968): 198–209.

Gutman, Herbert G. "Persistent Myths about the Afro-American Family." *Journal of Interdisciplinary History* 6 (1975): 181–220.

Hammack, David. "Problems of Power in the Historical Study of Cities, 1800–1960." *American Historical Review* 83 (Apr. 1978): 323–49.

Hareven, Tamara K. "Modernization and Family History: Perspectives on Social Change." *Signs* 2 (1976): 190–206.

Hazel, Michael V. "The Dallas Symphony Club: Inaugurating a Musical Tradition." *Heritage News* 11 (Fall 1986): 8–10, 14.

———. "Dallas Women's Clubs: Vehicles for Change." *Heritage News* 11 (Spring 1986): 18–21.

———. "May Smith and the Dallas Baby Camp." *Heritage News* 10 (Summer 1985): 19–25.

———. "A Mother's Touch: The First Two Women Elected to the Dallas School Board." *Heritage News* 12 (Spring 1987): 9–12.

Jackson, Susan. "Movin' On: Mobility Through Houston in the 1850s." *Southwestern Historical Quarterly* 81 (Jan. 1978): 251–82.

Jensen, Joan M. "Cloth, Butter, and Boarders: Women's Household Production for the Market." *Review of Radical Political Economics* 12 (Summer 1980): 14–24.

Jensen, Joan M., and Darlis A. Miller. "The Gentle Tamers Revisited: New Approaches to the History of Women in the American West." *Pacific Historical Review* 49 (May 1980): 173–213.

Jenson, Carol Elizabeth. "The Equity Jurisdiction and Married Women's Property in Ante-Bellum America: A Revisionist View." *International Journal of Women's Studies* 2 (Mar.–Apr. 1979): 144–54.

Kerber, Linda K. "Separate Spheres, Female Worlds, Woman's Place: The Rhetoric of Women's History." *Journal of American History* 75 (June 1988): 9–39.

Kretch, Shepard, III. "Black Family Organization in the Nineteenth Century: An Ethnological Perspective." *Journal of Interdisciplinary History* 12 (Winter 1982): 429–52.

Lasser, Carol. "'Let Us Be Sisters Forever': The Sororal Model of Nineteenth-Century Female Friendship." *Signs* 14 (Autumn 1988): 158–81.

Lerner, Gerda. "Priorities and Challenges in Women's History Research." *Perspectives: American Historical Association Newsletter* 26 (Apr. 1988): 17–20.

Magruder, Julia. "Club Life in the New South." *Arena* 6 (1892): 374–78.

———. "The Typical Woman of the New South." *Harper's Bazaar* 33 (Nov. 3, 1900): 1685–87.

Matsuda, Mari J. "The West and the Legal Status of Women: Explanations of Frontier Feminism." *Journal of the West* 24 (Jan. 1985): 47–52.

McCall, Laura. "'The Reign of Brute Force Is Now Over': A Content Analysis of *Godey's Lady's Book,* 1830–1860." *Journal of the Early Republic* 3 (Summer 1989): 217–36.

McDonagh, Eileen L., and H. Douglas Price. "Woman Suffrage in the Progressive Era: Patterns of Opposition and Support in Referenda Voting, 1910–1918." *American Political Science Review* 79 (June 1985): 415–35.

McDonald, Forrest, and Grady McWhiney. "The South from Self-Sufficiency to Peonage: An Interpretation." *American Historical Review* 85 (Dec. 1980): 1095–1118.

McElhaney, Jackie. "Pauline Periwinkle: Crusading Columnist." *Heritage News* 10 (Summer 1985): 15–18.

McGerr, Michael. "Political Style and Women's Power, 1830–1930." *Journal of American History* 77 (Dec. 1990): 804–85.

Mendenhall, Marjorie Stratford. "Southern Women of a 'Lost Generation.'" *South Atlantic Quarterly* 33 (Oct. 1934): 334–53.

Modell, John, and Tamara K. Hareven. "Urbanization and the Malleable Household: An Examination of Boarding and Lodging in American Families." *Journal of Marriage and the Family* 35 (Aug. 1973): 467–79.

Moore, Ellen S. "'A Certain Restless Ambition': Women Physicians and World War I." *American Quarterly* 41 (Dec. 1989): 636–60.

Papachristou, Judith. "The Woman Suffrage Movement: New Research and New Perspectives." *OAH Newsletter* 14 (Aug. 1986): 6–8.

Potter, David M. "American Women and the American Character." *Stetson University Bulletin* 62 (Jan. 1962): 1–22.

Prude, Jonathan. "Cash Is Good to Eat: Self-Sufficiency and Exchange in the Rural Economy of the United States." *Radical History Review* 17 (Winter 1977): 42–71.

Richardson, Eudora Ramsay. "The Case of the Women's Colleges in the South." *South Atlantic Quarterly* 29 (1930): 126–39.

Riefler, Robert F. "Nineteenth-Century Urbanization Patterns in the United States." *Journal of Economic History* 39 (Dec. 1979): 961–74.

Rindfuss, Donald R. "Changing Patterns of Fertility in the South: A Social-Demographic Examination." *Social Forces* 57 (Dec. 1978): 621–35.

Rosenzweig, Roy. "Middle-Class Parks and Working-Class Play: The Struggle Over Recreational Space in Worcester, Massachusetts, 1870–1910." *Radical History Review* 21 (Fall 1979): 31–46.

Rotella, Elyce J. "Women's Labor Force Participation and the Decline of the Family Economy in the United States." *Explorations in Economic History* 17 (Apr. 1980): 95–117.

Ryan, Mary P. "The Power of Women's Networks: A Case Study of Female Moral Reform in Antebellum America." *Feminist Studies* 5 (Spring 1979): 66–85.

Salmon, Lucy M. "The Woman's Exchange: Charity or Business?" *Forum* 13 (1892): 394–406.

Schmelzer, Janet. "Thomas M. Campbell: Progressive Governor of Texas." *Red River Valley Historical Review* 3 (Fall 1978): 52–63.

Scott, Anne Firor. "On Seeing and Not Seeing." *Journal of American History* 71 (June 1984): 7–21.

———. "A Progressive Wind from the South, 1906–1913." *Journal of Southern History* 29 (Feb. 1963): 53–70.

Seller, Maxine. "G. Stanley Hall and Edward Thorndike on the Education of Women: Theory and Policy in the Progressive Era." *Educational Studies* 11 (1981): 365–74.

Skopcol, Theda; Marjorie Abend-Wein; Christopher Howard; and Susan Goodrich Lehmann. "Women's Associations and the Enactment of Mothers' Pensions in the United States." *American Political Science Review* 87 (Sept. 1993): 686–701.

Smallwood, James. "Emancipation and the Black Family: A Case Study in Texas." *Social Science Quarterly* 47 (Mar. 1977): 849–57.

Smith, Sherry L. "Single Women Homesteaders: The Perplexing Case of Elinor Pruitt Stewart." *Western Historical Quarterly* 22 (May 1991): 163–83.

Smith, Thomas H. "Blacks in Dallas: From Slavery to Freedom." *Heritage News* 10 (Spring 1985): 18–22.

———. "Conflict and Corruption: The Dallas Establishment vs. the Freedman's Bureau." *Legacies: A History Journal for Dallas and North Central Texas* vol. 1, no. 2 (Fall 1989): 24–30.

Smuts, Robert W. "The Female Labor Force: A Case Study in the Interpretation of Historical Statistics." *Journal of the American Statistical Association* 44 (Mar. 1960): 71–79.

Taylor, Caroline. "Domestic Arts and Crafts in Illinois, 1800–1860." *Journal of the Illinois Historical Society* 33 (Sept. 1940): 278–303.

Testi, Arnaldo. "The Gender of Reform Politics: Theodore Roosevelt and the Culture of Masculinity." *Journal of American History* 81 (Mar. 1995): 1509–33.

Tilly, Louise A. "Gender, Women's History, and Social History." *Social Science History* 13 (Winter 1989): 439–62.

Underwood, June O. "Western Women and True Womanhood: Culture and Symbol in History and Literature." *Great Plains Quarterly* 5 (Spring 1985): 93–106.

Warren, John. "The Women Who Are Making a Musical America." *Delineator* 76 (Sept. 1910): 164, 210.

Wein, Roberta A. "Women's Colleges and Domesticity." *History of Education Quarterly* 14 (Spring 1974): 31–47.

Wells, Robert V. "Demographic Change and the Life Cycle of American Families." *Journal of Interdisciplinary History* 2 (Autumn 1971): 273–82.

White, Martha E. D. "The Work of the Woman's Club." *Atlantic Monthly* 93 (May 1904): 614–23.

Winslow, Helen M. "The Story of the Woman's Club Movement." *New England Magazine* 38 (July 1908): 532–57.

Wirth, Louis. "Urbanism as a Way of Life." *American Journal of Sociology* 44 (1938): 1–24.

Woodbury, Marion. "Time Required for Housework in a Family of Five with Small Children." *Journal of Home Economics* 10 (1918): 226–30.

Zagarri, Rosemarie. "Morals, Manners, and the Republican Mother." *American Quarterly* 44 (June 1992): 192–215.

C. UNPUBLISHED WORKS

Bailón, Gilbert. "Little Mexico: An Enduring Hub of Mexican Culture in Dallas." Senior paper, University of Texas at Arlington, 1991.

Bourland, Ellen Persons. "History of the Dallas Symphony Orchestra: 1900–1980." M.A. thesis, Southern Methodist University, 1981.

Bowles, Willie D. "The History of the Woman Suffrage Movement in Texas." M.A. thesis, University of Texas at Austin, 1939.

Brucken, Carolyn. "Manners and Morals: Women and Etiquette of the City, 1830–60." Paper presented at the Fourth Southern Conference on Women's History, Charleston, South Carolina, June 14, 1997; copy in author's possession.

Cockrell, Frank M. "A History of Early Dallas." 1944. Texas/Dallas Collection, Dallas Public Library; Dallas Historical Society.

Cristol, Geraldine Propper. "The History of the Dallas Museum of Fine Arts." M.A. thesis, Southern Methodist University, 1970.

David, Ethelyn Clara. "Little Mexico: A Study of Horizontal and Vertical Mobility." M.A. thesis, Southern Methodist University, 1936.

Giles, Mary Louise. "Early History of Medicine in Dallas, 1841–1900." M.S. thesis, University of Texas at Austin, 1951.

Guzmán, Jane Bock. "Dallas Barrio Women of Power." M.A. thesis, University of North Texas, 1992.

Halbach, Mary Louise. "Domesticity in the American South: Catharine Bunting Coit, 1837–1883." M.A. thesis, University of Texas at Dallas, 1982.

Harris, Henry Camp, Sr. "Dallas: Acorn Planters of Yesterday, 1864–1924." Pamphlet, [1966]. DeGolyer Library, Southern Methodist University.

Hickey, Georgina. "Waging War on 'Loose Living Hotels . . . and Cheap Soda Water Joints': Urban Development and the Criminalization of Working-Women in Public Space." Paper presented at the Fourth Southern Conference on Women's History, Charleston, South Carolina, June 14, 1997; copy in author's possession.

Lazarou, Kathleen Elizabeth. "Concealed Under Petticoats: Married Women's Property and the Law of Texas, 1840–1980." Ph.D. dissertation, Rice University, 1980.

McArthur, Judith N. "Cracking the Solid South: Texas as a Case Study." Paper presented to the Third Annual American Heritage Center Symposium: Women in Public Life. University of Wyoming, Laramie, September 1994.

McElhaney, Jacquelyn Masur. "Childhood in Dallas, 1870–1900." M.A. thesis, Southern Methodist University, 1962.

Paulson, James W. "Women's Rights and the Antebellum Texas Supreme Court." Paper presented at the Texas State Historical Association meeting, Austin, February 29, 1996.

Pettit, Jennifer L. "Class, Consumerism, and Club Work: Racializing, Gendering, and Politicizing Socioeconomic Identity." Paper presented at the Fourth Southern Conference on Women's History, Charleston, South Carolina, June 12, 1997; copy in author's possession.

Sandell, Velma Irene. "The Effects of the Assimilation of the La Réunion Colonists on the Development of Dallas and Dallas County." M.A. thesis, North Texas State University, 1986.

Santerre, Eloise. "Réunion." M.A. thesis, Southern Methodist University, 1936.

Seaholm, Megan. "Earnest Women: The White Woman's Club Movement in Progressive Era Texas, 1880–1920." 2 parts. Ph.D. dissertation, Rice University, 1988.

Sharpless, Rebecca. "Choices Amid Constraints: Cultural Continuity on Early-Twentieth-Century Central Texas Farms." Paper presented at Annual Meeting, Texas State Historical Association, Austin, Texas, March 1, 1996.

Stein, Heidi Gale. "The Dallas Public Library's Association with Andrew Carnegie's Library Philanthropy." Professional paper. North Texas State University, 1987; copy available, TDCDPL.

Turner, Elizabeth Hayes. "Issues of Protection and Class: Galveston Women in the Progressive Era." Paper presented at Women and Texas History Conference, Austin, Oct. 6, 1990; copy in author's possession.

———. "Women Progressives and the Origins of Local Suffrage Societies in Texas." Paper presented at meeting of Houston Area Southern Historians, October 1991; copy in author's possession.

U.S. Works Progress Administration, Texas Writers' Project, Dallas Unit. "Dallas Guide in History" [known as "WPA Guide"]. American Guide Series, 1940. Photocopy of bound typescript, available, TDCDPL.

Index

Throughout the history of Dallas, women have worked both alongside and apart from the men now remembered as the city's founders and builders. In truth, women helped to create the definitive forms of urban life by establishing organizations and agencies that altered the responsibilities and functions of local government, amended the public conception of political issues, changed the city's physical structure, and affected the day-to-day lives of thousands of people.

In *Women and the Creation of Urban Life,* Elizabeth York Enstam examines how women stretched, redefined, and at times erased the essentially artificial boundaries between female and male, between "the private" and "the public" as aspects of human endeavor.

As Dallas evolved from a frontier town into a modern city, the varied facets of women's work revealed how their roles changed to shape, influence, and on occasion determine specific characteristics of urban life during times when female lives were supposed to be only private. The years after 1880, especially, opened a period of enormous change in women's roles in public life and in women's status in American society.

significance of these women's accomplishments in Dallas have echoed throughout the nation.

ELIZABETH YORK ENSTAM, an independent scholar of urban, community, and women's history, received her Ph.D. in history from Duke University. She lives in Dallas.